A Caring County?

Social welfare in Hertfordshire from 1600

A Caring County?

Social welfare in Hertfordshire from 1600

Edited by Steven King and Gillian Gear

Hertfordshire Publications
an imprint of
UNIVERSITY OF HERTFORDSHIRE PRESS

First published in Great Britain in 2013 by
University of Hertfordshire Press
College Lane
Hatfield
Hertfordshire
AL10 9AB

British Library Cataloguing in Publication Data
A catalogue record for this book is available from the British Library

ISBN 978-1-909291-12-6

Design by Arthouse Publishing Solutions
Printed in Great Britain by Henry Ling Ltd

Publication Grant

Publication has been made possible by a
generous grant from the Aurelius Trust.

Acknowledgements

IN NOVEMBER 2008 the Hertfordshire Association for Local History (HALH) annual symposium was held in Chipping Barnet. The host was the Barnet Museum and Local History Society, the theme 'Care and the Community'. Unfortunately, one of the invited speakers, historian Samantha Williams, was unable to attend. It was partly to ensure that the talk she had prepared, on the treatment of unmarried mothers, did not go unheard that I organised a meeting at Welwyn Library in December 2008. People interested in hearing Samantha's lecture and those who might be interested in developing research on social welfare in Hertfordshire were invited to attend. By the end of the day plans had been put in place to work towards producing a book.

A Caring County? Social welfare in Hertfordshire from 1600 is the result of the dedicated work of a team of local historians. The staff of Hertfordshire Archives and Local Studies (HALS) supported us and, with the much-appreciated guidance of Samantha Williams, the next few years were busy ones. Once our research began to produce chapters needing the skills of an editor, we were fortunate enough to find a 'volunteer' for the job: Professor Steven King of Leicester University. We greatly appreciate his help in bringing cohesion and structure to the chapters and with the addition of his excellent introduction we hope we have produced a book that will fill a gap in the published history of our county.

Throughout the whole process, all our contributors have received the help of fellow local historians, friends and colleagues and staff in the record offices and libraries listed in the bibliography, particularly those at HALS.

Many individuals and bodies kindly allowed us to use images from their collections. To them all we offer our thanks.

We would especially like to thank the following: Peter Greener at Ashwell Museum, Yasmine Webb at Barnet Archives, the Barnet Museum volunteers, Berkhamsted Local History & Museum Society, Katie Roberts and Roy Smith for the Duchy of Lancaster, Kate Godfrey and John Clark at Enfield Archives, Alison Duke at the Foundling Museum, London, Pirton Local History Group, Les Bedford, Janette Bright, Dr Gillian Clark, Chloe Gardner (deceased), Christine Mason, Jon Mein, William Pumfrey, Jean Riddell and Brian Warren.

Gillian Gear

Contents

Figures

Tables

CHAPTER ONE

Introduction: Hertfordshire in context

Steven King

AN EXPLOSION IN the historiography of poverty and poor relief over the last two decades has revealed and at the same time constructed a complex landscape of experience, practice and official sentiment. It has become clear, for instance, that the poor law was not simply imposed upon the poor. Historians differ on the degree to which the poor were free to exercise agency and to shape the decisions that were taken about their welfare.[1] Nonetheless, the analysis of narratives written by paupers seeking relief or disputing decisions under both the Old and New Poor Laws suggests definitively that the poor had, and felt themselves to have, a right to engage with the poor law as a process. Indeed, many of them believed that they had rights to receive welfare even where (as under the Old Poor Law) the law itself afforded them no such rights.[2] Observed from the outside, cumulative poor-law practice would seem to suggest that officials from the seventeenth through to the late nineteenth century concurred with this view. While vestries, overseers and boards of guardians might periodically slash the relief lists, refuse applications for relief or arbitrarily reduce allowances, increasingly rich studies of the experiences of poverty in old age, sickness or childhood point to a long-term sense (shared by officials, paupers and communities) that certain groups were simply 'deserving', whatever the law said.

This is not to say that poor-law practice and sentiment were uniform or predictable, on either a spatial or chronological basis. Historians continue to differ strongly on the relationship between space and welfare. Steve Hindle, Samantha Williams and others point persuasively to notable differences in the resources devoted to poor relief, the character of spending and the sentiment with which welfare was dispensed between communities within the same county, let alone more widely.[3] In this sense, intra-regional variation might be seen as the defining characteristic of the Old Poor Law and even the New, precisely as the Webbs argued in the early twentieth century.[4] Other historians have been less accepting of the idea that the poor law comprised a series of welfare republics. Jack Langton, for instance, suggests that intra-county variation in Old Poor Law practice in Oxfordshire was not random and situational, but instead reflected deeply ingrained differences in sentiment related to culture in a number of natural topographical sub-regions.[5] Equally, I have argued that if one tolerates a certain amount of 'noise' – that is, short-term variation in practice and some communities that simply break the mould – it is possible to discern and classify practice on an inter-regional and cross-state basis in the form of poor-law regimes.[6] Resolving this question of spatiality requires the sort of systematic county studies of welfare practice which are conspicuous by their absence in the wider historiographical literature. In this sense, the chapters collected together for this volume mark an important advance, suggesting as they do that Hertfordshire was in essence a 'caring county'.

The issue of chronological changes in welfare practice and sentiment is no less contentious. Anchoring their periodisations variously in chronologies of proletarianisation[7], philanthropy, public commentary[8], law[9], actual relief practice, affordability or the role of institutions, historians have created and demolished multiple turning points in the character and role of welfare. The idea that the New Poor Law marked a radical departure from older practice has been intensively questioned. For most paupers, the new threat of the union workhouse has to be balanced by the fact that almost all relief was still given 'outdoors' after 1834. Indeed, Elizabeth Hurren has argued that it was not until the crusade against outdoor relief in the 1870s and 1880s that the full intent of the New Poor Law was first implemented.[10] Looking backwards from 1834, historians have disagreed on the issue of when the Old Poor Law was at its most generous and whether and when the poor lost the support of the ratepayers who financed their welfare.[11] The sense that we can somehow discern a uniform 'crisis of the Old Poor Law' running from the spiralling of relief bills in the 1790s through to reform in the 1830s has fractured. It is absolutely clear that, whatever the public and pamphlet rhetoric of this period, at the coal face of the parish the poor in many communities retained a deeply embedded fellow feeling with other parishioners. The very chronologies of the chapters assembled for this volume, running seamlessly from the seventeenth century through to the 1950s, are an expression of the problems associated with fixed boundaries and a confirmation of the importance of fluidity in these terms.

Of course, matters of chronological and spatial variation are in some senses red herrings. The welfare literature over the last two decades has increasingly focused not on 'the poor' as a lumpen mass, but on particular life-cycle or economic groups, such as the aged, the mad, children or the unemployed. The experience of, and policies towards, these groups might cut across wider considerations of space or chronology, suggesting that we should talk about multiple poor laws rather than a single encompassing entity. Thus, the historiographical literature has increasingly constructed the elderly as a definitive sub-group of the poor. While issues such as the generosity and regularity of allowances for the aged need more empirical work, there is wide agreement that those who yoked together increasing age and a progressive inability to work could expect to achieve a *de facto* entitlement to communal allowances.[12] This did not mean that life was easy or that officials under the Old and New Poor Laws were not capable of excruciating acts of unkindness, but a relatively positive sentiment towards the aged can be found across the country under both systems.

The mad have also been identified by researchers as one of a number of definitive sub-groups of the poor and labouring sorts. Indeed, the historiographical literature on this group is richer than any other and Gary Moyle's chapter for this volume thus fits into a complex framework. An early focus on the construction of public asylums and the experiences of inmates in those asylums has given way to a more nuanced discussion about the circulation of the insane through different societal institutions.[13] Most of those who went to the public asylum did so only temporarily and, prior to admission and subsequently, they might move through workhouses, private homes/family situations, private institutions, independent living and voluntary hospitals. Against this backdrop, parishes and unions often went to quite extraordinary expense with the insane of the labouring classes. While some of the explanation for such expense is incarceration and the desire simply to be rid of problematic individuals, most of those who have looked in detail at the letters of families or the detailed decision-making of officials have detected a genuine desire for communities to 'do their best'.[14] Chapters by Gary Moyle and Gillian Gear in this volume use the prism of Hertfordshire to extend such discussions, Moyle focusing on the private mental institutions of the county[15] and Gear on certified industrial schools. The latter is particularly important in the sense that one of the continuing lacunae of the secondary literature is a picture of how those with milder mental problems or learning difficulties percolated through the welfare and institutional system.

For another sub-group of the poor – children under fifteen – the historiographical literature has become particularly vibrant. Katrina Honeyman, for instance, has revisited the issue of parish apprenticeship. While not ignoring instances of abuse, gerrymandering and casual attempts to offload problematic children, she has argued that parish apprenticeship often played a positive role in the subsequent life-chances of pauper children.[16] Gillian Gear, in her contribution to this volume, suggests that certified industrial schools may have played a similarly positive role, while discussions of attempts to send foundlings out to apprentice in chapters by David Allin and Jennifer Sherwood also result in relatively positive conclusions. Not all children benefited, however. Jane Humphries has used a series of autobiographical accounts to suggest that children who came into contact with the Poor Law, Old and New, suffered a definite socio-economic penalty across the life-course, mirroring the argument that modern politicians use to extol the value of working families or to lambast the failures of the welfare system.[17] On the other hand, Alannah Tomkins' use of a range of autobiographical sources to look at attitudes towards the workhouse suggests that, even if there was a life-cycle penalty, adults often retrospectively constructed workhouse residence as children in positive terms. For many, the workhouse represented family and community. Jennifer Sherwood's observation in her chapter for this volume that ex-foundlings can reflect positively on the self-reliance that residence in the Berkhamsted Foundling Hospital instilled in them is, similarly, a reminder not to apply modern yardsticks to historical situations. So is the work of Alysa Levene on the children of the urban poor and on foundlings. Acknowledging enhanced risks of mortality for these groups alongside sometimes appalling instances of cruelty and abandonment, she nonetheless shows how children could be sensitively, not to say generously, treated even as the urban Old Poor Law found itself under intense strain from the mid-eighteenth century.[18]

A final sub-group of the poor – the sick – has not attracted anything like the same attention. For many commentators, sickness was such an integral part of poverty – in terms of both cause and effect – that it is indistinguishable from a wide variety of life-cycle conditions. Thus, to be old was not of itself a cause for relief, but to be aged, sick and increasingly unable to engage with the labour market gave a *de facto* case for support in the minds of both overseers and paupers. Yet under both the Old and New Poor Laws sickness posed a central dilemma for officials. While they had no legal responsibilities to the sick, other influences – moral, economic, customary, religious and humanitarian – also impinged on their world view. Not to deal with individual and family sickness in its early stages might threaten both large future bills and the possibility of wider communal infection. Failing to provide nourishment, medical aid, nursing and cash relief to sick people might also provoke a community backlash where elites were seen to have a spiritual or philanthropic duty to their fellow citizens. Yet providing relief might generate explicit assumptions that sickness and entitlement could be yoked together. Unemployment could easily be disguised underneath a bout of sickness and, indeed, officials themselves colluded in just such a fiction when seeking to avoid using the workhouse for the temporarily unemployed under the New Poor Law. Linking sickness and relief also gave the poor a fixed reference point from which they could engage officials in a process of negotiation about the scale, form and duration of relief. Indeed, I have argued that sickness represents the key battleground over entitlement under the Old Poor Law.[19] Yet we know surprisingly little about the sick poor and their treatment. Systematic studies of multiple communities, such as that conducted by Samantha Williams on doctoring contracts in Bedfordshire, are rare and we remain heavily dependent upon the broad brush generalisation of commentators such as Joan Lane or the targeted micro-studies of Mary Fissell.[20] In this sense, our chapters by Robert Dimsdale and Carla Herrmann, both reflecting (favourably) on the scale and nature of medical relief across multiple Hertfordshire parishes, constitute an important advance.

Things neglected and forgotten

Yet if the literature of the last two decades has created an intricate picture of the English and Welsh poor laws, much remains for consideration. Detailed empirical work on the New Poor Law is remarkably thin on the ground outside David Green's sparkling work on London.[21] For the Old Poor Law, our appreciation of the nature and scale of welfare spending rests on a remarkably slim base and chapters in this volume by Alan Thomson, David Short and Helen Hofton add much-needed nuance to the existing stock of work, and for a county which has been rather neglected by welfare historians. Collectively, they create a picture of a Hertfordshire poor law which was fleet of foot and relatively sensitive in finding and treating the needs of the poor. Many of the conventional chronological turning points visible in the existing historiographical literature apply only lightly to these Hertfordshire parishes. Moreover, while each community had its own matrix of care, read together these chapters suggest a considerable regularity of approach and experience rather than the operation of innumerable welfare republics.

The question of where the poor law fitted into the wider economy of makeshifts accessed by the poor has also received limited attention. Sarah Lloyd and others have at last begun to address the ingrained, and mistaken, assumption that the relative importance of tax-funded welfare grew inexorably at the expense of philanthropic activity as the cost of relief spiralled upwards from the eighteenth century.[22] As Tim Hitchcock reminds us, to be masculine was also to be philanthropic, and innumerable acts of individual charity could and did add up to a considerable resource.[23] This is also the lesson from pauper letters, which frequently detail extraordinary records of individual and neighbourhood charity prior to the pauper writing for relief. The interlocking of the wider economy of makeshifts – crime, pawning, poor relief, boarding-out children, borrowing and lending, familial support, work and the abandonment of families or children – has been subject to relatively little theoretical and empirical attention. Against this backdrop, Yvonne Tomlinson's reconstruction of the work of Mrs Prudence West with the foundlings of the Barnet Hospital is a timely reminder that the access of the poor to a wider economy of makeshifts could often be dependent upon the willingness and ability of those with power to join the dots.

Other lacunae are also obvious. Some of the most exciting work of recent years has been on the voices of the poor. Pauper letters written by those away from their place of settlement when they fell into need have been analysed for rhetorical structure, strategic appeal, linguistic singularity and development of argument, resulting in a clear sense that such paupers had agency and shared a common linguistic and rhetorical platform with officials and those who advocated on their behalf. Those who have used them have played down issues of representativeness, honesty, orthographic irregularity and selectivity, arguing that they provide an important window onto the lives and experiences of the poor.[24] Carla Herrmann's chapter for this volume thus fits into an increasingly rich picture of the words of the poor, and for a county not thus far covered in the literature. Yet we must also acknowledge that most pauper letters thus far collected were written in the period between the 1790s and 1830s. The voices of the poor for later periods have been muted and little has been done to systematically exploit the letters sent by paupers to the central authorities and to boards of guardians under the New Poor Law. Our chapters do little to address this issue, but Jennifer Sherwood's engagement with oral histories of foundlings in the twentieth century begins to suggest other avenues for reconstructing the more recent words of the very poorest.

These are important observations, but four gaps in our understanding of the broad welfare system loom particularly large. The first is a failure to reconstruct the life-cycles of the poor. Early work on the demographic life-cycle by Tim Wales and the poor relief histories of individual paupers by Richard Smith is taken up by Samantha Williams in her analysis of two Bedfordshire parishes and by Samantha Shave.[25] Yet our grasp of where poor relief, workhouse residence, hospital admission, receipt of charity, parish apprenticeship and other welfare-related experiences fitted into the life-cycles of individuals and families remains at best tenuous. In turn, our ability to properly characterise the purpose, impact and role of the Old and New Poor Laws is held back by this empirical gap. It matters, for instance, whether an accelerating dependence on poor relief at the end of life and during a last illness came at the end of a life lived independently of parochial resources or of a life lived slipping in and out of dependence. Both scenarios might result in a pauper funeral but its meaning for both officials and bereaved families would be rather different. And, as Elizabeth Hurren reminds us, after 1832 the sort of life-cycle that paupers had led could influence strongly whether they ended up on the anatomy table.[26] Against this backdrop, several of our chapters – by David Short, Sheila White, David Allin, Yvonne Tomlinson and Jennifer Sherwood – offer models of the sort of detailed record linkage needed to embellish and reconstruct the lives of the poor. That by Tomlinson is particularly instructive, pulling together very disparate sources – from reports through letters to wills – in order to understand the life-chances of foundlings under the care of Mrs Prudence West.

A second weakness of the existing literature centres on the issue of personality. While the earliest commentators on the poor laws and associated institutions implicitly recognised the importance of who filled official positions, the matter is not one that has weighed heavily in the recent historiography. Yet a wide variety of welfare issues – how parishes reacted to pauper letters; whether poor relief was paid regularly; the form in which it was paid; the duration of periodic attempts to cut the relief lists; whether pauper children were boarded out; reactions to ill-health; and how paupers were treated in the workhouse – were crucially dependent upon the respective personalities of official and pauper. A workhouse master long in post might set a permissive and even paternalistic tone, or he might oversee a repressive regime. Paid overseers often reacted in a more businesslike manner to the payment of pauper allowances than did their amateur counterparts. Overseers who disagreed with periodic slashing of the relief lists might simply defy the vestry. Others were a law unto themselves, refusing to respond to the requests of the poor or to the advocates who wrote for them. And all poor-law historians are aware of the importance of personality in how the New Poor Law was received and instituted. In turn, personality was tied up with issues of social position, religion, belonging and ideology. Several of our chapters reinstate personality as an important variable in the character of care and welfare. David Allin and Yvonne Tomlinson both note the way in which the experiences of foundlings sent to the provinces – whether they lived or died as well as their everyday experiences – were crucially dependent upon those who supervised their carers. Gary Moyle places the issue of personality at the very heart of his consideration of the private madhouse system in Hertfordshire, while Robert Dimsdale demonstrates the central importance of the personalities of vestrymen and their officials to the character of the parochial relief system. In Hertfordshire the issue of who administered welfare was one of the key factors in shaping how that welfare was administered and with what sentiment.

Nowhere, perhaps, was personality more important than in the institutions that housed or confined the poor. Yet, notwithstanding the development of historiography over the last decade, we have remarkably little purchase on the character, role and operation of some of these institutions. Under the Old Poor Law problems over the very definition of what a workhouse was coalesce with poor record survival, so that relatively little is known, outside of interesting *ad hoc* examples and the large London workhouses, about who workhouse inmates were, how they were treated and where workhouse residence fitted into their life-cycle of dependence and independence.[27] The broad and widely accepted generalisation that workhouses under the Old Poor Law were receptacles for the most costly paupers, those without kin and those with the most entrenched causes of poverty (advanced old age, single women with children, orphans and so on) is not unproblematic. There is evidence that such institutions experienced high 'churn factors' and might sometimes house significant numbers of working-age paupers.[28] Sheila White's chapter on the Cheshunt workhouse for this volume confirms the need for a more complex understanding of the Old Poor Law workhouse, portraying it as a multi-purpose, fluid and flexible institution overseen by men who saw it as an essential part not of 'economy' (that is, a means of saving money) but of fulfilling their duties to the poor.

The situation is clearer for the post-1834 period, when the broad chronology of workhouse building and improvement is well-established if still London-focused.[29] Moreover, while the exact composition of workhouse populations varied according to area, chronology and local economy, census work by Nigel Goose, Andrew Hinde and others has confirmed Jean Robin's 1990 observation that New Poor Law workhouses became institutions in which children, women, the sick, the insane and, above all, the most aged were confined.[30] Yet our understanding of workhouse life remains far from complete. Counties such as Hertfordshire have figured little in the recent reshaping of our view of the New Poor Law and, more widely, studies of workhouse life beyond the nuances revealed by the study of autobiographies have been limited by a striking lack of sources. Just as importantly, the question of where the workhouse fitted in the institutional welfare matrix of eighteenth- and nineteenth-century England is unclear. As Gillian Gear demonstrates in her chapter, it was perfectly possible for children to be shunted between school, workhouse, certified industrial school and prison, a list to which one might add the public and private asylum. A clearer understanding of where the workhouse sat in this picture is thus essential, rather than merely desirable. On the resolution of this puzzle depends a proper understanding of the character of the workhouse as it was experienced rather than as it was constructed and reconstructed in both literary and literate public discourse.

Finally we might return to the vexed question of the spatial variation of poor-law practice and sentiment. While there are those who suggest that the poor law was merely an accumulation of the highly individualistic practice of parochial welfare republics, spatial variation in practice is so unpredictable and situational that one can say little about regional patterning. Other commentators, including myself, have suggested that there were more regularities of practice and experience on a regional basis than has usually been allowed. Framed in a different way, how should one understand the character of the Old Poor Law in Hertfordshire? The county demonstrates well the essential problems in resolving this question. Officials in Carla Herrmann's Royston seem to have been driven by a relatively narrow sense of their obligations to the poor. Some of the inspectors whose activities emerge in David Allin's discussion of the role of Hertfordshire in reacting to the General Reception at the London Foundling Hospital appear to have given only the most cursory attention to their charges if indicators such as death rates are anything to go by. Most of the Ashwell pensions reconstructed by David Short were nowhere near enough to live on. Balancing these experiences, officials in Sheila White's Cheshunt appear to have tailored welfare packages to the exact needs of the poor, while Mrs Prudence West restores the reputation of foundling inspectors with her careful attention to the needs of her foundlings and a determination to confront administrative authority to ensure the best outcomes for the children. Parishes around Hertford seem to have been remarkably sensitive to the claims of their resident poor.

Making sense of such diversity is not easy and there is clearly a need for more, and more systematic, work of the sort offered in this volume. Yet, if we exclude Royston as an outlier and make some allowance for the variations of policy linked to particular crises – if we tolerate noise – the impression is of a county with a conscience. In the twenty or so communities whose detailed experiences underpin the work reported here it is possible to detect ingrained individual and communal obligations to the poor, obligations which were not necessarily trumped either by questions of cost or by supposedly national changes in sentiment. While not exactly a welfare state in miniature, the welfare system in Hertfordshire was rather more comprehensive than appears to be the case in northern and western counties of England.[31]

Conclusion

When the pauper Thomas Marne wrote from his parish of residence in Hertford to his parish of settlement in Rotherthorpe (Northamptonshire) in June 1833 he detailed at length the support that he had received from people and officials in his host community.[32] The overseers of Hertford had managed to free him from the nursing of his brother – a 'lunatik' – by getting a recommendation to the Peckham asylum from a local benefactor. They had in turn relieved him with 'trifles' at need rather than requiring him to write to 'my parish'. Neighbours had offered Marne and other family members work, food and access to charitable resources. And a doctor had treated his daughter 'freely' – that is to say, charitably. Only after two years of 'making do' had Marne turned to his parish of settlement. Thirteen years later Marne was one of those – one of very many in Hertfordshire – whose belonging was regularised in the first state attempts at dealing with the entitlements of the migrant poor by introducing residence-based entitlement to welfare. While Hertfordshire poor-law unions joined many others in reacting with dismay to such rewriting of the settlement laws, there is little evidence that they sought to undermine the new legislation in the way that guardians in Northamptonshire did. Later in the nineteenth century most Hertfordshire unions were reluctant participants in the crusade against outdoor relief, and the county appears (on the basis of census data) to have confined relatively few of its blind, deaf and lunatic paupers to institutions compared with Norfolk, Kent or Surrey. There is evidence, in other words, that Hertfordshire really was a caring county.

Notes

1. For the two sides of this debate see P. King, 'The summary courts and social relations in eighteenth-century England', *Past and Present*, 183 (2004), pp. 124–72 and S. King, '"Stop this overwhelming torment of destiny': negotiating financial aid at times of sickness under the English Old Poor Law, 1800–1840", *Bulletin of the History of Medicine*, 79 (2005), pp. 228–60.

2. See S. King, 'Negotiating the law of poor relief in England 1800–1840', *History*, 96 (2011), pp. 410–35.

3. S. Hindle, *On the parish? The micro-politics of poor relief in rural England c.1550–1750* (Oxford, 2004) and S. Williams, *Poverty, gender and life-cycle under the English Poor Law 1760–1834* (Woodbridge, 2011).

4. S. Webb and B. Webb, *English poor law history Part I: the Old Poor Law* (London, 1963 edn), pp. 406–31.

5. J. Langton, *The geography of poor relief in rural Oxfordshire during the late eighteenth and nineteenth centuries* (Oxford, 2000).

6. S. King, 'Welfare regimes and welfare regions in Britain and Europe, c.1750–1860', *Journal of Modern European History*, 9 (2011), pp. 42–66.

7. L. Patriquin, *Agrarian capitalism and poor relief in England 1500–1860* (Basingstoke, 2007).

8. J. Innes, 'The mixed economy of welfare: assessment of the options from Hale to Malthus (1683–1803)', in M. Daunton (ed.), *Charity, self-interest and welfare in the English past* (London, 1996), pp. 139–80.

9. L. Charlesworth, *Welfare's forgotten past: a socio-legal history of the poor law* (Basingstoke, 2010).

10. E. Hurren, *Protesting about pauperism: poverty, politics and poor relief in late-Victorian England, 1870–1900* (Woodbridge, 2007).

11. L. Hollen Lees, *The solidarities of strangers: the English poor laws and the people, 1700–1948* (Cambridge, 1998), pp. 46–60.

12. On the entitlements of the aged see S. Ottaway, *The decline of life: old age in eighteenth-century England* (Cambridge, 2004) and P. Thane, *Old age in English history: past experiences, present issues* (Oxford, 2000).

13. For a flavour of the very extensive literature on these matters see L. Smith, *Lunatic hospitals in Georgian England, 1750–1830* (London, 2007); C. Smith, 'Family, community and the Victorian asylum: a case study of the Northampton General Lunatic Asylum and its pauper lunatics', *Family and Community History*, 9 (2006), pp. 23–46; B. Forsythe et al., 'The New Poor Law and the county pauper lunatic asylum: the Devon experience 1834–1884', *Social History of Medicine*, 9 (1996), pp. 335–55; A. Suzuki, 'The household and the care of lunatics in eighteenth century London', in P. Horden and R. Smith (eds), *The locus of care: families, communities, institutions and the provision of welfare since antiquity* (London, 1998), pp. 153–75.

14. On such sentiment see E. Murphy, 'Workhouse care of the insane, 1845–1890', in P. Dale and J. Melling (eds), *Mental illness and learning disability since 1850* (London, 2006), pp. 24–45.

15. For private institutions see W. Parry-Jones, *The trade in lunacy: a study of private madhouses in England in the eighteenth and nineteenth centuries* (London, 1972) and C. Philo, *A geographical history of institutional provision for the insane from medieval times to the 1960s in England and Wales: This space reserved for insanity* (Lewiston, NY, 2004).

16. K. Honeyman, *Child workers in England, 1780–1820: parish apprentices and the making of the early industrial labour force* (Aldershot, 2007).

17. J. Humphries, *Childhood and child labour in the British Industrial Revolution* (Cambridge, 2010).

18. See A. Levene, *Childcare, health, and mortality at the London Foundling Hospital, 1741–1800: 'Left to the mercy of the world'* (Manchester, 2007); A. Levene, 'Children, childhood and the workhouse: St Marylebone, 1769–1781', *London Journal*, 33 (2008), pp. 41–59; A. Levene, *The childhood of the poor: welfare in eighteenth-century London* (Basingstoke, 2012).

19. S. King and A. Stringer, '"I have once more taken the Leberty to say as you well know": the development of rhetoric in the letters of the English, Welsh and Scottish sick and poor 1780s–1830s', in A. Gestrich *et al.* (eds.), *Poverty and sickness in modern Europe: narratives of the sick poor, 1780–1938* (London, 2012), pp. 63–94.

20. S. Williams, 'Practitioners' income and provision for the poor: parish doctors in the late eighteenth and early nineteenth centuries', *Social History of Medicine*, 18 (2005), pp. 159–86; J. Lane, *A social history of medicine: health, healing and disease in England, 1750–1950* (London, 2001); M. Fissell, *Patients, power and the poor in eighteenth-century Bristol* (Cambridge, 1991).

21. D. Green, *Pauper capital: London and the poor law, 1790–1870* (Farnham, 2010).

22. S. Lloyd, *Charity and poverty in England, c.1680–1820: wild and visionary schemes* (Manchester, 2009), pp. 1–35.

23. T. Hitchcock, 'Begging on the streets of eighteenth century London', *Journal of British Studies*, 44 (2005), pp. 47–98.

24. For the definitive overview of pauper letters see T. Sokoll, *Essex pauper letters, 1731–1837* (Oxford, 2001), pp. 1–72. Also A. Gestrich *et al.*, 'Narratives of poverty and sickness in Europe 1780–1938: sources, methods and experiences', in Gestrich *et al.*, *Poverty and sickness*, pp. 1–34.

25. T. Wales, 'Poverty, poor relief and the life-cycle: some evidence from seventeenth-century Norfolk', in R.M. Smith (ed.), *Land, kinship and life-cycle* (Cambridge, 1984), pp. 351–404; R.M. Smith, 'Ageing and well-being in early modern England: pension trends and gender preference under the English Old Poor Law 1650–1800', in P. Johnson and P. Thane (eds), *Old age from antiquity to postmodernity* (London, 1998), pp. 64–95; Williams, *Poverty, gender*; S. Shave, 'The dependent poor? (Re) constructing individual lives "on the parish" in rural Dorset 1800–1832', *Rural History*, 20 (2009), pp. 67–98.

26. See E. Hurren and S. King, 'Begging for a burial: death and the poor law in eighteenth and nineteenth century England', *Social History*, 30 (2005), pp. 321–41 and E. Hurren, *Dying for Victorian medicine: English anatomy and its trade in the dead poor c.1834–1929* (Abingdon, 2011).

27. Although see Fissell, *Patients, power and the poor* and T. Hitchcock, 'The English workhouse: a study in institutional poor relief in selected counties, 1696–1750', D.Phil. thesis (Oxford, 1985); T. Hitchcock, 'Paupers and preachers: the SPCK and the parochial workhouse movement', in L. Davison *et al.* (eds), *Stilling the grumbling hive* (Stroud, 1992), pp. 145–66.

28. Shave, 'The dependent poor?'

29. See Green, *Pauper capital*.

30. N. Goose, 'Workhouse populations in the mid-nineteenth century: the case of Hertfordshire', *Local Population Studies*, 62 (1999), pp. 52–69; N. Goose, 'Poverty, old age and gender in nineteenth-century England: the case of Hertfordshire', *Continuity and Change*, 20 (2005), pp. 351–84; A. Hinde and F. Turnbull, 'The population of two Hampshire workhouses, 1851–1861', *Local Population Studies*, 61 (1998), pp. 38–53; R. Hall, 'The vanishing unemployed, hidden disabled, and embezzling master: researching Coventry workhouse registers', *Local Historian*, 38 (2008), pp. 111–21; J. Robin, 'The relief of poverty in mid-nineteenth century Colyton', *Rural History*, 1 (1990), pp. 193–218.

31. S. King, *Poverty and welfare in England 1700–1850: a regional perspective* (Manchester, 2000), pp. 142–68.

32. Rothersthorpe parish church: Thomas Marne, Hertford, to Rotherthorpe, 15 June 1833. On the asylum see E. Murphy, 'The metropolitan pauper farms 1722–1834', *London Journal*, 27 (2002), pp. 1–18.

CHAPTER TWO

The Old Poor Law and medicine in and around Hertford, 1700–1834

Robert Dimsdale

It has been remarked, that death, though often defied in the field, seldom fails to terrify when it approaches the bed of sickness in its natural horror; so poverty may easily be endured, while associated with dignity and reputation, but will always be shunned and dreaded, when it is accompanied with ignominy and contempt.

S. Johnson, *The Rambler* (London, 1750–52)

A S STEVEN KING has suggested in his introduction to this volume, enhanced understanding of the character and scale of medical relief offered by the Old Poor Law is held back by the lack of systematic multi-community studies. Hertfordshire offers a wealth of such possibilities, and this chapter focuses on the records of parishes located within a three-mile radius of All Saints Church in Hertford (Figure 2.1). Only three of the parishes have records for the seventeenth century.[1] None contains medical references and so the period of the study runs from 1700 to the end of the Old Poor Law in 1834. All the parishes, vestries, liberties and hamlets, with the exception of Bayford and Little Amwell, provide records for at least part of this period. Hoddesdon's records are the most complete (covering the entire period), while those of Stanstead St Margarets and Stapleford cover only two decades each. As in other counties, the volume and depth of records steadily increase over the period and there are significant overlaps, particularly involving Hertford All Saints and Hertford St John. The coverage, therefore, while far from complete, is relatively good and no decades are devoid of information.[2]

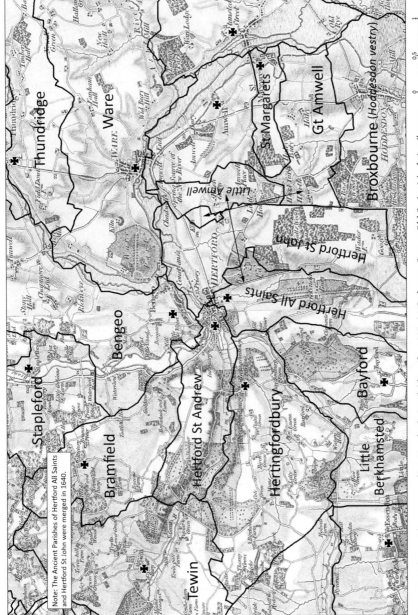

Note: The Ancient Parishes of Hertford All Saints and Hertford St John were merged in 1640.

Figure 2.1 The parishes surrounding Hertford. Overlaid on the 1805–34 Ordnance Survey Old Series 1 inch:1 mile map
© Cassini Publishing Ltd. Used by permission.

Table 2.1   Parish statistics at the close of the eighteenth century.

Parish/Liberty	Population	Families	Occupied dwellings	Workhouse places
Great Amwell	772	162	135	20
Little Amwell	403	84	78	4
Bayford	235	45	31	
Bengeo	584	112	95	15
Little Berkhamsted	314	71	71	
Bramfield	192	41	28	
Brickendon	463	94	86	
Hertford All Saints	872	193	147	30
Hertford St Andrew	1,277	254	224	50
Hertford St John	638	167	111	24
Hertingfordbury	625	115	104	30
Hoddesdon	1,227	255	224	35
St Margaret's	65	14	10	
Stapleford	111	22	24	
Tewin	494	74	74	20
Thundridge	503	93	93	
Ware	2,950	604	557	90
Total	11,725	2,400	2,092	318

Source: Based on R. Clutterbuck, *The history and antiquities of the county of Hertford*, 3 volumes (London, 1815–27). Workhouse places from 1776–7 Parliamentary Survey in *Abstracts of the returns made by the overseers of the poor...* (London, 1777).

Table 2.1 provides summative statistics on population and workhouse coverage for the sample parishes and shows that in 1800 the population of the area was approaching 12,000. The 1776–7 Parliamentary survey of poor-relief expenditure in England and Wales indicated 318 workhouse places within the survey area, which, with out-relief pensioners,[3] might imply between 500 and 1,000 dependent poor. Alternative indicators also point to significant poverty. In 1804, for instance, Hertingfordbury submitted a list of 39 people – just over 6 per cent of their inhabitants – to the Commissioners for Taxes to be exempted on account of poverty from the duties on windows and lights.[4]

Operation of the poor law

Responses to this poverty problem were the responsibility of the parish and its amateur overseers, often themselves overseen by vestries of elected ratepayers. Between six and eight people might be present at vestry meetings in the villages and in Ware, but the three Hertford vestries – All Saints, St Andrews and St Johns between 1732 and 1823 – show ten on average, with the largest – St Andrews – having consistently higher attendance than the other two. Meetings were formal and might take place three or four times a month (as at Ware), or monthly (as at Hertingfordbury). Their primary purposes were to provide direction to the overseer, hear appeals for support and monitor the collection and spending of the poor rate. For the sample parishes the issue of rating proved very problematic. The poor and those who became poor were themselves exempt, but Quakers[5] and others regularly refused to pay and were as regularly challenged by the parishes, obliging their overseers to get warrants for distraint in order to obtain payment. In the early eighteenth century a major ratepayer – William Cowper of Hertingfordbury – protested that his share was too heavy in proportion to the rest of the parishioners, which entailed legal expense for the parish,[6] while further legal costs were incurred at Hertford St Andrew in 1741[7] and at Brickendon in 1775–6.[8] In any event rates were often in arrear and individual cases were noted in the annual accounts or those of outgoing overseers as 'bad money'.[9]

What rates were made and how often is well illustrated in a Hertingfordbury series running from 1722 until 1764.[10] This shows a single increase in the product of a penny rate from £5 10s to nearly £7 occurring in 1729, no doubt attributable to re-rating, as well as a further slight increase at the end of the period. Varying numbers of rates were made annually over the same period: most often two, but sometimes one or three. Evidence from Brickendon between 1741 and 1772 shows that an increase in the product of a penny rate from £3 6s to nearer £3 18s occurred at some time between 1741 and 1763.[11] In general about one quarter of all households paid rates and the cost to the average ratepayer was about ten shillings per rate, multiplied by the number of rates made in the course of the year. There was a distinct tendency for this rate burden to increase over time. In the 1720s Hertingfordbury was raising 2s 6d per ratepaying inhabitant. From the mid-eighteenth century and up to the early 1790s the Hertford parishes and Brickendon were raising 3s to 5s, with Great Amwell raising 8s 6d in 1788. But from 1795 onwards Ware, Hertford All Saints and

Stapleford had reached 19s to 25s per head, a trend we see played out too in other counties at this time. Yet there were also considerable disparities in payments between parishioners. The top 10 per cent of ratepayers in predominantly rural parishes paid nearly three-quarters of the total rate, whereas in urban parishes they paid less than a third of it. The parish of St John, Hertford, combined both rural and urban populations, and there the top 5 per cent of ratepayers in the urban parts paid only half of what the corresponding 5 per cent in the rural parts did.[12]

A new regime for workhouses was introduced with the passing of Knatchbull's Act in 1723, which empowered 'the churchwardens and overseers of the poor of any parish, with the consent of the major part of the parishioners, in vestry ... to purchase or hire any house or houses in the parish ... and contract with persons for the lodging, keeping, and employing of poor persons'.[13] Houses called poor houses or even workhouses were already in existence, Hoddesdon having a workhouse in 1703[14] and Hertford All Saints having Parish Houses in Back Street.[15] Hertford St Andrew took the passing of the 1723 Act as the occasion to build a workhouse by June of the following year for £320 on land leased for 99 years.[16] At first it was shared between St Andrews and All Saints,[17] but the arrangement did not last long and by 1734 All Saints vestry was pressing for changes to the arrangements, which St Andrews was unwilling to accept.[18] All Saints then started putting their Parish Houses into repair and by 1737 was taking in Brickendon Poor as well as their own.[19] By 1744 it was St Johns vestry which was making arrangements with Brickendon instead, albeit on strict conditions.[20] Both All Saints and St Andrews made improvements especially to cater for work in their workhouses,[21] but Hoddesdon was already doing this at the beginning of the century and was making further arrangements to incorporate organised spinning much later on.[22] In 1777 the Hertford parishes, except for Brickendon, were operating separately – St Andrews having 50 places in their workhouse, All Saints 30 and St Johns 24.[23] At the same date Ware, which was not subdivided into several parishes as was Hertford, had a workhouse with 90 places and Hoddesdon had one with 35.[24] In 1802 there was an agreement to establish a joint Hertford workhouse, based in St Andrews, with the other parishes in the town.[25] Another long-lasting workhouse near Hertford was that of Hertingfordbury. In 1761 there had been a proposal for that parish's poor to go to St Johns,[26] but in 1772 existing premises – already a poorhouse – were made into a workhouse,[27] which had 30 places in 1777 and was still in use well into the nineteenth century. Great Amwell had a workhouse by 1769[28] showing 20 places in 1777[29] and a decision to build a new one was taken in 1803. Even Little Amwell had four places in 1777.[30] Of those villages not reporting workhouse places in 1777, Bramfield had one which was burned down in 1802[31] and Bayford had a poorhouse by 1830.[32]

Workhouses entailed rules for their management and vestries progressively handed over the supervision of the poor and of workhouses to managers referred to as 'farmers', who, for a price, took on the job by agreement. In 1737[33] and 1744[34] two of these agreements – probably because they involved more than one parish and a workhouse manager – took the form of full-blown indentures prepared by lawyers, but usually statements in vestry minutes signed by the parties sufficed. The agreements provide an important part of the context for medical treatment of the poor. Hertingfordbury records include a listing of their arrangements between 1772 and 1818.[35] It appears that three members of the Field family held the job of manager for two-thirds of the period. For the first twenty years (with figures missing for only one year) the rate of remuneration remained relatively steady – indeed, it declined in the first ten from £165 to £125. Then, in the next ten, although it fell from £145 to £125 after seven years, it rose after ten to £150. Thereafter it rose steeply to £200 in 1797, £270 in 1802 and £400 in 1809.

By no means all of those poor who were in receipt of pensions came to live in the workhouses and many remained in their homes; on occasion, a choice was available. In 1741 Hertford St Andrew ordered 'that Thomas Scott & his family have one shilling per week or go to the workhouse',[36] but in 1748 the same vestry ordered 'that all the out pensioners come to the work[house] or … have no relief'.[37] At Hoddesdon in 1777 there were 12 or 13 people in the workhouse and nearly 30 poor pensioners outside it, some of whom had their rent paid by the parish in addition to their pension.[38] At Hertingfordbury in 1802, 44 per cent of the resources detailed in the accounts of outgoing overseers were directly attributable to poor in the workhouse and 9 per cent to out-pensioners.[39] And by the 1830s about 75 per cent of Brickendon pensioners were living outside the workhouse.[40] It may be concluded that it was rarely the case that all poor patients were conveniently assembled for the doctor in one place, and that medical visits had to be made to many in their own homes.

The records contain several lists of the poor over the period, a rarity in poor-law records more generally. There are four for Ware, dating from

1705, 1708, 1709 and 1719,[41] all made in late November or December. That of 1705 was a 'list of persons who have been called over at a vestry … and admitted to receive a weekly pension for one month wearing a badge WP with the several occasions which brought them under the necessity of receiving such relief'. Of the approximately 50 people named, 32 were stated as aged, 7 as lame, 2 as blind, 1 as crazy, 1 as a lunatic, 1 as sickly and 4 as widows with children. In 1708 the list of those called over at the vestry included 25 aged, 5 lame, 1 lame and sick and 1 lunatic. Over the next year there were 26 aged, 1 sick, 2 aged and lame and 14 children, and a total of 72 entries. The 1718 list of pensioners is more thorough: 83 people were named on it, all of whom were in receipt of sums between 6d and 4s, with the total weekly payment amounting to over £5. There were more than 120 individuals in all, over 50 of whom were women and nearly 40 children. Of the rest, only 17 at most can be identified as men with certainty. Hertford St John made a list of 34 people in 1769[42] that included 2 married couples, 6 single men, 3 widows, 5 women and 14 children. Hoddesdon's lists of 1774, 1776 and 1777 included 10, 13 and 12 people respectively, equally divided between men and women and never with more than one child.[43] Hertford All Saints made a list on 24 April 1784[44] of 41 names accompanied by exact ages and in some cases other information as well, such as 'useful woman' in three cases, 'not able' in two (both small children), and 'cripple' and 'infirm' one each. For this cohort the average age is 31, with nine children under 10 years old (including two infants, one a month old), three teenagers, five in their twenties, three in their thirties, three in their forties, nine in their fifties and three aged 60 or more. The two eldest, both men, were 74. At Great Amwell, in three years between 1803 and 1810 when there were about 12 people in the workhouse, women outnumbered men by more than two to one, again with no more than one child present.[45]

Medical relief

For these populations health issues were often very important. At Great Amwell in 1754 Ware End distinguished between pensions at £4 6s 10d and 'accidentals' at £4 2s 6d, while at Hoddesdon End pensions were £2 11s and 'accidentals' £5 14s 8d.[46] The terminology reflects well the relative steadiness of the weekly pension bills and the unpredictability of other bills, which were usually health-related and often significant. At Hertford St Andrew in 1759 it was agreed that workhouse manager

Thomas Wells [should] pay and discharge all charges and expenses
of casualties illness deaths and burials that shall happen to the ...
poor except that in case a doctor or surgeon's bill for any one person
in any one illness or casualty shall amount to more than five pounds
in which case the overplus shall be paid by the parish.[47]

At Hertingfordbury the same arrangement was in operation in 1773
and 1798[48] and the records for the study area contain further agreements
with similar wording for Hertford St John[49] and Hertford St Andrew.[50]
This, then, was the usual framework for the management of medical
treatment of the poor, laying out the costs to be met by the parish. Most
expenditures and fees, it thus appears, could be contained within the terms
of agreements between overseers and farmers, but it is also apparent that
medical expenses could be so substantial as to unbalance the budget and
require regular and detailed supervision by the vestry. In effect, there were
two tiers of expenditure, with one being negotiated annually, or for a
longer period, with the farmer, and the other negotiated with a doctor or
doctors. It is within this framework that the medical activities of the Old
Poor Law fit.

Fractures were the most obviously costly form of 'accidental'. An
example of the order of expense which might arise was Frost's bill for 15
guineas for attending John Sadler with a broken leg at Hertford All Saints in
1785.[51] In turn, the risk to vestries was defined in agreements with doctors.
John Frost agreed with the vestry of Hertford St Johns on 21 April 1769

to attend the parish house of every disorder that may happen to
[the poor] in the physical profession at the rate of five guineas a
year all cases in surgery of any common nature included in the
same sum [but] all fractured limbs, large swellings, fractured skulls
... and smallpox excepted ...[52]

William Baker excluded fractures in his agreement with Hoddesdon in
1782 and in 1791 Hertford All Saints made a similar agreement with Mr
Jope for annual attendance on the poor, but excluding fractures.[53] In 1798
Ware vestry agreed an annual salary of £28 for Mr Burr, but he was 'to
be paid [separately] for broken bones and other violent accidents as may
appear to be necessary'.[54] Two of Burr's bills for broken bones survive, both
at Great Amwell. In 1801 he charged four guineas for setting a fractured

thigh and a fractured arm in July, but visits and dressings cost a further £2 15s, in part because in the second week in October the thigh 'broke a second time', an event for which Burr did not bill.[55] On 24 May 1802 he charged £2 for 'bleeding, reducing a fractured leg Cass the father' and on 14 June the same year £3 for 'reducing a fractured thigh Cass the son'.[56] These charges were in addition to his Easter yearly salary of £6.[57] The 'overplus' of the cost of treatment of breaks had to be agreed, and in 1794 the All Saints vestry appointed 'Mr William George on the one part and the overseers Mr Thomas North to settle the expenses in regard to the fracture of James Nunn's leg'.[58] Part of the problem in these cases was the suddenness of the need and one finds periodic cases such as that of Hertingfordbury in 1739 where the vestry directed that

> no bill [should] be paid to any surgeon or apothecary for
> medicines or attendance given to any of the poor of this parish
> unless they have a written order from under the hand of the
> overseer or churchwarden for the time being and the overseer is
> desired to give notice to Mr Wellington Mr Dimsdale Mr Patient
> and Mr Poultney.[59]

On the other hand, in 1740 the Brickendon overseers were authorised to relieve 'any accidental desperate cases' until they could call a vestry.[60]

Childbirth rarely occasioned such sudden need, but as a condition requiring medical relief it was no less problematic for overseers and vestries. Allowances were made to women 'lying in' in Ware in the first decade of the eighteenth century. In December 1708 Ann Bird was allowed £1 6s per week for keeping Susan Duffill a month 'for the time of her lying in with all things needful for her in that condition'.[61] At the same date 'the overseers were allowed one Pound for the lying in of ... widow Bossey for a month'. In the following month widow Shepherd was paid 3s 6d 'for keeping [a woman] with all things needful for eating & drinking & washing ... for her in her condition'.[62] A midwife's charge at Ware in 1706 was 2s 6d.[63] More than 20 years later Dr Worby received two guineas from the Ware vestry 'for delivering Will Tailor's wife',[64] the same fee that Brickendon paid Dr Yates in 1762 for delivering Mary Green.[65] These were doctors' fees, whereas the midwife, Mrs Welch, received one guinea at Hertford St Andrew in 1763. By the end of the period at Great Amwell the midwife, Mrs White, was receiving only 6s.[66] At Ware in 1798 an agreement with the vestry stated that 'respecting midwifery if a woman find it necessary for the time being to call in further advice, the parish doctor for the time being to attend and to receive one guinea. Jno Burr & M O Tice'.[67] In 1826 the Hoddesdon doctors' fee for difficult cases of labour was one guinea, but in some cases all three elements – doctor, midwife and carer – might be included. At All Saints in 1734, for instance, it was ordered

> that the overseers of the poor do pay Edward Skinner ten shillings
> for the support of his daughter in her lying in and also half a
> crown to Mrs Halcey as a midwife to her. And it is desired that Mr
> Pountney do attend the said Skinner's daughter and do the best he
> can for her and report the condition she is in as soon as he can to
> the overseers of the poor of this parish.[68]

Unless there were complications it seems that the vestries' finances were not unduly tested by childbirth, which remained a relatively minor and predictable component of medical-relief expenditure, albeit with case-by-case variations in the charges.

The opposite is true of cases of mental illness, especially those that required institutionalisation. In 1757 Hertingfordbury vestry ordered that the expenses of getting Richard Bigg to Bedlam be paid, as well as allowing his family 5s per week.[69] In 1776 the vestry of St Andrews was concerned for John Catline, 'who is a lunatic[,] in order to get him into St Luke's or some other hospital for cure'[70] (St Luke's was a private asylum in London). In 1777 a workhouse contract for John Randall, the manager at St Andrews, stipulated that he was 'not to be at any expense in removing any mad or frenzied person who shall be sent into the said workhouse to any place whatsoever' and should leave the 'overplus' element to the vestry as an extra.[71] In 1787 Brickendon paid for expenses at 'Bethlem'[72] and by the beginning of the nineteenth century there were major payments for lunacy costs at Ware, a Mrs Burrows being paid £51 5s 8d for the year 1800/01, £51 6s 10d for the next year and £41 10s 7d for the year 1802/03.[73] And the Hoddesdon overseer in 1821 was in receipt of a well-stated request indicating a going rate for maintenance at that time:

> Dear Sir, I have been applied to as an act of Charity to write to
> you on behalf of a poor insane woman of the name of Mrs Mason
> (who in 1819 kept a School in your place, & by her occupancy of

a House there gained her Settlement with you) to beg the favor
of your making some arrangements for her support without
her being removed to you, as she is under the care of those who
will see she has that care and attention her distressing situation
requires, and who w[oul]d have been happy, had they the means
to have supported her without troubling you at all. There being
not the least prospect of her recovery, it is desirable that whatever
arrangement takes place sho[ul]d be with a view of continuance
for some time – You will be pleased therefore to consider what
sum it is in your power consistently to allow for her, & proper
persons to be constantly with her, per week; I believe 7/- is the
usual one, and I will endeavour on hearing from you to get the
same so arranged that it may be received as most convenient to
yourselves at the Bankers in Town, ... at Lutterworth or this place
– I am Gentn your very obdt Servt ... Rugby.[74]

By 1821 St Luke's were operating a strict system, informing Hoddesdon
that

Ann Edwards continues a Lunatick and from the present
circumstances of the Patient's case, there is not sufficient reason
to expect a speedy recovery; you are therefore required, at your
own Cost and Charges, to remove and take away the said patient
from the said Hospital, on Friday next, pursuant to the Condition
of your Bond entered into on Admission. I am Sir Your humble
servant John Webster Secretary. N.B. The Committee desire you
will give no fee whatever to the Officers or Servants, it being
against the Rules and Orders of this Hospital. P.S. If the friends of
the above Patient desire it, the Patient will be upon the Incurable
list; and, when the Turn comes, will be re-admitted at Seven
Shillings a Week; but as there is at present no Vacancy, the Patient
must be taken out of the House. – The Committee desire your
answer next Friday.[75]

Vestries had recourse to several other hospitals as well. In 1732 All Saints
ordered the overseers to 'apply to Dr Clarke or some other proper person
for that purpose to get Richard Mills a poor man in the workhouse to be
admitted into St Thomas's Hospital London or some other proper hospital

there'.[76] And in 1743 the same vestry ordered 'that overseers of the poor do forthwith make a proper application for sending Robert Tite to one of the hospitals in London'.[77] But ten years later they had to pay the vestry £2 9s 6d 'by cash received of Dr Dimsdale on account of Robert Tites being sent to Bath which was returned and is charged to [the overseers'] account'.[78] A special hospital was used by Little Berkhamsted in 1831, when the vestry

> agreed that the sum of £2 2d be paid to defray the expenses of Marie Maynard's journey to London in order [for her] to be placed in the 'Deaf and Dumb';[79] and of the clothes purchased for her upon her being admitted there, in pursuance of a letter from the asylum describing the things required for her.[80]

They used St George's hospital in the same year.[81] Brickendon vestry paid the Steward of Guy's Hospital for 'a protection for Chalkley' (an individual) in 1763,[82] while Hoddesdon sent a man to St Bartholomew's in 1770.[83]

More generally, the sheer range of medical relief is striking. Stanstead St Margarets provided milk for 12 weeks in 1828 to help with the recovery of a sick child and meat for a sick woman in 1831.[84] Mary Plum was ordered wine, tea, sugar, and 'lickers' at Great Amwell at some date between 1806 and 1813. Moreover, vestries often went to great pains to underpin subsistence in the long term. At Hoddesdon in 1778 the workhouse master Thomas Collerson was to 'have the produce of the garden belonging to the said Workhouse for the use of the house only and to keep the garden in constant cropping and always to continue the same ... and no part of the crop of the said garden to be sold or destroyed at leaving the same'.[85] And Ware had been at pains in 1727 to plant apple, pear and walnut trees for the workhouse.[86] Often food relief was entwined with other aspects of medical welfare. In Ware in 1708 the vestry ordered 'that Mary Sheperd wid[ow] be allowed five shill[ings] that is two shillings and six for curing her family of the Itch & the other towards her sustenance',[87] and in the following year 'that doctor [John] Dimsdale do take care of Ann Birds child to cure him of the Evil'.[88] 'Itch ointment' was prescribed in Hoddesdon for four boys at 5s and two others at 6s in 1797,[89] while the St Andrews vestry in 1777 attempted payment by results and agreed

> that if Mr Abraham Levi may cure of a scald head [probably ringworm] of Joseph Draper son of Daniel Draper, that the

overseers shall pay him one guinea for the said cure: but if the
scald head should break out again with the same disorder the said
Abraham Levi will undertake it again at his own expense.[90]

Itch (usually scabies) was, ultimately, curable. Other diseases, such as
rabies, were more of a problem and the dangers they posed were perhaps
particularly exaggerated in the public imagination. On 3 September 1760
the St Andrews vestry noted that

> as well from the knowledge of several accidents which have
> happened in this neighbourhood as by repeated advices from the
> City of London & County of Middlesex … that many dogs have
> lately run mad and bit both man and beast who have thereby lost
> their lives to the great terror of the public, and it being known by
> fatal experience that these unhappy incidents are greatly increased
> by the number of dogs which are suffered to run about the streets
> and highways and are bit by those that run mad. We do therefore
> … resolve that public notice be given in this church likewise fixed
> on the church door and town post on Sunday next that all dogs
> which are found loose … for one month after Sunday next will be
> killed and that this parish [together with All Saints, St Johns and
> Brickendon] will pay one shilling per head for each dog which
> shall be so killed and buried.[91]

The churchwardens also required that the hides of the dogs be 'slashed and
rendered unfit for use'.[92] However, on 12 October it was noted that 'the
agreement concerning the misfortunes happening by mad dogs has not
had the desired effect for want of being continued longer than the month
therein mentioned for that upon the tenth day of this [month] several
dogs & hogs were bit in this town by a mad dog'.[93] The vestry ordered
a further month of the campaign,[94] but this danger was not eliminated.
Leprosy was equally feared in the public imagination, and at Thundridge
in 1765 a woman was sent to London having caught the disease.[95]

Some of the forms of expenditure to be found in this sample of parishes
are less often seen in the secondary literature. For example, in 1832
Hoddesdon 'Bought of S Smith Truss Maker to the City of London Truss
Society No 40 Grays-Inn Lane, Holborn, To left side 24 Inches Truss 12/–'.[96]
A century earlier Hertingfordbury vestry had authorised a particularly

unusual treatment, ordering that 'Jno Harlow be allowed 10s or 12s at the most to bear his charges … in order to see for a cure by having his leg stroked by a person that comes thither at certain times, he having done (as we are informed) several cures that way, and this money to be allowed besides his pension'.[97] Expenditure on hartshorn shavings (deer horn) was authorised at Tewin in 1753,[98] while Hoddesdon purchased frankincense in 1798[99] and 'fungous testicle applications' for John Sharpe in 1829.[100]

Epidemics

Yet, and as elsewhere in England, it was epidemics that put the most pressure on parochial resources. The passage of 'fever' went unrecorded in vestry minutes except for an All Saints entry of October 1801 which 'Ordered … that the overseers do pay to Mr Colebeck the doctor of the parish the sum of twenty five pounds as a present for his extra trouble occasioned by a bad fever among the poor People of the Parish'.[101] By contrast, smallpox appears in vestry minutes throughout the period. At intervals the disease provoked exceptional strains on parish finances – more severe than any other medical contingency or 'accidental'. Nationally there were smallpox epidemics in 1679–82, 1719–20, 1727, 1729, 1740–2, 1763, 1766 and 1768,[102] and to an extent the local records reflect this. A total of 31 occurrences was minuted by Ware vestry between 1705 and 1709 and in 1722, occasioning payments for nursing ranging from 1s to £1.[103] In 1731 a particular set of complications arose at Hertingfordbury. John Harlow had just died and the vestry clerk recorded

> that whereas an order was made … that in case widow Harlow should have the smallpox (which was then in her family) 7s.6d should be allowed per week to widow Warner to look after her, and she [widow Harlow] now having the smallpox the said widow Warner has refused to come to her to look after her but has withdrawn herself & gone to some other place by means whereof the said widow Harlow is destitute of a nurse & both she and the child she lies in with having the said distemper the overseer is now obliged to find another nurse for her but can find none that will nurse her for less than 10s per week. And [she] also expects some help, and the said Harlow being in great danger of her life if due care be not taken of her, we therefore agree to leave it to the discretion of Mr Grubb the overseer, to make the best agree[ment]

he can with such person he can find to the best advantage for the benefit of the parish until further order of [the] vestry.[104]

Mrs Harlow died and the vestry put the surviving child to William Faulkner (a relation of the Harlows at Bayford) at 18d per week until further notice. The overseer resorted to distraining on the family's goods in order to pay the rent. All was accounted for on 10 April the following year, with aggregated costs of £2 7s 6d for relief, £1 1s for burial-related payments, £1 2s 6d for nursing, 2s 6d for a person to sit up and £1 9s 8d for other expenses.[105]

In March 1734 All Saints ordered that the overseers 'permit a young man who lodges at the widow Walker's and is taken ill of the smallpox to have the use of some convenient room in one of the parish houses in the Back Street until his illness be over'.[106] At a time when there were already a few relatively isolated pesthouses the crowded Back Street location was far from ideal. In the same year the vestry ordered

> that the ... clerk do write a letter to the churchwardens and
> overseers of the poor of Paul's Walden to acquaint them that if
> they don't pay all the charge and expense of one John Handley
> who now lies ill of the smallpox within this parish that then if he
> recovers the parish will certainly send him to that parish by virtue
> of an order of two justices as soon as possible and a physician shall
> judge [if] it may be safe to send him And it is further ordered that
> in case he does recover that the officers of this parish do remove
> the said John Handley accordingly.[107]

Two years later, and motivated by the same concern, All Saints vestry ordered 'that the mother of the poor boy who is ill of the smallpox be forthwith removed to the parish to which she belongs'.[108] Brickendon vestry agreed with the new workhouse manager in 1745 that those poor in the workhouse with any infectious disease, including smallpox, should not be ejected but be treated as necessary at the parish's expense.[109]

An outbreak of smallpox in Hertford in December 1761 induced St Johns vestry, which was negotiating at the time about the possibility of admitting six Hertingfordbury poor to St Johns, to react in its own defence:

> ... at this vestry came one Harding belonging to the ... parish of
> Hertingfordbury and said he had an order from Mr Gosling Wm

Flindell and Danl Robins to come to the said workhouse of Saint
John Hertford on Monday seven[n]ight with his wife and four
children and further said that John Wright and family Collarbone
and others living near the said Harding had received notice or
warning to quit their respective places of abode and to go to the said
workhouse at the same time with the above Harding to the number
of twenty two persons or thereabouts[.] It is agreed by us who
constitute this vestry that as we are already engaged with the liberty
of Brickendon and as the Smallpox now is spreading in the Town
that we will not agree to take in or give or grant leave to take in the
poor of any parish whatsoever into the said workhouse except the
poor of ... Saint John H[e]rtford and the liberty of Brickendon.[110]

In 1793 Ware agreed to let three people remain at Widford to be
inoculated there on the same terms as the Widford poor, 'the parish of
Ware to be answerable for the same but these families [were] not to be
inoculated for the small pox unless a general order [were] given by the
parish of Widford for inoculating their own poor'.[111] Great Amwell
resolved in 1805 'to take into consideration the necessity of an inoculation
of the poor Children belonging to this Parish when it was unanimously
resolved that the Overseers do give an order for all such as shall apply
for the same to be inoculated with the Cow pock'.[112] Vaccination slowly
replaced inoculation as the most acceptable defence against smallpox
from the beginning of the nineteenth century.[113] By 1809 Hertingfordbury
was prepared to vaccinate children and others in the parish who had not
had the smallpox, but would not help those who preferred inoculation.[114]
However, as late as 1817 inoculation was still preferred by some and the
Ware vestry

agreed to prevent as much as possible the spreading of the
contagion of the smallpox which is of a very dangerous sort by
vaccination generally and in such parts of the town where the
distemper is now prevalent, and where vaccination will not be
submitted to, to mitigate the disease, it was resolved to inoculate
with the Smallpox. This operation to be performed by Mr Tice
[who] is to have his authority for such families as are to be
inoculated, from the present acting overseers.[115]

Moreover, both Stapleford[116] and Little Berkhamsted[117] vestries were paying for inoculation in addition to vaccination in 1820.

Practitioners

In some ways, of course, sudden and widespread epidemic disease drove parishes into the arms of medical practitioners and Hertfordshire, like other areas of southern England, saw a marked engagement with this group as the eighteenth century progressed. Of all the practitioners named in various records one was from Hatfield, 18 were based in or near Hertford, 6 were at Hoddesdon and 12 were at Ware. Two businesses were named as father and son – Frost of Hertford and Baker of Hoddesdon. Vestry records are most plentiful between 1730 and 1745 and then again between 1760 and 1805: 16 names occur in the first period and 22 in the second. Of the first group, four appear in vestry records for All Saints, three in those for St Andrew and two in those for Hertingfordbury. In Brickendon six separate names occur from 1760 to 1785, whereas there are only two in Hertingfordbury. For both the earlier and later periods it appears that Ware doctors did not practise in Hertford, nor did Hertford doctors practise in Ware: four doctors were taking business in the Hertford parishes, including Bengeo and Hertingfordbury, in the early 1730s and another four in Ware. Combining references in vestry minutes with those in trade directories identifies more than 60 doctors working in the area across our period. Only one (M.B. Walley of Ware, who was listed in the Medical Register in 1779, 1780 and 1783[118]) was a university-trained physician; his degree was from Cambridge. The 1779 Register states that he lived near Hertford and he is recorded at Hertingfordbury in 1799. An earlier Walley occurred at St Andrews in 1738.[119] Thomas Dimsdale eventually obtained a degree from Aberdeen,[120] but at the time he appeared in vestry records at Brickendon, Hertingfordbury, St Andrew, All Saints and Little Berkhamsted between 1738 and 1745 he had no qualification. His son Nathaniel Dimsdale qualified at Edinburgh but was less active as a physician than as a politician. Another son, Joseph, was also qualified but did not feature in vestry records. John Andree MD is named in the *Universal Directory* as being at Hertford, but he does not appear in vestry records either.

Some practitioners were known primarily as surgeons, and in the 1770s this category included William Chandler and John Frost. An example of a bill made out specifically by a surgeon is that of Mr Edwards in 1816 to All

Saints 'for Hawkes child having an accident'.[121] In the same way others were known primarily as apothecaries. Mr Patient was referred to as such by All Saints in 1732 and 1734 and the vestry paid his bills six times between 1732 and 1735 for 'diverse medicines', 'phisick' and looking after sick families.[122] Richard Clarke was also referred to by All Saints as an apothecary in 1742, when he supplied physic and medicines,[123] as was Mr Nash in 1746.[124] These bills were for various sums between one guinea and £17 3s 9d. John Watford's bill to Great Amwell vestry in 1794[125] amounted to £4 16s 6d and covered a period between 29 November 1793 and 15 April 1794. Ten patients were mentioned and the charges (all for 6d, 1s, 1s 6d and 2s) were for mixtures (febrile, balsamic and astringent), powders (including emetic), embrocation, emulsion, pectoral linctus, draughts, nervous drops and 'gargarism' (a gargle).

From the 1760s onwards it became usual for parishes to make exclusive agreements with doctors for varying periods. The first of these was Hertford St Andrew, which in 1761

> agreed with Mr Cutler for his attendance and necessary medicines
> for the poor in cases of illness which now are or shall become
> chargeable to the Parish for one year from the 5th day of this
> instant May at the sum of six pounds to be paid by the overseers of
> the poor of this parish.[126]

There were price rises, and in 1776 Mr Frost agreed for two years with Hertford St Johns for ten guineas, whereas seven years previously he had agreed half that amount.[127] At Hoddesdon – a larger place – William Baker agreed in 1782 on 12 guineas per year for an indefinite period but with the possibility of three months' notice on either side.[128] This continued until 1789, when, on Baker's death, he was succeeded by Samuel James on the same terms.[129] James was still being paid 12 guineas in 1797,[130] but by 1825 the rate had doubled[131] and in 1826 two surgeons were being paid a total of £40.[132] Mr Burr in Ware was receiving his 'usual salary' of £28 in 1798,[133] but by 1815 the contract must have lapsed because the vestry required that 'in future the Medical Gentleman attending this Parish shall have a stipulated salary and any Surgeon residing in the Parish may be at liberty to propose terms to the next meeting'.[134] Straightaway the post was filled and the vestry 'resolved that Mr Tice take the office of apothecary for this parish till Easter next at his usual salary of thirty five pounds and that no extra charges be paid until the Bill has been laid before and allowed by a vestry called for that particular purpose'.[135] Small parishes also made agreements, as Stapleford did with Mr Cheese on an annual basis for 5 guineas between 1796 and 1799[136] and Bramfield did to the tune of 10 guineas with Mr Dickens in 1818,[137] rising to 12 guineas in 1821[138] but falling to 8 guineas in 1822.[139] In fact the figure was different in almost every year until nearly the end of the period, in 1833, when it was down to £5.[140] Little Berkhamsted had an agreement with Doctor Darbey in 1795 for 5 guineas[141] and with Mr Dickens in 1826 for 15.[142] In the late 1820s and the 1830s even little Stanstead St Margarets had an arrangement, with Mr Horley, which lasted for at least 12 years.[143]

What drove the need for agreements must have been difficulties in getting a doctor for the poor when one was needed. As a vestry at All Saints, Hertford noted on 12 February 1798:

> it appearing to the parishioners that the poor are left destitute of a ~~doctor~~[144] surgeon & apothecary the churchwarden and overseers of the poor now proceed to appoint a proper gentleman for that purpose It is agreed at this vestry that Messrs Frost & Colebeck be appointed.[145]

As elsewhere in provincial England, doctors balanced their private and public practice, and, notwithstanding evidence from elite correspondence in the area that the medical marketplace was crowded,[146] the needs of parishes not already under contract might be a distant priority for local medical men.

Charitable and voluntary aspects

Of course, the poor of some parishes could also turn to a wider medical economy of makeshifts. The poor in Little Berkhamsted benefited from a payment of £15 shared between 24 persons in 1796,[147] receiving sums from 7s 6d to a guinea under the terms of the Maurice Hunt charity. The parish also had a 'club' and in the same year reported that 'likewise any members sick or lame belonging to the club held at Mr Turner's 3 Horse Shoes Little Berkhamstead to be paid 2 shilling per week when they receive 8s per week from the club, and 1s per week to those who are allowed 4s'.[148] As elsewhere in provincial England, the plight of the sick poor might occasion special philanthropic initiatives. At Hertingfordbury in 1809 the vestry noted that

> A letter was produced from Samuel Whitbread Esq, stating that
> Sarah Stone, a parishioner of this parish being a lunatic was placed
> by him in … private confinement with Mrs Burrows of Hoxton
> & that the charge of maintaining her there will amount to 10s per
> week and the parish taking the same into consideration Resolved
> that they would bear the said charge as long as she should remain
> there it being understood that Mr Whitbread had generously
> promised to add the annual sum of 20 guineas to be expended in
> supplying her with various articles of comfort.[149]

In the same vein a Lying in Society was set up in 1795 for the relief of poor married women in the town of Hertford and its vicinity,[150] while a dispensary had been founded in Hertford prior to 1824, at which date the vestry appointed the profits of a sermon to be appropriated to the charity.[151]

But it was smallpox which gave rise to some of the most significant non-parish-based efforts and achievements. There had been an isolation building at a place called the Stant in St Johns parish,[152] but in 1763 T.P. Byde of Ware Hall conveyed a piece of ground in Port Hill Close in Bengeo for 10s to Dr Yates and 29 others 'upon trust to build thereon a house for the reception of persons afflicted with smallpox … only, in Hertford and Bengeo'.[153] The trust, which involved the Mayor and Aldermen of Hertford, the Vicar of All Saints, the Rector of St Andrews, a dissenting minister and trustees of Hertford charities, using money raised by subscription, erected a small isolation hospital known as the Pesthouse, which served its purpose until the disease ceased to be such a threat.[154] This benefited more people than just the poor.

Dr Levett, rector of Little Berkhamsted, recorded several general statements in his parish registers. On one occasion he wrote that

> About the year 1754 the Small Pox broke out in the Parish a poor
> person came with it … which spread very fast … Benevolence seized
> upon the neighbouring gentry who sent us in near an hundred and
> sixty pounds so that everybody who chose it was supplied with all
> necessaries. This was begun by William Strode Esq who lived at
> Ponsbourne, unhappily pulled down in 1761 and died about the
> year 1756. A gentleman of the best breeding and greatest goodness
> of Heart that perhaps the County ever produced: the numbers who
> had it were eighty four out of which eleven died.[155]

Another outbreak of smallpox took place at Little Berkhamsted in 1768, and this too was recorded by Levett:

> About the beginning of the year 1768, George Hodges (he was buried February 12th), a youth of 10 years of age, was taken desperately ill. His Parents imagined, but did not know, it was the smallpox. After being ill some days, they waited upon Mr (since Baron) Dimsdale for his advice, who kindly came over in the evening tho' the snow was above a foot deep and his servant got a dangerous fall. He insisted upon me going with him to his patient. We found him in a bad situation, full of dirt and sores. The doctor, with a humanity peculiar to himself, washed him, removed all nasty obstructions and by his care, preserved his life some days. Upon our return to the parsonage, he told me it was the smallpox of the worst sort, the infection of which would certainly go thro' the parish but if I and the parish choose it, he would inoculate the whole Gratis in two days. I immediately used what persuasions I could; many complied with great cheerfulness and the rest, seeing they cou[l]d not prevent inoculation taking place, soon came in to it; all succeeded and did well. He kindly gave them medicine and attendance. Dr [Ingen Housz], afterwards physician to the empress queen [Maria Theresa] and who inoculated all her family, was for the purpose of experience attending upon Dimsdale. The inhabitants of Bayford, upon seeing our people so cheerfully enter upon it, beg'd of the Dr at the same time to exert the same charity to them. Their request was complied with and they did well.[156]

Hoddesdon experienced a smallpox crisis in 1769 and

> At a legal vestry called this day at the Parish Church of Broxbourne and there held to consider if it was proper to inoculate such poor of the hamlet of Hodsdon as are willing to receive that benefit which this vestry [is] induced to think the most likely means under God to stem the infection of that calamity of the Small pox which rages in the said hamlet: already to the Destruction of many and from the numbers that fall every day it is greatly to be feared few would escape: and many more might die.

This vestry came to the following Resolution – that the Revd Mr Jones & Mr Philipson be Desired to wait on Baron Dimsdale to know of his opinion if it was proper to inoculate at this season of the year or not and to adjourn this Vestry to the Black Lion Inn at Hoddesdon on the morrow eve at 7 o clock to receive their report concerning the same and to consider further on this matter.[157]

At the adjourned meeting on the next day the vestry heard

the Revd Mr Jones & Mr Philipson[, who] reported the opinion of Baron Dimsdale concerning inoculation which he was so obliging to give under his hand & is as follows

'I do not think the season of the year any objection to the inoculation of the poor since experience has convinced me that the distemper produced by inoculation is generally very favourable in hot weather provided the patients take fresh air and are lightly covered'.

Whereupon it was moved and agreed to inoculate such of the poor of the said hamlet that were willing to receive that benefit. But a question arising who was to pay the expense this vestry was told by Mr Philipson that a subscription was set on foot by some gentlemen in this parish to defray the apothecary's charge of inoculating one hundred persons upon which it was further agreed that this parish should sustain the expenses that might happen by maintaining such of the said poor as should be inoculated and the following persons were appointed a committee to carry the same into execution.[158]

Thomas Dimsdale's success in launching inoculation in Russia shortly afterwards removed any necessity for him to work as a doctor, although he continued to do so to some extent. It was claimed for him in his obituary of 1801[159] that he continued to work as a doctor in local cases without fees, and William Baker's letter provides grudging confirmation from a political opponent:

The two Barons [Thomas and his son Nathaniel], for the sake of preserving their parliamentary interest … are disposed to attend many of the inferior families in the town gratuitously; This of course operates something to the prejudice of the other persons of the profession.[160]

Conclusion

While parish archives are inevitably uneven in quality and chronological coverage, this chapter has attempted to explore the administrative devices used to manage health-related issues. Vestries appear to have shouldered their responsibilities for the health of their poor, even against the backdrop of funding constraints. There was, however, outright rejection of heavy charges for outsiders unless and until settlement was proved, particularly vehement in smallpox cases, even between parishes that were co-operating with each other over their poor with arrangements for sharing a workhouse. But by the 1730s the growth in importance of workhouse managers and their appreciation of the financial risks which they faced brought in a £5 rule for the costs of treating individual cases, above which figure the vestries paid. This rule was in use up to the end of the eighteenth century but not in the nineteenth, perhaps because medical emergencies became a much smaller – or at least a less noticeable – proportion of total expenses. And there were other expensive cases as well which the managers were careful to leave to the vestries in their agreements with them. Such arrangements were not always thought necessary, especially in smaller parishes, where the risks to the farmer of the poor were not deemed to be very great, but also, although many exceptions were still to be found in the managers' agreements, these no longer included all the medical emergencies which had once been included as a matter of course.

Vestries well knew what high fees doctors might charge for their services, as instanced by Hertingfordbury's warning to four of them in 1726, and they also clearly understood the threat to their budgets of 'accidentals' and 'overpluses', as opposed to their other, more predictable, expenditures on pensions and workhouse routine. A frequently inevitable result of incapacitation was that many families that were not usually in need of help were thrust into poverty so long as illness lasted, so that the vestry had not only to pay for the doctor but also for everything else – that is, pensions to cover shelter, fuel, clothing, food and drink. This multiplier effect must have increased the value to vestries of good doctors.

Unsurprisingly, vestries' contracts with workhouse managers were supplemented by agreements with doctors, which occur from 1760 until the end of the period in 1834. These too contained exceptions which protected practitioners from having to meet the heaviest expenses. Nowhere is the calculation of the fee explained. It was often in the order of 2½d per head of parish population, but up to four times this in villages. After 1770 parishes were often in long relationships with doctors, who might themselves deal with more than one parish at a time. Private practice offered better rewards and conditions to doctors – indeed, some may never have taken the poor's business at all, perhaps even because it was better for their own health not to[161] – and the occasional difficulties experienced by vestries in engaging them may have been due to this, but on the whole the business offered by the vestries was not only taken up but to an extent competed for. Prospects for doctors may have been better in Hertford than in Ware, judging by the number of practitioners in the two centres, but the Ware business must have been more economical and cost effective to run. In short, concern with the poor's health was a key issue for vestries throughout the eighteenth century but rather less so in the nineteenth, when it was just one among many cost concerns.

The other principal categories of record in the sources are the disorders from which people suffered and the ways in which they were treated. In some cases – such as scrofula (the King's Evil) and leprosy – there is only one mention, which may be attributable to the increasing rarity of these two diseases. Blisters and bleeding are not often mentioned either, but for a quite different reason, namely that they were routine. The itch (usually scabies) – not a rare condition – and 'scald head' (sometimes ringworm) took time and management to cure in serious cases, so accounting for their occasional presence in the sources. But smallpox occurs in the sources with the greatest regularity, reflecting both the fear that it engendered and the consequences for vestries. In one sense its onset was predictable, as when protection through immunity resulting from a previous outbreak in any area wore off the disease was increasingly likely to strike as a new epidemic. But in another it was unpredictable, because it was impossible to foretell when the worst might occur and crises in the study area appear not to have been particularly closely related to epidemic years in neighbouring parts of the south-east.[162] From the mid-1760s the Hertford and Ware area was quick to emulate the increasing use of the known practice of inoculation, which had been pioneered on a large scale in neighbouring Essex in the 1750s.[163] It had been used in Hertfordshire in the 1750s as well and events in Little Berkhamsted in both 1754 and 1768 provide examples of the backing which local subscriptions or free emergency treatment provided for vestries. Periodic village- and town-wide inoculations had some beneficial effects during the rest of the century, but the impact of the disease was substantially reduced only in the nineteenth century, with the introduction of vaccination. The two treatments ran in tandem for the rest of the period, but with inoculation being increasingly frowned upon by vestries.

The sources used are virtually silent on much else relating to the health of the poor, in particular fevers, and it took a very serious and prolonged outbreak for a vestry (Hertford All Saints) to gratuitously reward its hard-pressed doctor afterwards.[164] The Quaker-led preoccupation with the health of the poor in London, which was specifically based on combating fever and which led to the establishment of dispensaries in the last thirty years of the eighteenth century, finds no echo in the study area except for the public dispensary in Hertford referred to above. This may partly be because the problem was not so pressing in small towns and rural areas as it was in the metropolis.[165] But it may also be due to the fact that doctors' routine attention to the poor closely resembled the work of the London dispensaries. Dr Baker's very detailed bill to the overseers for the last quarter of 1781 in Hoddesdon shows that he was primarily and routinely treating 'fever' with a variety of cordials, powders, juleps, tinctures and the like, much as went on in London practice.[166] Rheumatism, arthritis, gastric disorders and consumption get no mention, nor do folk medicine, and – commonest and most self-evident of all – age and infirmity. To some extent support for the poor was, however, at least in workhouses, underwritten by attention to proper diet.

There is little evidence, then, that the administration of the Old Poor Law generated a medical service for the poor that was inferior to that enjoyed by the rest of the population. It is worth noting, however, that there was a widespread view in the later eighteenth century (propounded by supporters of the London-based campaign for the inoculation of the poor in their homes) that the poor were getting a bad deal, and this contention was allied to a criticism that smallpox doctors were happy to make money from the rich but unwilling to help the poor.[167] The well-intentioned proposals of the campaign foundered on popular fear of hospitals and on the impossibility of limiting the spread of the natural disease from the inoculated poor to their neighbours who had not had the smallpox in the natural way. Neither was opposition disarmed by the observation that quarantining the rich could be unsuccessful and that their servants and neighbours were sometimes infected. And it was, in any event, mainly a London issue. Certainly, well-off people came from far and wide in relative safety and isolation to a private inoculation clinic established in 1766 by Thomas Dimsdale close to the 'Pesthouse' at Bengeo, and although this shows that, in this respect, it was better to be well-off than not, the campaign of major inoculations of entire towns and villages in the Hertford area appears to have been on the whole successful. It certainly put Essex and Hertfordshire years ahead of most of the rest of the country in this respect.[168] Both rich and poor alike benefited from the effects of placebos, which often conferred psychological buoyancy and hope.[169] And it may be doubted whether the expensive services consumed by the rich did them that much good. In any event there was widespread scepticism – much of it quite justified – as to the efficacy of many, if not most, of the medical practices of the day.

No discussion, however, should be left on the table without reference to John Scott (1731–1783), a Quaker and sometime Great Amwell vestry member and overseer, who lived at Amwell End on the edge of Ware. In 1773 he published anonymously his *Observations on the present state of the parochial and vagrant poor*.[170] This was a forthright, informed and eloquently argued call for reform of the poor law, reflecting his intense dislike of most of the system as it stood. He was repelled by the workhouses and by what he regarded as the abdication of their responsibilities by those vestries that handed over management of their poor to 'farmers', whose management would inevitably be – in Scott's view – dictated by avarice. So in our consideration of the medical treatment of the poor – in which we have not overlooked their accommodation, which Scott found woefully and dangerously deficient in fresh air – it would be wrong to pass by his view of the matter:

> One thing is too publicly known to admit of denial, that those workhouses are scenes of filthiness and confusion; that old and young, sick and healthy, are promiscuously crowded into ill-contrived apartments, not of sufficient capacity to contain with convenience half the number of miserable beings condemned to such deplorable habitation; and that speedy death is almost ever to the aged and infirm, and often to the useful and robust, the consequence of a removal from more salubrious air to such mansions of putridity.

Notes

1.   Bengeo, Hertingfordbury and Hoddesdon.
2.   The parishes, liberties and hamlets are: Great Amwell, Little Amwell, Bayford, Bengeo, Little Berkhamsted, Bramfield, Broxbourne (Hoddesdon only), Hertford All Saints, Hertford St Andrew, Hertford St John, Hertingfordbury, Stanstead St Margarets, Stapleford, Tewin, Thundridge and Ware.
3.   Throughout the period this term refers to people who are still living in their own homes but who are in receipt of regular money payments.
4.   Hertfordshire Archives and Local Studies, Hertford (hereafter HALS) DP/50/8/2.
5.   Their main objection was to church rates.
6.   HALS DP/50/8/5.
7.   HALS DP/49/8/1.
8.   HALS DP/48/8/18.
9.   HALS DP/24A/8/11. This reached 6 per cent of a rate at Hoddesdon in 1770.
10.   HALS DP/50/11/2.
11.   HALS DP/48/8/16–17.
12.   Estimates based on poor-rate records for Brickendon, Hertingfordbury, Hertford All Saints, Hertford St Johns, Little Amwell and Ware.
13.   L. Turnor, *History of the ancient town and borough of Hertford* (Hertford, 1830), pp. 274–5.
14.   HALS DP/24A/8/8.
15.   HALS DP/48/8/8.
16.   Turnor, *History of the ancient town*, pp. 274–5.
17.   HALS DP/48/8/8.
18.   Ibid.
19.   HALS DP/48/18/2.
20.   HALS DP/48/18/3.
21.   HALS DP/48/8/8 and DP/49/8/1.
22.   HALS DP/24A/8/9.
23.   *Abstracts of the returns made by the overseers of the poor...* (London, 1777).
24.   Ibid.
25.   HALS DP/48/8/9.
26.   HALS DP/48/8/12.
27.   HALS DP/50/8/2.
28.   HALS DP/4/8/1.
29.   *Abstract of the returns made by the overseers of the poor.*
30.   Ibid.
31.   HALS DE/X3 Carrington Diary.
32.   HALS DP/20/8/3.
33.   HALS DP/48/18/2.
34.   HALS DP/48/18/3.
35.   HALS DP/50/8/3.
36.   HALS DP/49/8/1.
37.   Ibid.

38. HALS DP/24A/8/11.

39. HALS DP/50/8/2.

40. HALS DP/48/8/21.

41. HALS DP/116/8/1.

42. HALS DP/48/8/12.

43. HALS DP/24A/8/11.

44. HALS DP/48/8/9.

45. HALS DP/4/8/3. The vestry proposed a new workhouse for 40 persons in 1803 on the back of the increased rate base resulting from the new East India College, presumably to bring in more of the poor under one roof, but there were objections.

46. HALS DP/4/8/1.

47. HALS DP/49/8/1.

48. HALS DP/50/8/2.

49. HALS DP/48/8/12.

50. HALS DP/49/8/2.

51. HALS DP/48/8/9.

52. HALS DP/48/8/12.

53. HALS DP/48/8/9.

54. HALS DP/116/8/2.

55. HALS DP/4/8/8.

56. Ibid.

57. Ibid.

58. HALS DP/48/8/9+.

59. HALS DP/50/8/5.

60. HALS DP/48/8/16.

61. HALS DP/116/8/1.

62. Ibid.

63. Ibid.

64. HALS DP/116/12/2.

65. HALS DP/48/8/17.

66. HALS DP/4/11/26.

67. HALS DP/49/8/2.

68. HALS DP/48/8/8.

69. HALS DP/50/8/6.

70. HALS DP/49/8/2.

71. Ibid.

72. HALS DP/48/8/18.

73. HALS DP/116/11/1.

74. HALS DP/24A/18/18.

75. HALS DP/24A/18/19.

76. HALS DP/48/8/8.

77. Ibid.

78. Ibid.

79. Founded 1792.

80. HALS DP/20/8/3.
81. Ibid.
82. HALS DP/48/8/17.
83. HALS DP/24A/8/11.
84. HALS DP/103/12/1.
85. HALS DP/24A/8/10.
86. HALS DP/116/12/1.
87. HALS DP/116/8/1.
88. Ibid.; Queen Anne was still touching sufferers to cure them three years later.
89. HALS DP/24A/18/1/21.
90. HALS DP/49/8/2.
91. HALS DP/49/8/1.
92. Ibid.
93. Ibid.
94. Ibid.
95. HALS DP/110/8/1. Hansen's disease.
96. HALS DP/24A/18.
97. HALS DP/50/8/5.
98. HALS DP/106/5/1.
99. HALS DP/24A/18/1.
100. HALS DP/24A/18/6/7.
101. HALS DP/48/8/9.
102. M.J. Dobson, *Contours of death and disease in early modern England* (Cambridge, 1997), p. 371, fig. 7.2.
103. HALS DP/116/8/1.
104. HALS DP/50/8/5.
105. Ibid.
106. HALS DP/48/8/8.
107. Ibid.
108. HALS DP/48/8/8.
109. HALS DP/48/8/17.
110. HALS DP/48/8/12.
111. HALS DP/116/8/2.
112. HALS DP/4/8/3.
113. Vaccination, as introduced by Jenner, involved the use of cowpox, and this competed with and eventually superseded inoculation using smallpox (variolation).
114. HALS DP/50/8/2.
115. HALS DP/116/8/2.
116. HALS DP/104/12/2.
117. HALS DP/20/8/3.
118. S.F. Simmons, *The medical register for the year 1779* (London, 1779); S.F. Simmons, *The medical register for the year 1780* (London, 1780); S.F. Simmons, *The medical register for the year 1783* (London, 1783).
119. HALS DP/49/8/1.

120. W. Munk, *Roll of the Royal College of Physicians of London* (London, 1878).
121. HALS DP/48/8/9.
122. HALS DP/48/8/8.
123. Ibid.
124. Ibid.
125. HALS DP/4/8/8.
126. HALS DP/49/8/1.
127. HALS DP/48/8/13.
128. HALS DP/24A/18.
129. Ibid.
130. Ibid.
131. Ibid.
132. HALS DP/24A/8/1.
133. HALS DP/116/8/2.
134. Ibid.
135. Ibid.
136. HALS DP/104/12/1.
137. HALS DP/22/12/4.
138. Ibid.
139. Ibid.
140. Ibid.
141. HALS DP/20/8/3.
142. Ibid.
143. HALS DP/103/12/1.
144. It seems that the vestry specifically needed both a surgeon and an apothecary and that the term 'doctor' would not have been precise enough.
145. HALS DP/48/8/9, amendments in the original.
146. University of Nottingham PwF 230/1 Portland Papers.
147. HALS DP/20/25/2.
148. HALS DP/20/8/3.
149. Ibid.
150. Turnor, *History of the ancient town*, pp. 377–8.
151. HALS 252.034/Le Bas.
152. HALS DP/48/8/1 (location only).
153. Hertford Museum Andrews Collection, printed note.
154. Ibid.
155. HALS DP/20/1/2.
156. HALS DP/20/1/2.
157. HALS DP/24A/8/9–10.
158. Ibid.
159. *Gentleman's Magazine* (1801).
160. University of Nottingham PwF 230/1 Portland Papers.
161. ERO D/Z 15/1. Records of the Benevolent Medical Society for the united Counties of Essex and Hertford 1786–1804. There was a 'fund for the relief … of Widows and

Orphans of Physicians, Surgeons and Apothecaries in Essex and Herts, [who are] exposed to numerous sources of infection and suffer premature death frequently thereby and the fair prospects of a family suddenly blasted and a painful reverse presented to persons well brought up but thus cut off from future resources'.

162. Dobson, *Contours of death and disease*, pp. 383–449.

163. J.R. Smith, *The speckled monster* (Chelmsford, 1987), pp. 40–68. J. Beckett, *Writing local history* (Manchester, 2007), pp. 106–23.

164. HALS DP/48/8/9.

165. R. Kilpatrick, '"Living in the light": dispensaries, philanthropy and medical reform in late-eighteenth-century London', in A. Cunningham and R. French (eds), *The medical enlightenment of the eighteenth century* (Cambridge, 1990), pp. 254–80.

166. HALS DP/24A/18.

167. J.J. Abraham, *Lettsom. His life times friends and descendants* (London, 1933), pp. 185–205.

168. F.M. Lobo, 'John Haygarth, smallpox and religious dissent in eighteenth-century England', in Cunningham and French, *The medical enlightenment*, pp. 217–53.

169. A. Digby, *Making a medical living: doctors and patients in the English market for medicine, 1720–1911* (Cambridge, 1994), p. 302.

170. For a full treatment of Scott's work on this subject see D. Perman, *Scott of Amwell: Dr. Johnson's Quaker critic* (Ware, 2001), ch. 9.

CHAPTER THREE

Caring for the sick and poor in eighteenth-century Royston

Carla Herrmann

I N THE 1790S Royston was described as 'A good market town on the utmost northern border of Hertfordshire, where it joins to the county of Cambridge'.[1] The town had developed in what would have been regarded by contemporaries as a healthy position on chalk downs situated at the important intersection of the ancient east–west route the Icknield Way and Roman Ermine Street (the Old North Road), which ran from London to Lincoln (Figure 3.1). Royston was a busy thoroughfare town served by both daily coaches to London, Carlisle, Cambridge, Boston and Stamford and a network of wagons which linked it to the nearby villages. There were a large number of inns, taverns and other services dependent on the coaching trades, such as smithies and wheelwrights. Royston was also a trading centre for maltsters and corn factors, many of whom also farmed cereals, principally barley, in the surrounding countryside. These men employed varying numbers of mostly day-labourers throughout the year in their fields and maltings. In 1801 the town had a population of 975[2] but by 1821 this had grown to 2,474.[3] It is not possible to know how many of these people were paupers, but there is an earlier figure for 10 June 1788 which gives a total of 354 pauper men, women and children. On that day their smallpox inoculations – by deliberate infection with matter from smallpox sufferers – were paid for by the town because they could not afford the necessary 2s 6d per person themselves.[4] However, this figure may also have included paupers from outlying villages such as Barkway, Bassingbourn and Therfield.

One of those being vaccinated in 1788 could well have been Widow Sarah Fordham, who was certainly a pauper and is known to have been

Figure 3.1 Royston Cross, *c.*1750, where the ancient Ermine Street and Icknield Way crossed. By Robert Clutterbuck, courtesy HALS.

living in the Back Street in Royston several years previously with her son and daughter. More than 30 years earlier, as Sarah Reeves of Bassingbourn, she had married John Fordham, a widower and farm servant. He subsequently became an ostler and later had sufficient resources to set up as a victualler and a vintner.[5] John may have been older than his wife, as he died in 1772,[6] but appears to have been sufficiently healthy to serve in the Hertfordshire Militia until the year of his death.[7] He could have been under 45 when he died, as this was the upper age limit for the Militia. Sarah and her family survived on their earnings and possibly some form of widow's allowance for ten years before Royston Vestry seized the opportunity of her sickness to save the expense of her maintenance. Her case throws some light on how Royston treated its poor and on parish officials' attitude towards them, as well as – particularly interestingly – showing a female pauper somehow winning the right to keep her independence. This was an unusual outcome for a parish dependent pitted against the oligarchy which ran Royston. She may possibly have been a poor relation of one of the up-and-coming vestrymen, Edward King Fordham, who was a woolcomber and stapler and later rose to banker and workhouse overseer.[8] He might have used his influence or she might have argued her case exceptionally well, because she did not meekly move into the workhouse when she recovered from her illness but seems to have convinced the Vestry that she should remain on outdoor relief.

Throughout their lives paupers commonly existed on the edge of complete destitution. They were almost certain to be obliged to seek parish help if they were orphaned or deserted in childhood; if they suffered unemployment through injury or illness when their young children were totally dependent on them; and when their children had grown and moved away and they became chronically sick and unemployable during old age. These life-cycle poverty crises have been studied for some counties but not to date in Hertfordshire. The intricate connection between life-cycle stress points and the medical problems suffered by all but exacerbated by extreme poverty have been even less thoroughly researched. Children were often mortally endangered by sickness and accidents and any medical costs further weakened the vulnerable pauper family, with the mother often unable to contribute to the family income because she was engaged in caring for her sick child or children. Older children, especially boys, were liable to accidents both when playing and in their first jobs or apprenticeships. They suffered injuries when working unsupervised with horses and carts[9] or herding cattle and sheep, and they could be permanently damaged when lifting and labouring beyond their strength. Boys, when not working, were prone to accepting life-threatening 'dares' such as testing thin ice or climbing dangerous structures.[10] Girls were usually kept closer to home or in domestic service and given less independence, but were constantly at risk from scalds and cuts when preparing food or doing laundry and might also develop muscle strains and injuries when house-cleaning. A child could enter the labour market but then almost immediately be injured through inexperience or lack of supervision, and some of these injuries, such as blindness or a crippled limb, would affect the child's prospects throughout life. Epidemic diseases, fevers and accidents could strike at any time and devastate families, as could death in childbirth. Old age was a time of increasing infirmity, as the chances of suffering from conditions such as arthritis, rheumatism and dropsy (indicating the existence of heart and circulatory problems) increased. Apoplexy, paralysis or strokes could threaten and frequently abruptly end the life of a pauper.

Against such a backdrop, this chapter will focus on the hitherto largely unknown pauper patients of eighteenth-century Royston. It will

Figure 3.2 The Old Workhouse, London Road, Royston. It is the colonnaded building on the right-hand side of the photograph (which was probably taken in the early twentieth century). HALS photographic collection.

not consider medical institutions – only a few became patients at the nearest hospital, Addenbrookes in Cambridge, because Royston chose not to hospitalise very sick paupers. Royston paupers do not appear to have required admission to lunatic asylums at this time. The idea of taking out a hospital subscription was discussed by the Vestry[11] but they eventually decided on the much cheaper option of creating an infirmary in the workhouse instead.

The Royston town oligarchy certainly recognised some obligations towards its sick and unemployable paupers because it spent money on constructing and later improving its workhouse (Figure 3.2), but it does not appear to have been primarily concerned with their welfare. Royston's interpretation of the Old Poor Law was essentially a response to the problem of poverty in the town that needed to be solved as simply and economically as possible. The town's policy was centred on identifying those people who could not, or could no longer, maintain themselves by working. These sick and destitute people could not be allowed to disgrace Royston by 'going about the town abegging',[12] and nor was Royston prepared to maintain them in their own homes. It was far cheaper to put them in a workhouse under a Master and Mistress so they could be lodged, fed, cared for and encouraged to do what work they still could in a strictly controlled environment.

Pauper patients

Royston's pauper patients can be divided into three distinct groupings based on probably the most important factor in their lives, their employability. The first group consisted of infants and children not yet strong enough to be apprenticed or able to work outside the home and usually aged below 7 or 8 years. The second and largest group was formed of regularly employed or semi-employed paupers, of both sexes, aged from 7 to 70 or even 80 plus. Some particularly robust children of even younger age fall into this group. The third contained paupers of any age who were not capable of supporting themselves owing to disability, chronic sickness, senility or debility. Most of these rejects from the job market would still be employed in spinning, gardening, cooking, cleaning and nursing one another in the workhouse unless they were too young, totally 'impotent' or plainly in their last illnesses.

No medical bills seem to have survived for sick workhouse inmates, but as they were already in the care of the parish these might well have seemed unnecessary. It was left to the Master to choose a medical man and send for him at his discretion to 'visit any such of the persons afors[d] who shall be Visited with Sickness or any Disease whatsoever'.[13] In the 1785 Workhouse Inmates List, which was probably compiled by the workhouse master, there are very brief notes on the 'condition' of 41 workhouse inmates.[14] Most were described as 'healthy' but two old men were 'infirm' and the elder, aged 80, was going blind and died the following September. Two children had 'bad eyes', one 'has had fitts' and two had 'the Evil' (scrofula). One of these, Daniel Gaylor, whose treatment the Vestry had refused to fund, 'won't work'. He died in 1787 and was buried from the workhouse (see below). One girl was described as 'sickly' and she died in the following July. Of the disabled inmates, John Brown had one leg and a boy was described as 'lame' and 'in the hospital'.

Living conditions in the Royston workhouse at this time could not be described as 'Dickensian'. The workhouse was well furnished compared to most paupers' hovels; there was a collection of miscellaneous clothing for the most destitute[15] and all inmates were considerably better fed and more comfortable than they could hope to be outside.[16] If the apothecary so ordered, sick paupers could be provided with extras, including wine,[17] but he was called out and paid by the workhouse master, who may well have had a vested interest in rationing such items.[18] The only appearance of a workhouse apothecary in official records was in 1799, when William

Crespin Junior appeared before the Vestry to give his opinion on Charlotte Knights, a young and possibly deranged workhouse inmate, and advised the standard treatment for such problems: 'that She should have a Blister laid on head as the only remedy of doing her Service'.[19]

Outside the workhouse the Vestry could act as gatekeepers to medical services for undeserving paupers, rationing the amount and quality they received. Vestry members carried out regular workhouse inspections and in 1789 had expanded Royston medical services, possibly prompted by problems in dealing with infectious diseases in the workhouse: 'October 5 1789 Order'd that at the Vestry meeting at Church it be taken into Consideration respecting the Building an Infirmary to the Workhouse', while on 18 March 1790 it was

> likewise found the Lodging Room insufficient to Lodge the poor in a proper and commodious manner and especially when any Illness or bad disorder happen in the House. It is therefore proposed that two new Rooms be Erected on the South End of the Workhouse for Bed Rooms that two Rooms at the North End of the House be kept entirely for Sick paupers and to be made no other Use of whatsoever.[20]

The amount of information available on pauper patients living outside the workhouse is very uneven. All detailed medical and pharmaceutical information for Royston paupers is drawn from the 16 surviving annual medical bills submitted by parish doctors in payment for their services to sick paupers, which are scattered in no discernible order throughout the bundles of overseers' bills and vouchers held at Hertfordshire Archives and Local Studies (HALS). The lives and health problems of both female and child pauper patients are particularly difficult to trace. There must have been many who remain completely 'hidden' because they did not appear in any official records. Women patients living outside the workhouse did not often feature in Vestry orders or medical bills. They could bring themselves to the attention of parish officials as potential workhouse inmates, as did Widow Fordham, or by suffering incapacitating illnesses. These anonymous sick women obtained varying degrees of assistance from their parish. Thus, the Royston Vestry in 1791 'Order'd that the Overseer at his discretion allow Ew^d Reynolds for a Woman to look after his Wife who has the Use of her Limbs taken away'.[21] According to a note by the curate in the Royston Burial Register, Edward Reynolds had been the Royston parish clerk for 'near 30 years' when his wife died in 1780.[22] He would therefore have been considered a 'deserving pauper'. By 1791 he had remarried and his usefulness to the parish may have influenced the Vestry to pay for a 'carer' for his wife who was possibly a victim of paralysis or stroke, as there was apparently no female relative available. However, by 12 January 1795, when Reynolds himself was also ill, the Vestry set limits on its generosity, ordering 'that the Overseer Allow Ew^d Reynolds what he thinks necessary /he being Ill and his Wife/ not to exceed 10d Weekly'.[23] Another sick woman, Henry Sanson's wife, also suffered from a long-term illness, but Royston chose not to maintain her. She was ordered into hospital and may have died there, as both she and her husband subsequently disappeared from Royston records.[24] Other women, possibly older, suffered fractures and dislocations which required the doctor's expertise. Of the four women who were treated at different times for a broken arm,[25] a dislocated collar bone,[26] a fractured rib[27] and a badly bruised head,[28] three were widows (Brown, Fordham and Hall). They may have been frail, under-nourished and/or elderly. In the case of Brown the Vestry minutes recorded that she had suffered from a fall and should be in the workhouse.[29] It was not recorded how Widow Hall had received her head injury.

At the other end of the life-cycle, childbirth was regarded as a potentially fatal illness at this time by all sections of the community and by persons medical and lay. Pauper women sometimes appear on medical bills because they were exhausted and malnourished and suffered progressively greater difficulties with each birth. If there were complications with a pauper delivery a doctor had to be called in instead of the considerably cheaper midwife, who always received a set fee of 3s for each delivery. In the upper reaches of society man-midwives were progressively invading this lucrative branch of medicine by offering forceps delivery, but a pauper woman would have had to be in serious difficulties to receive such services. Daniel Crespin appears to have been the most consulted practitioner in these emergencies and charged a standard fee of 10s 6d per delivery. This was always recorded but whether his patients survived is more difficult to unravel. He delivered 'Dame Hankin' who apparently recovered, because she was not listed in the burial register for that year.[30] Thomas Kefford's wife also appears to have survived her delivery in December 1786, as her name was recorded in later medical bills. She may have had twins, as Crespin charged a double fee of one guinea. Joseph Hankin's wife was also delivered by Crespin on 18 April 1799[31] and she also survived. 'Crouch's Wife' may have suffered post-natal medical problems. She was delivered by Crespin on 27 November 1799 and a day later he prescribed eight unspecified powders and an unspecified mixture. There were no further references to her or the child in his later medical bills and as there is a gap in the burial records from April 1799 to January 1800 it cannot be known whether they survived. On 7 July 1801 Crespin charged 5s for 'midwifery in part' on Charles Docwra's wife, which would seem to indicate that some emergency situation had arisen which required his expertise, possibly with a forceps delivery.[32] Midwives were not permitted to learn how to use forceps.

Women were traditional providers of herbal and folk-medical knowledge. In the community women self-medicated for less serious illnesses and consulted one another. They might swap remedies for treating coughs and colds, but fevers were usually left to the doctor, probably because they developed with frightening speed and could be fatal. Most women would keep recipes for treatments such as salves and liniments for sores, strains, burns and bruises and pain-relieving or heating ointments for chronic illnesses such as rheumatism and arthritis. They would also have relied on one another for advice on the safest methods of using potentially lethal abortifacients and other cures for female problems. This kind of medicine was known to the medical profession as 'domestic' or 'kitchen' because women usually prepared their recipes in the kitchen and also frequently wrote cookery and medical recipes in the same book, which was then handed down from mother to daughter in the family. Crespin seems to have been the only Royston pauper practitioner to have recognised that such treatments might have some value and he encouraged a degree of self-medication by regularly supplying 'ingredients to boil' when he applied a blister to a sick patient. He did this frequently on a first visit and in all cases of epidemic fever. Presumably he wanted to enable the patients' carers to maintain the blister for several hours or days.[33] Other practitioners seem not to have trusted the carers but instead used the more standard and quickly applied blistering plasters, containing cantharides, made from Spanish Fly, or similar agents to raise blisters.

Sick infants and children were normally nursed and medicated at home. First-time mothers would have required advice and recipes for treatments for their children's ailments and they would tend to acquire these from their own mothers, female relatives and neighbours. If an infant had a sudden and potentially fatal attack of convulsions the mother would have to turn to her immediate neighbours for help because there would be no time to seek a doctor. There are no records of child patients being sent away to institutions, which would seem to indicate either that there were no chronically disabled or sick children (which is unlikely) or that Royston Vestry was not prepared to pay for their treatment. There was at least one Royston disabled child living outside the parish at Newmarket with her mother Mary Greenhow. She appears to have been a victim of infantile paralysis, which had crippled one leg so that she was dependent on crutches.[34] Indeed, Royston pauper children appear very seldom on medical bills except when they broke or dislocated a limb,[35] needed a tooth drawn[36] or required treatment for boils[37] or abscesses,[38] both of which could have been symptoms of malnutrition. Children were often among the first sufferers when infectious diseases such as smallpox or measles arrived in the parish, as they had no resistance. They became objects of almost palpable anxiety to the parish officials, who immediately began discussing preventative measures and even considered consulting with all the parishioners on inoculation:

> Order'd that as there is now one Child of Wm Walker [Labourer]
> taken with the smallpox and that the same be forthwith sent into
> the pesthouse and that if any others fall with the like disorder that
> they be sent into the same House until the same be full and if it
> shall happen that many others should fall with the smallpox, that
> the Overseers call a general Meeting at Church and take the voice
> of the parish whether a general Inoculation shall take place.[39]

The only recorded large-scale childhood infection was the epidemic of 1800–02 and, judging from the medical bills, this was *not* diagnosed by Crespin as smallpox, measles, diphtheria or scarlatina/scarlet fever, the major childhood diseases of the time. In some cases the sick children seem to have infected their families. In others their parents were the carriers, particularly when malarial ague was brought back by male relatives who had been working in areas of East Anglia where this disease was endemic. These cases can be traced through the almost immediate prescription of Peruvian Bark, then regarded as the most effective remedy for ague.[40]

Adult male patients aged from 18 to 50 years form the group about whom most medical information is known because the parish constable whose job it was to compile the militia ballot lists had to record any infirmities that would prevent an individual from serving. In 1762 the upper age limit was reduced to 45. In Royston, as for Hertfordshire as a whole, large and almost complete runs of these militia lists have survived, complete with details of occupations. These give insights into both common disabilities and probable work injuries and illnesses.[41] However, although the Royston parish constable was able to write reports and submit expenses he was unlikely to have had any specialist medical knowledge. He described his neighbours as he saw them and probably also recorded their verbal accounts of their health problems, some of which they may have exaggerated in order to avoid the militia ballot. Lameness, disability or obvious mental problems could not be hidden, however. During the period covered by the lists from 1758 to 1786 successive constables reported 28 men who were 'lame'. This meant disabled in some way, as it was possible to have a 'lame' thumb, as in the case of John Burden, a wool-sorter listed in 1775. There were, in addition, 26 men with leg or foot problems, 13 men with sight and eye defects, 2 men who were 'ill', 2 who were 'deformed', 2 who were 'infirm' and 4 who had fractures. Others had hand and finger injuries, back, neck and shoulder defects, ruptures or were deaf. Only one man, William Cackbread, was described as 'disordered in his head', which might have been either due to a mental problem or a form of vertigo induced by the intense concentration on a rotating object required in his job as a turner:

> moreover they [turners] must keep the eyes fixed on the work,
> and from that rotary motion of the wood the eyes contract some
> injury, since it stimulates the spirits and humours to a vertiginous
> sort of motion.[42]

Examples of other possible occupational 'infirmities' include two ruptured butchers, a jockey with a broken and apparently badly mended leg, a breeches-maker with a stiff neck and labourers 'blemished' or blind in one eye or 'lame'.

From the medical bills it appears that pauper surgery principally consisted of reducing fractures and dislocations probably caused by falls and work accidents. There was also a constant need to open and dress boils, abscesses, wounds and ulcers, which may also have been the legacies of work-related injuries. Surgery was appreciably more expensive than 'physick' and it is perhaps surprising that the Vestry allowed so much to be done, especially of the more 'cosmetic' variety, as skin infections and eruptions did not usually prevent a man from working unless very severe or awkwardly placed so as to make it difficult to work. Abscesses and ulcers could also be caused by scurvy and it is possible that some Royston paupers suffered from forms of malnutrition, particularly as they aged and grew debilitated and less capable of earning enough to feed themselves properly. There is one Essex pauper letter from 1822 in which an elderly agricultural labourer describes exactly how this vicious circle of slow deterioration had affected him:

> From William James in Chelmsford July 29 1822
> I find health and strength decaying fast, so that when I have a
> little work to do, I find myself, through Age, and fatigue, incapable
> to perform it. Walking into the Country five or six Miles in a
> morning, working the Day, and returning home at Night, is a
> task that I cannot, but without great difficulty perform, several
> times I have thought, I could not get home, and it have been the
> Occasion, of my being Ill, for two or three days, this I attribute in a
> great degree, to the want, of constant Nourishment, to keep up my
> strength, and of Age added there too, being now within one year of
> Seventy – at this time I am Unwell, and have been several days …[43]

Many of the male Royston paupers held down several jobs and might be both agricultural labourers and also, during the winter, malt-makers. In both of these occupations it would be possible to sustain fractures and dislocations to legs and arms or to receive wounds and injuries from animals, machines, lifting-gear or tools. At least two men may have been partially crushed; one 'fractured his breastbone'[44] and another 'damaged his back and loins'.[45] Sometimes men died at work: several fatal injuries are recorded in the Royston burial register. James Prior[46] and Charles Thurley[47] fell down wells; William Mead,[48] a labourer, was killed 'by a cart being overthrown'; and James Trigg[49] was killed by a 'fall from a horse'.

Three case studies demonstrate the abundance of information about the medical problems of male pauper patients in contrast with the paltry amounts regarding females and children. One of these men was John Britton, a sick labourer who was therefore targeted for the workhouse. On 7 March 1785 the Vestry ordered an un-named parish doctor to 'attend John

Britton and family to see if they are well enough to go into the Workhouse'.[50] It would seem that they were not because on 25 July the Vestry 'ordered payment for the Midwife [who] attended John Britton's wife'.[51] On 4 February 1787 Matthew Daniel prescribed dressings and medicines for John Britton, who then disappeared from the records. He may have survived until 1816, because there is a John Britain in the Royston burial records who died at the age of 84, but this might have been his son.[52] Hansell/Ansell Brown was a labourer who was treated by all three of the parish doctors for ten years from 1785. He had various 'stomachick' problems in 1785 and 1786. Hansell also required a 'bathing liniment' in 1786, when the Royston constable described him as 'lame' in the Militia List but did not specify in which part he was disabled. This was the only time that he was listed, so he may have been near the upper age limit of 45. He had fever in 1790 and 1794 and on 12 January 1795 the Vestry ordered that 'the Overseer Allow Ansell Brown about two Shillings a Week he being very Ill'. He does not appear in the Royston burial register, so may have recovered and moved away. John Brown was a workhouse inmate listed on 7 February 1785 as aged 26 and having lost one leg. He had already been recorded as 'lame' by the Royston constable in 1780, so this may have been a degenerative disease rather than an accidental injury.[53] By July 1787 he was having problems with his remaining leg. Matthew Daniel prescribed a 'General Embrocation' and a 'Purging Powder'. On 17 July he repeated the embrocation and on 23 July prescribed unspecified ointment, dressings and 'curing thigh'. This cost 7s 6d and involved expensive surgery, possibly by incision or cautery. On 3 and 5 August Daniel repeated the embrocation and the treatment appeared to have worked because no more was heard until 1 June 1790, when Daniel bled Brown and ordered another embrocation, repeated on 29 June. On 29 August Daniel treated an ulcer in Brown's leg – not his thigh, so this may have been a new problem – and on 23 November he 'cured' a large laceration and wound in Brown's leg and foot: this injury was possibly the result of an accident and its treatment was certainly a very expensive operation for a pauper (£2 2s); however, it prolonged his life for three more years. He was buried 'from the workhouse' on 29 December 1793.[54]

What is particularly interesting is that comparatively few pauper men seem to have used Royston parish healthcare, which would seem to show that a great deal of self-medication and consultation of friends, relatives and local 'unorthodox experts' went on in preference to parish provision. The parish doctor was used in an emergency, when surgery or bone-setting were required or when sudden, debilitating fevers struck, but he does not appear to have been the first resort of the sick male pauper. A man may well have wanted to avoid entanglement in the Royston poor law system and possible consignment of himself and his family to the workhouse, where he would completely lose his independence. Sick men were anxious to assure the Vestry that any health problems were purely temporary and easily cured: 'Order'd that Mr Butler allow Corn[elius] Hankin two Shillings a Week he having a sore Leg which he says will be well in the Course of a Week or two'.[55]

The parish doctor appears to have reported directly to the Vestry and taken orders from the overseer. The more politically astute paupers would have been well aware of this relationship and its implications for them. Male workers, both married and unmarried, survived by 'makeshifts' and had to know what was going on in their community in order to take advantage of every opportunity of local employment and/or transport to other parts of the country to find work. During the hungry winter months work was rarely available except to the specialist workers, such as horsemen, cattlemen and shepherds. General labourers were now responsible for themselves since the former residential-farm-servant system was becoming an unnecessary burden to farmers. In the workhouse men would be cut off from their contacts, from friends and from local gossip. The Workhouse Rules allowed paupers out of the workhouse on Sundays to attend church and in the summer evenings from Lady Day to Michaelmas but this freedom was very brief and strictly controlled by the Master. It was laid down that 'the Master shall allow such paupers as he thinks proper to walk out of the House in the Summer half year after their Working Hours [5.30 p.m.] until Supper time [set at 7.30 p.m. throughout the year] but never later.'[56]

Women, who were nearly always dependent on a male 'breadwinner' – husband, father, brother or son – were more likely to be absorbed into the system. They tended to consult doctors more frequently, particularly if their children were seriously ill. Sarah Gaylor, a Royston pauper living in London with a sick husband and son, was determined to get the best possible treatment for her child. Her son suffered from what had been diagnosed as a degenerative 'Scorbutic disorder nearly in the last stage', and she had spared no effort to find a cure for him: she 'ha[d] had the advice of every Eminent Surgeon', as her host parish officials reported back to Royston in 1784. Royston Vestry would neither pay for any treatment nor agree to repay the host parish if they loaned her the money and advised her to return to the workhouse; her son subsequently died there in January 1787.[57] A surprising level of detail can be gleaned about the medical practitioners sick paupers consulted and the workings of the medical practices they used.

Royston medical men

Traditionally, the medical marketplace has been seen as divided between the elite physicians, the craftsman surgeons and the tradesman apothecaries. Royston paupers would have been likely to have encountered the hybrid 'surgeon-apothecary', a role that was developing at that time and is now generally considered the ancestor of the general practitioner.[58] The Vestry-appointed parish doctors worked an annual rota, but it is not known exactly when this system began. There seem to have been early attempts to experiment with annual contracts from 1770 onwards,[59] but these appear to have been biased towards the practitioner, providing insufficient detail (usually only referring to the amount paid) and failing to satisfy Vestry requirements to know the exact cost of the services being provided. Royston Vestry preferred to control both the doctors and their patients. A list that survives for the period 1782 to 1789 appears to form part of a cost–benefit analysis by the treasurer. In this analysis Thomas Nunn emerged as the worst 'bargain', having charged the parish £37 1s 9d for two years of pauper medical treatment, whereas Daniel Crespin cost £17 1s 3d for the same period and Matthew Daniel £25 15s 7d for three years.[60] During this period Royston paupers were attended by two established and probably Royston-born medical practitioners, both of whom were surgeon-apothecaries: Daniel Crespin[61] and Matthew Daniel,[62] who had been apprenticed to the Royston surgeon-apothecary, Luke Wayman, in 1755.[63] Daniel Crespin's master is not recorded. These two were joined by an incomer, Thomas Nunn, in 1785,[64] who had formally applied to be added to the rota:

> To the Gentlemen of the Royston Easter Meeting
> Gentlemen
> As I am now Settled in Royston as a Medical Practitioner I hope
> there will not be any Impropriety in Soliciting the favour to Attend
> the poor of Royston in Rotation with the others of the Faculty
> Y^rs respectfully
> Thos J Nunn
> P.S. Indisposition <u>prevents</u> a Personal Application.[65]

He disappeared from the records after 1798 and may have moved away.

Many paupers appear to have been living in and around the town in the back streets and outlying rural areas. They probably came into daily contact with the townsfolk as sellers of services and market produce or as direct, and sometimes live-in, employees. Therefore, it made sense, from the town oligarchy's point of view, to ensure that they were kept as healthy as possible even when it cost a steadily increasing amount of money. Royston Vestry had to weigh the costs of keeping paupers relatively healthy against the dangers of allowing them to degenerate into a dangerously diseased underclass, as was already happening in London and other rapidly expanding new towns. Self-preservation and a drive for efficient town and worker management won out against savings. When the threat of epidemics loomed Royston initiated an inoculation programme and paupers suspected of being infected, as with the Walker child above, were usually immediately isolated in the pesthouse. Food, medical and nursing aid were made available to all those affected, including dependent families. For ordinary sickness the Vestry treasurer received a detailed annual bill from the outgoing parish doctor on the rota and could thus monitor each item prescribed to every man, woman and child. It is probable that he did this and also queried items because bills were regularly paid at least several months in arrears, as can be seen from the practitioners' dated signatures on the bills. Initially separate bills from Royston, Hertfordshire, and Royston, Cambridgeshire, were provided by practitioners even after the two parts of the town were united in 1781 in a deliberate strategy to save money on provision for the poor.[66] Itemised bills for individual pauper families were submitted separately, especially where a high level of expenditure had been incurred, as in the typhus-like fever outbreak among the Docwra family.[67] When the patient/s came from other parishes, such as neighbouring Basingbourn and more distant Standon, as in the Cherry smallpox cases,[68] their parishes were expected to reimburse Royston for all costs.

The parish doctor appears also to have served Vestry members and their circle on demand. Thomas Nunn was instructed to attend Robert Walker's wife in labour 'By order of Mr Abbott', as recorded on his medical bill.[69] Robert Walker was one of Mr Abbott's labourers and probably a valued worker. There may have been many more verbal directions given to parish doctors regarding the treatment of paupers; certainly, it is difficult to believe that vestrymen would not intervene informally in the provision of medicine when given the opportunity. Indeed, judged by its orders, bills

and invoices Royston Vestry seems to have been run by an authoritarian
and highly managerial group of men which collected and kept even the
most minute pieces of information. The Crespin family may have proved
the most amenable to Vestry control, as they were more frequently chosen
to serve consecutive years and evolved into Royston's *de facto* parish doctors
without any official decision being recorded in the minutes. Not everyone
was satisfied by this. In 1796 an anonymous 'sick person' complained that
W.R. Crespin (who was possibly the Workhouse apothecary and son of
Daniel Crespin, the William Crespin Junior mentioned above) 'does not
give proper Attendance'. A verbal reprimand seems to have been given by
the Vestry Clerk, who 'is desired to acquaint Mr Crespin of the same'.[70]

Treatments

From the amount and variety of prescriptions used it would appear that
the Royston surgeon-apothecaries aimed to 'cure', in the sense of alleviate,
the most troubling symptoms: it was rarely possible to do away with them
entirely. They probably tended to use the cheapest ingredients in 'pauper
mixtures' and 'draughts' because poor people, even when sick, were
believed by practitioners to be able to tolerate drastic purges and 'rougher'
and cheaper types of medicines:

> But this latter Form [Mixtures in the form of Draughts] is not so
> neat for Persons of any Delicacy, the solid Ingredients being much
> better made into Boles, and washed down with a Draught made
> of the Liquids, unless it be to such who are poor, and to whom
> Charity requires as much to be done in as small a compass as
> possible.[71]

While the Vestry needed and wanted a healthy workforce, medicine
was regarded as a commodity 'charitably' bought by the vestrymen for
'their' paupers in the same way that they purchased gentler medicines
for themselves and their families. Against this backdrop, costs rose
rapidly from the eighteenth century onwards, particularly when a major
epidemic struck in 1800. There is no evidence that Royston Vestry tried
to economise by reducing pauper prescriptions or limiting treatments to
sick but normally employable men. On the contrary, money was thrown
at the problem and remedies were provided for all the sick, irrespective
of age or sex, with a resulting and unprecedented total bill of £69 17s 5d

during the period covered 1801–02, entirely for 'physick' (the bill for 1800–01 is missing from the record). A contemporary Hertfordshire vicar put the reasoning that lay behind this attitude very succinctly: 'it is certainly for the benefit of the rich that the poor should be healthy; for 'the Head cannot say to the Foot "I have no need of you".[72]

Two of the Royston surgeon-apothecaries had radically different styles of prescribing. Thomas Nunn would tend to throw everything in his pharmacy at a medical problem and await the results. Daniel Crespin adopted a more cautious approach. He seems to have painstakingly sought to match the remedy to the patient and would use repeat prescriptions, usually consisting of one item, and then observe its effects. If he could see no signs of improvement he would then concoct another treatment and try that. To what extent the pauper patient had any input into his decisions or those of his colleagues is unknowable.

Medicine was neither designed nor expected to be pleasant to take, although some effort was probably made to sweeten children's prescriptions. Nunn initially used a large number of syrupy juleps for his adult patients, probably to hide the taste of unpleasant-tasting medicines such as antimony, which he briefly experimented with in his early days in Royston. He may well have been an enthusiast for such 'chemical' medicines, many of which, such as mercury, were deadly.[73] A suspicious patient could quietly dispose of unpleasant medicines and consult friends and neighbours or the local herbalists and wise-folk, all of whom would have been well known in this essentially rural and close-knit community. Patients were either allowed some element of choice among the practitioners or made their own decisions; several small bills made out to individuals survive, suggesting that some may have part-paid for their treatment when capable of doing so. Matthew Daniel, as a Royston-trained practitioner, appears to have been popular with some patients, who may have known him from an apprentice and therefore sought him out. They were apparently allowed to do so, even when the serving parish doctor was Crespin. Daniel appears to have been a 'general' practitioner who did comparatively more surgical procedures than his colleagues, who may have referred patients to him for surgery. He was also rather more adventurous than Crespin in his prescribing.

The Vestry treasurer, Joseph Beldam, signed off every medical bill in the 1780s and 1790s and appears to have demanded that a great deal of information be provided in those documents, including the form in which the medicine was given, the cost of it, the patient's name and the date/s of prescription. Practitioners sometimes also included the type of medicine: for example, a 'Stomachik Mixture' or a 'Carthartick Powder'. This gives some indication of the illness that the patient may have suffered from, or at least what the practitioner had diagnosed and was attempting to cure. Most physick was intended to remove over-production of some bodily fluid, such as bile, which was considered to be causing the illness. Some prescriptions appear to have been mixed for individual complaints and were described as 'Cordials' or 'Specific' mixtures, but these were frequently used as a last resort for dying patients primarily to stimulate failing organs, particularly the heart. The surgeon-apothecaries often record several different prescriptions for one patient and, particularly at the onset of an illness, more than one prescription could be given in a day. The aim here appears to have been to match and encourage the symptoms: if a patient had a high temperature they would be encouraged to sweat and if they complained of feeling sick they would be encouraged to vomit. These medicines were intended to clean the patient inside and enable the prescribed 'remedies' to work effectively. Close observation of the patient was required, so the doctor might make several visits a day. In fevers very large quantities of mixtures and powders could be prescribed, particularly where entire families were infected. The Rose and Hankin children were several times jointly given two pints of 'Mixture' between them.[74] There is very little evidence of the 'vast array of ready-mixed medicines' that Joan Lane found being prescribed in Warwickshire.[75] The Royston-concocted 'Anodyne Mixtures' may well have resembled in composition 'Dr James Powders', which were very popular painkillers, and the 'Night Mixtures' may also have contained opiates or sedatives similar to those found in the long-established 'Daffy's Cordial'.

Physick was the most frequently used remedy on pauper patients, but the parish doctors could also use the more invasive and often more elaborate treatments of bleeding and blistering, common at that time. These were generally used when physick had failed to cure the problem, on patients with life-threatening fevers, inflammations or infections or when epidemics threatened to get out of hand and a rapid reduction of symptoms was required so that the doctor could go on to his next patient. It certainly does not appear that bleeding was an 'essential' element of everyday Royston medical practice, as it apparently was in Warwickshire.[76] Only during the 1800–02 epidemic, which seems to have caused severe and often painful inflammation, was it regularly used by Daniel Crespin, who appears then to have been the sole pauper doctor. None of the practitioners seem to have found it particularly efficacious in everyday use and as it cost 6d it may well have been regarded as an unnecessary expense.

Although frequent bleeding was a popular practice at this time, this treatment was not used much on Royston paupers. The parish doctors bled their patients very infrequently and sometimes not at all throughout an entire year. They did not bleed patients after 'reducing' fractures or dislocations, although William Buchan, an experienced practitioner and author of the highly popular *Domestic Medicine*, a very detailed home first-aid guide, recommended this.[77] Nor did they use bleeding after operations. Occasionally they seem to have used bleeding as part of a general 'cleansing' treatment with certain mixtures and powders. In 1797 Thomas Nunn experimented briefly with leeches, but only on two patients.[78] Matthew Daniel does not seem to have employed them and Daniel Crespin used them once in 1799. Leeches usually cost 8d to 1s because they had to be collected, usually by elderly pauper leech-women, and applied at exactly the right place to work properly. They then had to be observed as they did their work and removed before they took too much blood. They were both more expensive and more time-consuming than the usual method of cutting a vein. 'Cupping' to heat the skin and form blisters, which could then be scratched to draw blood, does not seem to have been employed on paupers, although all of the practitioners used blistering agents. These were generally recommended for dangerous symptoms of inflammatory fever, such as a racing pulse and delirium.[79] Daniel Crespin regularly employed them at the onset of fevers as well as of other illnesses which do not appear to have been fevers as he was not using fever medicines. He provided blistering ingredients, possibly herbal, for which he charged an extra 6d, and generally administered a 'Mixture' or pills at the same time. Presumably all were supposed to work together. As noted above, he may have left supplies of these ingredients to enable the patients' carers to maintain the blisters.

Conclusion

An appreciable amount of information can be obtained from Royston's primary sources relating to the medical relief of paupers and the policies which lay behind it. We can uncover at least part of the lives of male Royston pauper patients, although female paupers and children remain largely hidden except on those occasions that they brought themselves to official attention. How parish officials managed their poor can, to some extent, be revealed, particularly in a parish as well organised and extensively documented as Royston. Although paupers who used the parish healthcare system were subjected to micro-management they appear to have received medical attention and treatment literally from 'cradle to grave'. The number of prescriptions recorded in the medical bills indicate that some effort was put into curing paupers and speedily dealing with accidents and injuries. However, there are still many unanswered questions. It is not known what proportion of paupers used the parish system and what proportion avoided it. Were some 'undeserving' poor excluded from it? Was Royston, despite its supposedly healthy situation, in fact a particularly good place to live for paupers? Fever appears to have been endemic, flaring up into epidemics periodically – but was this restricted to the poor areas or did it affect the whole town? These severe fevers appear to have been primarily of the 'remitting' type, as they repeatedly died down and recurred in individual patients. The symptoms of those illnesses recorded as appearing in winter appear to represent a form of typhus fever,[80] which tended to attack the poor. Whether the remitting summer fevers recorded were actually an eighteenth-century version of typhoid, drinking-water pollution or episodes of food poisoning is an interesting question. Paupers, as we have seen, were popularly believed to have strong stomachs and were therefore considered to be capable of digesting bad food; thus, according to William Ellis, a contemporary Hertfordshire farmer, 'hashing or mincing [of left-over meat] is best, because if it is a little tainted, it is thus taken off by a Mixture of shred Onions and Parsley'.[81]

It is not possible to know how successful the Royston practitioners generally were in their cures. To achieve this, further work is required on the parish burial registers to match up patients to outcomes. This chapter has aimed at a detailed holistic investigation into the lives and treatment of the sick poor in one Hertfordshire town. The primary aims have been to contextualise the town's sick paupers within Royston Vestry's interpretation of its role in the medical relief system and to attempt to gain some understanding of how the medical relief system evolved. The work is intended to act both as a model for further studies and a contribution to this previously little-researched area of the Old Poor Law in Hertfordshire. Further work on Royston and other Hertfordshire towns will examine both the providers and the consumers of medical relief during the early modern period, and will seek to reveal both the experiences of the sick pauper and the influences which shaped the parochial medical relief with which he or she was provided.

Notes

1. *Universal British Directory* (London, 1791–8), p. 341.
2. L. Munby, *Hertfordshire population statistics 1563–1801* (Hitchin, 1964), p. 37.
3. *Pigot's Directory of Hertfordshire* (London, 1823–4), p. 173.
4. HALS DP/87/18/10.
5. S. and J. Ralls, *Royston 1200–1800: a list of residents* (Royston, 2011), p. 31.
6. M.J. Cawdell, *Royston St. John Hertfordshire burials from 1800–1852* (Royston, 2004), p. 1, entry 54 for Sarah Fordham widow 27 July 1802 (age not given).
7. Royston & District Family History Society, *Royston burial register* (unpaginated) entry 3313 for John Fordham 30 Dec 1772.
8. Ralls and Ralls, *Royston 1200–1800*, p. 31.
9. E. Wallace, *Children of the labouring poor: the working lives of children in nineteenth-century Hertfordshire* (Hatfield, 2010).
10. J. Parkinson, *Dangerous sports. A tale addressed to children* (London, 1800).
11. HALS DP/87/8/2, 26 July.
12. HALS DP/87/8/1.
13. HALS DP/87/18/4 Miscellaneous papers 1778–1808 16 February 1785 Workhouse Agreement (extract) with Master (James Serle/Searle).
14. HALS DP/87/18/19.
15. HALS DP/87/18/4 16 February 1785 (listed on the back of the Workhouse Inventory for 20 April 1778).
16. HALS DP/87/18/4 Table of Food April 25th 1788? (in response to Paupers who complained about not being given enough bread at Breakfast Misc note March 1788?).
17. HALS DP/87/18/4 Miscellaneous papers 1778–1808 Rules & Orders for the Regulation of the Parish Poor and Workhouse. Undated but Workhouse Rules being read to paupers is referred to in vestry minutes 31 May 1785.
18. HALS DP/87/18/4 16 Feb 1785 (extract) with Master (James Serle/Searle).
19. HALS DP/87/8/2, 20 May 1799.
20. HALS DP/87/8/2, 5 October 1789.
21. HALS DP/87/8/2, 24 January 1791.
22. Royston & District Family History Society, *Royston burial register* (unpaginated), entry 3561 for Elizabeth Reynolds wife of Edward, 18 Sept 1780.
23. HALS DP/87/8/2, 12 January 1795.
24. HALS DP/87/8/2, 21 July 1788.
25. 4 March 1800 – Reducing fractured Arm, Lotions, Medicines, Bandages, Plaisters &c – W Hill's Wife – 10s 6d (did not bleed her).
26. 20 August 1792: Reducing Dislocated Collar Bone, Embrocations, Bandage – Anne Brown 15s 6d.
27. 23 February 1796: Reducing fractured Ribb Bandages etc – Widow Brown – 5s.

28. 22 May 1790: Opening a large contusion in her head Dressings & Cure – Widow Hall – £1 1s 0d.

29. HALS DP/87/8/2.

30. HALS DP/87/18/18.

31. HALS DP/87/18/22.

32. HALS DP/87/18/19 Royston Overseers' Bills & Vouchers 1782–1807 Daniel Crespin's Bill April 1801–April 1802, 7 July 1801.

33. HALS DP/87/18/26.

34. HALS DP/87/18/2 and 18/3. Letters from Widow Mary Greenhow to Royston Vestry Clerk and letters written on her behalf by the Newmarket Overseer.

35. HALS DP/87/18/8–35.

36. HALS DP/87/18/10.

37. HALS DP/87/18/12; DP/87/18/20.

38. HALS DP/87/18/15; DP/87/18/20.

39. HALS DP/87/8/2, 22 March 1797.

40. HALS DP/87/18/19 Royston Overseers' Bills & Vouchers 1782–1807 Daniel Crespin's Bill April 1801–April 1802: 3 November 1801 J Hankin & Wife; 11 November 1801 Jos Hankin's family; 2 December 1801; Then Powdered Bark Farr's Son; Shepherd's wife; 9 December 1801 Farr's Son; 16 December 1801 Shepherd's daughter; 4 February 1802 Webb's wife.

41. John Hill, *Hertfordshire militia ballot lists: Royston 1758–86* (Ware, 2000). The Royston lists run from 1758 to 1786 with gaps and cover the years 1758, 1759, 1760, 1761, 1762 (February), 1763, 1764, 1765, 1768, 1769, 1772, 1773, 1775, 1778 (April), 1778 (December), 1780, 1781, 1782, 1783, 1784, 1785 and 1786.

42. B. Ramazzini, *Diseases of workers: the Latin text of 1713 revised with translation and notes by W. C. Wright* (Chicago, IL, 1940), p. 443.

43. T. Sokoll, *Essex pauper letters 1731–1837* (Oxford, 2001), pp. 417–18.

44. HALS DP/87/18/19 Royston Overseers' Bills & Vouchers 1782–1807 Thomas Nunn's Bill April 1797–April 1798.

45. HALS DP/87/18/12.

46. Royston & District Family History Society, *Royston burial register* (unpaginated), entry 3637 for 23 Aug 1782 James Prior 'killed by a fall into a well'.

47. Ibid., entry 3918 for 10 April 1790 Charles Thurley 'killed by falling into a well'.

48. Ibid., entry 3871 for 4 Jan 1789 William Mead – 1778–84 'killed by a cart being overthrown'.

49. Ibid., entry 3876 for 14 Feb 1789 James Trigg 'killed by a fall from a horse'.

50. HALS DP/87/8/2, 7 March 1785.

51. Ibid., 25 July 1785.

52. Cawdell, *Royston St. John Hertfordshire*, entry 366 for 6 July 1816.

53. HALS DP/87/18/19 Names of the Poor in the Workhouse 7 February 1785.

54. Royston & District Family History Society, *Royston burial register* (unpaginated), entry 4061 for 29 Dec 1793 from the workhouse.

55. HALS DP/87/8/2, 25 July 1785.

56. HALS DP/87/18/4 Rules & Orders for the Regulation of the parish Poor and Workhouse.

57. HALS DP/87/18/2 Letter and draft reply from Royston Vestry Clerk 1 and 4 May 1784.

58. J.G.L. Burnby, *A study of the English apothecary from 1660 to 1760*, *Medical History*, Supplement No. 3 (London, 1983); A. Digby, *Making a medical living: doctors and patients in the English market for medicine, 1720–1911* (Cambridge, 1994); I. Loudon, 'The nature of provincial medical practice in eighteenth-century England', *Medical History*, 29 (1985), pp. 1–32; S. Williams, *Poverty, gender and life-cycle under the English Poor Law 1760–1834* (Woodbridge, 2011).

59. HALS DP/87/12/1.

60. HALS DP/87/18/11 An Accn'of Doctors Bills from Easter 1782 to Easter 1789.

61. P.I. and R.V. Wallis (eds), *Eighteenth century medics: subscriptions, licenses, apprenticeships* (Newcastle upon Tyne, 1988), p. 143: Daniel Crespin: Born 1745 – Died 11 March 1823.

62. Ibid., p. 152. Matthew Daniel: Born 1741 – Died 27 June 1793.

63. Ibid., p. 152.

64. Ibid., p. 242.

65. HALS DP/87/18/4 Miscellaneous papers 1778–1808 (Undated but was sent before he was appointed parish doctor in April 1785).

66. HALS DP/87/8/2.

67. HALS DP/87/18/17.

68. HALS DP/87/18/10 (on outside of bill 'Dr Nunns Bill for the Cherrys May 1788 Bills for their expences sent by agreement to Basingbourn (their parish) and Standon (William Cherry's parish)'.

69. HALS DP/87/18/15, 29 March 1786.

70. HALS DP/87/8/2 19 December 1796: 'Order'd that as Complaint having been made by (a) Sick person (a pauper?) that W. R. Crespin the Doctor for the parish this year does not give proper Attendance And that the Vestry Clerk is desired to acquaint Mr Crespin of the same'.

71. J. Quincy, *Pharmacopoeia officinalis & extemporanea: or, a complete English dispensatory, in two parts…*, 5th edn (London, 1724), p. 585.

72. O.F. Christie (ed.), *Diary of the Revd. William Jones, 1777–1821: curate and vicar of Broxbourne and the hamlet of Hoddesdon 1781–1821* (London, 1929), p. 138: 19 April 1802.

73. HALS DP/87/18/15.

74. HALS DP/87/18/19 Royston Overseers' Bills & Vouchers 1782–1807. Daniel Crespin's Bill April 1801–April 1802. March 1802 and several others.

75. J. Lane, *A social history of medicine: health, healing and disease in England, 1750–1950* (London, 2001), p. 46.

76. Ibid., p. 46.

77. W. Buchan, *Domestic medicine: or a treatise on the prevention and cure of diseases by regimen and simple medicines…* 7th edn corrected (London, 1781; facsimile ECCO, 2011), p. 459.

78. HALS DP/87/18/19 Royston Overseers' Bills & Vouchers 1782–1807 Thomas Nunn's Bill April 1797–April 1798.

79. Buchan, *Domestic medicine*, p. 127.

80. HALS DP/87/12/1, 4 January 1770.

81. W. Ellis, *The country housewife's family companion...* (London, 1750; facsimile ECCO, 2011), p. 71.

CHAPTER FOUR

Madhouses of Hertfordshire
1735–1903

Gary Moyle

THE HISTORIOGRAPHICAL LITERATURE on madhouses, their patients and their treatment regimes is very extensive. Historians now have a strong grasp of the ways in which madness was defined, the sorts of patients who were confined, the iconography of the asylum and the complex intertwining of statutory, voluntary and private provision. Studies of individual asylums have multiplied considerably since early studies of Bethlem highlighted the rich records available to historians of insanity.[1] Against this backdrop, Hertfordshire is a much-neglected county. It probably saw no madhouses until the 1730s and certainly no county asylum of its own until the very late date of 1899. Hertfordshire could benefit from not being London and yet adjoining it. An 1853 return[2] lists Hertfordshire pauper lunatics sent to private asylums. Most commonly used then were Middlesex's Hanwell and Colney Hatch and the 'commended' Warburton's house in Bethnal Green. Also used were Kent Asylum, Surrey Asylum, Grove Hall in Bow, Miles' house in Hoxton, Peckham House and the 'severely censured' Hoxton House.

There was, however, a two-way flow of lunatics: Hertfordshire paupers were consigned to London while the wealthy of London (and elsewhere) were ushered away to enjoy the clean air of Hertfordshire. Fuelled by the fear that respectable people could be unnecessarily locked away, the 1774 Madhouses Act had introduced licensing and visiting.[3] Hertfordshire Justices of the Peace granted annual licences to madhouse proprietors, who would be running 'private licensed houses'. These were subject to regular inspection by two Justices of the Peace and a physician, being the 'visitors'. Further regulatory Acts built on that of 1774 and culminated in measures during the late 1820s and thereafter to lay the foundations for County Asylums and the tighter regulation and monitoring of private institutions[4] up until the point at which further licensing was banned by the 1890 Lunacy Act.[5]

The records of individual asylums for the county are rare but centrally held records include the *County Register of Madhouses* 1798–1812[6] and the substantial series of Patients' Admissions Registers 1846–1913.[7] Once civil registration and detailed census records begin (in 1837 and 1841 respectively) a reasonable insight into the private licensed houses becomes possible and this study is the first to survey Hertfordshire madhouses using such sources.[8] For each institution a tentative list of patients is offered. These lists do not claim to be complete, and nor is their detail: dates of patients' births and deaths are sketchy, dates of residence are given only where there is evidence, and 'place of association' may be either birthplace or the place from where admitted. Occupation or equivalent is noted, as are dates of known Chancery inquisitions. Even if patchy, however, this survey is an important step forward in attempts to understand the complexion of county lunatic provision.

The madhouses of Hertfordshire
St Albans St Peter (1735–c.1757; proprietor Dr Nathaniel Cotton)
The death (exact date unknown) of a Dr Thomas Crawley at Dunstable, Bedfordshire, heralded the demise of his madhouse, but also the creation of Hertfordshire's first. Nathaniel Cotton 'engaged Dr Crawley's house-keeper, and a few of his remaining patients, to remove with him to St Albans, where he opened a house of a similar kind on a small scale'.[9] Cotton (c.1706–88; Figure 4.1) is fairly well documented elsewhere.[10] Before assisting Crawley he trained at Leiden in the Netherlands under the physician Hermann Boerhaave. The dates and locations of Cotton's asylums have been a matter of debate and warrant some discussion. As early as the 1740s he held land locally,[11] was practising medicine and was able to comment on an outbreak of scarlet fever in St Albans,[12] but it is the St Albans St Peters poor rate assessment of 5 November 1735[13] which is the earliest to place him in St Albans. As Cotton arrived with patients the asylum establishment date of 1735 seems reasonable. Its location may have been fluid, but the assessment for 1750, for example, lists for Cotton a house and barn on the east side of St Peters Street, probably halfway

Drawn by J. Thurston. Engraved by W.H. Worthington.

Figure 4.1 Portrait of Nathaniel Cotton. Drawing by J. Thurston, engraving by W.H. Worthington, first published 1820. HALS DE/Cl/27/60.

Figure 4.2 Side view of the assemblage of buildings of the 'Collegium Insanorum', College Street, St Albans. Photograph by Stanley Kent, *c*.1909, HALS Acc 4473/1a/37.

between the modern Hatfield Road and Victoria Street. Although nothing is known of the patients, their numbers must have been sufficient to warrant the hiring of larger premises. Cotton's grandly named Collegium Insanorum (St Albans, Abbey parish, *c*.1757–1813) had been operating for nearly twenty years when the advent of licensing in 1774 created records enabling future researchers to unveil the county's asylums. The Abbey poor rates first record this site, with a rental value of £22 until 1795, in Cotton's name in 1757.[14] County Quarter Sessions granted his licence until at least 1783, Borough Quarter Sessions from at least 1786.

For a couple of years either side of the *c*.1757 'moving date' Cotton had two houses on Market Place. The Collegium itself occupied land on the northern side of the junction of Spicer Street and Dagnall Street, where College Street would later extend northwards. Early twentieth-century photographs looking down College Street (before the old buildings there had been demolished) claim to show the building (Figure 4.2),[15] but it has been suggested[16] that the building is not the same as that drawn by George Henry Oldfield,[17] his being the only contemporary image we know of (Figure 4.3). The differences are, indeed, stark. Was the Collegium

Figure 4.3 The 'Collegium Insanorum', St Albans, c.1790s. By Henry George Oldfield. The Collegium was run from c.1757 to 1813 by Nathaniel Cotton and then Stephen Pellett. HALS DE/Of/8/498.

actually somewhere in this area? Land tax and poor rate assessments do place a property of Cotton's at this location. College Street and College Place do run to either side of the site. Regarding the exact building, the following theory may confirm that the building which stood on the corner was indeed the Collegium.

The Dury and Andrews map of 1766 shows a detached east–west College on the north side of Dagnall Street. Oldfield drew that in the early 1790s: fronting the road which slopes down to the left (west), four windows across, and no College Street yet visible to its right. In 1795 the property was substantially extended out from the rear-left, as supported by the Abbey poor-rate assessments which leapt from a longstanding rental value of £22 to £35 between February and April.[18] On the 1818 Abbey parish map by Godman, held by the Abbey, a much larger building is indeed shown. But the construction of College Street in the 1820s necessitated slicing from both the 'wings' in its path, one of which was actually the right (east) half of the original building. This left a corner building fronting Dagnall Street but extending round into the new College Street. What Kitton and Holmes Winter later drew was the whole assemblage: half of the original together with the rear extension.[19] An extension, new street and corner aspect have contrived to cast doubt on the location of Cotton's house. If correct, this theory allows for all known views of it to be trustworthy.

Among the most famous of Cotton's patients was William Cowper. His account of treatment under Cotton celebrated the doctor and his Collegium. Born in Berkhamsted in 1731, Cowper was the most famous poet of his day, but crumpled at the prospect of sitting an examination for a new job. His friend and biographer William Hayley wrote that 'the mind of Cowper seems to have laboured under the severest sufferings of morbid depression; but [by way of] the medical skill of Dr Cotton and the cheerful, benignant manners of that accomplished physician … his ideas of religion were changed from the gloom of terror and despair to the lustre of comfort and delight'.[20]

Cotton 'continued the oversight [of the Collegium] till his death, when he was succeeded in it by the present occupier Stephen Pellet, M.D.'.[21] The caption to Oldfield's undated but contemporary drawing states that it is 'now Dr Pallats'. Stephen Pellett (the more common of the various spellings) was both a Justice of the Peace for the Liberty of St Albans and a medical man, termed a 'Doctor of Physick' in the *Liberty Reports of the Visiting Magistrates and Physician appointed to inspect Houses for the reception of lunaticks*.[22] This volume records visits made from 1792 to 1798 and from 1810 to 1819. The 12-year gap in visiting accords with a 4-year gap, 1798–1802, at the start of the *County Register* described below, suggesting that the asylum may have suspended its operations for a short period. The *County Register of Madhouses* provides a list of patients from 1802 to 1809 (Table 4.1) and suggests that residents were generally from outside the county. Moreover, the first appearance of a Chancery case confirms they were people of considerable wealth.

Although visitors' books do not survive for the County Quarter Sessions, two do for the sessions of the Liberty of St Albans and both refer to the post-Cotton Collegium. Statistics rather than names are recorded: five men and two women in 1792, five men and one woman from 1793 to 1797, and five men and two women in 1798. Later figures are lower: three men and two women in 1810, one man and two women in 1811, and one

Table 4.1 Patients at the Collegium from 1802 to 1809.

Patient's name	Admission/residence	Details
Miss Mary Boldington	4 Jun 1808	From Beds
Charles Burton	25 Jul 1806	From Bucks
Edmund Calamy	9 Aug 1802	
Maria [Clack]	24 Nov 1807	Referred from Bethlem
William Cowper (1731–1800)	1763–5	Poet, born Berkhamsted
Elizabeth Drew (–1765)	1765	
James Finlayson (–1771)	1771	
Thomas Harkham	2 Aug 1805	
Benjamin Kingston	26 Feb 1809	From Buckinghamshire
Sir John Knightley (1746–1812)	10 Jan 1803	1st Bart Knightley of Fawsley, Northants
Hannah Paget	2 Aug 1807	From Lambeth
Humphrey Praed	29 Jul 1805; 1 Nov 1808–11	From Bucks or Somerset. Chancery 1811
Thomas Willis	8 Apr 1809	From London

man and one woman from 1812 to 1813. Perhaps these were not enough to make it viable, and perhaps the opening of the Rumballs' asylum in St Albans was the final nail in the coffin. A Mrs Blow occupied the building subsequently left empty by Pellett and in 1830 she sold the contents and moved. Occupied well into the 1920s,[23] including periods as a warehouse and a boot factory, both the newer then the older part of the College would ultimately be demolished.

Cheshunt (1774–9; proprietors Mary Thornton and then Thomas Baldwin)

Bethlem Hospital, London, already had a presence in Cheshunt, holding numerous properties in Waltham Cross, but the onset of licensing in 1774 recorded not just Cotton in St Albans but also a house run somewhere in Cheshunt by a Mary Thornton. Soon after the Act created the first record of her asylum she married Thomas Baldwin in Cheshunt in 1775. Henceforth the licensing was in his name, in 1775, and then renewed to

him in 1776, 1778 and 1779.[24] Thomas continued to hold land, including
that on which the asylum may have operated, but Mary died, being buried
at Cheshunt in 1780. Two months before her death Essex Quarter Sessions
were appointing visitors to an asylum of Thomas's in Waltham Holy Cross,
Essex.[25] Unless this is indicative of the long-running boundary disputes
between Cheshunt and Waltham Abbey, and is actually the same building,
it appears that a joint venture to Essex was intended. But widower Thomas
continued alone, licensed by Essex in 1780 to keep a madhouse at 'Waltham',
presumably Waltham Holy Cross. Records exist of an inspection there in
1781 and, more specifically, of a visit to the asylum at Waltham Abbey in
Waltham Holy Cross, Essex, in 1787.[26]

   Although the enterprise was now an Essex one there remains the
question of whether it later became the famous asylum of Dr Matthew
Allen (1783–1845). His group of madhouses at High Beach, Waltham
Holy Cross, Essex, were to care for the escapee John Clare from 1837 to
1841 and to a bankrupt Tennyson. Bridging the gap between Thomas
Baldwin's settling in the 1780s and Allen's venture in the 1820s, there was
a licence awarded in 1819 to a George Hammond in the same parish.[27] It is
a tantalising possibility that there was continuity and that High Beach had
its origins in Hertfordshire. Nothing, however, is known of the patients
in Hertfordshire. Although a Liberty Sessions visitors' book survives, a
County one does not. Unfortunately Thomas Baldwin had moved over the
border well before the *County Register* began in 1798.

Northaw (1799; proprietor William Vernon)

In 1799 the Liberty Sessions licensed William Vernon to keep a house for
no more than ten lunatics at Northaw,[28] but it was not licensed further
and did not appear in the contemporary *County Register*. Presumably no
patients were ever admitted. The circumstances of Vernon, a gentleman,
may have improved after being granted lands as part of the 1803 enclosure.
Regarding the possible location of this madhouse, there is an Abstract
of Title[29] to a messuage with waste to the north and a garden called the
'pease ground' next to the street to the south. In 1790 William Vernon was
admitted to the property. The Abstract refers to his will of 1828 and to the
one messuage, but not to Vernon House, which may have been connected.
What looks to be the property is shown labelled with his name on a map of
c.1811.[30] Across the road from the church, exactly where the building itself
was remains unclear.

Hadham Palace, Much Hadham (1803–88; proprietors Robert Jacob, then Mary Jacob, then Mary Monro, then James Smith, then Dr Frederic Moore Smith, and then Dr William Blundell Willans)

When the historic former country residence of the bishops of London was advertised for sale in 1802[31] it was soon to become the first of the Hertfordshire madhouses whose patients' details would be subject to the census, run by the most renowned of mad-doctor dynasties. Like its 'competition', Harpenden Hall, it would last for most of the nineteenth century.

Robert Jacob (*c.*1749–1825), who had married into the fringe of the eminent Monro family, physicians to Bethlem Hospital for over a century, ran the asylum from its opening in 1803 until 1824. It was from one of the Monros' private licensed houses, Brooke House in Clapton, that Robert Jacob left for Much Hadham in 1804, having mismanaged it. There was an overlap of some months, as Hadham had been licensed to him in 1803 for no more than ten patients; this licence was renewed almost annually until 1824. The extent of the Monro involvement in, or ownership of, Hadham Palace is not always clear. When Robert Jacob died in 1825 his widow Mary tried to continue in his place. An elderly widow when she was granted the licence in 1825, Mary Jacob had previously been married to Thomas Monro. It was their unmarried daughter Mary Monro who was to manage Hadham in her mother's very old age and after her death, obtaining the licence in 1826 and renewing until 1828.

The asylum was purchased from Robert Jacob's executors and in 1829 Mary entered into a management partnership with surgeon and apothecary James Smith (1786–1859),[32] who was to run Hadham Palace for more than 30 years. The licence was in his name from 1829. The upper limit was then raised to 15 lunatics, clarified in 1833: 'in which number no parish Patients are included'. Presumably this indicated the high status expected of the residents rather than any further allowance for those on the parish. We do know something about the treatments available under Smith. For mania he would resort to 'local bloodletting', both from the temporal artery and also by simple 'cupping' of the neck. He recommended purging, exercise and clean air, but also the unfashionable warm body bath and cold head wash.[33] Smith said he avoided general bloodletting 'under a conviction that the lancet is always to be feared in cases of insanity'.[34] 'General' bloodletting involved taking a significant amount from an artery or vein, whereas 'local' bloodletting involved taking a smaller amount from smaller blood vessels.

Upon James's death in 1860 his son Frederic Moore Smith (*c*.1828–1900) managed Hadham Palace asylum for 11 years. The 13 acres were 'quiet and sequestered' and for 'only Patients of the higher class'.[35] One kept several horses. But Smith received a commission on 23 December 1871 to be assistant surgeon to 2nd Administrative Battalion of the Hertfordshire Rifle Volunteers, and after 42 years the Smith proprietorship had come to an end.

William Blundell Willans (*c*.1850–1915) took over in 1871 as a young man, but by the 1881 census he had only one patient in the house, William Haworth, besides his extended family and servants. The end was in sight for the Hadham Palace asylum and in 1888 the sale of the freehold residential estate was advertised. Months later the sale of household furniture and effects signified the complete winding-up of the business. Items are illustrative of the standard of decor and of the amusements: mahogany Arabian four-post and iron French bedsteads, three cottage pianofortes, a billiard table, a thousand books, a ladies' work-table from the Great Exhibition, a magic lantern, an American typewriter, choice orchids, horses, pigs and poultry.[36] Willans then moved to a smaller house in Much Hadham to live with his large family and work as a GP. As a curious endnote, after the closure he took into his family home one of his former patients, Caroline Novelli, who remained as a boarder rather than patient until her death in 1893. It is unclear whether the arrangement was borne out of necessity or the appeal the income represented, or resulted from a developed relationship. He gave up the general practice in 1914 and moved to Bedford, where he died the next year. A brass commemorates him and his son in Much Hadham church.

Table 4.2 provides details of the known patients, many of whom were from outside the county. Three cases suggest the level of detail that it is possible to reconstruct through detailed record linkage. Referring to the Spencer sisters, it was reported that 'coercion by means of belt and gloves is resorted to occasionally, in the case of two ladies … who are extremely violent, dirty, & destructive'.[37] For John Tharp, family papers reveal that his estates, including slave-worked plantations, were managed from an early age; after marrying young he spent 66 years at the Palace and died intestate.[38] Finally, Revd Lord Frederick Townshend was admitted in 1806 on the recommendation of his father, having probably killed his own brother ten years earlier. Travelling from Yarmouth, where their strange behaviour was noted, the brothers had arrived in Oxford Street, London,

Table 4.2   Known patients at Hadham Palace.

Patient's name	Admission/residence	Details
Mrs Mary Alston (*c.*1791–)	1828–41	
John [F]uller Baines	1847	
Miss Barr	8 Nov 1805	
Emma A. Beadon	18 Dec 1882–2 Sep 1886 (not improved)	
Hannah Bing	8 Jan 1874–27 Apr 1874 (not improved)	
Maria E. Blakey	28 May 1868–6 Aug 1868 (recovered)	
Mrs Bouchier	11 Dec 1808	
Elizabeth Bourchier	26 Apr 1852–28 Sep 1853 (relieved); 20 Jun 1854– 14 Sep 1854 (relieved); 10 Feb 1866–9 Apr 1866 (relieved)	
Revd William Brett (1797–1858)	3 Apr 1858–22 Dec 1858 (death)	Vicar of Linton, Cambs
Robert Bruce (–1885)	24 May 1884–13 Dec 1885 (death)	
Alfred P. Canning	25 Sep 1870–16 Jan 1871 (recovered)	
Susan Canning	9 Feb 1873–4 Sep 1873 (recovered)	
Revd Charles Chapman	3 Jul 1879–13 Aug 1884 (not improved)	Clerk in Holy Orders born Putney, Surrey
Sir Thomas Clarges	27 Mar 1806	
Marianne Chowne	1873	Chancery 1873
Frances C(l)aridge (*c.*1776–)	1841	
Martha Clarke	30 Aug 1866–7 Jan 1888 (not improved)	
Otto Clarke	30 Aug 1808	
James Robert Colebrooke (*c.*1791–)	1841	Military officer
Mary Ann Colebrooke (*c.*1801–)	1841–71	From Takeley, Essex
Henry Collins	14 Aug 1812	From London

Patient's name	Admission/residence	Details
Gideon Death	16 Oct 1852–7 Aug 1856 (relieved)	
Martha Dodd	24 Mar 1812	
Robert Ellice (–1849)	1 Mar 1848–22 Apr 1849 (death of marasmus)	
John Franklin	18 Jan 1806	
[Loker?] Franklin	30 Apr 1807	
William Golding (c.1796–)	1828–41	Chancery
William Griffith	12 Dec 1878–14 Feb 1881 (not improved)	
Mrs Hanbury	22 Jul 1811	
William Hannay	6 Jun 1805	
William Haworth (c.1815–)	1881	Solicitor, from Bolton-le-Moor, Lancs
Frances Hitch	15 Aug 1850–18 Jun 1851 (recovered); 26 Aug 1853–19 Nov 1853 (death of general dropsy)	
Jane Hobbs	30 Sep 1848–4 May 1849 (not improved)	
John Thomas Hopkinson (c.1791–)	7 May 1806–61	Chancery 1817
Thomas Horne	23 Nov 1861–26 May 1862 (relieved)	
George Howard	15 Jul 1803	
William Hurrell (c.1801–56)	1828–51	
Edmund James (c.1824–)	3 Feb 1864–30 Jan 1882 (not improved)	Barrister, from Middlesex
I.W. Jennings	9 Sep 1809	From Beds
Robert Lee	20 Dec 1808	
John Lindsell	16 Aug 1803	
Mary A. MacInnes (c.1833–)	15 Nov 1870–7 Aug 1871 (recovered)	From Canada
Joseph Madocks	3 Jun 1812	From London
James Mair	12 Apr 1803	
Lieut. George Martin	3 Sep 1811	

Patient's name	Admission/residence	Details
Robert Martin	2 May 1867–21 Sep 1867 (not improved)	
Charlotte Merciers	19 Feb 1805	
William Miller	1846–47	
Henry S. Morice	20 Jun 1882–9 May 1888 (relieved)	
Sarah Martha Morice (–1858)	22 Jun 1855–8 Sep 1856 (not improved)	
John Moseley	20 Feb 1808	
Charles Mott	24 Jun 1810	
Rev Newcome	20 Mar 1803–28	
Mrs Newman	24 Mar 1803	
Caroline Louisa Novelli (c.1817–1893)	15 Feb 1850–93	From Manchester
Mrs Olive	19 Sep 1812; 1828	From London
John Osborn	8 Aug 1809	
Hannah Overman (–1865)	1851–65 (death)	From Burnham Deepdale, Norfolk. Chancery 1864
Hindley Leigh Philips (c.1801–85)	1841–85 (death)	Merchant, from Stockport, Lancs. Chancery 1860. Left £129,848
Jenny Pickard	29 Oct 1809	From Essex
Mary Ann Pollard	1847	
Miss C. Quilter	1803; 20 Nov 1805	
Mr Rawling	4 Sep 1805	
William Rayment	10 Jul 1871–31 Jul 1871 (relieved)	
Daniel Richardson	15 Nov 1849–2 Jan 1850 (recovered)	
Christina Cockburn Ross (c.1796–1872)	1841–71	Of Shandwick? Ross-Shire, Scotland
Ernest Sharpe (–1878)	9 Dec 1873–18 Jan 1878 (death)	
John Shields	26 May 1810	
Susannah Simson	29 Sep 1852–29 Dec 1852 (recovered)	
Mary Smith	23 Jul 1807	Same as Smith below?
Miss Smith	1828	Chancery
Mr Soame	25 Jun 1806	

Patient's name	Admission/residence	Details
Mary Spencer	28 Jul 1849–18 Oct 1850 (relieved)	Chancery 1850
Sarah Spencer	28 Jul 1849–18 Oct 1850 (relieved)	Chancery 1850
Francis Stracey (c.1786–1857)	1841–10 Sep 1857 (death)	
John Tharp (1794–1883)	1817–83 (death)	From Chippenham, Cambs. Chancery 1816
Mrs Thompson	15 Jul 1805	
Ann Titchmarsh	29 May 1859–27 Sep 1859 (not improved)	
William Thomas Toke (1802–74)	1841–71	Attorney
Revd Lord Frederick Townshend (1767–1836)	30 May 1806–28	Chancery. Rector of Stiffkey, Norfolk
James Stewart Tulk	13 Sep 1850–22 Sep 1850 (relieved)	
George Charles Waller	20 Dec 1855–22 Dec 1856 (not improved)	
Mrs Wheatley	13 Jan 1809	From Wales
Ann Williamson	1876	Chancery 1876
Mr Wilson	31 Dec 1805	
Thomas [D?] Wright	31 Aug 1867–14 Feb 1871 (death)	
John Young	13 May 1811	From Bath
Miss Maria Zachary (c.1776–1843)	20 Mar 1803; 20 Mar 1809–41	Chancery 1824
Unknown (–1876)	1876 (death from tetanus following burns)	

whereupon 'Lord Frederick jumped out of the carriage, struck one of the post boys, and offered to fight with the persons attracted to the spot'. His brother, a newly elected MP, was found shot in the head in the carriage.[39]

Hertford (1805–06; proprietor Anne Cocks)

A private house in Hertford was licensed by the county to Anne Cocks in 1805 for the reception of no more than ten lunatics. A widow, her husband is likely to have been the surgeon John Cocks, who was buried at All Saints on 30 May 1805 aged 43. Presumably she was trying to make a living on her own. Land Tax assessments for 1805 and 1806 record her husband renting their property at £16 per annum from Baron Nathaniel Dimsdale. There is evidence of Dimsdale's land holdings in Hertford, but it is unclear where Anne's licensed house was. Her landlord also came to be the physician appointed to visit Anne's asylum. The assessment for 1807 seems to list a different tenant for the property and licensing does not continue. Perhaps she was unable to attract the patients to make the venture viable. We know of only one, Mary Smart, the daughter of a vestry clerk from Enfield, courtesy of the *County Register*. In 1783 a Mary Smart and her two sisters were admitted under the Manor of Enfield to a copyhold messuage at White Webbs but the property was surrendered in 1802.[40] It is likely that this Mary is the one who was then recommended for the asylum by her sister Elizabeth and on the advice of Enfield surgeon Mr John Durham. Anne Cocks' one patient, presumably quite unwell, died in 1806 aged 44 and was buried at Enfield St Andrew.

St Albans St Stephens (1812–at least 1820; proprietors John Rumball and James Quilter Rumball)

This was probably the first incarnation of the longest-lasting private asylum in Hertfordshire, initially run by John Rumball and James Quilter Rumball. Cotton's Collegium faded from St Albans as this was beginning and, while it is possible that there was continuity between the two, the case is not compelling. They were in different parishes. Pellett was visited in August 1813 whereas Rumball had been visited the previous month, so the institutions overlapped. There is no evidence as yet of any Pellett patients becoming Rumball patients. Finally, poor rates[41] do not indicate that Rumball replaced Pellett at the Collegium; indeed, it lay empty from 1814 until occupied by Mrs Blow in 1816. So this was a new and separate madhouse, licensed variously by the Liberty and the County to John Rumball from 1812 to 1818. James Quilter Rumball joined him on the licence in 1820.

A surgeon, John Rumball (1766–*c.*1821) came from Chipping Barnet and practised at Croydon, 1791–5, and Abingdon, 1795–9. Land tax assessments then record him in Windridge Ward, St Stephens, renting from Henry Field from 1802 to 1814, and in 1822 from Mr Church. Although probably practising in St Albans, Rumball's omission from the *County Register* indicates that his madhouse was not operating before 1812. His son James Quilter Rumball (1795–1872) is well documented. He claimed to have studied at Bethlem, under the Monros, and under the German phrenologist Johann Gaspar Spurzheim. Rumball was an ardent proponent of phrenology, undertaking lecture tours on which he condemned mesmerism; he read the head of biologist and philosopher Herbert Spencer. Although his focus on phrenology perhaps placed his medical works somewhat out of the mainstream, he did contribute to the momentum which created the McNaughton rules for the criminally insane.

This early period of the Rumball operation is not well documented, as the asylum records are lost or in private hands. It opened as the *County Register* ends and was active some years before the availability of admissions registers and relevant census data (only from 1841 onwards were individuals named in censuses). But details of patients begin to emerge in the Liberty Sessions: there was a man and woman in 1813, a man in 1814, two men in 1816 and in 1817 three men, probably Clerk, Mason and Tapster in Table 4.3.[42] After improved information in 1820 comes the period through to 1834 for which details become more elusive, there being no further county registers or Liberty visitors' books. Although care was probably continuous the financial stability of the house is revealed to be questionable by James Quilter Rumball's bankruptcy in October 1833. Nonetheless, continuity from this house to Harpenden Hall, where the operation finally settled, is evidenced by the extending of the Rumball management over 78 years, by longstanding patient William Clerk receiving care at all three sites and by claims in later advertising. In addition, upon the opening of business at Harpenden Hall in 1847 the visitors noted the need to complete an old entry in the medical journal dating back to 1814.[43] The same set of records was used at each of the locations.

Table 4.3   Patients at St Albans St Stephens from the Liberty Sessions.

Patient's name	Admission/residence	Details
William Clerk (1788–1863)	1817–20	Formerly seafaring, from Winchester, Hants
John Edwards	1819	
L.D. Hunt (1770–)	1820	From Aylesbury, Bucks
Richard Oswold Mason (1775–)	1817–20	From Elstree
Richard Tapster	1817–19	

St Albans St Michael, Oster/Oyster Hills (1834–c.1843; proprietor James Quilter Rumball)

The second incarnation of the Rumballs' asylum appears in a different St Albans parish following an indistinct winding up of the first. Arthur Griffin Rumball would later advertise the family business as established '40 years', suggesting a 'foundation date' of *c.*1823.[44] Land at Oster Hills was not advertised for sale until 1827 and the house then built. Although bankrupt in 1833, the following year Rumball leased Oyster Hills House from the Revd William Le Worthy of Harston, Cambridgeshire. An institutional licence was duly obtained for the 'house and buildings at Oyster Hills', where Rumball would reside, and for no more than 15 patients. From 1835 there could be no more than 10 of these private wealthy patients. None could be from the parish, but Justices could invoke 9 George IV c40 in times of need. Thus, when William Lane was found wandering in St Peter, St Albans, in 1836 they made an order for his confinement in Rumball's house. It was on their doorstep, the extended Rumball family officiated in St Albans, Lane's status or condition may have ruled out the workhouse and Bedford Asylum was not yet an option.

The census provides a snapshot of the asylum in the twilight of this transient precursor of Harpenden Hall. With James Rumball touring in Cornwall, Oster Hills was inhabited in 1841 by his wife Rebecca, their many children, John Calvert (brother of absent patient Anne Calvert), who was later buried next to Arthur Griffin Rumball, and one servant. The patients were the long-term William Clerke and Thomas 'Terry', possibly the same person as Thomas 'Toovey', who would be admitted in 1863.

Pursuant to the 1834 Poor Law (Amendment) Act, the St Albans Union opened its workhouse in 1835 between Oster Hills House and St Albans. As it was soon overcrowded, the board of guardians looked to Rumball's house for more space[45] and resolved in 1842 to temporarily hire Rumball's cottages. Old women from the workhouse would be moved there. This caused, contributed to or was subsequent to the decamping of Rumball's asylum to Harpenden Hall. Noting that the property was occupied by Rumball as the tenant at will, the freehold of 'The Oster, otherwise Ostorious Hills Estate' was advertised for sale in 1843.[46] This indistinct transition period is reflected in the fact of the Lunacy Commissioners not acknowledging Oster Hills as an active asylum in 1844.[47]

Harpenden Hall (1845–1903; proprietors James Quilter Rumball, then
Arthur Griffin Rumball, then Emma Elizabeth Rumball, then Dr Allan
MacLean, then Dr Arthur Henry Boys, and then Dr Hugh Fraser)

As the Rumball operation moved out of St Albans to rent Harpenden Hall
(Figure 4.4) James Quilter Rumball was still to dominate until about 1863.
Although doubt has been cast on Harpenden Hall's licensing, Rumball
certainly exhibited the required licence at the first visitors' meeting in
1847.[48] The same report also confirms that the proper records were being
kept and reveals that the 'occupations & amusement of the patients are
walking & carriage exercise – gardening and farming – music and whist,
these are adequate & beneficial'. By 1860 it was described as 'Established
by JQ Rumball, Surgeon, for the reception into his family circle, and for
the Phrenological treatment, of a limited number of First-class patients.
Conducted by himself and son.'[49]

Scandal hit James Quilter Rumball in 1865. Having just passed on the
proprietorship of Harpenden Hall to his son he advertised in 1863 for a
single lunatic to be taken into his private residence, The Limes, Harpenden.
But, without paperwork, on 6 July 1864 he took in and restrained Thomas
Landon Garratt, who then escaped. The unaccountable incarceration was
exposed and Rumball was seen to have acted against a century of legislation
designed to safeguard the liberty of the sane and monitor the conditions
of the insane. The case against Rumball was heard at Hemel Hempstead
Petty Sessions and an arrest warrant produced for him at the Assizes,
but he had apparently fled to the continent. Returning to be tried at the
Central Criminal Court for misdemeanour, Rumball pleaded guilty. He
tried, unsuccessfully, to claim that he was ignorant of the law and that the
person was not a lunatic but had *delirium tremens*, and was fined £20. It is
tempting to think that Rumball persisted thereafter, as a William Charles
Henry Dicken (1829–88) was 'boarding' with him in 1871. Dicken was
unmarried and was retired from the War Office by the age of 42. However,
the census does not indicate his lunacy and he soon married and raised
children in Bengeo.

Compared with his father's frenetic lifestyle, the tenure of Arthur
Griffin Rumball from c.1863–80 suggests that he wanted the quiet life. As
his father had before him, Arthur suffered bankruptcy in the 1870s, but
he would have benefited from his intestate father's death in 1872. He had
already been advertising for 'quiet cases only'[50] and, shortly before his own
death, for a 'lady or gentleman who is only slightly mentally afflicted'. This

INSANITY.

ONE of the most common forms of this disease unfits the Patient for general society, but still more unfits him for that strict confinement to which he must be necessarily exposed in a large Asylum.

There are many also, who, having been thus confined, are so improved that a change into the green fields and country air would probably restore them quite. Their friends are unable, however, to procure this for them without risking their safety, and depriving them of that peculiar medical experience which their cases may still require.

A medical gentleman, (formerly pupil to Sir George Tuthil and Dr. Munro), who resides an easy distance from London, in one of the most retired and beautiful villages in England, offers to any such, an ....it by his own fire-side, horse or carriage exercise, and the personal attendance of some fit member of his family in the walks and rides about him. By this treatment he has cured those pronounced incurable, and after recovery, some who have come to him as patients, have continued to reside with him as friends.

This one fact speaks volumes! His references are of the first description, and terms suited to the wants and means of the party applying.

A Treatise upon Insanity, Price One Shilling, embodying his experience and treatment, and pointing out the premonitory symptoms, may be had by applying to J. Q. RUMBALL, Surgeon, Harpenden Hall, St. Albans, Herts.

Figure 4.4 Rumball's advert for his private asylum at Harpenden Hall, *c*.1850. HALS QS/Misc/B/9/4.

may reflect the ill health of his father and himself, but also perhaps an acknowledged lack of expertise.

Upon Arthur's death in 1880 his wife Emma Elizabeth Rumball (1839– 85) continued the proprietorship. This unqualified gentleman's daughter from Hornsey continued to specify potential patients' gender and class, advertising in 1883 her 'Private Asylum for Ladies of the Upper and Middle Classes'. Upon the splitting up of the estate in 1882 she purchased the Hall from J.M. Pott: the asylum finally belonged to the Rumballs. In turn, Emma's trustees let Harpenden Hall to two further doctors. But for later events, the tenancy of Allan MacLean, 1885–92, would have been a swansong in the dying days of the private asylum. The court of Quarter Sessions notes 'complete satisfaction with the conduct of the house' as MacLean confidently applied to take in three extra females.[51] To die there later in the year was his aunt Octavia, a resident. The long-term male patients, Thompson and Pattison, remained in what had become a ladies' asylum. But domestic disaster struck MacLean. In 1890, having spent a month away with his patients in Felixstowe, it emerged on his return that his wife was no longer living with him. After nine years of marriage Eva had taken up with neighbouring farmer William Edward Duckworth, of Hammonds End. On the grounds of adultery MacLean divorced her and she married the farmer a year later. The case was widely reported and in the wake of the scandal the tenancy was given up.[52]

From 1894 Arthur Henry Boys held Harpenden Hall on a repairing lease, paying rent of £120 per year. It was still for ladies only. But the surviving trustee of Emma Rumball rang its death knell, advertising it to be sold at auction on 4 March 1901. No mention was made of the history of the 'charming old-fashioned freehold family residence known as Harpenden Hall'.[53] H.C. Wright bought the freehold of the Hall, but Hugh Fraser, the Medical Officer of Health for Harpenden Urban District Council, administered its last rites. Resident there in the 1901 census, he inherited six lunatic females for whose care he employed two 'mental nurses'. The last of the Hertfordshire private licensed houses, Harpenden Hall would not survive the decade. The patients – Law, Bullock and Moordaff – were discharged as relieved during 1901–02 and the freehold was sold by H.C. Wright to Frank Gough in 1903, whereupon the remaining patients were removed. Grant and Halse were discharged on 14 October 1903, which can be taken as the closing date. Charlotte Grant went to live in Chequer Street, St Albans, with the former proprietor Dr Boys and his family, until her death in 1911. Halse was sent to Otto House asylum, Kensington, but was admitted to Hill End Hospital, St Albans, in 1932, where she died five years later. By 1909 Harpenden Hall was a school for girls.

Table 4.4 provides a list of the patients that can be traced to the asylum. Wider record linkage allows us to discern a surprising amount of detail about their lives and history. Thus, Anne Calvert's 'dirty habits' repeatedly concerned visitors. Part of the walled garden was sectioned off for her personal use in 1850, with which she was 'well pleased'.[54] However, the walls had to be raised as she was still stripping naked and attempting to escape. On Commissioners' advice a strong dress was obtained for her. In April 1851 they found her 'restrained in the use of her hands and arms by straps', and in September reported that 'the case of Miss Calvert is truly deplorable'.[55] A report on Jean Low noted her 'perpetual talking in a strange purposeless manner', her 'extreme violence & bad language a habit of abusing persons out of windows haranguing a crowd on the commons & spending her money foolishly', and that she 'Dresses in a extraordinary manner [and] excites ridicule in the streets'.[56] William Houston Pattison was a repeat escapee who was retrieved from a pub in Witham and from his father's place in Coggeshall. On one occasion he gave the slip during an outing to Hatfield races.[57] Thomas Toovey was a hallucinatory maniac with delusions of grandeur who 'imagines he is possessed of immense wealth which he says he intends distributing by millions to his numerous friends'. More specifically, Dr Wotton was told 'he had millions of Horses – That he was going to give one to each person he saw – That he intended giving a state dinner to which the Prince of Orange had been invited'; 'he is continuously writing letters to various postmasters to send him carriages with four horses each to take him to different places to dance'. Toovey's brother John lamented that he 'had Telegraphed for several carriages and four to take him and his friends to hunt'. As to the source of his wealth, he was 'imagining the house in which he resides is infested by witches'; they surround him and 'purloin his clothes etc but have brought him immense riches'. Within days of admission he was dead from 'maniacal exhaustion' and 'phlegmonous erysipelas', a deep-tissue form of the inflammatory fever known as St Anthony's fire.[58]

Hilfield, Aldenham (c.1900)
Sale particulars of 1903[59] advertise the house's leasehold for sale as a going concern, being 'a Licensed Private Asylum For Ladies of the Upper Classes suffering from Nervous and Mental Affections'. But these were the

Table 4.4   Patients at Harpenden Hall.

Patient's name	Admission/residence	Details
William John Alexander (1796–)	1866–9	Merchant, from Kilburn. Chancery 1865
Julia S. Allen	29 May 1899–1 Sep 1900 (not improved)	
Rosa Clemence Ashwell (c.1841–1922)	7 Jun 1890–4 Aug 1896 (not improved)	Daughter of clergyman, from Wales
Mr Badger	1863–6	
John Bare	1879	Chancery 1879
Ellen Annette Eliza Bertlin (1863–1919)	2 Oct 1889–7 Nov 1891 (relieved)	Daughter of merchant's widow, from Hampstead
Phillip Ca[r]teret Bertrand (c.1827–)	1 Nov 1852–2 Feb 1853 (recovered); 6 Feb 1853–7 Jan 1854 (recovered)	
Sarah J. Blake	29 Nov 1889–21 Mar 1890 (not improved)	
Eliza[beth] Glinn Bullock (1842–)	19 Jun 1900–18 Dec 1901 (relieved)	From Chappel, Essex
Anne Calvert (c.1795–1866)	21 Sep 1849–25 Sep 1866 (death)	Lady
Mr Charrington	1858	
William Clerk	1847–56; 1861–26 Dec 1863 (death)	[as before]
Revd Woodthorpe Scholefield Collett (1826–1913)	3 Mar 1859–30 Jun 1862 (not improved)	Clergyman, from Market Rasen, Lincs. Chancery 1861
Blanche Marie Collis (1863–1920)	5 Nov 1888–27 Apr 1889 (relieved)	From Brixton. Died in Bethlem Hospital
Eleanor Dennistoun Cross (–1898)	30 May 1895–19 Oct 1898 (death)	
Ellen Mary Crump (c.1860–)	10 Nov 1888–25 Dec 1893 (not improved)	Solicitor's daughter, from Primrose Hill Road
Mary Debar[r]y (1766–1854)	1847; 15 Jan 1848–8 Apr 1854 (relieved)	Lady, from Hurstbourne Tarrant, Hants
Sarah A. Fitton	22 Nov 1894–13 Sep 1895 (recovered)	
Mr [Thomas?] Fowler	1854	[Possibly bricklayer of St Albans – see above]
Anne B. Gardner	10 Feb 1890–22 Dec 1890 (not improved)	

Patient's name	Admission/residence	Details
Thomas Landon Garratt	c.1865	Unauthorised, Rumball indicted at Assizes
Charlotte Elizabeth Grant (c.1845–1911)	3 Jun 1894–14 Oct 1903 (discharged)	
Charlotte Radclyffe Russell Hall (c.1817–86)	6 Oct 1886–27 Oct 1886 (death)	From Bedford
Gertrude Anna Otton Halse (c.1855–1937)	27 Jul 1889–14 Oct 1903 (discharged to Otto House)	Daughter of merchant, from Wandsworth
F. William Thomas Hammond	12 Jul 1854–21 Oct 1854 (relieved)	
Mary Anne Francis Coleman Hancock (c.1827–1906)	27 Feb 1873–1901	Daughter of rubber manufacturer, from London
Eliza Herbert	11 Apr 1891–11 Apr 1892 (recovered)	
Ethel A. Hitch	3 Jun 1888–17 Dec 1888 (recovered)	
Emma Hubbard	Jun 1899–24 Jul 1899 (not improved)	
James Stuart Jarvis/ Jarvie/Jawie (c.1819–)	20 Mar 1871–28 Apr 1871 (recovered)	Gentleman from Glasgow, Scotland
Mary A.B. Johnson	17 Mar 1896–18 Mar 1896	Irregular admission
Elizabeth R. Landell	10 Feb 1894–10 Mar 1894 (recovered)	
Mary Lathbury (–1854)	2 Jul 1851–30 Aug 1851 (relieved)	From Burton-on-Trent
Anna Louisa Law (1851–)	1891; 22 Dec 1899–31 Oct 1901 (relieved)	From Orwell, Cambs
Henrietta R. Lawson	26 May 1887–15 Jun 1889 (relieved)	
Cecilia Isabella Loraine (c.1835–1905)	1890–1	From London
Jean Low(e) (c.1801–82)	24 May 1869–25 Mar 1882 (death)	Gentlewoman, from Forfarshire, Scotland
Octavia MacLean (c.1809–89)	25 Jan 1888–20 Aug 1889 (death)	Proprietor's aunt, from South Kensington
Maria Eliza Macquoid (c.1811–94)	4 Oct 1894–11 Oct 1894 (death)	From St Albans

Patient's name	Admission/residence	Details
James Manb(e)y (c.1811–57)	25 Apr 1848–15 Feb 1857 (death of dropsy)	Surgeon. Buried next to Ann Calvert
Esther C. Mead	30 Nov 1887–27 Nov 1888 (recovered); 4 Mar 1890–4 Mar 1891 (relieved)	
Annie R. Mercier	28 Apr 1888–31 Oct 1888 (recovered)	
Catherine Moordaff (1865–1949)	20 Jan 1893–20 Jan 1902 (relieved)	Daughter of solicitor, from Cockermouth
Catherine A. Nelson	2 Mar 1895–11 Jul 1895 (not improved)	
Emily Norton	30 Aug 1893–29 Nov 1893 (not improved)	
Edith Osborn	13 Jan 1893–20 Apr 1893 (not improved)	
William Houston Pattison (c.1830–95)	17 Dec 1861–14 Dec 1894 (not improved)	Gentleman/Surveying Engineer, from Coggeshall, Essex. Chancery 1886
Alfred Pigott	15 Jun 1873–2 Sep 1873 (recovered); 23 Dec 1873–7 May 1874 (not improved)	
Henry Pigott (c.1816–53)	11 May 1850–20 Mar 1853 (death of epilepsy)	Former stock broker's clerk, from St Albans
Ann Rogers	10 May 1889–31 Oct 1889 (recovered)	
George Shaw	13 May 1874–10 Jun 1874 (relieved)	
Eliza Slack	1890–1	
Maude Agnes Smith (c.1867–)	1890–1	Daughter of solicitor's widow, from Whittlesey, Cambs
Frances M. Style	17 Dec 1896–9 Jan 1897 (recovered)	
Elizabeth Wilhelmina Galliers Swinton (c.1823–1908)	17 Dec 1890–11 Nov 1891 (recovered)	Widow of solicitor, from Scotland
Frederic[k] Taylor	24 Apr 1858–28 Nov 1859 (not improved)	
Peter Thompson (c.1817–93)	1848–93	Gentleman, former army tailor, from Soho, Middlesex

Patient's name	Admission/residence	Details
Armstrong Todd (1824–73)	23 Nov 1871–20 May 1873 (not improved)	
Louisa C. Tomlinson	8 Mar 1890–23 Oct 1890 (recovered)	
Thomas Toovey (1823–63)	1 Jun 1863–21 Jun 1863 (death)	Miller, from Kings Langley
Frederick James Townend (1853–)	1868	From Turnham Green, Middlesex
Clara Louisa Udal (1841–1925)	18 Apr 1892–16 May 1892 (recovered)	From Bromley, Kent
Louisa White	1 Apr 1899–25 Apr 1899 (recovered)	
Emily A. Wilkinson	16 Feb 1893–17 Feb 1893; 17 Feb 1893–16 Feb 1895 (relieved); 19 Feb 1895–15 Sep 1898 (not improved)	Initially an irregular admission
Sarah Wyatt	2 Sep 1859–20 Sep 1859 (relieved)	

dying embers of the age of the private madhouse. The particulars' general remarks state that the

> Premises comprised in this Sale are licensed by H.M.
> Commissioners in Lunacy to be used for the reception of 13
> Female Residents, and special attention is drawn to the fact that
> this Asylum is one of the few remaining Private Asylums owing to
> H.M. Commissioners having been debarred granting fresh licenses
> since the Lunacy Act, 1890, was passed.

It was the last of the attempts, especially typical of the later asylums, to adorn a beautiful house with genteel ladies. Perhaps they would not be so ill as to require incarceration as private patients in county asylums, but would simply be somewhat distracted or nervous and guarantee a good income. However, the national admissions register which runs to 1900[60] records no patients admitted to Hilfield. The 1891 and 1901 censuses indicate no patients or medical staff at Hilfield, Hilfield Lodge or Hilfield Farm. Indeed, the sessions rolls of 1889–91 refer only to Harpenden Hall's licensing and not to Hilfield.

Conclusion

The madhouse system's heyday was the early nineteenth century, building towards an 1848 peak of 145 institutions in England and Wales. Many of these were soaking up the pauper lunatic trade that would be so lucrative until the county asylums became more numerous. Madhouses in Hertfordshire differed in that they were all intended for the elite. Proximity to London determines much in Hertfordshire. The city had private and charitable pauper institutions, so poor London lunatics usually need not be sent out to expensive houses in the shires, while paupers from Hertfordshire might make do with parish provision such as workhouses or be sent to spacious cheap asylums in London.[61] The exclusive houses on their doorsteps would not want them, and nor would their parishes pay their astronomical fees. For rich London lunatics, naturally there were madhouses in the City. But they could not offer the clean air, space and distant discretion that easily accessible Hertfordshire could. It is no accident that the county's madhouses are all in the south rather than the north. Completing the equation, that issue of discretion meant that rich lunatics from Hertfordshire would only rarely be installed in the nearest respectable house. Some element of distance appears to have been the convention.

For a small county, proximity to London led to a fairly healthy number of institutions compared with other counties. There were about 40 nationally in 1800. The 1799–1813 period saw five madhouses active in Hertfordshire, sometimes three at a time. Nonetheless, a distinction can be made between the three established 'proper' houses and the more transient amateur enterprises. Two of those three, at Hadham and Harpenden, vied for the Hertfordshire trade over much of the nineteenth century. There is no evidence of fierce competition, but neither is there for respectful professional co-operation. Standing sentinel in the county's far-east and west, the gap would have helped them both survive.

Yet if each projected the image of a restful country retreat for distracted gentlefolk, a detailed comparison reveals subtle differences. Both processed an average of about one patient per year, so had a similar turnover. But the proportion of women at Hadham, about 43 per cent, is outweighed by the 68 per cent at Harpenden, where the admissions policy became women-only. Perhaps unfairly, it could be suggested that this not uncommon tendency to advertise only for ladies reflects an ill-informed attempt at an 'easy option' to make up for a lack of expertise or staff while maintaining that veneer of attentive care in a refined environment. About 11 per cent of the Hadham patients became Chancery cases, compared to 5 per cent in Harpenden, an indicator that the patients there were a little less well-heeled than at Hadham. In turn, the ratio of medical staff to patients averaged 1 to 1.2 at Hadham but only 1 to 2 at Harpenden. Essentially the difference lay in the Rumballs' 'inclusion' of patients in the family, something which could not only be interpreted as brave, progressive and respectful but also greatly reduced outgoings on staff. In this context Harpenden Hall emerges as the underdog. Run on a more informal, family basis alongside J.Q. Rumball's phrenological and lecturing pursuits, it had fewer staff, less wealthy patients and had to scale down to welcome only ladies. It was plagued by questioning of its licensing, its record-keeping and irregular admissions, and by the scandals of a court case, divorce and bankruptcies. The Hadham asylum, however, occupied a palace. At times it had the backing of the renowned Monro dynasty, physicians to Bethlem. The staffing was better and the patients richer.

Although medical and proactive attempts at cures may have been lacking, the Rumballs' easier approach to their patients is reflected in the policy of non-coercion and non-restraint, which suggests a degree of respect. Applying for his licence, James Quilter Rumball wrote that

> there is ample means for separating the sexes … the airy grounds
> are front and back comprising together half an acre … with 600
> acres of Common in front of the house. Besides this there is a
> walled in garden and seven acres of Meadow Land … I only intend
> to take first class Patients, and consider carriage exercise our most
> sovereign remedy. As my father was the first to adopt the non
> restraint principle and as I have had ample reasons to test its value
> and pursue it, confined spaces are less necessary than they would
> be at a house conducted on different principles. Vigilance and care
> are better than walls. Both I and my son will reside in the House.[62]

The visitors reported that the 'system of non-coercion is steadily pursued'.[63]

Reassured by the proprietors' medical qualifications, what seemed to matter to the relatives and proprietors was comfort and environment. The law, especially the Court of Chancery, was concerned with whether respectable patients needed to be incarcerated and the predicament of their property. Visitors were focused on paperwork, the contentedness, cleanliness and restraint of patients and whether they attended divine service. Real detail as to treatment and its success rate was not a feature of their reports, but would have been in the lost Case Books. At times the work of the Commissioners could be more probing, but aside from the clinical relationship and administrative process a surprising and intriguing level of connection between proprietors and patients is to be seen. Cowper was Cotton's friend and fellow poet. Octavia MacLean was Allan MacLean's rich aunt. Calverts were friends with Rumballs. A female patient remained with the proprietors of both Hadham and Harpenden after closure. Some patients stayed long term; escaping the standard label of 'idiot', a therapeutic relationship may have been fostered over time, but so was a guaranteed income. There could be real concern and humanity in dealing with the escaped or lost. Burials of proprietor and patient could be adjacent. For all the commercial basis of a private licensed house, the patient–doctor relationship is often seen to be informal rather than distant and clinical.

Notes

1. For a flavour of this extensive material, see L. Smith, *Lunatic hospitals in Georgian England, 1750–1830* (London, 2007); C. Smith, 'Family, community and the Victorian asylum: a case study of the Northampton General Lunatic Asylum and its pauper lunatics', *Family and Community History*, 9 (2006), pp. 23–46; B. Forsythe *et al.*, 'The New Poor Law and the county pauper lunatic asylum: the Devon experience 1834–1884', *Social History of Medicine*, 9 (1996), pp. 335–55; A. Suzuki, 'The household and the care of lunatics in eighteenth century London', in P. Horden and R. Smith (eds), *The locus of care: families, communities institutions and the provision of welfare since antiquity* (London, 1998), pp. 153–75; J. Melling and B. Forsythe, *The politics of madness: the state, insanity, and society in England, 1845–1914* (London, 2006); S. Cherry, *Mental health care in modern England: the Norfolk Lunatic Asylum/St. Andrew's Hospital c.1810–1998* (Woodbridge, 2003); A. Scull, *The most solitary of afflictions: madness and society in Britain, 1700–1900* (New Haven, CT, 1993).

2. Hertfordshire Archives and Local Studies, Hertford (hereafter HALS) QS/Misc/B/3/12.

3. An Act for Regulating Madhouses 1774, 14 Geo III c. 49.

4. An Act to Regulate the Care and Treatment of Insane Persons in England 1828, 9 Geo IV c. 41; Madhouses Act 1832, 2 and 3 William IV c. 107; Lunacy Act 1845, 8 and 9 Victoria c. 100.

5. Lunacy Act 1890, 53 Victoria c. 5.

6. The National Archives (hereafter TNA) MH 51/735.

7. TNA MH 94/11.

8. These institutions include St Albans, Cheshunt, Northaw, Much Hadham, Hertford, Harpenden and Aldenham.

9. *Gentleman's Magazine* (June 1807) pp. 500–1.

10. C.E. Jones, 'A St Albans worthy: Dr. Nathaniel Cotton, 1705 to 1788', *St Albans and Hertfordshire Architectural and Archaeological Society Transactions* (1936), pp. 57–63; M.F. Thwaite, 'Doctor Nathaniel Cotton: physician and minor poet', *Hertfordshire Past & Present*, 6 (1966), pp. 29–33; Rev F.A. Harding, 'Dr Nathaniel Cotton of St Albans', *Hertfordshire Countryside*, 23 (1969), pp. 46–8.

11. An Act for vesting part of the settled estate of Nathaniel Cotton Doctor in Physic, lying in the county of Hertford, in trustees, in trust, to sell the same, and to lay out the money arising by such sale in the purchase of another estate to be settled to the uses of his marriage settlement 1748, 22 George II c. 30.

12. N. Cotton, *Observations on a particular kind of scarlet fever that lately prevailed in and about St Albans* (London, 1749).

13. HALS DP/93/11/3.

14. HALS DP/90/11/3.

15. HALS Acc 4473/1a/37 by Stanley Kent; Local Studies Library image collection, by RCHME, c1910; Acc 4104/17(Neg80/W/3a) in Local Studies Library image collection.

16. J.T. Smith, 'Nine hundred years of St Albans: architecture and social history', *Hertfordshire Archaeology*, 11 (1993), p. 13.

17. HALS DE/Of/8/498.

18. HALS DP/90/11/4–5.

19. C.H. Ashdown, *St Albans historical and picturesque* (London, 1893); H. Winter, *The last of old St Albans*, pt. 7 (1898), pl. 69/100 dated 24 September 1898.

20. E.M. Alty, 'Cowper and St Albans', *Hertfordshire Countryside*, 30 (1975), p. 35; W. Hayley, *The life and letters of William Cowper*, Vol. 1 (London, 1812), pp. 94–9.

21. *Gentleman's Magazine*, Vol. 77 (June 1807), p. 500.

22. HALS SBR/949.

23. HALS IR/1/385 b–c and IR/2/65/1 (plot 440); *Kelly's Directories* (1907–28).

24. Regarding the location of the asylum, there is some evidence from the 1780s concerning where Thomas held land in Cheshunt. See HALS DE/Cr/109/1; HALS court book dated 1775–89 in Off Acc 590.

25. Essex Record Office (hereafter ERO) Q/SBb 301/18.

26. ERO Q/SBb301/10; Q/SBb 303/11; Q/SBb 329/33, 35, 36.

27. ERO Q/SBb 457/16.

28. HALS LS/B/2, pp. 269–70; HALS LS/MB/3.

29. HALS 29075.

30. HALS 66568.

31. *Morning Post*, 30 April 1802, pp. 1, 4.

32. London Metropolitan Archives (hereafter LMA), ACC/1063/164.

33. Great Britain Commissioners in Lunacy, *Further report of the Commissioners in Lunacy* (London, 1847), p. 410.

34. P. Earle, *An examination of the practice of blood-letting in mental disorders* (New York, 1854) p. 36.

35. Great Britain Commissioners in Lunacy, *Sixteenth report of the Commissioners in Lunacy* (London, 1862).

36. *Hertfordshire Mercury*, 7 January 1888, p. 2; 2 June 1888, p. 2.

37. HALS QS/Misc/B/8/3.
38. Cambridgeshire Archives R55/7.
39. C.J. Palmer, *Perlustration of Great Yarmouth* (Great Yarmouth, 1872).
40. LMA ACC/1057/034; LMA ACC/1057/061.
41. HALS DP/90/11/8.
42. HALS LS/B/3; LS/MB/5–6.
43. HALS QS/Misc/B/10/7.
44. *The Times*, 14 February 1863.
45. HALS SBR/1700A.
46. *The Reformer*, 23 September 1843.
47. Great Britain Commissioners in Lunacy, *Report of the Metropolitan Commissioners in Lunacy* (London, 1844), p. 212.
48. HALS QS/Misc/B/10/7.
49. *The London and provincial medical directory and general medical register* (London, 1860), p. 1083.
50. *The Times*, 27 May 1872.
51. HALS QSR/112, letter dated 19 March 1889.
52. TNA J77/456/3889; *The Herts Advertiser*, 25 April 1891, p. 7.
53. *The Herts Advertiser*, 16 February 1901, p. 1.
54. HALS QS/Misc/B/10/26.
55. HALS QS/Misc/B/9/7, 22.
56. HALS QS/Misc/B/9/24.
57. HALS QS/Misc/B/9/10, 12–13, 17.
58. HALS QS/Misc/B/9/14–16, 18.
59. HALS DE/Gr/5.
60. TNA MH94/11.
61. HALS QS/Misc/B/4c.
62. HALS QS/Misc/B/10/1.
63. HALS QS/Misc/B/10/7.

CHAPTER FIVE

Caring for the poor in East Hertfordshire c.1620–50

Alan Thomson

THE POOR RECEIVED care and support in a number of different ways in the mid-seventeenth century. Firstly there were the products of the medieval and post-medieval charities, whose benefactors specified the purposes to which the charities should be put, which might include hand-outs of cash or in kind at specified times, support for the building and maintenance of almshouses or income from grants of land aimed at specific groups, such as poor widows.[1] In theory these charities were perpetual, in contrast, secondly, to the one-off payments that arose from the bequests in individual wills whose authors specified the amount of their estate that should be distributed, usually to the poor of their own parish.[2] Thirdly, there were the charitable collections, often on a weekly basis, through the poor box in the parish church, which were seldom recorded in the churchwardens' accounts. These were sometimes supplemented by charitable giving on feast days such as Christmas or Easter, when either a special collection was made for the poor or hospitality was extended from the wealthy to others in the wider community.[3] These were also seldom recorded except in the detailed accounts of the great estates, churchwardens, traders or businessmen. However, from the late sixteenth century there was, fourthly, provision for a parish poor rate to be levied on the better-off members of the community to support the poorer, which was often raised only in years of particular hardship.[4] These were increasingly recorded in the accounts of the overseers of the poor. Lastly, in an emergency which had arisen through harvest failure or high bread prices specific funds were raised locally, as was the case in the early 1630s.

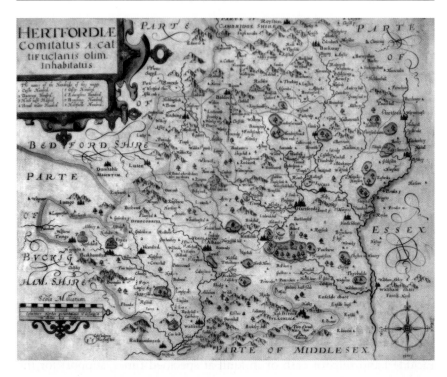

Figure 5.1 *Hertfordiae Comitatus*, 1607. Christopher Saxton's map of Hertfordshire, engraved by William Kip for Camden's *Britannia*.

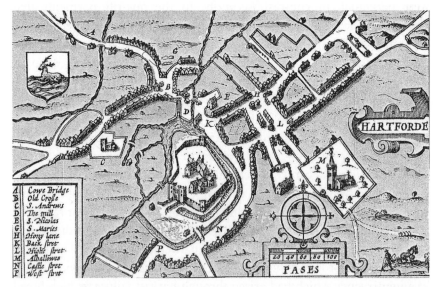

Figure 5.2 Map of Hertford, 1610. Detail from John Speed's Hertfordshire map for *Theatre of the Empire of Great Britaine*.

Against this broad backdrop, the current chapter focuses on significant developments in poor relief (widely defined) in the rural parishes and small towns of East Hertfordshire (Figures 5.1 and 5.2) in the middle decades of the seventeenth century, when political policies and social and economic circumstances changed dramatically. The first part deals with parochial charitable provision. Contemporary bequests made in wills to the poor can be partly found in the *Victoria County History of Hertfordshire* and other local histories and partly in the wills proved by both the Prerogative Court of Canterbury and the local archdeacons' and bishops' courts. Parts of East Hertfordshire were in the archdeaconry of Middlesex in the bishopric of London, many of whose records are held in the Essex County Record Office at Chelmsford. Other wills in the hundred of Hertford were part of the archdeaconry of Huntingdon, in the southernmost part of the vast Lincoln diocese.

The second part of the chapter deals with the crises of the 1630s. Following poor harvests at the beginning of the decade the 1630s witnessed rising bread prices, increasing vagrancy and poverty and endemic attacks of the plague and smallpox, which led to the implementation of the Book of Orders (instructions, issued to all local magistrates, on how to cope with bread shortages and mass poverty), attempts to more tightly control the local markets, the extension of pauper apprenticeship and a variety of local responses to care for different categories of poor.[5] Evidence for this decade is particularly found in reports sent from divisional magistrates to the Privy Council[6] and printed *Acts of the Privy Council*. Parochial records, particularly those from Hertford borough, and the County Quarter Sessions[7] give a more detailed perspective on the experiences of individual localities.

The chapter's final part focuses on the impact of the civil war in the 1640s on the parishes and their ability to care for the poor, and on post-war provision. The war brought massive increases in taxation, the loss of manpower to parliamentary armies and the increasing burden of free quarter (the practice of soldiers taking free board and lodging in houses and inns, the owners of which were not paid until much later). These all resulted in there being fewer people to implement poor-law provisions as well as less money to support them. Additional resources had to be found for those injured or maimed during the conflict and for war widows.[8] Demobilisation of armies, including the local volunteer regiments, the army of the Eastern Association and the National Armies created an increase in vagabonds, particularly in the east of the county through which ran the Old North Road, the main road from London to the north. County and divisional magistrates had to respond to this situation in a variety of ways, including repairing houses of correction and, later, paying constables to remove vagrants.[9] In turn, policies of the 1650s were influenced partly by the continuing problems created by war, the disastrous summer of 1648 and the harsher moral climate of the Cromwellian Protectorate. Apprenticeship, bastardy orders and legal settlements became prominent as means of getting young men off the streets, discouraging them from having illegitimate children and limiting those who could claim a legal settlement in a particular parish.[10] Policies of maintaining law and order, moral imperatives and a drive to reduce those on the poor rates influenced how communities acted.

Charitable provision for the poor in East Hertfordshire to 1640

East Hertfordshire in the seventeenth century consisted of the communities in the old divisions of the hundreds of Hertford and Braughing and surrounding parishes then in other hundreds. Included were the borough of Hertford and the market towns of Ware, Bishops Stortford, Buntingford and Sawbridgeworth, along with other villages north and east of Braughing and settlements down the Lea Valley to Broxbourne and Cheshunt. Charities for the poor existed in many parishes, some of which involved payments from the rental of lands or buildings. In Ware there were a number of such properties, the town's charities going back to the early fifteenth century at least. In 1407 the Ware feoffees or trustees (then in the guise of the Guild of Corpus Christi) acquired a house and garden in Mill Lane (now Priory Street) which by the 1630s had become two almshouses. Other land and buildings produced rent, such as the Bell Close, containing about four acres, and that on which the former Corpus Christi Barn had stood, as well as two inns, the Saracen's Head (possibly acquired as early as 1365) together with a piece of land called the Netherhoe and the White Hart with appurtenances (Figures 5.3 and 5.4). This latter had been obtained by 1479, or possibly as early as 1426.[11]

The Ware Guild had political and religious imperatives until the sixteenth century, when it was reformed. It changed its name to the Jesus Brotherhood and used its income to meet the common charges of the town, such as cleaning the streets and repairing the roads. After dissolution in 1539 the properties passed to the 'Feoffees of the Town Land

Figure 5.3 White Hart Inn, High Street, Ware.

Figure 5.4 Blue Plaque for the White Hart Inn, Ware.

Rents' whose purpose was to administer the trust and 'to distribute the income to the benefit of the inhabitants of Ware'. With the establishment of the overseers of the poor in Elizabeth's reign the vestry and the trustees shared responsibility for looking after the local poor, the vestry levying the poor rate and paying for the workhouse, the trustees both keeping up the almshouses and giving hand-outs to the 'necessitous poor'. In 1612 all the properties were brought together under one trust and a new trust deed stipulated that the profits were to be used for the public charges and to relieve the poor of the parish 'as shall fortune to be in such great poverty or necessitie' as charity would relieve. By then the trustees had obtained various acres of meadow on the Meads, an almshouse and other properties in Crib Street and the schoolhouse. A similar situation had arisen in Stevenage from the late fifteenth century, when almshouses and other charities were accumulated.[12]

Further donations to the stock of charitable resources were made before 1640. In 1619 George Mead MD gave a post-mortem bequest of £5 yearly issuing out of the George Inn, and in 1622 John Elmer made a post-mortem bequest of Baldock House for the benefit of the poor of Ware and Stevenage. The Charity of Ellen Bridge, founded in 1628, consisted of a garden formerly known as Pope's or Doulton's Pightle, situated in Watton Road, and the Charity of Humphrey Spencer, founded on 26 June 1630, consisted of a cottage in Kibes Lane. Following Spencer's death in 1633 £200 from his will enabled the trustees to buy the Holy Lamb inn at Colliers End with eight acres of land and a cottage, the rent from which came to the trust. The schoolhouse was also established with £100 from his will to pay for a master to 'teach and instruct so many of the children of the poorest sort of the inhabitants of the town of Ware to write and read, freely and for nothing'. Thus in this one town there were already, before the 1630s, a considerable number of charities which focused on caring for the urban poor and providing an education for their children.[13]

Hertford, being a borough, had more resources than most towns for helping the poor.[14] In 1645 a review was carried out of the use to which the profits from the Chequer (a covered building containing shops and stalls which were rented out) and other sources of income had been put over the previous 16 years. The rents on properties, including shops, in the Chequer[15] had raised a total of £288. Other rents and income came to £192 and fees for innkeepers' and victuallers' licences brought in £49. Rents from two purchased properties had brought in £60, where the initial purchase price had been £55. Only £13, however, had gone to the poor on the direction of Sir Thomas Gardiner, along with £18 for those visited by the plague, a further £11 that was lent to poor men for trading purposes, £10 to set the poor on work and £64 to provide fuel for the poor at £4 a year. A vast amount had been spent on rebuilding the Chequer and the neighbouring Red Lyon Inn after a disastrous fire, as well as on legal fees for this and other purposes.[16]

As well as receiving borough income, groups of the 'deserving poor' were identified in bequests from benefactors with links to Hertford. The will of Roger Daniel in 1625 left an annuity of £10, of which £5 was payable for a monthly sermon, £4 for the 14 poorest householders of All Saints and 6 of the parish of St Andrew, 12s for bread and drink for poor prisoners in the 'Maine Gaol' and 8s for a breakfast for the administering trustees. In 1649 Mary Pettyt, widow, gave two tenements near Cowbridge for as many poor widows. Other towns were not as lucky or as well organised as Ware and Hertford but donations from various wills served similar purposes from the 1620s to the 1650s. The church and poor lands in Sawbridgeworth, in an indenture dated 20 July 1652, consisted of a moiety of the income derived from the following property: the bowling green, containing 3 roods 22 perches and used as a recreation ground for boys; three cottages occupied as almshouses by three poor women who received parochial relief; Pishocroft Gardens, containing about five acres near High Wych, and a rood of land in Church Street. Almshouses for widows were also the object of William Bonest, who left his tenement in Overbury in Braughing to the churchwardens in trust for four widows to dwell in rent-free and £1 yearly out of a field called Dassel Field to be distributed equally among them.[17]

Bishops Stortford also had five almshouses founded by Richard Pilston in 1572. This was in a long tradition: it has been estimated that about 1,300 almshouses, hospitals and so on were constructed in England and Wales during the medieval period.[18] In addition, the tradition of leaving land or a rent-charge on land in a will was regularly followed in Stortford in the Tudor and early Stuart periods by people such as Robert Adison in 1554, Margaret Dane in 1579, William Ellis in 1616 and William Gilby in 1630. Cheshunt was exceptional in that it had accumulated a considerable sum of money for the poor which had derived from the compensation given by King James I for inclosing a large piece of common to increase the size of Theobalds Park. The compensation totalled £500: £180 was expended

Figure 5.5 Clock House, formerly Baesh's Grammar School, Cappell Lane, Stanstead Abbots.

in the erection of almshouses at Turners Hill and the balance of £320 was used in the purchase of Curtis Farm, Nazeing. The total of the gifts was brought to £1000 by £200 from the will of Humphrey Flint in 1610, £100 left by Richard Coulter in 1620 and a further £200 from the will of Sir Edmund Scott in 1638. In addition, Robert Dewhurst set up an almshouse charity in 1643.[19]

In some cases, as at Stanstead Abbots, an extensive charity was set up by a single wealthy benefactor, in this instance Sir Edward Baesh. In 1635 he left the vicarage house and grounds, land in Chapel Lane producing £2 yearly, almshouses with land and other pieces of land including 'a piece of meadow ground called the Pitansey Meadow alias Parentase', and a rent-charge of £25 issuing out of the manor of Stanstead Baesh (Figure 5.5). Similarly, in Braughing in 1595 Matthew Wall had given a rent-charge of 20s out of a house and about 12 acres of land at Green End in Braughing, 3s 6d of which went to the poor, 6s 8d to 20 school children, 4s 10d to the sexton and clerk and 5s to the vicar and churchwardens for their trouble. These bequests were given by men – many of whom were of puritan persuasion – who were aware of the privations of the poor and who responded positively to the economic and social conditions of the time to help the poor, particularly widows and children, who could not fend for themselves.[20]

In other cases, as at Standon, the parish charities accumulated a considerable quantity of land, the income from which was dedicated to the poor. In 1554 George Crowch had left land in a trust fund and between 1614 and 1658 64 acres were bequeathed to the poor from three different wills. How the income was derived varied with the particular will. In 1556 George Clerke of Bennington left a rent-charge of £2 10s issuing out of Boxbury Tithe, Walkern, and in 1617 William Purvey of Great Amwell left a yearly rent-charge of 13s 4d from the Wormley Bury estate, whereas Sylvester Elwes, also of Amwell, whose will was proved in 1639, left a legacy of £40 out of which land for the poor was purchased. Thus not all land was left from the same parish or even the same county. In 1603 Sir George Carey, K.G. Lord Hunsdon, had given money to the poor of Eastwick and Hunsdon that was later invested in lands in Great Parndon in Essex, and in 1613 Grace Ellis gave 40s yearly for the poor, charged upon property in Norton Folgate in London.[21]

Whatever the source, it is clear that before and immediately after 1630 income over and above that stemming from the poor rate was available to particular parishes from charitable bequests to care for the poor. In some cases the purpose of the money was specified, as when William Thorowgood left a yearly sum of £4 from land in Hoddesdon for the distribution of bread and a further rent-charge of £4 4s for the distribution of bread and beef from the rents from Balls Park, Hertford. In 1602 Richard Turner of Reed gave 20s a year to the poor paid out of the close called 'Barton's' which was distributed in bread, and Thomas Hall of Little Munden left money to buy bread for the poor in 1643, as did the Gore family at Gilston. It was thought that gifts in kind would benefit the poor more than cash hand-outs, which might be wasted on alcoholic drink, gambling or other excesses.[22]

Apart from these ongoing charities, legacies were left in the wills of the better-off to be distributed among the poor of the parish or parishes with which the deceased had been associated. A sample of the various wills from communities in the area reveals that a custom seems to have developed whereby a standard fraction of a pound, such as one- or two-thirds, was given to the poor of the parish to be distributed either by the executor or executrix or by the churchwardens and overseers of the poor, either at the funeral or one, three or six months after it. The later period may have given the officials some discretion to give the money at seasons of greatest need.[23]

These sums vary in rural parishes from the 10s given by Henry Campe, husbandman of Hunsdon, to the £4 given by Benedict Beawcock, a gentleman from Anstey. Often the bequest was to the poor of one rural parish, implying the potential for widespread benefit, as, for example, in 1634 when Henry Wootton, yeoman, gave 20s to the poor of Furneaux Pelham and in 1641 when John Parnell, yeoman, gave £2 to the poor of Hunsdon. In the urban context John Lyndsell, yeoman, gave 50s to the poor of Stortford and the same to the poor of Sawbridgeworth, both in 1640. In urban parishes as much as £5 was given by, for example, James Byrche of Ware to the poor widows of the town in 1632, a time of particular poverty, whereas in 1627 Thomas Haggard, grocer in the town, gave as little as 5s and in 1624 Bennet Beltoft only 3s 4d. Similarly, in Stortford yeoman William Sumpner gave £3 in 1641 and in 1640 William Bayford, husbandman, gave 10s. Prudence Bird, widow of Stortford, gave 6s 8d specifically to the poor of the district of Hockerill within the town.[24]

To some extent the sum given to the poor related to the status and wealth of the deceased. Some husbandmen, such as William Bayford of Stortford, or the poorer sort of yeoman, such as Henry Shuttleworth of Widford in 1627, gave 10s. However, Anthony Wheeler of Great Hormead, a yeoman farmer with land in three parishes, gave only 10s to the local poor in 1627, which had to be distributed within a week of his death. In contrast, Oliver Harvey, yeoman of Ware, gave £2 in 1627. Businessmen such as Leonard Knight the Elder, tanner of Stortford, gave £1 in 1642, whereas the wealthier butcher John Miller, of the same town, gave £2 to be distributed at his funeral, which presumably ensured a good turnout, a practice also stipulated in 1648 by Henry Neates, a tailor of Anstey. George Meade senior, a doctor and apothecary from Ware, gave £3 in 1621 to be equally divided among the poor of Ware at the discretion of the churchwardens, who would presumably know who were the most worthy cases for relief.[25]

Sometimes more precise stipulations were made in wills. In 1629 George Channcy of Sawbridgeworth, gentleman, gave £3 to be distributed to 30 poor householders of the town, half on the day of his funeral and half a year later on its anniversary. His executrix was his wife Lucy, who in her will, made 11 years later in 1640, gave £2 to be distributed to the poor at her burial.[26] The innholder from Ware, Robert Wilson, gave not just 10s to the poor of Ware in 1620 but also a dozen bread loaves. These payments in kind in the form of loaves meant, of course, that there was no additional money to spend on drink. Servants were often left items of clothing, as in the case of Alice Thirgood, maidservant to the widow Elizabeth Duke, who in 1650 was left a cloth petticoat.[27]

Parishes also collected for the poor through church services, sometimes at special communions. At Stortford in 1626 the churchwardens 'layd out and disburst to poore and sicke folke & charitable uses out of the money gathered at the communion £4 2s 6d'. Ten years later there was a special collection 'at the fasts' when over £7 was collected, £4 15s being spent on bread for the poor and £3 12s 9d being given to 'divers poor people visited with the poxe & others sick and lame'. In Braughing ten named people were identified at the time of the town feast on Easter Wednesday to benefit from local charity. Also in 1635 Braughing vestry caused Mr Edmonds to distribute £2 10s to the poor and throughout the 1630s continued to support young people getting married through the maids' marriages fund, by which couples who did not produce a child within nine months of marriage could claim anything from 6s 8d to £1 from the parish, depending on the number of claimants in any one year. By the late 1650s charitable giving and poor rate income were often put together as the overseers of the poor in Stortford were paying out regular sums from charitable income and from the poor rate, more than £88 being given in 1656, £76 in 1658 and £102 in 1660.[28]

Poor rates had been authorised to be collected in parishes from late Tudor times but few lists of assessments or disbursements are available for this area before the 1630s. At Cheshunt, however, there was an assessment in 1606 for Cheshunt Street Ward, those able to pay contributing up to 20d a quarter. By 1630 the assessment was collected every half year, the earl of Tullibardine paying as much as 10s, Mr Lazenby 6s 8d and widows and others no more than 6d. The total of £6 7s 4d was countersigned by the local JPs, Sir Thomas Dacres and Henry Atkins. Detailed accounts exist in the intervening decades for Aldenham in the west and Totteridge in the south of the county and these give an idea of what was possible within a parish where there were a number of wealthy landowners, financiers or merchants.[29] There is also evidence that other Elizabethan measures, such as the Statute of Artificers (which encouraged parishes to apprentice young people) were being implemented in some areas to find employment for the children of the poor. A large number of apprenticeship indentures for Cheshunt indicate that the churchwardens and overseers were regularly apprenticing children in the 1620s, one girl aged 9 being apprenticed to a victualler until she was 21, a 12-year-old boy to a basketmaker until he was 24 and others to a brewer, gardener, buttermaker and shoemaker. These children would have learnt a skill and a trade, but it is not clear what the 7-year-old Elizabeth Paston, who was born in and kept at the charge of the parish, would have learnt from being apprenticed to a labourer for seven years. The number of paupers apprenticed did, however, increase with the grain crisis of the 1630s.[30]

The grain crisis and poor relief in East Hertfordshire in the early 1630s

In 1629 and 1630 there were two consecutive poor harvests, that of the latter year being 50 per cent deficient across England. This had devastating effects on the poor, whose diet included large quantities of bread. Charles I, who was ruling without parliament, having dismissed it in 1629, resurrected the Jacobean device of the Book of Orders. These were instructions, issued to all local magistrates, on how to cope with bread shortages and mass poverty. They involved the local JPs, in their divisions of the shire, controlling local markets, trying to provide a variety of bread grains at an affordable price to the poor and raising poor rates to provide a local subsidy. They were then required to report back to the king's Privy Council, the main executive arm of government, in principle once a month, on a variety of issues associated with poverty and law and order. All seventeenth-century governments feared revolution from below, notably when hunger drove the poor to desperate measures. The Book of Orders was therefore just as much about controlling the poor as feeding them.[31]

The device laid down by Charles I and his ministers for achieving these aims was the monthly meeting of magistrates in their divisions. There are in the National Archives more than 100 reports of these monthly meetings from various parts of the county that were sent to the Privy Council; many of them are from East Hertfordshire.[32] The County and Borough

Quarter Sessions for Hertford and the local parish accounts also contain some details of how magistrates tried to carry out the orders of central government within their jurisdictions and how parishioners coped with the problems that arose. The magistrates succeeded in preventing the London corn chandlers from buying in markets less than 35 miles from London as a measure to protect the local poor. This meant that the chandlers were banned from the markets in Hertford and Ware but could buy grain in Royston. Nevertheless, in the period from September 1630 to April 1631, the price of wheat, normally about 3s 4d per bushel, trebled in price to 10s per bushel. In London it even rose as high as 12s 4d. This resulted in a major crisis in the county, as reflected in reports coming from different parishes and divisions in the first six months of 1631.[33]

In Ware the constables, overseers and churchwardens, the local parish officials with responsibility towards the poor, reported to the JPs for the hundred of Braughing, of which Ware was a part, that they had £30 of stock accumulated to set the poor on work (a parish stock was a stock of raw materials and tools with which the poor could manufacture goods to be sold to pay for their upkeep). They had managed to get three young people apprenticed but had nine more for whom they still had to find a master. They normally had £80 from the annually levied poor rate, but had collected more than that since the previous September. A total of £93 had been raised and bread corn was sold to the poor at 4s a bushel.[34] The local inhabitants had given a further £26 at Christmas, which had been distributed to the poor to buy essentials. As Ware was on the Old North Road, the main route between London and York, its inhabitants also had to keep watch for sturdy rogues and vagabonds coming through the parish, 13 of whom had been rounded up, punished and given passes to go elsewhere. The town was clearly well organised and had enough wealth to look after its own poor, but was not going to countenance providing for the vagrant poor from other parishes. Standon and Braughing, in contrast, distributed bread to the poor each Sunday.[35]

Most of these reports were responses to particular questions that were laid down in the Book of Orders. Magistrates had to show they were responding to the crisis not only by subsidising bread but also by punishing rogues (Figure 5.6). They were asked if there were unlicensed alehouses, of which Ware had three, and whether local charities were providing sums according to the details of bequests. The parish officials of Stortford claimed not only to have no unlicensed alehouses but also that they had a stock to

Figure 5.6 Whipping a vagabond. Woodcut, *c*.16th century.

set the poor on work to make cloth out of hemp and flax: 22 poor spinners had been set to work and 24 children apprenticed. In Sawbridgeworth, too, there were no unlicensed alehouses and, moreover, 10s had been raised from fines on drunkards. These sums were used to help the poor, as was a stock of corn which was sold to the poor at the old price of 3s 4d a bushel. Gabriel Whittacre and his wife and daughter were said 'to live idly and are hedge-breakers', but otherwise all the poor were set to work. For all these towns, keeping the local poor busy by making them work and providing them with cheap bread would prevent disorder breaking out. Keeping out the poor from other areas was equally important as the weather improved and men sought work elsewhere; the Braughing divisional JPs punished 16 such people in April, 30 in May and more than 50 in June.[36]

In May 1631 the JPs reported to the Privy Council on the grain supply in the area. They showed that a whole variety of bread grains was still available, including 552 quarters of wheat and 424 quarters of barley, as well as rye, meslin (mixed wheat and rye sown and harvested together) and oats. The JPs Thomas Leventhorpe of Sawbridgeworth and Sir John Watts of Mardocks, near Ware, had also accumulated 374 quarters of malt, made from barley, which was an essential ingredient of ale. In the following September the High Sheriff, John Boteler, reported to the Privy Council, among other things, that four rogues had been punished at Standon and 10s given weekly to the poor along with five dozen loaves of bread. He had received a certificate the month before from Sir Thomas Dacres of Cheshunt and Sir Richard Lucy of Broxbourne, JPs for the hundred of Hertford, which painted an optimistic picture in terms of falling grain prices and the availability of work at harvest time. They claimed that there were then no able-bodied poor, only the old and infirm. One reason was that 134 poor children, who would otherwise have been a burden on the rates, had been apprenticed, their new masters having to provide food and accommodation for them. Child labour was not seen to be a problem: the magistrates commented that, as for those who were not yet fit for service, 'order taken for the setting of them to such worke as they are able to undergoe according to their severall years towards their better maintenance & provision of living'. In another report this view was reiterated: those not old enough to be apprenticed 'we have caused to be set to spinning and such small work as is most meet for them, according to the tenderness of their age, that idleness may not fasten in them'.[37]

Cheshunt, too, took advantage of the scheme for pauper apprenticeship, which enabled the magistrates, churchwardens and overseers to get poor children off the parish rates either at a younger age, or for longer, or to different masters than would have been the case in a normal seven-year craft apprenticeship. Dacres and Lucy apprenticed 12-year-old William Cullens to Nathaniel Coles, tanner, for nine years, and Anthony Andrewe, a poor child aged 17, to a yeoman for six years 'by virtue of the Book of Orders'. He was thus becoming a farm labourer with virtually no pay, but would receive board and lodging for six years. However, he was provided with two suits of clothes, 'both decent and manly'. Whether these young people were exploited by the system is open to question, but it should be noted that Rachell Steward of Cheshunt, a poor child, was apprenticed for ten years in 'housewifery' to Anne Blacksedge, an illiterate widow of the parish. In March 1633 Robert Needham, a poor child, was apprenticed to Henry Cock, yeoman, for a total of 12 years and in March 1634 Elizabeth Nicholson was apprenticed to Widow Joan Robson for 13 years. Young men normally came of age at 21, but under the Book of Orders pauper apprentices could serve their masters until they were 24 if male or 21 if female, unless of course they ran away, which some did. Clearly some men and women would have benefited from the cheap labour provided by these paupers, and poor Elizabeth Nicholson may have been aged only 8 when apprenticed to become what was possibly just a household skivvy.[38]

Even small communities were expected to keep their youngsters out of trouble. A report for Brickendon in July 1631 noted that 'Penelope Ockamye, daughter of John Ockamye, a Moare [i.e. Moor], lyveth ydely at home with her father', but that four other children had been apprenticed, including William Hancock to Henry Browne, a Hertford tanner, and two girls, one to a husbandman, the other to a yeoman, presumably as farm servants. A return of the constables and overseers of Hertford Borough also reveals the destinations of the wandering poor who had been punished and sent on their way. Some went only to places in the home counties, such as Lewes in Sussex, Swallowfield in Berkshire and various places in Kent, while another was sent back to Warwickshire and two as far as Lancashire. Although 39 local youngsters were apprenticed to men in Hertford one found a master in Hoddesdon and another in Hatfield. Significantly, fines levied on local people for drunkenness and swearing foul oaths in public amounting to £5 3s were used for relieving the poor in Hertford, as was the money raised by selling the grass from the Meads.[39]

The borough authorities, as well as providing food for the poor, controlled the market and fined those who sold lightweight bread. Those who 'forestalled', or bought up the grain before it got to the market, were also controlled and punished in the court of the Market. They also levied a special rate in 1625 to help the sick when the plague struck the town, relieving them either in their homes or in the pesthouse. In 1636, when the plague struck again, they tightened up controls and appointed ten warders to ensure that no one with plague symptoms entered the town. The situation was so bad that in 1637 they levied a special rate for the building of two further pesthouses. More than £29 was spent on them and various sums were also spent providing bread and beer for those afflicted. They spent a further £22 to care for the poor who were sick either at home or in the pesthouse in 1636 and in 1637; All Saints parish alone spent over £15. It was also calculated that they had spent over £18 above the amount raised by the special rate, which might well have included the cost of some of a list of items bought for the sick, including butter, candles, currants, sugar, eggs and cheese. It was clearly realised that falling ill with the plague was not the fault of the poor and that the community had a responsibility to care for them while they were sick (between 70 and 100 per cent of plague victims were likely to die).

Apart from helping the sick, the borough also gave loads of wooden faggots to keep the resident poor warm in winter – the equivalent of a modern winter-fuel allowance. A list indicates how much was spent each year in the early 1630s: 28 loads at 8s a load in 1631, 33 loads in 1632 and as many as 70 loads in 1633, totalling nearly £19 out of borough funds. Individuals such as Thomas Gardener of the Inner Temple gave rental income to the poor at Christmas 1630, and the borough also lent money to poor freemen: 'upon securities to make them stockes for the mayntenance of their trades'. These included loans of £2 to a shoemaker and £3 each to a glover and a smith, which loans by 1635 totalled £21. This came out of the rent for the Chequer, which also helped apprentice youngsters to the tune of £22. The Borough also gave money to the parishes to 'set the poor on work' and subsequently audited them. Hertford, because it had jurisdictional privileges as a borough and had other sources of income, was better placed than some other towns and most of the surrounding villages, some of which had little or no stock and few wealthy families to support the poor.[40]

Magistrates worked not only in their divisions and parishes but also in quarter sessions to ensure that the system of poor relief worked across the county. One aspect that particularly concerned them was the claiming or asserting of a claim by individuals to be legally settled, as settlement gave rights to apply for (but not necessarily receive) poor relief.[41] In January 1630 they had to make a judgement about a certain Susan who had been ordered to be removed from Wethersfield in Suffolk to Stocking Pelham in Hertfordshire, where she had been supposedly legally settled with Edward Wasdell. This was found to be false, however, and her last place of legal settlement was her parish of birth, which was Sible Hedingham in Essex. The constables of Stocking Pelham then had the job of taking her back to Wethersfield, so that neither the county nor the parish would be responsible for her welfare. Even within the county the inhabitants of one parish did not want to support the poor of a neighbouring parish. On the same day that Susan was ordered to be removed to Suffolk it was reported that, although John Cannon had been taken up by the constable of Great Munden as a vagrant and punished and then sent with a pass to Aspenden, where he had been born, the inhabitants there had refused to provide him with any relief. However, the following April the JPs changed their mind and decided that he should return to Munden as it appeared that he did have a legal settlement there. The parishes continued to dispute this and in July the matter had to be referred to the Judges of Assize to decide.[42]

The county justices also had to implement the law with regard to those who broke the regulations on regrating and forestalling, which related to the buying and selling of corn on the open market, particularly where county boundaries were crossed ('regrating' was holding back large quantities of corn from the market until the price rose, then selling it at the higher price). Two men from Essex were said to have unlawfully bought wheat and barley at Stortford market, which corn was 'stayed'. They were bound over by Thomas Leventhorpe and when discharged their punishment was that 26 bushels of their wheat and 3 of barley were retained by the magistrates to be distributed to the poor.

Other matters that crossed county boundaries and were dealt with by magistrates included bastardy cases. Anne Crouch of Ware had a bastard child by Anthony Mugge, son of Robert Mugge of Tottenham in Middlesex. As Mugge senior was supposed to have caused his son to leave the area he was bound over to pay the overseers of the parish of Ware £4 'to discharge both Mugges'. In Much Hadham in 1634 the death of a couple who had been nursing the illegitimate child of a London mercer caused a thorny problem for the parish, which sought out the mercer in order that he might reclaim his child. He was difficult to find, but where the father was local, as with James Parrat, the reputed father of a Little Hadham child, he was ordered by the magistrates to pay the local overseers 2s every Saturday afternoon for 12 years for the child's maintenance. On appeal he was allowed to reduce this to 1s 6d a week but bound in the sum of £40, which he would forfeit if he refused payment.

To pay for all the additional expenditure during the early 1630s the poor rate in most parishes had to be increased. This sometimes involved a reassessment of the land and wealth of the inhabitants, as happened at Little Munden. On 26 February 1631 a new rate was agreed by which every inhabitant paid 8d for every score of acres he or she held. Thus Thomas Rowley, with 48 acres in the parish, paid a total of 2s 9d, but the following year, when the rate was raised to 10d per score of acres, he paid 3s 6d. Those with very little land paid no more than 2d. These reassessments were useful and relatively fair at the time, but later, as they were classed as 'common payments', they were used by Charles I as the basis for the notorious and much resisted 'Ship Money'. They also created problems where inhabitants disputed their assessments, as happened at Sawbridgeworth in 1630.[43]

Even as the grain crisis receded the JPs for the hundreds of Hertford and Braughing were, in March 1633, still reporting to the Privy Council on local conditions. Leventhorpe, Lucy, Dacres, Watts and Thomas Fanshawe of Ware Park reported that the market towns of Hertford, Hoddesdon, Ware and Stortford had plenty of corn of all sorts, their Provost Marshall had apprehended a total of 136 rogues and 49 children had been apprenticed. More positively, 'The weekly pencon to the impotent poor is dulie and carefully continued according to their several necessities.' However, they also commented, 'Those that are willing to labour are set on work, those that can, but will not, are sent by us to the House of Correction.' This house was 'amply furnished and duly imployed according to instructions', the governor receiving a quarterly salary from the county. Thus military-style officers were used for controlling the wandering poor and special institutions set up for punishing them.[44]

The people of Bengeo seem to have been more generous than others. In the churchwardens' accounts for 1632–3 it is recorded that they gave 6d to a soldier who was passing through and also 6d to an Irishman 'for his relief'. In 1633 they levied over £33 on the poor rate, using part of the sum to pay for clothing 'for a bastard childe', for a load of faggots for fuel, for rent for three widows' houses and for repairing the almshouse.[45] The churchwardens in Benington spent £18 in 1630 – the worst year in terms of harvest yield – and just over £9 in the following two years, but £30 in 1636, the year that plague hit Hertfordshire.[46]

Local children continued to be apprenticed throughout the period. The table of apprenticeship enrolments within the borough of Hertford indicates that children as young as 11 were apprenticed for up to 13 years, in the case of males until they were aged 24, to a variety of trades. This enabled the son of a labourer to become a weaver, the son of a poor butcher and an orphan to become tanners and two poor children, one aged 11, the other 13, to be apprenticed into gentlemen's households.

The authorities in Hertford borough were also concerned about their own children when 'nurse children', infant foundlings (see Chapters 9 and 10) sent out of London to the area, were found to be suffering from, or had died of, the plague in 1648. The nurse children who were still alive were subsequently sent back to London. Concern was not just for the children but for the future of the borough as, once their craft apprenticeship had

Figure 5.7 Brent Pelham stocks. HALS photographic collection.

been completed, the foundlings could become freemen of the borough, thus helping to ensure its future as a productive trading community.[47]

So the local communities in East Hertfordshire dealt reasonably effectively with the grain crisis of 1630–1 and, following the lead of central government, established monthly meetings of local magistrates who were prepared to spend time and money relieving the local impotent poor, finding work for the idle or unemployed and punishing and sending on their way those who were not from the area. The aged were looked after, but the young were put to work and the lazy or apparently idle punished (Figure 5.7). The pauper and illegitimate children probably suffered most, but immorality was punished alongside criminality. All of this followed in the spirit of the Elizabethan poor law, but it also reflected Charles I's obsession with keeping the poor in their place and in good order. Unfortunately for him his policies of the later 1630s undid much of the good of the earlier period and came to alienate so many in the shire that few sided with him in the civil war of the 1640s.

The impact of the civil wars

The civil wars that started in 1642 took many men away from the shire to serve in a variety of local, regional and national armies on behalf of Parliament, creating gaps in the administration of the poor laws. In July 1643 local JPs

Figure 5.8 Cromwell inflicts injuries on Royalists at the Battle of Worcester 1651. Engraving by James Caldwall for *Cromwelliana: A chronological detail of events in which Oliver Cromwell was engaged from the year 1642 to his death 1658*. Published by Machell Stace, Westinster, 1810.

were required to ensure that constables were sworn in for a large number of parishes, thus enabling them to control sturdy rogues and vagabonds. In the following April new high constables were sworn in for the hundreds of Hertford and Edwinstree and in July two JPs took the accounts of the High Constable of Braughing hundred. The local parochial government continued working at the start of the civil war and although few records survive we know, for example, that more than £26 was paid to the poor in Braughing. Some parishes, such as Little Munden, continued to elect two each of the four statutory officials throughout the 1640s and revised their rating system for poor relief based on landholders paying 20d for every score of acres they owned, which in May 1646 raised £18 17s 7d. Rates continued to be collected on this basis throughout the 1640s and 1650s and there is no real sign of disruption to the system. However, after the war the poor rates at Cheshunt 'shalbee henceforth by land rates with this caution that where there is not considerable lands to rate by for and towards the rates there for the poore, in such cases the rates for the reliefe of the poore shalbee made by mens' abilities'. This principle was also applied to Hertingfordbury in 1649 'for the best advantage of the poore there and not otherwise'.[48]

As men came to be impressed into the armed forces local parishes had to make arrangements to look after their dependents. Michael Crosse of Great Amwell was paid 20d a week to look after the child of William Heath, who had been impressed on behalf of the parish, and 9s for nursing it when unwell. Even in 1649 Joan Whitacres of Hertford, whose husband was killed at Edgehill in 1642, received the large sum of 12s 6d for her relief. As a result of war a number of maimed soldiers of local origin sought relief (Figure 5.8). The county treasurer for Hospitals and Maimed Soldiers, who had been appointed since Queen Elizabeth's time, continued to operate, Mr Minors of Hertford acting in that role in 1646. He had to provide money for the maintenance of William Trymor and James Webb, who had been injured in the First Civil War; the other treasurer, Mr Lamas of Ware, also paid for James Burgess, a maimed soldier from the same town who was then living in London. Alice Hale of Hertford, widow of William Hale of Datchworth, 'whoe lately dyed souldier at Alisbury Garryson in the service of the state', was given 2s 6d a week for herself and her five children and in 1648 the treasurer was paying other war widows. One maimed soldier was allowed to inhabit a cottage built on the lands of the manor of Essendon and John Gilderson of Amwell was given a pensioner's place and 40s back pay.[49]

Charity to the poor continued both in donations and in bequests, and schemes for employing the poor were further developed. When William Leman of Northaw, Treasurer of the Eastern Association, gave £100 in December 1645 to pay off the debts of the corporation, the £10 left over was given to the poor. In January 1646 the Mayor and burgesses met with Henry Chalkley 'about the setting of poore children to worke by spynnynge of jearsy' and the parishioners of both All Saints and St Andrews parishes were called together to meet them about it. The house of correction was maintained for the whipping of rogues and vagabonds and William Burgess was appointed both master of the house and Town Marshall in February 1655. In the following year two wardens were appointed to arrest all travellers and tipplers on the Sabbath and were clearly carrying out their duties, as can be seen by the fining in the next year of a man who was travelling on a Sunday.[50]

In order to prevent teenagers becoming a burden on the poor rates, the borough authorities in Hertford were assiduous during the 1640s in apprenticing orphans or the sons of widows or widowers to a master in the town. For example, in August 1644 William Green, one of the sons of the deceased Thomas Green, was apprenticed to John Taylor, a Hertford cordwainer, with the consent of Green's grandmother. The 11-year-old Robert Rogers, son of the deceased John Rogers, was apprenticed to William Tufnell, a basketmaker of All Saints, as was another 11-year-old, Robert Stoughton, to Henry Browne of All Saints, tanner. Thus the processes of pauper apprenticeship were still working even in the middle of the first civil war.[51]

Conclusion

The authorities in East Hertfordshire were, throughout the tumultuous period covered by this chapter, able to operate a system of poor relief conceived at the end of the previous century but developed only piecemeal over the first half of the seventeenth century. Established charities were supplemented by bequests in wills across the area and local magistrates and parochial officials raised poor rates where they were needed and coped with the extraordinary circumstances of dearth and civil war. The mechanisms of the monthly meetings of magistrates devised in the 1630s were revived again in the 1650s and some of the principles of the post-1660 poor laws, particularly those relating to settlement, can be seen to have developed over the previous 30 years. Widows were cared for, youngsters apprenticed and the idle put to work. However, concern over revolt from below may have been a more important motive in giving relief than actual compassion for the poor.

Notes

1.   For an overview, see W.K. Jordan, *Philanthropy in England, 1480–1660. A study of the changing pattern of English social aspirations* (New York, 1959).

2.   On post-mortem giving see S. Hindle, '"Good, godly and charitable uses": endowed charity and the relief of poverty in rural England, *c.*1550–1750', in A. Goldgar and R. Frost (eds), *Institutional culture in early modern society* (Leiden, 2004), pp. 164–88.

3.   On *inter vivos* charitable giving see I.W. Archer, 'The charity of early modern Londoners', *Transactions of the Royal Historical Society*, 12 (2002), pp. 240–73.

4.   On the early history of poor rates see S. Hindle, *On the parish? The micro-politics of poor relief in rural England c.1550–1750* (Oxford, 2004), pp. 229–56.

5.   On the 1630s crisis see P. Slack, *Poverty and policy in Tudor and Stuart England* (Harlow, 1988).

6.   The National Archives (hereafter TNA) SP16 series.

7.   Hertfordshire Archives and Local Studies, Hertford (hereafter HALS) QSB/2A/2B Quarter Sessions Rolls Series & Quarter Sessions Books.

8.   See also E. Gruber von Arni, *Justice to the maimed soldier: nursing, medical care and welfare for sick and wounded soldiers and their families during the English civil wars and interregnum, 1642–60* (Aldershot, 2001).

9.   On vagrants and vagabonds see T.J. Kelly, *Thorns on the Tudor rose: monks, rogues, vagabonds and sturdy beggars* (Jackson, WY, 1977), pp. 55–80; R. Houston, 'Vagrants and society in early modern England', *Cambridge Anthropology*, 6 (1980), pp. 18–32: A. Beier, *Masterless men: the vagrancy problem in England 1560–1640* (London, 1985), pp. 123–6; K. Crassons, *The claims of poverty: literature, culture and ideology in late medieval England* (New York, 2010).

10. On these issues see K.D.M. Snell, *Parish and belonging: community, identity and welfare in England and Wales 1700–1950* (Cambridge, 2006).

11. D. Perman, *600 years of charity: a brief history of the Ware Charity Trustees* (Ware, 1991), p. 5; W. Page (ed.), *The Victoria County History of the county of Hertford*, 4 volumes (London, 1902–14), Vol. III, pp. 380–97 (hereafter *VCH Herts*).

12. Perman, *600 years*, pp. 9–15; M. Ashby, *The Hellard Almshouses and other Stevenage charities 1482–2005* (Hertford, 2005), pp. xv, 1–25.

13. Perman, *600 years*, pp. 14–16; D. Perman, *A new history of Ware, its people and its buildings* (Ware, 2010), pp. 106–7; *VCH Herts*, III, pp. 380–97.

14. For the concentration of philanthropic resources in towns, see Hindle, 'Good, godly and charitable uses'.

15. The Chequer or Cheker had in 1621 contained at least eight shops rented by buyers of corn, including men from Enfield, Cheshunt and Waltham Cross. HALS Hertford Borough Records (hereafter HBR) Vol. 25 fo.1.

16. HALS DE/L/Q/5 The account of the Commissioners 1645.

17. HALS DE/L/Q/5 Will of Roger Daniels 1634; *VCH Herts*, III, pp. 332–47, 501–11.

18. For a recent survey of almshouse research see N. Goose, 'The English almshouse and the mixed economy of welfare: medieval to modern', *Local Historian*, 40 (2010), pp. 3–14.

19. *VCH Herts*, III, pp. 292–306.

20. *VCH Herts*, III, pp. 306–17, 366–73. On motivations for giving see L.M McGranahan, 'Charity and the bequest motive: evidence from seventeenth-century wills', *Journal of Political Economy*, 108 (2000), pp. 1270–91.

21. *VCH Herts*, III, pp. 73–7, 317–19, 347–66, 414–19, 462–8.

22. *VCH Herts*, III, pp. 129–35, 247–53, 319–23, 430–40.

23. Essex Record Office D/ABW wills series, Archdeaconry Records, Commissary of Bishop of London Wills also online on the SEAX Database (henceforth ERO D/ABW).

24. ERO D/ABW 45/1: Will of Bennet Beltoft; 45/67: Will of Henry Campe; 49/256: Will of Anthony Cramphorne; 49/330: Will of Thomas Haggard; 52/67: Will of Henry Wootton; 52/297: Will of Benedict Beawcock; 55/62: Will of Prudence Bird; 56/274: Will of William Bayford: 56/275: Will of John Lyndsell; 57/94: Will of William Sumpner; 57/148: Will of John Parnell; 151/42: Will of Thomas Byrche.

25. ERO D/ABW 43/54: Will of George Meade; 48/112: Will of Henry Shuttleworth; 48/130: Will of Anthony Wheeler; 48/258: Will of Oliver Harvey; 56/241: Will of John Miller; 57/164: Will of Leonard Knight; 60/88: Will of Henry Neates.

26. ERO D/ABW 49/1: Will of George Channcy; ABW 57/40: Will of Lucy Channcy, Widow.

27. ERO D/ABW 43/125: Will of Robert Wilson; ABW 60/170: Will of Elizabeth Duke. On servants and inheritance see J. Styles, *The dress of the people: everyday fashion in eighteenth-century England* (New Haven, CT, 2007).

28. HALS DP/21/5/2 fos 34, 43; DP/21/12/1; DP/23/8/1 fos 1, 5, 6, 8, 9, 10, 13, 14.

29. HALS DP/29/11/156; DP/3/12/1; DP/46B/5/1. On the Aldenham poor law see W. Newman Brown, 'The receipt of poor relief and family situation: Aldenham, Hertfordshire, 1630–90', in R.M. Smith (ed.), *Land, kinship and life-cycle* (Cambridge, 1984), pp. 405–22.

30. HALS DP/29/14/1 Apprenticeship Indentures for Cheshunt Bundle I, Nos 1–16.

31. W.G. Hoskins, 'Harvest fluctuations and English economic history 1620–1759', *Agricultural History Review*, XVI, Pt I (1968), pp. 17–18; B.W. Quintrell, 'Making of Charles I's Book of Orders', *English Historical Review*, XCV (1980), pp. 553–72; P. Slack, 'Books of Orders: the making of English social policy 1577–1631', *Transactions of the Royal Historical Society*, 30 (1980), pp. 2–4.

32. TNA SP16 State Papers Domestic for the reign of Charles I.

33. J. Larkin (ed.) *Stuart proclamations Vol. II, royal proclamations of King Charles I 1625–1646* (Oxford, 1983), pp. 271–3, 298, 300–1, 304, 312–14.

34. TNA SP16/182 fo. 40; 183 fo. 37; 185 fo. 27; PC 2/40 f 289 Registers of the Privy Council.

35. TNA SP16/189 fos 80, 98.

36. TNA SP16/197 fo. 69; 203 fo. 84; 211 fo. 3; 233 fo. 90.

37. TNA SP16/189 fos 79, 80.

38. HALS DP/29/14/1 Apprenticeship Indentures for Cheshunt: Bundle 1 Nos 17–26; Bundle 2 Nos 1–3.

39. HALS HBR Vol. 9 No 125 List of vagrants passed by the constables 1636; Vol. 25 fos 7–9.

40. HALS HBR Vol. 9 fos 102, 127, 189; Vol. 20 fos 136, 139v, 144r, 144v, 176, 178; Vol. 46 fo. 896, 909–10; Vol. 48 fos 29, 32, 34.

41. On this issue see S. King, 'Negotiating the law of poor relief in England 1800–1840', *History*, 96 (2011), pp. 410–35.

42. HALS QSB/2A.

43. HALS DP/71/5/2.

44. TNA SP16/233 fo. 90.

45. HALS DP/17/12/1.

46. HALS DP/18/5/1.

47. HALS HBR Vol. 20 fos 232, 264v; Vol. 26 Table of Apprenticeship enrolments fos 46, 47, 50, 164, 167, 168, 184, 187.

48. HALS QSB/2B fos 39d, 43d, 49d–51d, 93d; DP/23/8/1 fo. 20; DP/71/5/2 fos 6, 81–88.

49. HALS QSB/2B fos 55, 67, 75d, 90–91d, 93d, 105d. See also Gruber von Arni, *Justice to the maimed soldier*.

50. HALS HBR Vol. 20 fos 231d, 232, 339, 376d.

51. HALS HBR Vol. 26 fos 44–59.

CHAPTER SIX

Pensions and the care of
the elderly in Ashwell, 1670–1770

David Short

WELFARE HISTORIANS HAVE long debated the character and role of the Old Poor Law after it was initially codified between 1597 and 1601. Innes has argued persuasively that for most of the country the property taxes which underpinned parochial welfare came to be applied relatively quickly, and there is general agreement that tax-funded welfare rapidly came to outstrip that provided by endowed and informal charity.[1] At the other end of the Old Poor Law's life-cycle, historians have been quick to identify a 'crisis' period from the 1790s until the advent of the New Poor Law in 1834. During these decades, it has often been argued, the poor lost their legitimacy in the eyes of ratepayers as welfare bills spiralled and blame for the tenacity of the poverty problem came to be foisted squarely on the shoulders of paupers themselves.[2] Notwithstanding recent work by Keith Snell and Samantha Williams,[3] however, the period between the late seventeenth and late eighteenth centuries remains remarkably neglected, in terms of both national survey and detailed micro-studies of the operation of the relief system. Yet, as Richard Smith has persuasively pointed out in relation to Whitchurch in Oxfordshire, this was the period at which (at least in relation to its treatment of the elderly) one can argue that the Old Poor Law was at its most generous and humane.[4] It was certainly the period in which custom, paternalism and legal responsibility entwined in complex ways to create *de facto* rights for certain groups of the poor where the law itself gave no such rights.[5] This chapter will thus explore the key 1670–1770 period in the context of the Hertfordshire parish of Ashwell, providing an overview

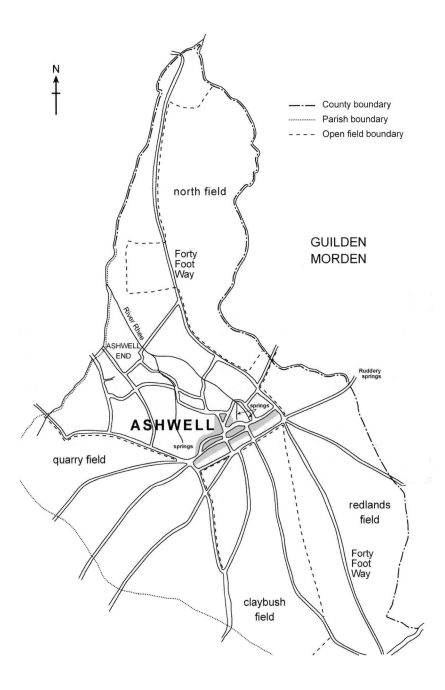

Figure 6.1 Ashwell before enclosure, showing field names. © David Short.

of the range, character and role of parochial provision which, when allied with other studies, can begin to locate the spatial and ideological nuances of the Old Poor Law.

Ashwell 1670 to 1770

In its heyday in the late Anglo-Saxon/medieval period Ashwell was a borough, a market town, serving a wide hinterland.[6] During the twelfth and thirteenth centuries new towns grew up in the area and must have taken some trade away from Ashwell,[7] which resulted in the settlement not growing as it might otherwise have done. The 1524/5 lay subsidies, a tax levied by government on those who were not clergy, show that Ashwell had 128 taxpayers. As it has been reckoned that there were about 4.75 people per taxpayer, the population of Ashwell would have been around 585 at this date, making it the largest town in the northern part of Hertfordshire after Hitchin.[8]

However, although the population of England as a whole rose by nearly 30 per cent between the mid-sixteenth century and the mid-seventeenth century, the population of Ashwell did not match that growth. The 1676 Compton Census lists Ashwell as having 471 communicants, which implies a total population of around 680.[9] The first national census in 1801 gives Ashwell a population of 715, suggesting a very slow growth trajectory.[10] The market that was so important in the economic life of the town probably still played an important role in the sixteenth century; there were more people living there than in other nearby towns and the wills and inventories that have survived from the period suggest an active commercial economy. By the end of the eighteenth century, however, Ashwell's market had declined to the extent that it is not mentioned in Owen's book of markets of 1792.[11] Yet there must have been some market activity at that stage, as a small market carried on until the early twentieth century.[12]

In the seventeenth and eighteenth centuries Ashwell was a traditional Midland open three-field parish (see Figure 6.1) most of whose population lived an area of the village including High Street, Swan Street (formerly Old Chipping), Mill Street, Hodwell and Silver Street (see Figure 6.2). There would have been a small but significant focus at West End, a smaller one at Townsend and another small one at Ashwell End/ Glytton, a mile to the west of the town. All of the farms, houses and yards, barring those at Ashwell End/Glytton, were in or at least close to the village, West End or Townsend. Although there were four open fields

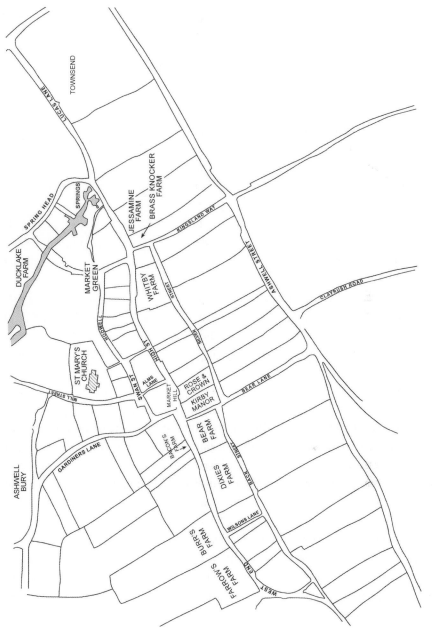

Figure 6.2 The settlement centre of Ashwell, showing road and farm names. © David Short.

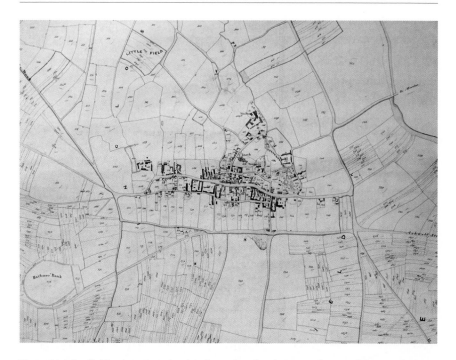

Figure 6.3 Ashwell tithe map, 1841, showing the nucleated settlement with parts of the open fields and ancient enclosures. HALS DSA4/6/2.

the land was farmed as if there were three, with some of the furlongs of Northfield farmed as if an integral part of Quarry Field and the rest as an integral part of Claybush/Middle Field.[13] There was a further area (see Figures 6.1 and 6.3) which had already been enclosed, possibly in the fourteenth century, most of which was to the north and west of the settlement.

Although the economy of Ashwell, like that of many small towns of the period, was based on agriculture, there were a significant number of occupations that show that it was a centre of significance in the area and therefore attracting people from some distance. The ubiquitous carpenter, blacksmith, shoemaker and shepherd stood alongside occupations often found in larger 'hub' centres, such as glazier, screw-maker, haggler, stay-maker, victualler and cordwainer, wheelwright, tailor, maltster, grocer, barber, hatter, fruiterer, weaver and stationer.[14] During the period Ashwell was also home to the Merchant Taylors' School, which catered for the education of boys, although it is unlikely that the number of scholars ever exceeded ten.[15] The community thus provides an excellent prism for the analysis of the operation of the Old Poor Law when at its height.

The Ashwell records

The first overseer's account book in Ashwell has either been lost or is in private hands. The surviving volumes date from 1676 to 1722,[16] 1722 to 1770, 1770 to 1810 and 1810 to 1830,[17] and are supported by settlement certificates, removal orders, apprenticeship indentures and bastardy records. In common with most other communities, the accounts are highly structured: weekly payments come first and are followed by casual payment, income, a reconciliation, a statement that the accounts have been proved by the vestry and the signatures of those who have approved them. At their earliest date the records are opaque. The initial item in the first account (23 April 1676) is for 15s but there is no mention of what the money was spent on. The second item, a week later, once again gives only the amount spent, in this case 17s. A second part of this account lists items bought or money spent in what must be disbursements, suggesting that the first set of figures represent pensions (regular payments to recipients, rather than an age-related payment) and, as the amount paid per week was irregular, that not all pensioners received the same amount.

The second part of the 1676/7 account gives a picture of what the overseers were spending the money on; a 'shurt for Thomas Turner 3s 4d' is followed by money spent on watching him and then burying him. No coffin is mentioned, but there is an amount for 'winging' (winding), which suggests he was bound in a shroud. Money was also spent on the almshouses, mending the town buckets and paying rent for the 'clunch pits' (clunch being hard chalk such as that used in the construction of St Mary's church in Ashwell and also probably used to mend the roads). In all there were only 23 items, which suggests that the poor of all ages were being given money and told to look after themselves. After finalising the account and showing the 'recepts', 'disbursements' and what was owing to the overseers, there is a section explaining that the interest on money lent to John Parsell was being paid in cloth and that lengths of this cloth were given to three widows and a man. It was also noted that £5 1s 4d was paid out for 'wooll given to the poore', and two other payments. This wool and the use of the clunch pits probably indicates a work regime for the poor in line with the original requirements of the legislation establishing the Old Poor Law.

While these accounting practices and the range of strategies for dealing with the poor which they embody will be unsurprising to historians of the Old Poor Law, the accounts themselves are remarkably detailed and provide the means to attempt a detailed reconstruction of the shape of welfare in Ashwell and the sorts of detailed case studies of individual paupers rarely seen in the secondary literature.

Disbursements

Disbursements were payments made by the overseers to individuals when 'in need'. For example, if the breadwinner was incapacitated and there was little or no income for a short period and the family did not need to be housed, one-off payments or a series of payments would be made until the recipient was back at work. These payments could cover a considerable variety of purposes: rent, as in 1696/7, when John Shipsea was paid 9s 3d for a quarter's rent for Widow Blott, and in 1772/3, when Widow Wilson's rent of £1 7s was paid at Hitchin; clothing, as in 1722/3, when 1s 6d was paid for 'a paire of shows for the Widow Sells boy', in 1736/7, when 3s was paid out for '2½ yards of stuff to make Ann Rayner junior a coat', and in 1754, when Ann Tickle received stockings costing 1s and a gown costing 8½d; medical supplies and attention, as in 1762/3, when 8d was paid for 'salve for John Swain', in 1725/6, when Dr Miles was paid £4 10s for 'curing Hawkins and family', in 1752/3, when Susan Horsley was paid for 'nursing Horsley family with smallpox', and in 1757/8, when Jeremiah Bailey was paid £3 3s 6d 'when his family had the small-pox several times'; household goods, as in 1695/6, when 12s 7d paid for 'a bed and bolster and a paire of sheets for Jane Thickens'; and paying the expenses for burying the dead.

A single case could occasion multiple payments, as in the case of an unnamed 'drowned man'[18] for whom the accounts record:

Paid the coroner his fee for the drowned man	13s 4d
Paid Mr Christy for going for him	5s 0d
Paid the watchman for him	1s 0d
Paid for his coffin	7s 6d
For digging his grave	1s 0d
Paid for beer for the men that carried him	2s 0d

Other sums were paid to people for services rendered, including nursing, work on the almshouses, assisting in burying people, 'cleaning Common

Brook', covering legal matters, providing clothes, travel expenses, paying the clerk (usually the schoolmaster at the Merchant Taylors' School) and fostering children.

The workhouse

After legislation in 1723 individual parishes or unions of parishes could, on a discretionary basis, provide relief to the poor or sub-contract ('farm') the work out to those who would feed, clothe and house the poor in return for a weekly rate from the parish.[19] The first indication that Ashwell had a workhouse is in the accounts of the overseer Thomas Hart, when in October 1727 Thomas Clark was paid 10d for 'setting up beds at the Workhouse'. Later that year Thomas Baldwin made the entry 'Due to Mr Carter upon note for goods and to the Workhouse £2 14s 0d', and further in the same account he recorded the following expenditure:

Balance of the Workhouse from the earnings etc. to Mar 7th 1727[20]

£8 1s 11d

Ditto to April 4th 1728   £4 9s 8d

The accounts of shopkeeper John Carter (from May 1728 to 30 September 1728) listed expenditure under the headings of 'Out of the House' and 'In the House'. The 'out of house' payments were to individuals, whereas money spent 'In the House' (from 4 May to 10 May he spent £4 5s 0½d and from 8 June to 4 July £8 9s 9¾d) bought mainly food but also items of clothing such as shifts, bodices, breeches and aprons. His fellow overseer, Thomas Cocke, did not set out his accounts under these headings but he did include 'earnings', presumably from the work undertaken in the house under the stipulation of the 1723 Act.

Within two years of opening a workhouse it appears that the people of Ashwell decided it was not needed and passed a motion to that effect at the vestry meeting. A note in the accounts, dated 7 April 1729, states: 'it was agreed upon by the majority thereof that the Workhouse be no more us'd for the use of the poor people of Ashwell and that no Overseers do supply the Poor there (as has been) any longer than the time of the new Overseers to come on upon their office'. In common with that reached in other places highlighted in the historiographical literature, this resolve was short-lived. Although no vestry minute is recorded, the accounts of 5 March–11 April 1730 record that half a year's rent, £4, was paid 'for the workhouse'. The

Figure 6.4 Workhouse Yard, Swan Street, Ashwell.

following accounts show £8 *per annum* being paid first to John Carter and then after, July 1730, to Mary Carter, his widow. In 1738 Mary was to become one of the overseers in her own right[21] and, as her accounts of 1738 show, during her time in office she was invoicing for 'shop goods' as well as food. Perhaps the Carters were protecting their interests, in that they not only leased the workhouse to the parish but also sold food for consumption and goods to be used in the workhouse. During her six months in office Mary paid herself £22 14s 9d out of a total of £58 5s 6½d, roughly 38 per cent, considerably more than she received in other years.

Ashwell never owned a workhouse, opting instead to rent property when needed. We are not sure where in Ashwell the Carters lived but it is more than likely that they owned the property on the north side of Swan Street, west of Mill Street (see Figure 6.4). In the 1841 tithe apportionment this block of buildings was referred to as 'Workhouse Yard', a name still in use today. The area on the corner of Swan Street and Mill Street in front of Ashwell Village Museum has been called Carter's Pond at least since the late eighteenth century.[22]

Over the years a lease was signed for Limekiln House, which must have been on Kingsland Way, previously called Limekiln Way. The accounts in

1749 note 'I hired the house of Mr Westrope for one year and entered on it the 18th November 1749 to pay 2 pound for the rent when due'. Today there is only one house in Kingsland Way (on the corner of Ashwell Street) that is old enough to be the workhouse, although it seems too small to have served that purpose.

In the overseers' accounts there is evidence of the work that occupants of the workhouse did. Thus, for the period 5 February–7 March 1728 a total of £2 8s 3¼d was listed as 'Earnings', with a further £2 9s 4d from the following four weeks. Later that year there is a reference to 'spinning that has not yet been accounted for at the vestry £1 5s 0d'. Other entries regarding earnings give the name of the buyer and the amount paid: there are a couple of references to Mr Carter paying for spinning and a couple for Brown's son's board and for 'bran and chaff'. There are also some entries which do not state what is being paid for; Mr Chapman of Westbury Farm paid 9s 4d, so it is possible that some paupers were working on his farm, which might also account for the bran and chaff.

From 1728 records of earnings were seldom listed, although the evidence does suggest some of the work to which people were being put. From the earliest accounts – that is, before the parish had a workhouse – rent of £1 was recorded for the clunch pits. These pits were probably those on the road to Hinxworth that are now a nature reserve. Once Ashwell had a workhouse it is possible that men were sent to these quarries to dig clunch for road repairs and to make the lime wash which covered most of the timber-framed houses, as well as making some available to farmers for soil improvement. In a number of accounts rent was also paid for gravel pits, the gravel from which, presumably, was also used on the roads.

We have already seen that Mr Carter was buying wool, probably to be spun by the women in the house. In other years, however, an amount of cloth and sewing material was bought but nothing sold, as in January 1748, when the overseers' accounts record the purchase of '2 ounces thead 3 yards of binding 5¾d; 1 ell and half Oxinbrid 2 ounces of thred 3½d; Hook and eye and half ounce thred 2d'. Such entries suggest, as John Styles has argued, that inmates made their own clothes.[23]

As in other communities, the governance of the workhouse was an important matter for the vestry. In 1737 Thomas Godfrey is named as the master, being paid his 'salary and disbursements'. In accounts for 1739 the master, John Allen, was paid the equivalent of 4s a week and on 3 September 1741, just before his last payment, he was referred to as 'Master

Alin'. In May 1747 the pensioners were listed and at the top of the list was 'Elliz Weeb 12 purson 13s 0d'. The detail of '12 purson' is an intriguing indicator that Elizabeth Webb was master of the workhouse, which housed 12 paupers.[24] This is confirmed in the 1750 account, where she was referred to as 'Eliz. Webb at the Workhouse'. She carried on in office until 9 April 1757, when Elizabeth Wilson took over for a fortnight before being replaced by her husband Matthew, who was still in office in 1770. The succession of female workhouse governors in Ashwell is highly unusual in the broader historiographical literature. In turn, there is little evidence that gender played a role in remuneration. Payments in the early years of the workhouse were a fixed amount of 2s 0d per week. When Elizabeth Webb took office, and thereafter, things changed and they received 1s per person plus 1s per week for themselves. As food was not mentioned in this part of the accounts it seems that the master paid for the food of the inmates from the salary, although repairs to the workhouse and clothing were still paid for by the overseers.

From 1729 to 1742 the Ashwell accounts give details of food and other items bought: in July 1736 we find 8d spent on 'calves pluck' and 5s 6d on 'beef 24 pounds at 2½d per lb'; in January 1738, '1 qr and ½ and 3 pound of cheese 13s 11d' and '5 pecks of malt 3s 9d'; and in the four weeks from 4 March to 2 April 1741 the following:

A fagot 2d flower 7d oyle 2½	0s 11½d
Money to buy bear	2d
½ a bushel grist ½ a bushel wheat	4s 4d
Wheat 1s 2d sugar 4d m[h]oney ½ pot ½ fagot 2	1s 9d
[...] Canes 1d fagot 2d chese 4½d pease 9d	1s 4½d
Peper ¾d salt ¾d sope 5d fagot 2d	8½d
M[H]oney ½d Eggs 1d bacon 8d Jeem [jam] 4½d	1s 2d
Starch ¾d flower 7d oatmeal 3d salt 3d	9¼d
Sugar 4d flower 7d fagot 2d m[h]ony ½d	1s 1½d
Vinigar 2d pins 1d	3d

While there is evidence from workhouse records elsewhere of food being sold and distributed out of the workhouse to the wider parochial poor, it seems likely that these accounts relate to food for the residents of the workhouse itself. In this sense, one might argue that institutional residence occasioned a better diet than that which the poor could afford outside.[25]

A wider sense of living conditions in the workhouse can be found in an undated inventory, probably taken around 1730. The document is badly damaged but nonetheless suggestive and worth recounting at length:

John Win[…]r's apartment.
One Feather Flock Bed Bedsted and Bedding, valencs & Cushions.
one Hatt and Box two Chairs one Trenchers Case. One Delph
Bowle & Cups & plates & other od Things. Two Chairs more. one
Brass pott, two Kettles & a skillett, an old Cupboard. Earthen […]
one pewter Dish. A Kneading [tr]ough, a Frying pan, a Warming
pan. wooden Trencher Dishes. One Barrell little tub

In the Wid[ow] Andrews apartment
One Flock Bed Bedsted & Bedding. three Wheels. A Boel. a pottage
pott. One Tub. A pair of pott hooks. One Stool & Chaire & other
od things.

In Tho[mas] Squire's Apartment
one Flock Bed, Bedsted & Bedding two pair of sheets Curtains &
valences, one Chest, eight Chairs. Two Tables. One Cupboard, a
pott hook Tonges. A looking glass a p[ai]r of Bellows, another little
bed, a Blanket & Bolster. A pair of Bellows, a kneading Trough a
Barrell a pottage pott & & Kit[…] Frying pan & other od Thing
In Passell Mason's Apartment
one Flock Bed a Bedsted one Blankett one coverlid a Bolster two
Hutts a Grid Iron, two Chairs one Candlestick one pewter dish.
Earthen Ware. One kittle a little Table. Hand Bowle a pudding
Maid a Frying pan & other od Things

In Tho[mas] Clarke's Apartment lately deceased.
one Feather Bed Flock Bolster pillow one sacking. Bedsted. Two
C[…]rds. & other od Things

In Tho[ma]s Horsley's Apartment
three Chairs a Joynt Stool & a B[…]e one Flock Bed. Bedsted and
Bedding a Bolster two Blanketts and a coverlet three Tables, one
Coffer. Seven Chairs two wheels and one [Beel]. One Frying pan[26]

From this inventory we note that the residents each had their own apartment, which would seem to have been of one room. This is in itself a useful corrective to perceptions of Old Poor Law workhouses, which have often portrayed them as communal, and often poor-quality, spaces. The variety of items in some of the apartments suggests that residents brought their own possessions into the house: it is unlikely that the parish would be paying for a Delft bowl. Whether such goods were 'marked' with the parish initials to indicate that their ownership had been forfeited and they were no longer the possessions of the inmate is unclear, but the sense that paupers entering the workhouse were not necessarily in dire straits is important.[27] Moreover, the presence of cooking utensils such as frying pans, brass pots, kettles and skillets would suggest that there was a fireplace and that the residents were doing their own cooking. Coal and faggots were provided by the parish.

Almshouses

The literature on almshouses has recently developed exponentially, but the records for Ashwell are particularly rich.[28] Whatever their form and whatever the rules that governed them, their function was essentially that of homes for the elderly who did not have the resources to look after themselves. In the early twentieth century George Moss set up a trust in Ashwell in memory of his mother and had eight almshouses built in Hodwell. Prior to 1834, the year of the introduction of the New Poor Law, the overseers' accounts and other documents tell us that the parish owned some almshouses; perhaps they were located in Alms Lane, in the centre of the village, a name going back to at least the late eighteenth century. The 1841 tithe apportionment lists three properties in Alms Lane, each described as 'cottages' and the owner being given as the 'Parish Authorities'. One of these cottages was occupied by three men, one by two men and one by a man and a widow. The tithe map (Figure 6.5) as well as the 1:2,500 Ordnance Survey maps of 1877 and later (Figure 6.6) show these properties. There is also a photograph which shows houses on this site (Figure 6.7). The almshouses were pulled down when a telephone exchange was built on the site, probably in the 1930s.

Details of these cottages can be found in the 1829 Rate Survey of Ashwell,[29] which listed Ashwell Parish as the proprietor of property number 126, but, unfortunately, omitted the names of the occupiers.

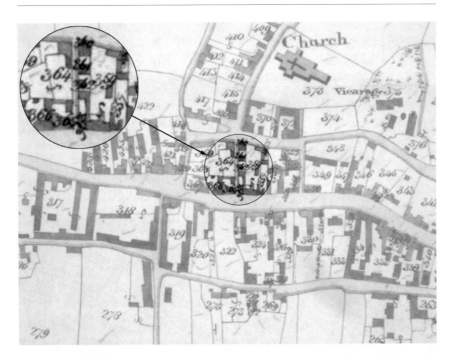

Figure 6.5 Detail of Ashwell tithe map, showing the almshouses numbered 360, 361 and 362. HALS DSA4/6/2.

The description gives details of a 'dwelling house' and ten cottages. The 'dwelling house', with stud and plastered walls and a tiled roof, contained three rooms and a pantry on the ground floor and four bedrooms upstairs, as well as a cellar, a 'coal place' and a 'Piece of Garden Ground in front'. Adjoining the 'dwelling house' was a block of four cottages with stud and plastered walls and thatched roofs, each with a sitting room and bedroom. Two also had pantries and three had 'a piece of Garden Ground'. Next was a second block of three cottages with stud and clayed walls and thatched roofs, one of which had two bedrooms and a pantry, the others having only one bedroom and no pantry. Each had a sitting room. A third block consisted of two cottages with stud and clayed walls and tiled roofs, each with a single bedroom and a sitting room. None of these cottages had 'a piece of Garden Ground'.

The overseers occasionally spent money repairing the almshouses. In 1769 no reason was given for spending 2s 10d, but a further 2d was spent on cleaning. Thatching cost £2 19s 11½d in 1768 and a further £1

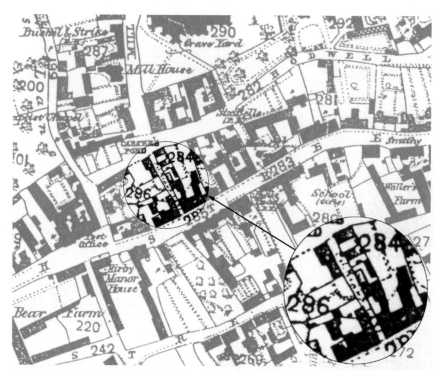

Figure 6.6 Detail of the 1877 1:2,500 Ordnance Survey map, showing the almshouses to the right of Alms Lane which runs from Carter's Pond to High Street.

7s 3d was spent on repairs the following year. On 10 November 1686 a bed for the 'Almes house that Elizabeth Wenham and Margaret Reed is in' was paid for and the entry clearly suggests that two people lived in each cottage, sharing a bed. Early in 1702 more than £1 was spent 'for laying a floore at the Twone [i.e. Town] House the Widow Rayner lives in' and later the same year 3s 2d was paid for '18 (s)plents and raills to the Twon House'. We cannot be sure which building is being referred to but it seems to have been one separate from the almshouses. The probability is that it refers to the building which now houses Ashwell Village Museum, which is across Alms Lane from the site of the almshouses. Tradition has it that the museum building was the Town House and was the place where the officials of the Lord of Ashwell manor, the abbot of Westminster, collected rents and so on. That is unlikely to have been the case, however, as the building was owned by St John's College, Cambridge, who were Lords of Kirby manor, another Ashwell manor. It was probably built as a shop in the

Figure 6.7 Detail of view from St Mary's church tower, showing the almshouses to the left of the photograph. P1439 ©Ashwell Museum.

early sixteenth century and since then has been used for various purposes, including a tailor's shop, a straw barn and, possibly, a school.

Pensions

The 1601 Poor Law Act did not stipulate that pensions were to be paid but in reality those who were too old or infirm to work were given an amount each week – in other words, a pension. In the 1670s the overseers listed only total expenditure on such allowances for the week or even in some cases for the whole six-month period. The amount of money paid out in total varied, ranging from 8s 3d to 17s 0d, and as it cannot always be divided by a whole number this suggests that pensions were being paid according to individual need, rather than at a set amount for everyone each week. It is not until 1733 that the word 'pension' is first used. John Dixon started his term of duty on 5 April of that year and his accounts show the amount spent weekly on pensions and also the total amount spent in 'disbursements'. The following year, 1734, pensioners' names were given for the first time – the heading 'For the 1st half year (weekly pensions)' was followed by a list of 22 entries including:

Paid to Ell: Saby for 24 weeks at 18d per week	£1 16s 0d
Paid to Jos: Bartlett 24 weeks at 2/- per week	£2 8s 0d
Paid to James Goodchild's children 24 weeks at 3/-	£3 12s 0d
John Brown senior 24 weeks at 18d	£1 16s 0d
Hunts boy 24 weeks at 15d	£1 10s 0d
Widow Bailey junior 24 weeks at 2/-	£2 8s 0d

Pensions were clearly tied to the needs of the pauper concerned but seem to have averaged about 8s per month for a standard case, somewhat about the norm for midland and northern England as traced by Steven King at a similar date.[30]

In 1742 the heading 'Weekly Pension' was used for the first time, suggesting a change in the way that pensions were both paid and conceived. The pensioners' names were again given, as were the number of weeks the pension was paid and the amount, which varied from 2s to 10s. Of the 13 pensioners listed, only three were men. By 1743/4 the accounting had become even more precise. Pensioners were again listed but this time after each name the number of weeks and the amount of the pension, varying from 6d to 2s 6d, were given. From that year it became normal to give the name of the pensioner and the weekly amount they received. It is interesting to compare the pensions paid in the seventeenth and eighteenth centuries with our contemporary situation. In 2012/3 the Agricultural Minimum Wage for a farm worker was £237.90 per week[31] and the basic state pension was £107.45. In other words, the basic state pension was 43 per cent of the basic wage for farm workers. By the 1760s many pensioners received 1s a week, although this varied according to circumstances. In 1795 'Day labourers employed the whole year by one master have 7 shillings and small beer, and 9 shillings and ale, for one month at hay time',[32] making the pension about 14 per cent of the weekly wage. Of course, some of the pensioners on 1s a week were living rent-free in the almshouses, whereas the farm workers usually paid rent. Nonetheless, Ashwell provides little support for Smith's idea[33] that the early to mid eighteenth-century poor law was relatively generous, even if the poor in this part of Hertfordshire were somewhat better off than their northern counterparts. This said, what perhaps mattered more than the amount of support was its regularity and place in the life-cycle of need, and it is to these and other themes that we move in the final part of the chapter.

John Swain

John Swain was baptised in Ashwell in 1702 and married Mary Clark, six years his junior, in St Mary's Church on 1 June 1729. The couple appear to have been childless, as there is no record of any children. The first mention of the Swains receiving money from the overseers was on 22 January 1746 when John, then 44, received 1s 2d as a casual disbursement. The year before, when Abraham Barber had collected his rate for the first half of 1745, John Swain was listed as having land to the value of £2 10s 0d and was assessed to pay 1s 3d. The following half year he was listed in Henry Mackaris's list of ratepayers, again for property valued at £2 10s 0d, but this time he did not have to pay anything, confirming the notion that he was suffering financially.

On 15 November 1746 John received a payment of 1s and a week later another 1s. The following week the payment was doubled to 2s and remained at this level until 1 January 1747, when it went back to 1s for four weeks, rising to 1s 6d for a week and then back to 1s. Indeed, there is no regular pattern to the amount he received or to the frequency. There was a period between August 1747 and December 1754 when he did not receive any payments. When he once again received money on 15 December 1754 he was 'in need'. He then received payments until his death in 1760, once again with no regular pattern. Between May and October 1760 he also received a shirt, costing 3s 6d, from the overseers. On 18 October 1760, now aged 58, the amount he received went up to 2s 3d and stayed constant, as if a pension, until 29 May 1761, when it was reduced to 2s. This was his last pension pay day. An entry on 20 May of that year was for 'removing Swain' at a cost of 1s 2d. The word 'removing' does not refer to 'removal' under the Settlement Act of 1662 as he was still in Ashwell on 20 May 1762, when 4s 4½d was spent on Mary's burial from the workhouse and three payments for salve for John were made in June, July and August 1762. The overseers paid 3s on John's funeral, which was also from the workhouse, in September that year, clearly signifying that the 'removal' in May 1761 had been from John and Mary's home to the workhouse.

The amounts paid for burials do not seem to cover all the costs, as the total paid for the funeral of Thomas German in August 1757 was 15s 0d and the cost of a coffin at this time was 7s 6d, being the amount paid for those of Thomas German, Elizabeth Andrews, Bailey, Widow Jennings, Widow

Hanscombe and Thomas Whittaker. This suggests that even though they were in the workhouse the Swains still had sufficient funds to pay some of the funeral costs.

Daniel and Anne Ingrey

Daniel Ingrey is an elusive character. There are no records of his baptism or burial but from documents in the parish chest we can get a glimpse of his life. The first reference to him in the parish records is on 13 February 1711, when he married Mary Everard, who had been baptised on 25 August 1689. This suggests that Daniel was born somewhere between 1680 and 1690. Their first child to be baptised, in Ashwell, was William in 1714. Thereafter a further six children were baptised, the last being Daniel in 1728. The gap of three years between marriage and the baptism of the first child is unusual and suggests that Mary miscarried a number of times, gave birth to stillborn children or that a child was born but baptised outside Ashwell. Mary died just 21 months after the baptism of Daniel, leaving Daniel senior with seven children to bring up. Daniel did not hold back and married Anne Everard, of Ashwell, five months later on 19 January 1731. As no baptisms were recorded in the registers it seems that they did not have any children. The marriage register suggests that Daniel was a tailor and the early entries relating to him in the overseers' accounts show that the parish used his professional services; in April 1742 he received 3s for 'making Barron cote and wascote' and in July he was given four yards of 'stuff' to make children's coats. The following January he was paid 1s for mending the coat of Richard Fairchild, who had just died. However, he was a man of many talents. On 10 May 1728 he was paid 2s 3d for '15 lbs 8 oz of veale', so it is possible that he, like many craftsmen of the time, kept some stock either on his own land or as a commoner. Early in 1742 he showed further talents when he was paid 5s 'for cureing her [Mary Winters] of the itch' and 6d for 'Bleeding How'. Twelve years later his medical services were once again called upon when he was paid 4s for 'for doctring her [Elizabeth Alder's] leg'. While many have suspected that parishes systematically turned to irregular practitioners in the eighteenth century, rarely do we have such direct evidence.

It is on 15 May 1744 that Daniel first received payment – 1s – from the overseers that was not for services rendered. Three days later, on 18 May, he received another 1s and two days after that a further 2s 3d. The accounts do not give a reason for him getting the money but, considering the way the accounts are laid out, the implication is that he was 'in need'. For the following six weeks he received 3s once a week except for one occasion, when it was 3s 9d and the account records that it was 'at times'. As these payments were listed under 'Other Disbursements' and not under 'Weekly Pensions' Daniel did not receive this money as a pensioner. Unwell into his fifties, Daniel was to receive irregular payments from the overseers for the next 20 years, all as disbursements, except for 17 weeks near the end of his life when he received a pension. However, it was while receiving the disbursements in March 1754 that he was paid 4s 0d for doctoring Elizabeth Alder's leg. All of this suggests that he was still working but, perhaps, just not capable of working the long hours that were necessary to earn a living.

In 1758 rent of £1 was paid, becoming an annual payment until December 1764. In 1758, 1759 and May 1760 he received payment as he was 'in need'. It was in the week following the May 1760 payment that, now in his seventies, he received a pension, but even then the payments were not continuous. In 1761 he skipped 22 weeks, but he received two payments of 1s 6d in July and then a lump sum of £1 2s 6d in November. These payments would have covered 17 weeks of pension at 1s 6d per week, so seem to have been backdated. After April 1763 he received neither a pension or disbursements, but on 14 January 1764 he was given a pension of 1s 6d a week. He carried on receiving this until 22 March 1766 and a week later, on 29 March, this was reduced to 9d. There were no further payments until 19 April, when he received a further 9d.

These last two payments are interesting as the parish had paid for his burial in December of the previous year. Strangely, there is no record of his burial in the Ashwell registers. To understand the last two payments we need to look at the entries for Widow Ingrey. On 5 April 1766 she received 9d as one of the 'weekly poor'. There was a further 9d on 12 April and then 1s on 26 April. The next week she received 1s, repeated weekly until 9 August 1766. It would seem from this that the entries for Daniel after his death refer to his widow.

Widow Gordge

Thomas Gordge died in March 1763. His first wife, Anne, had died in January 1758, when his four daughters, Mary, Elizabeth, Ann and Sarah were aged 4, 3, 14 months and 5 weeks respectively. One would have expected Thomas to remarry soon after Anne's death if for no other reason than to have someone to mother the children. However, it was four years later, on 29 January 1762, that he married Elizabeth Bester, who had been baptised in Guilden Morden on 8 July 1739 and was therefore 22. This second marriage lasted only 14 months as Thomas died on 18 March 1763, leaving Elizabeth with her four stepchildren, now aged 10, 9, 8 and 6.

Like Elizabeth, Thomas was not a native of Ashwell. A plumber and glazier by trade, he seems to have been one of the leading figures in Ashwell in the 1750s as in 1752, 1755 and 1756 he was one of the 'inhabitants' who signed off the previous year's accounts, 'seen examin'd and allow'd by us present', at the vestry meeting. His services as a glazier were of use to the overseers as he was paid 8s 9d in 1753 'for work done in the Workhouse' and further sums between 1s 0d and 12s 0½d between 1755 and 1761. His last bill of 7s 11d was paid to him in early 1762, a year before he died. No 'in need' payments were made to him by the overseers. From the land tax returns of 1753 to 1756 we gather that he owned some land which in 1753 was valued at £1 5s 0d. During the next 12 months he must have increased his acreage, as for the next three years the value of his holding was £3 10s 0d.

We do not know too much about Elizabeth, but it would seem that she was not capable of taking care of the children, as the four girls were apprenticed in housewifery, all to the age of 21, on 18 July 1763, just four months after the death of their father. However, it seems that the Ashwell overseers were trying to do their best for the girls. Mary, aged 10, and Sarah, aged 6, went to Henry Gordge, a labourer of Biggleswade, and William Gordge, a farmer of Wrestlingworth, respectively, suggesting that they went to relatives. Elizabeth, aged 9, went to John Handley, a carpenter of Wrestlingworth, and Ann, aged 8, went to Thomas Laurance, a farmer of Ashwell. A premium of £5 was paid by the overseers to each of the new masters for taking on the apprentice. This was normal practice as, when a child was apprenticed to a master, they became part of the family, living in their house and having all their necessities paid for.[34]

On 8 September 1764, a year after the apprenticeship of the children, Elizabeth, just 25, started receiving regular payments from the overseers – in other words a pension. Thomas Gordge did not leave a will and there is no inventory of his goods on his death so we have no idea how big his estate was. However, there was the property, which Elizabeth must have been able to live off for 13 months, after which she appears to have become destitute and had to rely on the parish. In the overseers' accounts it is usual to find two pensioners linked together and receiving a single payment, usually double that of a single person and suggesting that the two were living together in one of the almshouses. Initially Gordge was not linked with another widow and might therefore still have been living in her own home. On 30 November 1765 she was linked with someone else for the first time when she and 'German' were paid 1s 6d, and this suggests that she had moved into one of the almshouses. The week prior to this an Ann German received 6d, so presumably it was Ann German who lived with Elizabeth Gordge. These payments continued for five weeks, when the amount was raised to 1s 9d. For the rest of her life Elizabeth's name was linked with other widows – Hankin, Buck, Seamer, Gentle, Hunt and Betty Stavefly – but never with men. The amount that she and the widow she was linked to received varied from time to time but there is no indication as to why this might have been. She was buried on 29 June 1786, aged 46, having been a pensioner for 21 years.

Conclusion

In some senses Ashwell was, in poor law terms, a typical southern community. It had a relatively rich economy of makeshifts for those in different states of poverty and while not generous with its allowances nonetheless sought to do the best for everyone in the community. The parochial officials seem to have been flexible and to have tailored their allowances to the particular needs of individual paupers, including a range of disbursements in kind. The parish experimented with workhouses, but there seems to have been some reluctance to institutionalise people.

Yet there is also much that is new in the Ashwell material. The workhouse inventory suggests that the inmates of the workhouse did not lead harsh lives, having their own apartments and their own furniture around them. As people got older and were less likely to be able to support themselves there seems to have been a policy to help them live in their own homes for as long as possible, as we have seen with Daniel and Anne Ingrey. Where one person, such as Widow Gordge, was living on her own there were the almshouses where two people could live together. The provision of a pension was not dependent on age, as is particularly well demonstrated by the case of Elizabeth Gordge, who was 25 when she first received hers. For some, such as the Ingreys, it was a matter of receiving support when it was needed. Daniel seems to have been able to make some money some of the time, but when the income was low or non-existent they had to rely on the parish. Others, such as the Swains, received their pension and appear to have lived in their own home until they were unable to look after themselves. They then entered the workhouse, which in their case seems to have served the purpose of a nursing home rather than a place of work and correction.

Above all, the life stories reconstructed here point to two important conclusions: first, that the poor law was sensitive to the fluctuating needs of the poor, suggesting both an essential humanity and the monitoring of individual circumstances that allowed rapid and tailored action; and, second (and perhaps more importantly given the limitations of the secondary literature), that the poor themselves had a remarkably fluid engagement with parochial officials throughout the life-cycle. That Daniel Ingrey could move from being a supplier of services to the poor law to becoming a beneficiary of parochial rates suggests why such fluidity was needed and constructs the poor as an integral part of the communities from which they were drawn.

Notes

1. On the expanding role of the local state see J. Innes, *Inferior politics: social problems and social policies in eighteenth-century Britain* (Oxford, 2009) and S. Hindle, *On the parish? The micro-politics of poor relief in rural England c.1550–1750* (Oxford, 2004).

2. L. Hollen Lees, *The solidarities of strangers: the English poor laws and the people, 1700–1948* (Cambridge, 1998).

3. See K.D.M. Snell, *Parish and belonging: community, identity and welfare in England and Wales 1700–1950* (Cambridge, 2006) and S. Williams, *Poverty, gender and life-cycle under the English poor law 1760–1834* (Woodbridge, 2011).

4. See R.M. Smith, 'Ageing and well-being in early modern England: pension trends and gender preferences under the English Old Poor Law c. 1650–1800', in P. Johnson and P. Thane (eds) *Old age from antiquity to post-modernity* (London, 1998), pp. 64–95.

5. S. King, 'Negotiating the law of poor relief in England 1800–1840', *History*, 96 (2011), pp. 410–35.

6. D. Short, 'Ashwell, an example of Anglo-Saxon town planning', in T. Slater and N. Goose (eds), *A county of small towns* (Hatfield, 2008), pp. 159–72.

7. D. Short, *Snippets of Ashwell's history*, Vol. 1 (Ashwell, 1997), pp. 50–51.

8. N. Goose, 'Urban growth', in Slater and Goose, *A county of small towns*, pp. 96–126, and D. Short, *Snippets of Ashwell's history*, Vol. 2 (Ashwell, 2012), pp. xiv–xv.

9. Goose, 'Urban growth', p. 108, and Short, *Snippets of Ashwell's history*, Vol. 2, pp. xv–xvi.

10. British Parliamentary Papers 1801–2, *Census of Great Britain 1801*, VI (9), pp. 137–41.

11. W. Owen, *Owen's new book of fairs, published by the king's authority: being a complete and authentic account of all the fairs in England and Wales* (London, 1788).

12. For a full discussion of the population of Ashwell and the surrounding settlements 1086–2001 see Short, *Snippets of Ashwell's History*, Vol. 2, pp. vii–xx.

13. St John's College, Cambridge, D37 Terrier of Kirby Manor in Ashwell.

14. Hertfordshire Archives and Local Studies, Hertford (hereafter HALS) Mil 1, Ashwell

militia lists, 1756 to 1786. Also, those with denoted occupations in wills from the period 1670 to 1770, compiled by D. Short.

15.   D. Short, *The history of the Ashwell Merchant Taylors' School* (unpublished MS, n.d.).

16.   A few pages in the first surviving volume, 1676 to 1722, have been lost. Thereafter see Anon., *Accounts of the Ashwell Overseers of the Poor Vol. 2 Part 1 1722–1752* (Ashwell, 1983) and *Accounts of the Ashwell Overseers of the Poor Vol. 2 Part 2 1752–1769* (Ashwell, 1983).

17.   HALS DP/7/12/1–4.

18.   The man's name was not recorded but as Henry Bailey was the only burial in Ashwell around the date of the entries in the accounts, 17 August 1740, it is likely to have been him.

19.   The secondary literature on Old Poor Law workhouses remains remarkably slim. See, however, M. Fissell, *Patients, power and the poor in eighteenth-century Bristol* (Cambridge, 1991); T. Hitchcock, 'The English workhouse: a study in institutional poor relief in selected counties, 1696–1750', D.Phil. thesis (Oxford, 1985); T. Hitchcock, 'Paupers and preachers: the SPCK and the parochial workhouse movement', in L. Davison *et al.* (eds), *Stilling the grumbling hive* (Stroud, 1992), pp. 145–66.

20.   Under the Julian calendar, so 1728 in the modern calendar.

21.   On female overseers see Fissell, *Patients, power and the poor*, pp. 46–51.

22.   St John's College Cambridge, D37.

23.   J. Styles, *The dress of the people: everyday fashion in eighteenth-century England* (New Haven, CT, 2007).

24.   In 1776–7 a Parliamentary survey of poor-relief expenditure in England and Wales, published as the *Abstracts of the returns made by the overseers of the poor*, included an inventory of workhouse and the number of people each could house.

25.   J. Healey, 'Marginality and misfortune: poverty and social welfare in Lancashire c.1630–1760', D.Phil. thesis (Oxford, 2008).

26.   HALS DP/7/18/1.

27.   On pauper inventories more generally see P. King, 'Pauper inventories and the material lives of the poor in the eighteenth and early nineteenth centuries', in T. Hitchcock *et al.* (eds), *Chronicling poverty: the voices and strategies of the English poor, 1640–1840* (Basingstoke, 1997), pp. 155–91.

28.   For a survey see N. Goose, 'The English almshouse and the mixed economy of welfare: medieval to modern', *Local Historian*, 40 (2010), pp. 3–14.

29.   D. Short (ed.), *Survey of the farm homesteads, private dwelling-houses, shops, cottages, etc. at Ashwell, Hertfordshire made August 1829* (Ashwell, 2007), p. 30.

30.   See S. King, *Poverty and welfare in England 1700–1850: a regional perspective* (Manchester, 2000).

31.   See www.direct.gov.uk/en/employment/understandingyourworkstatus/agriculturalworkers/dg_179612.

32.   D. Walker, *A general view of the agriculture of the county of Hertford* (London, 1795), pp. 83–4.

33.   See Smith, 'Ageing and well-being in early modern England', pp. 64–95.

34.   K. Honeyman, *Child workers in England 1780–1820: parish apprentices and the making of the early industrial labour force* (Aldershot, 2007).

CHAPTER SEVEN

Looking after the poor: Cheshunt parish workhouse in the mid-eighteenth century

Sheila White

W HILE OUR KNOWLEDGE of how the eighteenth-century poor law operated has expanded considerably in the last two decades, significant gaps remain. Foremost among them is the issue of the character, administration and role of the Old Poor Law workhouse and associated issues to do with the experiences of institutional inmates and their attitudes towards workhouse 'care'. Problems over the very definition of the workhouse coalesce with poor record survival, so that relatively little is known, outside of interesting *ad hoc* examples and the large London workhouses, about these matters.[1] Even acknowledging that in 1803 only 12–15 per cent of the poor were relieved in provincial workhouses,[2] Richard Smith's observation that a poor grasp of who ended up in workhouses, why and for how long is a significant hindrance in attempts to understand the character and role of the Old Poor Law remains very pertinent.[3] Against this backdrop, the aim of the current chapter is to consider the circumstances of those entering Cheshunt Workhouse between 1753 and 1762 and the provisions made for their care. Evidence is derived from the workhouse committee minutes and admission book as well as other parish records of the period.

Cheshunt in the second half of the eighteenth century

Until the mid-nineteenth century Cheshunt was a sizeable parish encompassing the present town of Waltham Cross, the village of Goffs Oak

Figure 7.1 Waltham Cross, 1822. Drawn by E. Blore from a sketch by William Alexander, engraving by H. Le Keux. *Papers of Robert Clutterbuck 1773–1900*, vol. 3, p. 78, HALS DE/Cl/Z9/253.

and the district of Turnford.[4] Waltham Cross had long been established as
a post town (see Figure 7.1)[5] and the passage of traffic through the parish
to and from London was facilitated from 1725 by the establishment of a
turnpike trust to set up and repair the road from the 'Parish of Endfield
to the Great Bridge at Ware'.[6] Much of the population was concentrated
on the main road at Cheshunt Street (as Cheshunt High Street was then
known) and Waltham Cross. However, a settlement remained in the oldest
part of the parish around the church of St Mary the Virgin, near the manor
house of Andrews and Le Motte[7] and close to where the Roman road
(Ermine Street) had once run. More scattered housing lay west to Goffs
Oak, Flamstead End and Hammond Street.[8]

The population of Cheshunt recorded in the national census of 1801 was
3,173 – large compared to its rural neighbours, Wormley with a population
of 445 and Northaw with 440. It was, perhaps, more on a par with the parish
of Ware, whose population of 2,950 lived in an area just over half the size of
Cheshunt.[9] By the second half of the eighteenth century Cheshunt might
have been described as a small town or large village,[10] reliant on trade to and
from London. Positioned in the south of the county, close to the Essex and
Middlesex borders and on a main road out of London, the town found itself
under pressure in the mid-1750s because of the large number of vagrants
being passed from the City of London and parishes in Middlesex, Essex,
Suffolk and Norfolk.[11] This was exacerbated by the number of soldiers and
their families being moved in and out of the county.[12]

For administrative purposes the parish was divided into three wards,
each with its own overseer: Cheshunt Street, which included both the
commercial main road and the area east of the parish church; Waltham
Cross, which also included a large part of Theobalds Park; and Woodside,
which was largely rural and encompassed the free common, now part of
Goffs Oak. In terms of population these were certainly unequal in size
by 1821, when nearly half the population of the parish lived in Cheshunt
Street, under a third in Waltham Cross and just over a fifth in Woodside.
Trade and manufacture dominated Cheshunt Street, while the majority in
Woodside were employed in agriculture. Employment in Waltham Cross
was fairly evenly distributed between manufacture and trade, agriculture
and other employment.[13]

The disparity in the relative wealth of these wards had caused friction
among the overseers in the early eighteenth century. The overseer and
other inhabitants of Cheshunt Street ward complained that the poor there

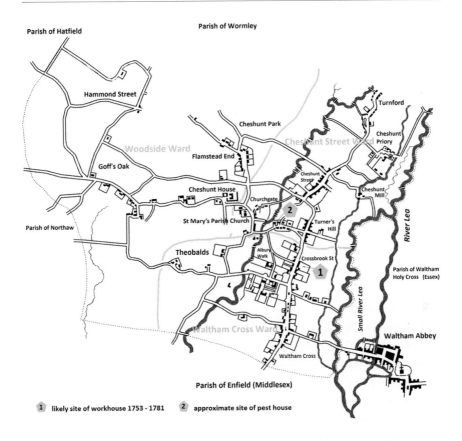

Figure 7.2 The parish of Cheshunt, *c.*1765, showing possible ward boundaries estimated from addresses given in militia lists and parish rate books. Based on a map from John Hill, *Hertfordshire militia lists: Cheshunt* (Ware, 1999).

were 'soe numerous and the charge of mainteyning and providing for them soe great and heavey' that the usual poor rates were insufficient without assistance from the other wards, where the poor were not so numerous.[14] Encroachment on the common fields had enabled the extension of the park at Theobalds by Lord Burleigh in 1561 and by James I in 1610 and 1620. There had been further acquisition of parts of the common fields by local estate owners, but the system of strip farming still prevailed, with common grazing rights on lammas fields,[15] the common at Goffs Oak and the marshes by the Lea. Until the Enclosure Act of 1799 was engrossed in 1804 many of the poorer parishioners had been able to eke out a living from the land.[16] Cheshunt (see Figure 7.2) could claim no large industry such as the maltings at Hertford and Ware, and so opportunities for unskilled labour would have been restricted to the service of wealthy landowners, farmers and gentlemen of the parish and employment with the local tradespeople – the shopkeepers, innkeepers and craftsmen.

The parish workhouse

The parish of Cheshunt maintained a workhouse from 1722 until 1837, leasing at least two different premises in Waltham Cross: one on the east side of Crossbrook Street between 1753 and 1781, the other on the west side of the High Street between 1781 and 1821. Reference is also made to an earlier premises in Marsh Lane.[17] In 1821 a decision was made to erect a purpose-built house in the west of the parish at Flamstead End.[18] In 1837 Cheshunt Parish became part of the new Edmonton Poor Law Union; the redundant building was demolished and the site, fabric, fixtures and fittings sold at auction.[19] A lease taken in 1753 on premises in Waltham Cross coincided with the appointment of a new master and mistress and the tightening up of the rules relating to the provision of outdoor relief. A committee of gentlemen chosen to oversee the running of the new house was to meet weekly on site. They were to approve admissions and discharges and sanction the expenditure required both to maintain the fabric of the building and to provide the poor with nourishment, clothing and work. Under the new regime the master was to keep a record of all those entering and leaving the house. The sole surviving example of the resultant admittance books begins with the very first admissions into the new premises on 17 December 1753 and covers admissions and discharges up to 24 July 1762.[20] This source, and the minutes kept by the workhouse committee during this period,[21] are the bedrock of this chapter. Along with additional information from vestry minutes and overseers' accounts, this nine-year continuous record provides an insight into the operation of a Hertfordshire parish workhouse in the mid-eighteenth century and a glimpse of the lives of many of those who passed through its doors.

It is known that a workhouse was being maintained by the parish in 1749 under the terms of Knatchbull's act, but this appears to have been wound up in the summer of that year. Beds, bedding and other materials were handed over and an agreement made with Samuel Tull of Edmonton to maintain and support the poor of the parish for the following three years. This arrangement, known as 'farming the poor', covered everything from clothing and housing the poor to paying the constables and the beadle. As was the case in most other communities, it did not last long; by May the following year Mr Tull's services were dispensed with and the overseers instructed to 'provide for the poor in there [*sic*] own wards in the cheapest and best manner they can till farther orders of the Vestry'. However, the premises re-equipped in 1753 on Crossbrook Street were also referred to as 'the late workhouse', so may have been those used for the purpose in the interim.

The 1722/23 'Workhouse Test Act' had envisaged institutions in which the poor were to be lodged, kept and maintained and to work for their keep.[22] In parishes where this discretionary legislation was adopted those who sought relief from the parish but refused to be lodged in such a workhouse were to be 'taken off the books' and denied any payment. The workhouse was to 'answer all the ends of charity to the poor, in regard to their souls and bodies; and yet at the same time prove effectual expedients for increasing our manufactures, as well as removing a heavy burden from the nation'.[23] The reality in Cheshunt, as in many other parishes,[24] was that most of those who entered the 'house' were incapable through circumstance, age or infirmity of earning their own living.

The new workhouse

When the newly equipped parish workhouse opened its doors on 17 December 1753 eight women, one man and one child were admitted as its first inmates. Five of the adults were aged 60 or over, one of the younger women was pregnant and soon delivered a son and the other two young women became permanent residents, perhaps because of sickness or incapacity. Their numbers quickly rose to 30 with the admission on Christmas Eve of ten children (under 18) and five elderly people (60 and over). On 31 December a further five people were admitted, including a child and another pregnant woman whose newborn child soon died. The first young mother and her baby were to leave in February 1754, but many of the others stayed on, some until their eventual deaths.

All pensions – that is, regular payments of relief to paupers of any age, and including those paid to people occupying the parish almshouses – were to stop from December 1753. For those unable to support themselves other than in the short term there was now little option but to enter the workhouse. Furthermore, no travellers or 'casual' poor (often referred to as 'casualties') were to be admitted by the master without permission from one of the parish officers. When a list of paupers being relieved by the parish was entered into the vestry minutes in April 1755 the number of inmates had risen to 48: 9 men aged between 58 and 87, 21 women aged 26 to 83, 13 boys and 5 girls.[25] By May 1756 there were 58 inmates and the number averaged 53 over the years to 1761, with men, women, boys and girls in much the same proportions throughout.[26]

None of the surviving documents tells us how many rooms were in the house that was used from 1753 and so it not possible to estimate how many people shared sleeping accommodation or communal facilities and whether families were split up. Separate accommodation was certainly provided for the sick and those deemed to be mad. An infirmary was one of the rooms fumigated with wormwood and the 'mad' room had a new partition, two new bedsteads and ladders made in February 1754; at the same time a lock was fitted to the door. However, other than being in a separate and presumably locked room, no details are given of how lunatics were treated once they entered the workhouse. Reference is also made in the minutes to the committee room, the master's room, a woolcombers' room, store room, lodging rooms, a brew house and a cellar, all suggesting a fairly substantial property. A watchtower and stocks had to be moved when the poor were housed in different premises in 1782.[27]

How those who were to make their home in the new workhouse viewed the prospect of entering an institution of over 30 inmates can only be guessed at. However, the new furniture and household goods with which the workhouse had been equipped may have provided a level of personal comfort superior to that which they had previously enjoyed. Beds, bolsters, tables and chairs, leather chairs, bed and table linen, towels, washing bowls, pots, pans, cutlery, small-beer horns and utensils were all bought in. The minutes record an initial order for 20 beds, but more were subsequently required. Some of these were described as flock beds, and one order was for two bedsteads for straw beds. Perhaps these were intended for the 'mad room' or for the travellers and casual poor. It is unclear if all this equipment was brand new, but expenditure on the new workhouse had made it necessary for the vestry to take out a loan of £300 'to furnish the workhouse and provide several other things in order to make it fitt for the reception of the poor'.[28] This was not a cheap undertaking and perhaps explains the longevity of workhouse use in the parish compared to elsewhere.

A plan of the Manor of Cheshunt, drawn up by Edward Richardson between 1782 and 1785, shows a building on the west side of Waltham Cross High Street (part of the main road) described as 'The Workhouse,

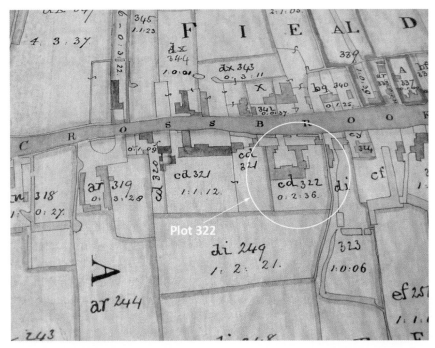

Figure 7.3 Detail from Edward Richardson's 'Plan of the Liberty, Manors and Parish of Cheshunt', showing plot 322, held by Francis Morland and likely to be the site of the 1753 workhouse. HALS DE/Cr/125/2 and DE/Cr/109/1.

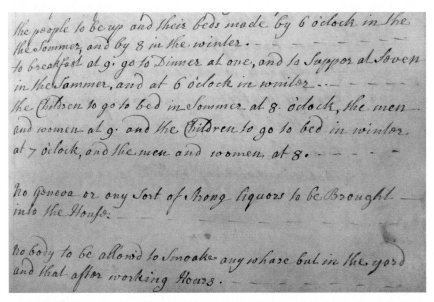

Figure 7.4 Rules of the house. Cheshunt poorhouse committee minutes and orders 1753–99, HALS DP/29/18/28.

Gardens etc'. Further north, on the east side of the main road (Crossbrook Street), is a plot described as 'House Garden C[our]tyard late the Workhouse' (see Figure 7.3).[29] As no new premises appear to have been taken until late 1781 it seems most likely that the latter is the site of the 1753 workhouse. Richardson's plan shows a sizeable property built on three sides of a courtyard on a plot measuring 2 rods 36 perches (just under three-quarters of an acre). A small outbuilding shown on the plan may have been the brew house or perhaps the 'necessary house', the emptying of which caused considerable offence to a Mr Satchwell in November 1760 when this was carried out during the daytime. From then on this task was to be performed only 'at a convenient hour on a moonlight night'!

There is evidence that the fabric of the buildings was kept in good repair and order: chimneys were swept, locks were fitted where pilfering might have been a problem, a pump was mended and another purchased for draining the cellar, windows were glazed and mended, holes were pointed, tiling was repaired over the 'necessary house' and the ditch was scoured.

House rules (see Figure 7.4) were essential to the running of such an institution. The people were to be up and their beds made by 6 a.m. in summer, 8 a.m. in winter. They were to go to breakfast at 9 a.m., dinner at 1 p.m. and supper at 7 p.m. or 6 p.m. in winter. All were to be in bed by 9 p.m. in summer or 8 p.m. in winter, with the children going an hour earlier. No Geneva (gin) or any strong liquor was to be brought into the house and smoking was permitted only outside in the yard and after working hours. The master and mistress had the authority to allow some of the inmates to go out of the house, but any who returned after the agreed time, or in a drunken state, would lose the privilege and be reported to the committee. They were also to be searched for strong liquor on their return. Visitors would be allowed only at the discretion of the master or mistress. Robert Timms, an 80-year-old resident, was to ring the bell at meal times and was also put in charge of the opening and closing of the gate, over which were to be painted the words 'Cheshunt Workhouse'.

Treating the poor

The 'Method for Dieting' (see Figure 7.5) appears unimaginative by modern standards, but three meals a day were provided which included meat three times a week. There was also the inevitable 'broth' made with 'Leggs and shins', pea soup and both baked and boiled puddings – presumably savoury, as they formed the main meal on two of the days. Tools and equipment

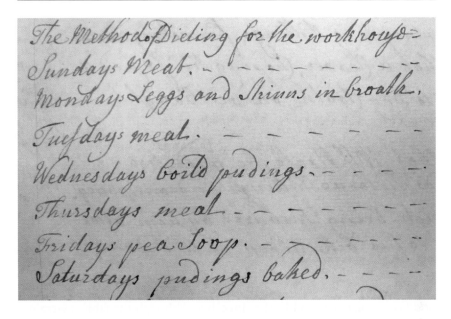

The Method of Dieting for the workhouse –
Sundays Meat. –
Mondays Leggs and Shinns in broath,
Tuesdays meat. –
Wednesdays boild pudings. –
Thursdays meat. –
Fridays pea Soop. –
Saturdays pudings baked. –

Figure 7.5 Method for dieting. Cheshunt poorhouse committee minutes and orders 1753–99, HALS DP/29/18/28.

were purchased for the garden, as were bean, pea and cabbage plants, so it would seem that a ready supply of fresh vegetables was available too. Peas for pease porridge, milk, flour and considerable quantities of cheese were also bought in along with the usual oatmeal, the basis for the staple workhouse gruel. Pigs were kept and the killing of one of them in April 1755 – no doubt quite an event for the inmates – was noted in the minutes. The committee was keen to see that the meat and provisions supplied to the workhouse were of an acceptable standard and weight and they met on Saturday mornings to inspect and weigh them personally. No doubt they wished to ensure value for money, but they heeded complaints that one lot of cheese was very bad and demanded that the next consignment be of better quality. To supplement this diet, each man and woman was to be allowed a daily quart of (small) beer, each child a pint; the roof of the brew house had been made good and brewing utensils purchased, and a brewing took place in early May of 1754, when malt and hops were purchased and a man hired to do the laborious part of the work.

Nearly fifty years later, when the Cheshunt overseers and churchwardens met to discuss the question of the nourishment of the parish poor, they expressed their belief that those applying for relief lived 'principally on bread, peas and potatoes'.[30] The workhouse fare of the 1750s seems varied and nutritious by this standard, and the opportunity to eat meat three times a week may have appeared a luxury to those scraping a living on the outside. Settlement examinations of the period show that male servants could expect to earn anything between £5 and £10 per annum and female servants between £2 and £4. The cost of meat agreed in September 1759 was 1s 8d per stone for ox beef and 8d per stone for legs and shins (cheap cuts).

In addition to the apparently well-equipped premises and a staple, if dull, diet, a degree of personal comfort was also afforded to the inmates. An instruction was given in December 1753 that six women from each ward should go into the workhouse and those wanting clothes should be sent to Pilleys in Church Lane to be measured. Fabric such as linsey for gowns, cloth for shirts and shifts and flannel for petticoats was ordered, as were ready-made caps, hose, bodices and stomachers and, for the men and boys, waistcoats and leather breeches. Although the fabrics were not luxurious, the clothes would be new and clean. Much of the business of the workhouse committee concerned the purchase of ready-made clothes or the fabric for making them, the purchase and repair of shoes and the allocation of clothing and shoes to inmates and to those receiving casual or outdoor relief.

The overall impression is that those on the inside were pretty well provided for, and this is particularly so in the case of the children, who inevitably grew out of their clothes and shoes.[31] Thus, Mary Allen, a 33-year-old woman arriving with three children in January 1756 and eventually leaving in June 1759, received during that time three pairs of shoes and nine items of clothing: three shifts; two caps; an apron; a gown; a coat and a handkerchief. Over the course of 18 months James Hall, a 13-year-old, received four pairs of stockings, three shirts, a pair of breeches and a pair of shoes with more clothing to send him off on his apprenticeship. Amy Halsey, who was admitted in February 1761 at the age of 1 and remained until her death in July 1769, was given six caps, five shifts, four aprons, two gowns, two pairs of stockings, a hat, a petticoat, stays and four pairs of shoes. The bill for making five pairs of shoes in 1754 amounted to 15s 5d: 3s 1d a pair. An idea of the affordability of new shoes is given by considering the workhouse master Richard Neale's annual salary of £30, including a gratuity – approximately 11s 6½d a week. By contrast, the weekly wage for a male yearly servant worked out at between roughly 2s and 4s a week. Many were naturally issued with clothing soon after arrival, and in December 1754 it was documented that inmates were not to go out of the house in any but the parish clothing. In some cases people appear to have arrived with clothes in such a poor or infested state that they needed to be 'entirely new cloath'd'. From November 1754 those relieved by the parish were also to wear badges.[32]

Among the earliest measures taken to underpin workhouse life were those related to hygiene. The shaving of 22 poor people's heads by John Stubbs, for which he was paid 5s, was no doubt to prevent or deal with head lice. It was also ordered that wormwood should be planted in the garden; this was to be used for fumigation, in the washing of linen and in the beds and sheets. Clearly the treatment of common parasites such as lice was not merely for the comfort of inmates; it made sense to run a clean and hygienic house and to prevent infestations which could easily spread. The committee ordered 'washhand Bowls or basons' as well, although no instructions about personal hygiene were issued. Soap was bought in on a monthly basis by the half firkin (about 14.5 kg) – most probably for the washing of clothes and linen – and washing troves and a clothes horse were purchased and clothes lines erected. One particular unhygienic habit was halted within a few weeks of the opening when the committee ordered that 'a Lattice in Each Lodging Room be put before the windows to prevent the potts being thrown out or Emptied There'. There are no descriptions of any routines for cleaning the house, but a scrubbing brush and a number of mops were purchased and a scraper acquired to be placed at the door of the committee room, no doubt to prevent the gentlemen bringing in mud.

A degree of preventative medicine was established from the outset. The apothecary, Mr (or Dr) Clark, was asked to attend a committee meeting in February 1754 to answer the complaint that he had neglected his duty, having promised to attend the workhouse every day 'to examine whether any were Sick and give them Immediate Assistance'. The following February he was given a final warning, but he continued to be paid a yearly salary of 20 guineas. There is no evidence of what 'assistance' he gave, but the use of this word suggests that the parish officers were concerned to help any sick inmates as well as merely deal with their illnesses. Besides, having access to a doctor or apothecary on a daily basis would have been more than ordinary folk could afford.

Clearly some medical problems were beyond the doctor's remit and the overseers displayed an enlightened attitude by funding treatment for a number of inmates at London hospitals. Perhaps Cheshunt's proximity to London and its situation on the turnpike road played a part in this. The case of 8-year-old Richard Underwood is possibly the most extreme. In July 1754 the workhouse committee asked Mr Hinde, one its members, to inform the 'Phisitions & Surgeons of Guys Hospital that they are at Liberty to act as they see Abslutely Nesscessary as to the Cutting off Richard Underwoods Leg or Omitting itt'. The cost of treatment and care in the hospital must have been considerable, as the beadle had been paid in February 1754 for taking the child up to London and a final payment was not made to the hospital until May 1755. This payment of 2s 6d, plus one guinea previously paid to Guy's, related to 'the washing etc of the said child who is now home cured'. We never learn whether the child lost his leg, but his recovery was sufficient for him to be apprenticed to a leather breeches maker in April 1762.

Although a few people were admitted to the house on the grounds of ill-health, the officers were careful not to take in those whose conditions were infectious. In addition to the 48 people maintained in the workhouse in April 1755, the vestry minutes also record relief paid to three men and four women described as 'Pentioners having Disorders upon them that they cannot be admitted in the workhouse' as well as three members of one family with smallpox who were being cared for in the parish pesthouse. A Widow Hall might have been admitted in July 1755 when she 'put her arm out', but could not be taken in as she 'had the itch upon her', and was cared for outside.

The philosophy of the workhouse

In considering the provisions made by parish authorities under the Old Poor Law, it is important to understand the political and economic climate of the day and to acknowledge the pressures under which the parish overseers operated. Today the rules for the payment of benefits are governed by state legislation and made both through means testing and by applying a strict set of rules about eligibility. Even so, the questions of eligibility and amount of benefit payable are the subject of much discussion and revision. The level of provision, while offering a reasonable level of benefit, must be balanced against the willingness of the taxpayer to pay. Such hard and fast rules and regulations were not available to the eighteenth-century overseers of the poor; they had in the main to 'work by custom, precedent and unwritten rule of thumb'.[33] Fundamental to the 1722 Act was the assertion that increases in parish rates had been due mainly to those obtaining relief by 'false and frivolous pretences'[34] and the 'workhouse test' embodied in the Act sought to remedy this. However, under the old system of poor relief, even in a parish the size of Cheshunt, ratepayers and paupers would be known to one another; as Oxley argues, it would be as difficult for parishioners to feign poverty as it would for parish officers to act in an inhumane way.[35] Still, it was the ratepayers who financed the upkeep of the poor and it was the responsibility of the overseers to ensure that their money was spent wisely and that the poor rate was maintained at an acceptable level. In the years leading up to the opening of the 1753 workhouse the rate had fluctuated between 10d and 1s 4d in the pound, but once the workhouse was established it remained stable at 1s, occasionally dropping to 10d.

What can be learnt from the records kept by the parish authorities about those entering Cheshunt workhouse between 1753 and 1764 and the kind of care they might have expected during their stay? Oxley asserts that although records of poor-law administration have come down to us in great quantities they tell us remarkably little about the poor themselves and the circumstances which brought them into dependence on poor relief. Among the formal records of expenditure and provision of relief by the Cheshunt Workhouse Committee are snippets of information about some of those who entered its doors.[36] Viewed alongside the admittance book these records enable us to make an analysis of the ages of the inmates, of the extent to which age was linked to circumstances and outcomes, and above all of whether the care given was appropriate to the needs and circumstances of those who received it.

In terms of age, those who came into the workhouse could be considered to fall into three fairly broad categories – those of working age, those too young to work and those too old. However, no strict age limit seems to have been applied when 'binding children apprentice' and it is known from the census returns of the mid-nineteenth century that many people continued to work into old age while they were still able. Clearly, recorded ages cannot be considered completely accurate, but it can be assumed that they at least represent either the age the inmates believed themselves and their children to be or the age estimated by the master.[37] For the purpose of this analysis, I have made an estimate of the age of inmates who entered the workhouse on more than one occasion but whose age was not stated each time. Some individuals were admitted on several occasions and each stay is treated as a separate instance for the purpose of analysis. The admittance book records

Table 7.1   Table of inmates 1755–61.

	Men	%	Women	%	Boys	%	Girls	%	Total
April 1755	9	18.75%	21	43.75%	13	27.08%	5	10.42%	48
May 1756	10	17.24%	25	43.10%	15	25.86%	8	13.79%	58
May 1757	9	17.31%	23	44.23%	12	23.08%	8	15.38%	52
June 1758	10	18.18%	25	45.45%	13	23.64%	7	12.73%	55
May 1759	9	15.79%	29	50.88%	15	26.32%	4	7.02%	57
June 1761	7	14.89%	20	42.55%	11	23.40%	9	19.15%	47
Average	9	17.03%	24	45.11%	13	24.92%	7	12.93%	53

most ages, but the workhouse minutes do not, although inmates lists in the vestry minutes of 1758 and 1759 also give ages. All in all, the ages of over 80 per cent of admissions are known or can be estimated.

In the nine years between December 1753 and July 1762 a total of 298 admissions was made, an average of around one every two weeks (see Table 7.1). In reality the intake tended to rise to around three a month in the winter and drop off to around one a month in summer.[38] It is estimated that the 298 admissions recorded during this period account for around 215 individuals,[39] 45 of whom were admitted on more than one occasion over the period. In addition to those taken in through the doors, 10 children were born in the workhouse during this time. The record keeping, however, was not quite as accurate as these statements might suggest: 18 of the discharges referred to in the admittance book[40] or the workhouse minutes are not matched by corresponding admission entries but admission has been assumed for the purpose of this study. Of the total 298 admissions and 10 births, it is known that 193 resulted in discharge from the house and that 76 died there. Although admissions were recorded in the surviving admittance book only up to September 1764, some later annotations relate to the discharge or death of a number of the inmates. By using this information and by examining the workhouse minute book, vestry minutes, removal orders, settlement examinations and certificates and burial records it is possible to determine the outcome of many of those whose admission occurred during the period of use of the admittance book, but whose stay extended beyond it. Clearly each admission resulted in the eventual discharge or death of an inmate, but inevitably there are some for which the outcome is completely unknown (25) and others for which the date of discharge or death is not recorded (40).

The elderly made up the largest proportion of admissions to the workhouse, and for the purpose of this study I have used the age of 60 as a cut-off point. Of the 267 admissions over the nine-year period for which age can be determined, over a third (90) were of adults known or estimated to be between 60 and 86. Oxley suggests that, taking into account the harshness of working life, limited diet and poor medical care, the age of 50 might be that at which advancing years contributed to dependence.[41] The evidence in Cheshunt is that those entering the workhouse from the age of 60 were the least likely to leave it again, and of the 90 admissions over half (53) are known to have died as inmates. Twenty-six were discharged, at least ten by their own request, including one who was to be cared for by a daughter. Sixty-year-old Widow Storey, admitted in December 1761, absconded the following April, but no more is known of the circumstances. One of the very first residents, 70-year-old Widow Susan Hall, was sent before the Justices of the Peace for 'abusing the master and mistress of the house and making a disturbance in the workhouse' on 8 April 1754, involving the parish in the expense of transporting her to Hertford. The only one of the older inmates known to have been expelled, she was ordered to go and to leave her (workhouse) clothes behind.

Of those discharged, 13 are known to have been re-admitted, including the runaway Widow Storey, who returned to the workhouse a year after her disappearance to live out the last nine months of her life. Charles Dickerson, first admitted in January 1754 aged 58, was to have six separate spells in the workhouse until he finally left in September 1763. In 1754 the parish made at least two payments to St Thomas's Hospital on his behalf, one to the Sister of Job's Ward for 'washing and other necessaries' and the other unspecified. Despite this history, he does not appear to have been an inmate when his burial was recorded in January 1767.[42] The troublesome widow Susan Hall was taken back into the house only a month after the 'disturbance' and re-admitted on at least two further occasions. Given responsibilities for nursing at the pesthouse, however – presumably she had smallpox immunity – she seems to have redeemed herself and the overseers were keen to encourage and reward her.[43]

To those not capable of hard physical labour such work perhaps offered a degree of dignity as well as some small financial reward. Elizabeth Miles, whose age was given as 60 when she entered the workhouse in November 1754, had already been sent to nurse an elderly parishioner in the March of that year. The following December she was sent out into the parish again, this time to nurse George Venables, until a week later when she was 'deemed no longer capable of nursing him'. Another elderly female resident, Joan (Joanna) Lowin, received 2s for nursing James Adams' family for two weeks in October 1754. Robert and Sarah Osborn, who were in their sixties, were sent out to the pesthouse in January 1755 and were to receive 4s a week for their care and labour. Besides payment for the occasional nursing jobs it is possible that the 6d received by six of the older women in December 1754 was for the knitting they had done in the house. Knitting needles and yarn were purchased very soon after the workhouse opened.

Some of the older men were allotted specific duties within the house. Eighty-year-old Robert Timms was put in charge of the gates and the dinner bell and Francis Coombes, 74, worked in the gardens: a gardener's apron was ordered for him just a few months after his admission. Besides this, he and two other older men were given the task of clearing the churchyard of weeds, nettles and rubbish in the autumn of 1755. It is not clear if many of the older men were engaged in any regular work in the house, but as those over 60 made up well over half the intake of adult males and tended to stay longer it is quite possible that they were involved in the net-making for the Free British Fisheries that took place from the outset.[44]

As they reached the end of their lives the elderly could expect to be nursed in the workhouse and finally to be buried at the expense of the parish. Although there are several references to bills paid for inmates' burials there is no indication of what was actually provided in terms of coffin, shroud or refreshment. Payment for the nursing care given to Widow Sarah Horseman was recorded in the workhouse minutes in mid-June 1755. Her burial took place less than two weeks later[45] and a payment was subsequently made to Mr Reeve for 'Sitting up with, Laying out and Burying the Widow Horseman'. Following the death of 70-year-old John Carter in March 1754 payment was made for laying him out and for his burial and 2s was paid to Widow Arnold 'for all her trouble with him'. This suggests that such care given to the old man was encouraged and his carer rewarded for performing her duties with compassion.

The committee also insisted that respect be shown to inmates who had died. An order recorded in the workhouse minutes in March 1756 declared that 'all the Buryings from the workhouse for the future be Carried to Church by five O'clock in the Summer and four in the winter and that the Master and Such of the poor as are able do Attend the Corpses'. This would have been a good mile and a half walk in each direction, even taking the old 'churchway' along Albury Walk. Particular respect was paid to one well-regarded inmate on his death in March 1754 when an extra 5s[46] was allowed for his funeral 'in consideration that the late Beadle Wm Hale hath behav'd well and Obliding to the parish and brought some Goods into the House with him'.

Children inevitably formed a large proportion of the 'impotent poor' and it is not surprising that they constituted the second largest category of admissions. Of the 267 admissions for which age is known or can be estimated 30 per cent (81) were of children aged between 6 months and 18 years. Under half of these admissions (35) were of children coming into the workhouse with their mother, and their circumstances as well as the length and outcome of their stay were in general related to those of their mothers: when mothers were destitute so were their children; when they were in a position to move on, their children generally went with them. However, some appear to have been orphaned in the workhouse or left behind when their mothers were discharged, perhaps in search of work.[47]

The remaining admissions were of lone children with ages ranging from 1 to 18. One 13-year-old girl had been removed from Edmonton and was known to be an orphan. However, in most cases it cannot be determined why these children were alone, although examination of the burial registers suggests that more than one of them had been orphaned. Some had already spent time in the workhouse with their mothers and were later admitted unaccompanied or returned after an unsuccessful attempt to place them in service or apprenticeship. Other children had living fathers who may have been widowed and not in a position to care for their offspring. Sisters Sarah and Letisha White, aged 6 and 3, were admitted on their own in October and November 1755 but discharged less than two years later at the request of their father, suggesting that he had not been able to look after them until then. There is evidence of the overseers putting pressure on fathers to take their children out of the workhouse, as in the case of James Gibson, a 5-year-old, whose father was ordered to remove him immediately in January 1756, and a later entry relating to an illegitimate child whose mother had died.[48] John Dudley was admitted at the age of 6 when the workhouse first opened in December 1753, although both his parents were still alive. The following May it was noted that his father, John, had abandoned the family, leaving his wife Ann pregnant with another child to whom she gave birth at the workhouse in March 1755.[49] When she was discharged two years later she took only her younger son Richard with her and John stayed on in the workhouse.

The fate of all those children who were not discharged and for whom the workhouse became their permanent home, with or without a parent, was to be apprenticed by the parish. Out of 78 child admissions 32 led to an apprenticeship, or at least to a trial apprenticeship – 25 for boys and 7 for girls. For the parish this made economic sense: indentures were drawn up, a fee of two guineas was paid to the master, the child was dispatched with a set of clothes and, in general, the parish's liability ended there. However, these arrangements were not always satisfactory, and three of the children sent out on trial had to be re-admitted. The most difficult child to place seems to have been Mark Hargood, who, at around the age of 10, was first sent to an Isaac Hooley of London. Hooley complained that the boy had misbehaved and so would not take him on and Hargood was 'sent for home'. Two months later he was sent on trial to Charles Lindsay, a breeches maker and glover in London, but was quickly returned on the grounds that he was 'not liked'. It was another nine months before the parish tried to place him again – this time to John Fearon, a weaver in Bethnal Green. No more was heard of the boy.

The age at which such children were indentured was generally 11.[50] Almost half were placed in London, most of the others in the parish – quite frequently with gentlemen who had served the workhouse committee – with a small number going to neighbouring parishes. The trades to which the boys were bound included those of chimney sweep, mariner, farmer, farrier, the Fleet,[51] barber, breeches and glove maker, stay maker, paper maker and watch gilder. Such skills might have led to a more prosperous lifestyle than that of their counterparts who did not did not learn trades through the parish system of apprenticeship. Of the seven apprenticeships arranged for girls, three may have been for the same person, Ann Harris, who had two local placements – one as a servant – and finally one in Bethnal Green to learn the art of cookery. Two further indentures show girls learning the art of housewifery and the minutes record another learning 'household work'. Although most apprentices were sent out 'on liking' and some masters were dissatisfied with their apprentices there is no evidence that the parish enquired after the welfare of those who had left their care.

Children were clearly expected to work while they lived in the workhouse; in December 1754 the committee ordered that the 'Children

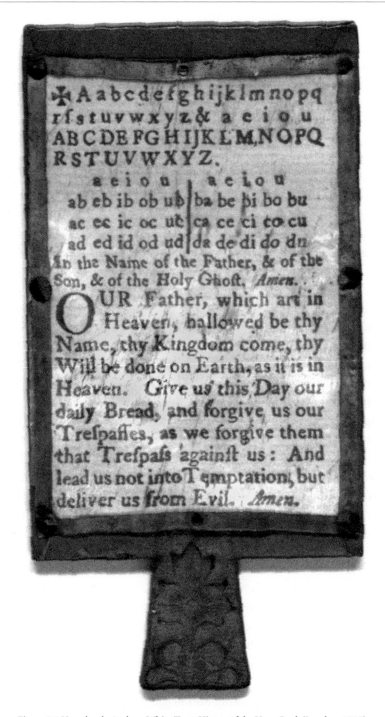

Figure 7.6 Horn book. Andrew White Tuer, *History of the Horn-Book* (London, 1897).

that Knit have sixpence a piece', although this is the only reference to children's work during this time. Some kind of education was offered as well; a dozen horn books (see Figure 7.6)[52] were purchased 'for the use of the children at the workhouse' in July 1754 and two school mistresses were given a Christmas box of 2s in 1757. In 1751 a boy attending the Robert Dewhurst Free School was discharged from the school as soon as he was admitted to the parish workhouse, suggesting that from then on his education would be provided there.[53] How much of their time was spent in lessons and how much in work, or indeed whether boys and girls were taught the same things, cannot be ascertained.

Over the course of nine years nearly all (92 out of 96) admissions of women aged between 18 and 85 were of those who found themselves alone for a variety of reasons. At least 25 of these (19 different individuals) were of young women, either pregnant with children to support or alone through widowhood, abandonment or illegitimate pregnancy. Some were merely described as 'the wife of', and it is not clear where the husbands were, nor do any attempts seem to have been made to track them down. Elizabeth Newitt, the wife of a soldier, first arrived in Cheshunt in May 1757. She and her two children had been 'pass'd as vagrants' from Berwick-upon-Tweed, an enormous distance to have travelled. Had they been moved from parish to parish all that way? To add to their woes they were suffering from smallpox and were immediately admitted to the pesthouse before, a month later, moving to the workhouse. Over the course of three years Elizabeth and her family were in and out of the workhouse five times. When she was admitted in September 1759 she had only her son with her, although her young daughter Elizabeth's burial was not recorded until May 1760 so perhaps the child was being cared for elsewhere. Elizabeth and her son Edward were discharged in June 1760, but it was only a matter of months before the 9-year-old was back, this time alone. A year later, Elizabeth returned. It was clear that this family was likely to be a perpetual drain on the parish and in March 1762 Edward was sent on a trial apprenticeship to a papermaker in Tottenham. His mother returned to Cheshunt in March 1775 and a settlement examination established that although she was settled in the parish, her travels – perhaps in search of her husband – had taken her to the West Riding of Yorkshire. There she had applied for relief from the parish of Wetherby and had been apprehended as a vagabond, accused of wandering and begging. In 1782 she reappeared in Cheshunt, described as a rogue and a vagabond, having been apprehended in Doncaster. Her soldier husband Edward, also settled in Cheshunt, was now dead.

Elizabeth Saunders arrived at the workhouse in December 1757 with one child, pregnant with another and abandoned by her soldier husband. No further reference is made to her pregnancy or to the death of an infant, only that she left the workhouse with her first child after eight months. The overseers were seemingly keen to support her, and allowed her 5s to buy a wheel so that she could spin 'out of the house'. Another abandoned wife, 29-year-old Mary Allum, was admitted in April 1758 with her three young children. They might have been admitted sooner but two weeks beforehand they were in receipt of outdoor relief, still not cured of 'the itch'. Three months previously Mary had given birth to a fourth child, the parish paying the midwife's bill and assisting her in having the baby placed at the Foundling Hospital.

Nearly a fifth (30) of the 164 female admissions during the nine years are known to have been of widows. Five were of widows aged 30 and under (including one re-admission), but the rest were all of women over 60. The younger widows arrived either pregnant or with young children to support. It is assumed that the parish officers believed the pregnancies of three young widows – aged 24, 30 and 35 – to have occurred during their deceased husbands' lifetimes, as no reference was made to illegitimacy. In all three cases it was at the expense of the parish that the newborn babies were sent to the Foundling Hospital; two are known to have been just one week old. Widow Judith Thorn, whose newborn child had been sent to the Foundling Hospital in September 1757, was still struggling to support herself and her 4-year-old son when they were admitted again in December 1759. Both needed to be 'entirely new cloath'd' on arrival and they remained in the workhouse for nearly 18 months. Some years later the overseers assisted her further by supplying a spinning wheel, enabling her to provide for herself in her own home.

Arranging for the newborn babies of young widows and abandoned wives to be taken in by the Foundling Hospital, as the examples above suggest, would seem to be a pragmatic approach by the parish authorities. An extra mouth to feed could well mean that the whole family would be a frequent or permanent drain on the poor rates, at least until the children were old enough to be apprenticed. The outlay at this point – making the arrangements and transporting the child to London – would have seemed a worthwhile investment. A four-year period of 'general reception', which started at the Hospital in 1756 (see Chapters 9 and 10 in this volume), no doubt provided the overseers with an easy and inexpensive solution.[54] From the mother's point of view another child would have been an extra financial burden and would prolong the period during which she would find it difficult to take up work. Perhaps this was felt to be the best possible outcome for babies whose mothers could not support them, and it is noted in two of the cases that the placement was at the mother's request.

If the parish displayed a degree of compassion towards widowed and abandoned pregnant women their attitude was somewhat different to those expecting an illegitimate child. Five such women were admitted over the nine-year period. The workhouse committee was keen to record that the admission of Judith Dover in December 1759 was not by order of the overseer but on that of the justice. She was described as 'big with child (or a bastard)', and her admission 'irregular Contrary to the Law and the rules of the House'. If the father of any illegitimate child could be found, he was made to pay for maintaining the child or made to marry the mother. In February 1754 a warrant was taken out against James Saunders 'on account of his getting Ann Scott now in the Workhouse with child', and he was made to pay 1s a week to the workhouse master during the child's lifetime. This did not last long, but despite the child having died two weeks after the warrant's issue Saunders was ordered to continue the payment until £3 had been paid off to defray the charge to the parish. Mary Want entered the workhouse in December 1753 following a removal order from Enfield the month before. The Enfield officers were no doubt keen to see her back over the border in her home parish: her illegitimate son was born a week after her admission to Cheshunt workhouse. Mary's discharge in February, with her son William, coincided with her marriage to William Wacket, noted in the minutes and no doubt speeded along and paid for by the overseers. Less than a year later the child was back, this time alone and now with the alias Wacket. He was to remain in the care of the workhouse until his apprenticeship 12 years later. The best efforts of the officers had failed to prevent him from becoming a financial burden to the parish.

Although the services of the midwife, Mrs Wigley, were recorded in only four instances of birth in the workhouse, it seems likely that all those who gave birth as inmates were afforded the same treatment and no distinction appears to have been made between legitimate and illegitimate births. The overseers paid the midwife 5s on each occasion, a sum which might have been beyond the means of those outside the workhouse and on low incomes.

Not all the younger lone women who entered the workhouse did so because of pregnancy or dependant children. Four admissions were of women arriving alone who appear to have been homeless, having their settlement in Cheshunt, but perhaps being without family there. However, it was rare for the minutes to record such a case of destitution as that of 20-year-old Mary Horseman. She was admitted in March 1758, having applied to the committee, 'being almost naked and destitute and not able to subsist herself'. It was not the first time she had been admitted. She had left in May 1756 after a five-month stay and it seems very likely that she went to London and worked as a prostitute. In January 1758, just a couple of months before her re-admission, the minutes record a payment of 7s 6d for the use of the parish officers of Bishopsgate for carrying her firstly to St Thomas's Hospital and then to Kingsland Lock – which at this time was treating female patients with venereal disease[55] – as well as for clothes and other charges. Whatever their opinion of her moral conduct, the overseers clearly felt that her pitiful state was worthy of note.

Other admissions of lone women appear to have been made primarily because of age, frailty, poverty or a combination of these factors. Over half of these women were to end their days in the workhouse; many died within months of admission, although for some the workhouse was home for many years. Those lone women who were able moved on; as we have seen, some were given spinning wheels to enable them to earn a living while others went into domestic service, but the fate of the majority is unknown.

In the years for which inmate numbers are known men consistently form a much smaller group than women, just less than 20 per cent of the total. Of the 59 admissions made over the nine years approximately half were aged 18 to 59, the rest were 60 and over. Of the younger men at least three were ill on admission or died shortly afterwards. Only one man with a wife and family is recorded entering the house. It is hard to know why the rest entered the workhouse; some at least were regulars (see below) and three had been removed from other parishes, so presumably had nowhere to stay. What is clear is that in Cheshunt workhouse there were no great numbers of able-bodied men, unencumbered by children, who were not in work. The majority came in the later years of their life, unable to support themselves.

As has been shown, there was a tendency for older people coming into the workhouse to remain there until they reached the end of their days.

In some cases this might be for some considerable time, and in the cases for which lengths of stay are known these range from five days to nearly 13 years. Widow Mary Carter was 70 when she came into the workhouse shortly after it opened in 1753 and she finally died there in January 1767. While in the house she received a gratuity, possibly for knitting or spinning, and was also granted leave go to London for a short period.

We have also seen how lone children had of necessity to remain in the workhouse until such time as they could be apprenticed. However, it was not only the young and the old who found themselves long-time residents. Arabella Wright, 34, was receiving a pension of 8s in March 1750 before she was admitted at the opening of the workhouse in December 1753. She remained there until her death in 1780[56] – a total of 26 years. Dorothy Wisbey, an 18-year-old, was a resident from the start, remaining until she died 15 years later. No explanation is given as to why these two young women were not encouraged to find work in service, so it can only be conjecture that they were not able, perhaps through illness or physical or mental incapacity, to make their own living. However, it is recorded that Arabella was among those who received 6d, possibly for knitting or spinning, while Dorothy was paid a gratuity for 25 weeks' spinning in July 1765.

In cases for which age is unrecorded it is not usually possible to deduce whether longer-term male residents were young or old. Only one case is noted of a lone man, John Anthony, being discharged with a child, but his admission date is unknown. Of the 24 admissions of men aged between 30 and 58 four might be described not so much as long-term residents but as 'regulars' – men who were in and out of the workhouse on several occasions. William Cass, a 30-year-old, was admitted and discharged at least four times, his final stay lasting nearly a year. There is no explanation of his circumstances, but it seems likely, given that most of his absences were during the summer months, that he was able to find only seasonal work. James Nixon, 27 when first admitted, was another young man who was frequently in and out of the workhouse – at least six times between November 1754 and May 1763. All we know of him is that when he left for the first time in November 1754 it was noted that it was because he was well. Perhaps he had a recurrent illness and could not always work. On most occasions he was discharged at his own request and on one occasion he was given a flannel waistcoat to see him on his way. Edward Vernon was 50 when first admitted in March 1756, and he was to return to the workhouse on at least two further occasions. It must have been his removal from the parish of West Malling in Kent that brought him to the workhouse initially,[57] but nothing else is known of him other than his six- and four-month stays that commenced in December 1758 and January 1762 respectively.

There is strong evidence that those who were able engaged in productive work in the house; the men initially made nets for the British Fisheries, the women spun and the children knitted. The presence of a woolcombers' room suggests that this was another process undertaken by the inmates. This was not work for work's sake; income was derived from knitted garments, the spun wool and the made-up nets and by October 1754 the workers had earned £33 8s 9d since the house had opened in December 1753. Gratuities were paid to the workers and the money was also used to buy clothing and equipment for the inmates' work. It seems likely that the women also did domestic work in the house and tended the lone children. Clothes were made on site, beer brewed and the garden worked. The older male inmates were found odd jobs and the older women were asked to nurse the sick and lay out the dead. These were functions for which the parish officers had responsibility outside of the workhouse and, although it is clear this was cheap labour, there is good evidence that some of the inmates performed these tasks with care and diligence.

Conclusion

Slack argues in *The English Poor Law, 1531–1782* that the 'more realistic scepticism about what workhouses could achieve' rather than a more 'generous way of thinking' became generally prevalent from the 1750s.[58] Others have located different transition points for the 'sentiment' of the Old Poor Law.[59] There is no doubt that many of the gentlemen who served on Cheshunt's workhouse committee took their role seriously. They operated a strict regime, but at no time does this regime appear to have been unnecessarily harsh. In all nine years there was only one case of whipping recorded, that of a runaway boy. Those being admitted were expected to bring their goods with them and to work and abide by the rules; and those who broke them were punished. Stealing and violence resulted in legal action, but these cases seem to have been very rare. Those who behaved well and did their work were rewarded with gratuities and occasional privileges, such as being allowed leave to visit relatives. One old man was allowed extra beer to take with his medicine, and one destitute widowed mother had her pawned goods redeemed by the overseers to enable her to bring them in with her.

Cheshunt workhouse acted as a children's home for the orphaned and abandoned, as a refuge for women in distress and as a care home for the sick and elderly. There was also continuity of regime over this period; the workhouse master and mistress, Richard and Mary Neale, remained in place until August 1762, when Richard Neale's scandalous behaviour with one of the young female inmates resulted in the couple's dismissal. Until this time his diligence had been regularly rewarded. The workhouse also provided personal care, medical care and funeral care. In terms of food, clothing and shoes the physical well-being of the inmates seems to have been well catered for. However, on one occasion the committee appeared to be sensitive to the suggestion that their treatment of an elderly inmate was lacking. In March 1755 70-year-old Joseph Starling, one of the few inmates whose words were recorded, described the care he received in the workhouse. When 'complaint [was] made without Doors that [he] has not proper care taken of him nor proper food for his Disorder he was call'd in said that he had no Complaint to make and that he had every thing Done for him that he desired'. This optimistic reading of the care offered by the poor law echoes recent work (outlined in Chapter 1 by Steven King) that has begun to emphasise the flexibility and often generosity of the Old Poor Law.

Notes

1. Although on workhouses see M. Fissell, *Patients, power and the poor in eighteenth-century Bristol* (Cambridge, 1991); T. Hitchcock, 'The English workhouse: a study in institutional poor relief in selected counties, 1696–1750', D.Phil. thesis (Oxford, 1985); T. Hitchcock, 'Paupers and preachers: the SPCK and the parochial workhouse movement', in L. Davison *et al.* (eds), *Stilling the grumbling hive* (Stroud, 1992), pp. 145–66.

2. *Abstract of Answers and Returns under the Act for Procuring Returns Relative to Expense and Maintenance of the Poor in England*, PP 1803–04 XIII, 378.

3. R.M. Smith, 'Ageing and well-being in early modern England: pension trends and gender preferences under the English Old Poor Law c. 1650–1800', in P. Johnson and P. Thane (eds), Old age from antiquity to post-modernity (London, 1998), pp. 64–95.

4. J. Edwards, *Cheshunt in Hertfordshire* (Cheshunt, 1974), p. 74. A chapel of ease built at Waltham Cross in 1832 became the parish church in 1855.

5. Ibid., p. 39.

6. Her Majesty's Stationery Office (hereafter HMSO), *Chronological table of statutes covering the period from 1235 to the end of 1973* (London, 1974); Parliamentary Papers 11 Geo 1, cap II, *Enfield Chase or Galley Corner Trust*, 1725.

7. Cardinal Wolsey's 'Great House'.

8. Hertfordshire Archives and Local Studies, Hertford (hereafter HALS) DE/Cr/109/1 *The liberty, manor and parish of Cheshunt* [tracing of 1785 plan] undated and HALS

DE/Cr/125/2 Field book to plan of *The liberty, manor and parish of Cheshunt* [original dated 1785], undated [1852 or later].

9. *A vision of Britain through time* population tables by parish unit: http://www.visionofbritain.org.uk/index.jsp: Hertford All Saints' population 1738, Hertford St Andrew population 1277.

10. P.C. Archer, *Historic Cheshunt* (Cheshunt, 1923), p. 1. Even as late as 1923 Percy Archer referred to Cheshunt as 'our Village'.

11. Hertfordshire Quarter Sessions Vol. 2, Christmas session 13 and 25 January 1755.

12. Hertfordshire Quarter Sessions Vol. 2, Midsummer session 12 July and 2 August 1756.

13. HALS DP/29/29/1 Cheshunt population returns 1821.

14. W. Le Hardy, *Hertfordshire county records calendar to the sessions books, sessions minute books and other sessions records* (Hertford, 1931), Vol. 7, 12 January 1712/13. The other two overseers had refused assistance but were ordered to contribute £10 each.

15. Fields used for common grazing after Lammas Day, 1 August – that is, after the end of the wheat harvest.

16. Edwards, *Cheshunt in Hertfordshire*, p. 63. In 1804 the hundred acre common at Goffs Oak was set aside for the use of 183 cottagers – that is, those possessing less than one rood of land with a cottage rent not exceeding £6.

17. HALS DP/29/8/48: a minute of 24 September 1722 refers to an agreement to lease houses and a courtyard for use as a parish workhouse. HALS DP/29/8/1: a minute of 26 June 1749 refers to the workhouse in Marsh Lane and HALS DE/Cr/125/2 Plan of *The liberty, manor and parish of Cheshunt* shows two roads in the parish called Marsh Lane, one now Trinity Lane, Waltham Cross, the other Windmill Lane Cheshunt.

18. HALS DP/29/8/52.

19. HALS DE/Cr/21 *A catalogue of well-conditioned building materials fixtures and fittings up of Cheshunt Poor-House* by H Crawter & Sons Wednesday 18 October 1837.

20. There follows a long gap until two final admissions are recorded in May and September 1764. For continuity the final two entries have not been included in this analysis.

21. Workhouse minutes were recorded and survive from 17 September 1753 to 18 April 1799.

22. HMSO *Chronological table of statutes*; Parliamentary Papers 9 Geo I, Cap VII, *Act for Amending the Laws relating to the Settlement, Employment and Relief of the Poor* (Workhouse Test Act 1723).

23. Society for the Promotion of Christian Knowledge (SPCK), *An account of several workhouses for employing and maintaining the poor* (1732).

24. G.W. Oxley, *Poor relief in England and Wales, 1601–1834* (Newton Abbot, 1974); P. Slack, *The English poor law, 1531–1782* (Cambridge, 1995), p. 34.

25. HALS DP/29/8/49 12 April 1755.

26. HALS DP/29/8/1 lists of inmates 1755–59 and 1761.

27. HALS DP/29/8/50.

28. HALS DP/29/8/1 2 April 1754.

29. HALS DE/Cr/125/2 *The liberty, manor and parish of Cheshunt*.

30. HALS DP/29/18/28. At a special meeting held on Wednesday 14 January 1801 to consider 'the proceedings under the Act of Parliament for the better provision for the maintenance of the poor etc' the overseers and churchwardens concluded that a

nutritious and wholesome diet of rice, herrings and pickled beef could be provided at reasonable prices.

31. See J. Styles, *The dress of the people: everyday fashion in eighteenth-century England* (New Haven, CT, 2007).

32. S. Hindle, 'Dependency, shame and belonging: badging the deserving poor, c.1550–1750', *Cultural & Social History*, 1.1 (2004), pp. 6–35.

33. Oxley, *Poor relief*, p. 51.

34. 9 Geo I, Cap VII.

35. Oxley, *Poor relief*, p. 42.

36. The workhouse committee included the three ward overseers and concerned itself as well with administering outdoor relief: that is, regular 'pensions', sickness payments and payments in kind (mainly clothing and shoes).

37. A number of entries show the age of certain individuals to have decreased or remained the same from one admission to the next.

38. The three initial intakes appear to relate to a number of paupers already permanently maintained by the parish and the average admission number has been adjusted to take this into account.

39. It is not always clear, without further evidence, that people with the same or similar names are the same individual.

40. The word 'expelled' is used throughout the admissions book, but corresponds with 'discharged at own request' in the minutes, and in any case its use is too frequent to imply the modern meaning of the word.

41. Oxley, *Poor relief*, p. 58. Respondents to an 1832 questionnaire (Parliamentary Papers 1834 XXV111–XXIX) used 50 as a threshold of old age.

42. HALS DP/29/1/8.

43. Workhouse minutes of 24 March 1755 said that she had 'behav'd in the pesthouse as nurse in the Small pox, with care and Diligence' and that ' the Committee for her Encouragement have agreed that Mr Neal [the master] Do Give her five Shillings more than their Agreement of two Shillings pr. Week'.

44. One of the reasons for selecting Richard Neale as master was his proposal to make 'netts of all sorts for sea and land'. Wrought nets were sent to London in August 1754 and more were ready in March 1755: workhouse Minutes 26 August 1754 and 31 March 1755.

45. HALS DP/29/1/8, 27 June 1755.

46. On burial standards see E.T. Hurren and S. King, 'Begging for a burial: death and the poor law in eighteenth and nineteenth century England', *Social History*, 30 (2005), pp. 321–41.

47. On workhouse children see A. Levene, 'Children, childhood and the workhouse: St Marylebone, 1769–1781', *London Journal*, 33 (2008), pp. 41–59.

48. Workhouse minutes of 28 October 1765 'Order'd that Samuel Govey aged abt. 8 Years born on the body of Elizabeth Davis in this sworn to Samuel Govey of Turnford Woolcomber be Discharg'd the House his Father Agreeing to take him home and provide for him'.

49. HALS DP/29/13/2 Settlement examination Ann Dudley 11 Nov 1754.

50. HALS D/P29/13 & 14. See also K. Honeyman, *Child workers in England, 1780–1820: parish apprentices and the making of the early industrial labour force* (Aldershot, 2007).

51. HALS DP/29/18/2, 2 June 1755 James Hall bound apprentice to the Free British Fisheries.

52. A primer with a single sheet often containing the alphabet and the Lord's prayer, set in wood and covered with transparent horn.

53. HALS DE/Ds/1/3 Orders relating to the Trustees at Cheshunt 1748 to 1778: Minute Book of the Charity School at Cheshunt Hertfordshire.

54. G. Pugh, *London's forgotten children: Thomas Coram and the Foundling Hospital* (Stroud, 2007), p. 44. A resolution was passed in the House of Commons in April 1756 backed by a grant of £10,000 'enabling the [Foundling] hospital for the maintenance of exposed and deserted young children to receive all the children which shall be offered'.

55. http://www.british-history.ac.uk/report.aspx?compid=65455&amp, *Survey of London: volume 25: St George's Fields (The parishes of St. George the Martyr Southwark and St. Mary Newington)*, pp. 121–6.

56. HALS DP/29/1/8, burial 3 May 1780.

57. HALS DP/29/18/27J removal order 6 October 1756.

58. Slack, *The English Poor Law*, p. 36.

59. For a broad discussion of this matter see S. Hindle, *On the parish? The micro-politics of poor relief in rural England c.1550–1750* (Oxford, 2004), pp. 361–449.

CHAPTER EIGHT

The Old Poor Law in a rural North Hertfordshire parish, 1731–1831

Helen Hofton

NOTWITHSTANDING THE SIGNIFICANT advances in the historiography of the Old Poor Law outlined by Steven King in his introduction to this volume, detailed long-term micro-studies of the changing character, administration and practice of parochial relief are noticeable by their relative absence.[1] In consequence, wider discussions of the nature of intra- and inter-regional variation in poor-law practice, the 'sentiment' of parishes towards their poor, the reactions of communities to particular crisis moments such as the Napoleonic Wars and the trends in the generosity and flexibility of parochial officials are based upon relatively slim empirical foundations. Situated within this broad framework, the aim of the current chapter is to provide a case study of how the Old Poor Law system worked in practice between 1731 and 1831 with reference to the north Hertfordshire parish of Pirton.[2] It takes account of the background of the general situation in England and provides an illustration of how a community took responsibility for looking after the poor who lived among them, as well as illustrating how the growing cost of applying the Old Poor Law factored into the Poor Law Amendment Act of 1834. The major sources for the research are the four surviving overseers' account books for Pirton (1731–1831).[3] The accounts give a list of ratepayers and the amounts paid in tax. Unfortunately, as poorer tenants were exempt from paying rates, the collection list is not a complete record of householders in the parish. The accounts also list sums spent weekly on the poor and give the name of the overseer, the name of the pauper, the amount given and, frequently, the reason for the payment. Such records are familiar to welfare

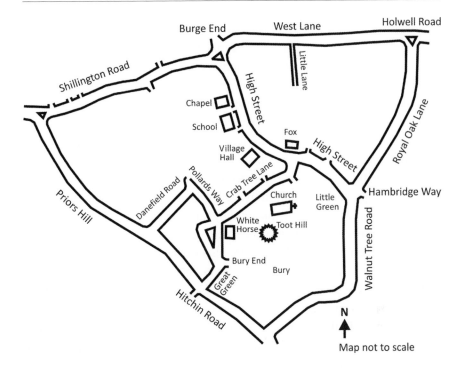

Figure 8.1 Street plan of Pirton. © Pirton Local History Group.

---

historians, but their relative richness for Pirton can allow a very detailed insight into the operation of the parochial welfare system.

Portrait of a community

In 1731 the parish had a total population of around 370, including 82 ratepayers.[4] By 1801 the population had risen to 481, who lived in 94 houses with a further 3 empty (the number of ratepayers is not known). Forty years later, in 1841, the population had increased to 758, but the number of ratepayers had reduced to 64.[5] In many ways Pirton was a typical agricultural village of the period (Figure 8.1). It was an 'open' village, receiving many incoming families from local single-landlord-dominated 'closed' villages such as Hexton. In open villages landlords often subdivided larger village buildings into tenements to let to these families and typically expected the parish to pay rents when their tenants could not.

Like other open villages, Pirton had a periodic and seasonal unemployment problem throughout the period. This may have been alleviated to a certain extent during the process of parliamentary enclosure begun in 1811, when 2,159 of the parish's 2,669 acres were enclosed. Hundreds of half-acre strips lying in the open fields surrounding the nucleated settlement were exchanged to make farming more efficient in a process that took seven years to complete. Land was drained, quickset hedges planted round the new, larger fields and new roads laid out. Although some labourers were worse off, as their common rights were extinguished, this process is likely to have brought some reduction in the levels of unemployment among the able-bodied as casual labour was used by farmers and landowners to create the new arrangements. The worst consequences of agricultural under-employment for men in Pirton were also offset to some extent by straw plaiting for the Luton hat trade. This was mainly undertaken by women and children, who could earn as much as 3s 6d a week from plaiting during the season from December to May (around half the average weekly wage for a male labourer). In the summer months they returned to working with their families on hay making and harvesting. This was very important, as in the winter months the men in the family were often 'laid off'. Evidence from Parliamentary Papers in 1818 noted that in straw-plaiting families the 'wife and children [together] can often earn more than the husband'.[6]

A government commission of 1824 to enquire into the practice of supplementing agricultural labourers' wages from the poor rate[7] provides important local context. The reply to the commissioners from the Pirton overseer John Woolston dated 28 April 1824 noted:

> First no labourers employed by farmers receive any money out of the poor rates.
> Secondly It is not any of our married labourers that receive any thing out of the rates unless being ill.
> Thirdly our labourers who cannot find work are sent round and then receive out of the rates sometimes one shilling per week and sometimes two and sometimes three according to there familys paid them by the overseer.
> Fourthly the number of unemployed labourers have increased within the last few years.
> Fifthly the lowest price given to an unmarried labourer is four shillings a week.[8]

This and other evidence given to the commission provides a clearer picture of what life was like for the able-bodied agricultural labourer at the time. The commission found that wages had decreased since the end of the Napoleonic Wars, as the labour market was flooded with 300,000 returning soldiers, and the conditions of the poor had worsened. A labourer in employment typically worked a 12-hour day in summer and a 10-hour day in winter. Weekly wages were 8s in summer and 6s in winter. Harvest was a good opportunity to work overtime and it was possible for a man to earn about 40s for that month as well as being fed. Boys of nine could earn around 2s a week, which would just pay the rent. Women also contributed to the family income by washing, making clothes for others, looking after children and nursing the sick. In effect, all members of the family had to work just to provide a basic standard of living. The labourer's diet was very plain and consisted of bread, cheese and potatoes from the garden. Meat was available only if the family could afford to buy and keep a pig.

Against this backdrop Elmsley has argued that the number of criminal offences was relatively steady until 1811, but rose sharply in rural areas after the return of the troops from the Napoleonic Wars, with peaks in 1817 and 1819. Thereafter was a brief decline until 1825 followed by a sharp trend upwards to another peak in 1832. These peaks coincided with years of economic depression and periods of social unrest, suggesting that rural labourers were being driven into crime out of necessity.[9] Thus, nine young men from Pirton were transported to Australia or Tasmania between 1818 and 1830 for sheep-, poultry- or pigeon-stealing. Many more individuals appeared at the Quarter Sessions for poaching or stealing food. These included Catherine Nicholls, a widow who received two weeks in gaol for stealing a peck of barley worth sixpence. George Pratt was sentenced to seven days' hard labour for stealing growing peas.

Such judicial responses, intertwining with rising prices and poor harvests (particularly 1828–30) were major factors in the 'Swing' riots of 1830. Pirton, however, occupies a relatively unusual place in the regional history of such riots: the availability of alternative work, albeit for women and children, seems to have made the labouring population less volatile than in other open villages. An interesting insight into this is provided by Pirton's reaction to the Swing riots of 1830 in nearby villages in Bedfordshire. The entry in the Overseer's Accounts notes: '1831 March 10th To Mr C Kingsley 47 special constables at 1 shilling each'. Pirton men were employed to put down the riots in the neighbouring Bedfordshire villages of Flitwick and Stotfold, although they must have been torn between loyalty to others fighting for higher wages and the shilling in their pockets.

The key question, then, is how the poor law operated in this complex community.

Administration

Pirton does not appear to have had a formal vestry. Monthly meetings were held between overseers and a small group of parishioners so that the former could present their accounts for ongoing approval. Unfortunately, no minute books have survived and so it is unclear whether applications for relief were adjudicated at these meetings, although this does seem likely. Meetings took place in private houses, not in the Church vestry, and the records show that beer, paid for out of the rates, was always served. The very fact that these meetings were convened marks out Pirton as a relatively unusual place in poor-law historiography.

The community was more conventional in terms of its relief funding. In common with other places, tenants were assessed for multiple poor rates on the basis of the rental value of their property, with any improvements made during the year being reflected in a new valuation. In 1731 the rate for Pirton was set at 14d in the pound and £58 19s 7d was raised from the village. The amounts contributed from individual households ranged from 7d to £9. The year 1801 saw a poor harvest and many people needed relief. As a result, in the following year in Pirton the rate was raised from 2s to 3s 6d in the pound. By 1830 individual contributions had risen to 1s 2d for a labourer and to £61 for the largest farmer. In that year the records show that the total amount collected was £234. In some years more money was disbursed than was collected. For example, in 1758 £161 9s 9d was collected and £165 3s 3d was disbursed, with the deficit made up the following year. The accounts often show money in hand, which may have allowed the overseers to set a lower rate in the following year or alternatively to continue to carry the balance forward to cover unexpected events.

During the century 1731–1831, and in common with most other places, there is some evidence in the Pirton accounts that a growing range of goods and services was seen as being essential, even for a pauper. The volume of payments also increased. Particularly after 1810 the task of the overseer appears to have become more onerous, with as many as 22 payments being made each week compared to half that number in 1731. Possibly

Figure 8.2 John Woolston's house on Shillington Road, Pirton, being repaired in 1933. © Pirton Local History Group.

as a result, the length of time an overseer in Pirton served was reduced to six months. At the start of the accounts a wide range of 'middling' people was carrying out the job and each individual's turn came round fairly infrequently. Nevertheless, by 1813 very few men were volunteering for the post. Possibly as a result of this, John Woolston, a local butcher (Figure 8.2), seems to have carried out the task more or less continually from 1813 until his death in 1830. It is possible that he was a paid official, as the Select Vestries Act of 1818 provided for the employment of salaried overseers.

Unsurprisingly for an open parish, Pirton overseers spent a great deal of time on settlement and removal cases. Officials had to collect the newcomers' settlement certificates or arrange for their removal if they did not have the appropriate permissions, and they dealt with litigation if an appeal arose, as for example in the following case: 'Jan 1811 going with George Weeding to sware him to is hablation [habitation]'. There are many references to 'taking people to the justices' and relief for 'a man on a pass'. In the opposite case, rather than accepting the return of paupers to Pirton, sometimes the local overseers paid other parishes to look after the Pirton poor. For example, in 1817 the overseers paid Ickleford £9 2s for Widow Ibbert as well as £2 10s for her rent. Great Brickhill was paid £5 11s

for Thomas Coleman and six guineas was paid to the parish of Weston to
accept the Turner family. In fact, Pirton paid Weston overseers around 3s
a week for the Turner family from 1782 right through to 1831, when the
accounts books come to an end.

A child's place of settlement at birth was taken to be the same as that
of its father. At marriage, a woman took on the same settlement as her
husband. Illegitimate children were granted settlement in the place
they were born and this often led overseers to try to remove unmarried
pregnant woman before the child was born, for example by transporting
her to another parish just before the birth or by paying a man from another
parish to marry her. Where this was impossible they obtained affiliation
orders from the father or even paid for a couple to be married. This could
be expensive, as shown by the marriage of Sarah Barber and John Gray at
St Mary's Church Pirton on 23 October 1764:

22 Oct the expenses of mareying John Grey to Sarra Barbur	
Examination	2s
waront	1s
my hors & self the jurney	1s 6d
at hitchin bear [beer] & brakfast	5s 6d
oats	8d
lissonce	£1 10s
the marrey fees,	10s
bearr at Ellins	
dinna at Ellins	

The Barber family had already been claiming relief at various times
during the previous eight years. Now Sarah Barber, a daughter aged 23,
seems to have 'got into trouble' and would therefore be a greater charge on
the parish. The overseers' accounts record that the final payment was 5s for
a 'reemufall [removal] order'.

These examples of the range and intensity of work, evidence of a
growing volume of payments and presumably appeals and the need for
officials to deal with a whole variety of non-poor-law activities linked to
their office[10] suggests that the administration of relief in Pirton placed a
heavy burden on individual ratepayers over and above the cost of the poor
rate. Such detailed perspectives on administration are often missing from
the wider literature.

Outdoor relief

The most regular form of engagement between official and pauper was via the payment of outdoor relief in cash and kind. This was typically a regular weekly, fortnightly or monthly occurrence and comprised payments to the elderly, widows, orphans, unemployed and the chronic sick. It was the simplest and most convenient way of distributing relief and also had the advantage of flexibility. It could be quickly increased or reduced to meet changing circumstances such as the birth of a child or the availability of seasonal work opportunities. The 1731 Pirton Accounts identify 13 pensioners by name who received cash payments of between 6d and 1s a week. Some widows with children received 1s 6d, but Elizabeth Bridgement, an elderly spinster, was given 2s a week until she died in 1744. Often if the widow died her children continued to receive the same amount of relief. Four of the 13 pensioners in the 1731 accounts had their board and lodging paid for in addition to their pension. At the time, lodging cost about 6d a week and board about 1s 3d a week. The total weekly amount paid out in Pirton increased over the 100 years from an average of about £1 8s to about £3 7s 6d. Individual pensions increased to between 1s and 3s a week.

Money for housing was often not included in a pension, but was provided as a separate item. One reason for this was that the rent was an annual or twice yearly payment made at Lady Day or Michaelmas. It was recognised that the recipient would not be able to save enough for such a large payment from a modest pension. In many instances married agricultural workers lived rent-free in tied cottages owned by their employers. These were usually the skilled workers such as horse keepers and shepherds, who needed to be close to their work. Single men 'lived in' at the farm and were described as farm servants.[11] Owners of rented properties in Pirton were mainly small farmers, craftsmen or shopkeepers. The rents of the poor were paid by the overseers right through the period, with individual amounts rising from under £1 a year in 1731 to £5 6s 0d a year in 1831. Pirton continued the tradition of providing families with a separate home despite all the pressure on housing resulting from the rapid increase in population that took place in the early nineteenth century. This was at a time when many commentators were advocating the use of workhouses as being a cheaper and more effective solution to the rising costs of caring for the poor.

An alternative to making payments for rent was to arrange for accommodation to be provided by a private contractor. Contractors were able to bid for the right to provide both outdoor and indoor (workhouse) relief. Sometimes payments were made for rented rooms and, in certain circumstances, for board and lodging. This was usually short term, but sometimes tenants brought all their worldly goods with them, as can be seen by the accounting entry for Robert Pearce on 10 October 1754, which read:

> One chest, one box, one trunk and three tables, a white dresser with two drawers, three common chairs and an elbow chair, one feather bed, three blankets, three sheets, a bedstead and curtains with iron curtain rods, one small barrell, one hand saw, a looking glass and a bill, a skillet, one kettle, one brass ladle, a pair of bellows and a candle box and two iron candlesticks, one pewter tankard and a hand bowl. This enmitary [inventory] was taken by John Hill, Mr Arnold being present 10th October 1754.

In 1754 Robert Pearce was living with his wife Mary in a cottage in Shillington Road. His annual rent of £1 had been paid by the parish for the previous three years and the family were receiving a pension of 3s a week. Mary died in May and, according to the accounts, was buried by the parish in a lace cloth cap, muffler and wool. The next month Robert became ill and was nursed by Mary Harding at 1s a week. A fortnight after the above inventory was taken the overseers paid 1s to Thomas Harding for removing Robert Pearce from the property and a further 4d for 'the first half week Robert Peirce was at his house'. By the following February Robert was well again and back in his rented cottage on Shillington Road.

Repairs to property were occasionally paid in addition to the pension because they were an unpredictable and infrequent expense. Thatching seems to have been the most common repair and it was carried out with straw, which was cheaper than reed. In Pirton the Hill family were the village thatchers. The records show that in 1742 John Hill did one day's work thatching Widow Nash's house at a cost of 1s 6d. He repaired it again 11 years later for 10s 1d. In 1782 'thecking Sam Walkers house' cost £2 17s 6d. This high cost suggests that it could have been for replacing the whole roof. Presumably these were rented properties not owned by the parish.

Shoes and clothing for the family were expensive items for a poor labourer and in the Pirton accounts there are many entries concerned with the making, buying or repairing of such items. Shoes were made either by

Thomas Campkin or John Crouch at the beginning of the period and by John Dawson and Francis Crouch towards the end. They made shoes, high shoes and pattens. There are many references to hobnails being hammered into leather soles to protect them from wear. In the 1730s children's shoes cost 2s 6d and men's shoes 4s, which was as much as two weeks' pension for some. Mending cost 7d. By 1828 the cost of both children's and men's shoes had risen threefold and, as part of the provision of clothes, men and boys were made britches, shirts, waistcoats, stockings and caps. Sometimes 'round frocks' – possibly working smocks – were mentioned. Girls received shifts, bodices, gowns, petticoats, stays, aprons, stockings and, in one case, a cloak.

Clothing was particularly likely to be given at times of sickness. Although the original Poor Laws of 1601 made no provision for medical relief, responsibility did seem to pass to the parish. Until 1790 the parish clearly employed doctors at need, rather than under contract, a chronology which sits well with that suggested by Samantha Williams.[12] In 1793 and 1796, however, Dr Meers was paid a four-guinea annual salary. He was followed by Dr Oswald Foster, initially at a rate of six guineas rising to between £8 and £19 in the 1820s. Various exclusions were made, as can be seen from his bill for 1827/28:

8 month 16 Attendance and reducing fractured thigh, medicines W. Burr	£4 4s 0d
9 month 29 Attendance and reducing fractured clavicle, medicines Geo Mails	£2 2s 0d
12 month 4 A patent truss for Titmuss	£1 1s 0d
1828	
2 month 19 twelve leeches George Hile	6 s
2 month 28 Journey to Hyde at Shillington	2s 6d
3 month 24 Four leeches Geo Hile	2s
One years' salary for medicine and attendance	£8 8s
Journey	2s 6d
On account of John Weedons son fractured thigh	£2 2s

These doctors treated a wide variety of ailments, including fevers, fits and smallpox. In 1801 Dr Bailly 'plaistered the children's heads' and later in 1828 a doctor was treating the 'Kings Evil', which was scrofula or tuberculosis of the lymph nodes in the neck. On another occasion Doctor Foster attended John Crouch's inquest. All of those commissioned by the parish set broken bones, and in the 100-year period only three paupers were sent to hospital. Most of the consequent nursing was carried out by local women. Their duties included midwifery, caring for patients in their own homes and the workhouse, sitting up with the dying and then laying out the dead. Local women nursed irregularly and usually for short periods, but the accounts show that Judith Pitts started nursing aged 37 and worked for the next 20 years until she was widowed and became a pensioner. She had one long-term patient named Turner whom she nursed for two years. Other nurses had more specialist skills: it is recorded in 1754 that Mary Carrington had physic for John Dunham and used salts to purge him. Mary was Pirton-born and seems to have started nursing when she was widowed ten years earlier. She continued working until her death at the age of 72. Occasionally, perhaps surprisingly infrequently compared to other parishes in the historiography, the records show that a midwife was used for a delivery, but it is unclear whether this was just a local woman or a specialist. Usually local women who were experienced in childbirth themselves aided mothers.[13]

There were many instances of smallpox in the late eighteenth century. Sometimes individuals and sometimes whole families caught the disease, including Samuel Moody's family. Many people survived, but John Campkin died after 11 days of nursing. In 1785 John Wright had 'smalpoke'. He survived, but his wife and two children died. The following year so many people had this contagious disease that a separate house was rented by the overseers. Normally sick people were nursed in their own homes by local women – the community was too small to warrant a pesthouse. Smallpox spread through the workhouse in 1799 and four village women were paid for nursing the inmates, none of whom died from the disease. The first inoculations took place in 1806, when Robert Taylor's children were treated. Three years later there was 'a parish account' and Dr Foster inoculated six people at 2s 6d a head. That year both Joseph and his mother Ruth Barber caught the disease. Ruth died, but her 18-year-old son survived. Perhaps his survival can be put down to the fact that he had received 5s 3d from the overseers for beer! The disease seems to have died out after this.[14]

Not all paupers were this lucky; another payment in kind was for all aspects of death. There were no undertakers and it was general practice for the villagers themselves to see to the preparation of the body. Village women 'sat up' with the dying and then washed and laid them out. Special clothes or items were bought, including 'cap and muffler 1s', 'cap and wool 2s' and a 'burying suite 7s 6d'. Coffins were made by the village carpenter, Peter Goldsmith, who charged 7s in the 1740s. By 1818 the price of a coffin had risen to £1. Burial fees for the minister and the clerk were 2s 6d per burial from 1730 to 1780 and had risen to 4s in 1819. Mrs Lake, the licensee of the White Horse on Pirton's Great Green, provided the beer at the funeral at 3d a quart and Mrs Walker was paid for bread and cheese. A poignant entry shows that Thomas Abbiss the sexton was paid 4d 'for briaring the grave of wife Conquest'. If the pauper had not left a will the overseers arranged for an affidavit to ensure that the dying person's last wishes were carried out. Moreover, the overseers also paid for Pirton people who were living elsewhere to be brought home to be buried. In March 1802 an entry in the overseers' accounts was made for 'fetching John Cordall's wife from Hitchin to be buried 3s' and a month later John himself, described in the parish register as a pauper, was bought back for burial and the overseers 'paid at Hitchin for ringing the knell for John Cordal 2s'. It was the custom to toll the passing bell when a death occurred, in the sequence of three lots of three chimes for a man, two lots of three for a woman, and one lot of three for a child.

At the opposite end of the age spectrum, children posed the threat of becoming a long-term cost to ratepayers. The 1601 Act had laid down two specific policies with regard to children. First, if parents could not support them overseers had to set them to work so that they could contribute to their own maintenance. Second, they were to be indentured as apprentices so that they could learn a skill and not be dependent on the parish. In Pirton there are records of children being paid to work, but it is not clear what they are doing. There are only two instances of apprentices in the accounts, one dated 1734 and the other 1762. A charity established in the mid-seventeenth century by John Hammond to fund apprenticeships may be one reason why few children relied on the parish directly.

Orphans were boarded out with villagers and their foster parents were paid a regular allowance. This happened to the Hunt children in the mid-eighteenth century. In 1731 Thomas Hunt was buried by the parish and then his widow was given a pension of between 1s and 2s a week until she too was given a pauper's burial ten years later. Their son George and his wife Ann also received relief until spring 1747, when two of their girls died.

By December of that year Ann Hunt was being nursed during her lying-in. The records show that her husband died and was buried on Christmas Day. The overseers helped Ann during the winter months by providing wood for cooking and heating, together with bread, cheese and beer for the family and clothes and shoes for the children. Another tragedy took place in May 1747 when 5-month-old Thomas was buried. Two years later the children, Elizabeth, Ann and George, were boarded with Charles Halfpenny at 2s a week. Charles had previously had his board paid from the poor rates, but now he was a married man of 38 with a wife and child. The Hunt children continued to board for six years. What happened next is not clear, but Ann was buried in 1760 and George three years later.

Illegitimate children, as we have seen earlier in the chapter, proved a particularly thorny issue for the administrators of the poor law. Fathers of illegitimate children had to reimburse the parish for the child's maintenance. Denials of paternity led to appeals and further legal expenses, for which the ratepayers had to pay. The cases were heard at the Quarter Sessions in Hitchin, which involved an expense. The Pirton overseers had different ways of collecting money. Local men tended to pay weekly and those from further afield in a lump sum. In 1823 William Worseley paid 18d a week for 20 weeks for Judith Pitts' child, but it cost the overseers 12s 'for having Judith Pitts to Hitchin and warrants'. Judith Pitts junior had three illegitimate children, as the parish register notes, by 'three different fathers'. Jemima Miles had two illegitimate children, Charlotte (in 1826) and James (in 1830), by two different men, who were described as a farmer from Redbourn and a servant from Lambeth. She received between 4s and 8s a week for a month from the overseer for Charlotte. Her two sisters also had illegitimate children.[15] Jemima, a straw-plaiter, married Richard Street in 1832 and they had two more children. In 1834 Richard was transported to Tasmania for 14 years for stealing pigeons. Seven years later Jemima was known as Jemima Abbiss and was living with her four children in West Lane.[16] She was head of the household and there is no record of Mr Abbiss. A year later she set sail for Tasmania with three of her four children to join her husband, who had been given his 'ticket' of leave. The family never returned to England. Of course, where no father was identified the child posed a significant potential burden to the ongoing finances of the poor law. In such cases apprenticeship was an option and the Pirton overseers often seem to have engaged in informal arrangements with local farmers, even for very young children, so as to remove the liability from the parish.

It is possible to argue that the arrangements described thus far in this chapter provided a workable system for the relief of the so-called deserving poor – for example, the aged, the sick, orphans and one-parent families. However, the 1601 Act also required that the able-bodied poor should be supported by the parish as this was an important part of the overall system. It was always going to be difficult for the overseers to find non-agricultural work for unskilled men in a parish such as Pirton, largely dependent on agriculture. For a start, it was hard to identify and classify the able-bodied poor. During the greater part of the period being considered able-bodied poor was essentially a short-term condition and often seasonal, though there were some exceptions, such as William Nicholls senior, who was 'on the books' for 43 years.

By the beginning of the nineteenth century, however, the burden on ratepayers had become much greater. The unemployed able-bodied were usually offered outdoor relief or a place in the workhouse. It was cheaper to offer outdoor relief, especially if the applicant had a large family. The overseer's duty was to set the poor to work and if the able-bodied could contribute to their own support by carrying out even a little work it was judged that this was better than doing nothing. Examples of temporary relief found for the able-bodied unemployed poor in Pirton included catching sparrows and moles, stone-picking and ditching. Another task that overseers found for the under- or unemployed was road-mending. The work was seasonal: baskets of stones were collected by individuals during the winter and the same gangs were 'pocking in the highways' in May. Men, women and children were all involved in this arduous work; baskets were bought by the overseers and workers were paid 1s a load. The entries suggest that it took a week to collect one load.[17] Wages for the road gangs fluctuated. In 1754 they earned 8d a day, but this had decreased to 2d a day 30 years later. Initially labourers were paid individually, but by the early 1780s groups of stone pickers were organised by the workhouse master or a local farmer and, working together, picked about 100 loads a year. As this process suggests, one option for dealing with the able-bodied poor was the use of the workhouse and it is to this iconic feature of the poor law that we now turn.

Relief in the workhouse

The Poor Law Act of 1601 stated that there was a need for 'necessary places of habitation for poor impotent people'. At first, the general trend was for

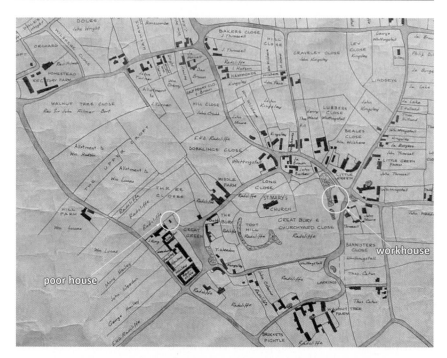

Figure 8.3 Pre-enclosure plan of Pirton, *c.*1811, showing the poor house on Great Green and the workhouse on Little Green, next to Blacksmiths Pond. © Pirton Local History Group.

parish administrators to try to make relatives care for the poor, or at least pay for their maintenance. Only those without relatives were cared for by the parish. A later 1722/23 Act empowered parishes to build workhouses or to contract paupers out to private institutions on a discretionary basis, as others have pointed out in this volume.

In Pirton there seem to have been two houses owned by the parish for accommodating the poor – what was called the Town House and, after 1769, a workhouse. Whether they were used concurrently is not clear from parish records, but the former was still referred to as the Town House in the Parliamentary Enclosure Award of 1811. A pre-enclosure map of 1811 shows that the Town House was in the north-west corner of Great Green, on the common land (Figure 8.3). It is mentioned on the award as being 'a town or poor house, a house with a garden of 5 perches'. It must have been demolished some time after this date. The first mention of it is in the records of 1734: 'one day's work altering the Town House for Widow Rollings'. Her husband had just died and she had three children aged 8, 4

Figure 8.4 Pirton's former workhouse as it looks today. © Chris Ryan.

and 1; perhaps she had no choice but to move into the house because they had been in a tied cottage. However, Widows Gravestock and Dearmer were 'moved' two years earlier in September 1732, possibly to the Town House, as rent was being paid for them before that. The Town House was in existence before this date and possibly as a result of the 1723 Act.

There are notes in the accounts of repair work being carried out on the Town House up until 1758, when references begin to be made to the 'workhouse'. Repairs were made in 1746, with George Lyle being paid 10s 6d for '400 bricks 18 parlins and 3 bushels of lime', and again in 1754: 'Paid to Samuel Circuit for seven ft. and a half of new glass for the Town House 4s 3d'.

In the 1760s more people were moved to the workhouse than ever before. This increase in paupers may explain the need for a new workhouse and in 1769 a barn on Little Green was converted into the new workhouse and an extension was added on the side (Figure 8.4). The records note that the carpenter Peter Goldsmith was paid £21 for building a workhouse and William Hill was paid £1 5s 7d for thatching it. Peter Goldsmith also built a 'necessary house' or lavatory a month later. The accommodation consisted of a dwelling house, a room next to the dwelling house, a room over the dwelling house, a further house and Jonas Goodwin's house.[18] It seems as if the workhouse was divided into three dwellings and a later census shows this to be the case. In 1776–7 a parliamentary survey of poor-relief expenditure in England and Wales revealed that Pirton had one workhouse with places for 40 inmates.[19]

An inventory of 1796, which included the possessions of the paupers themselves (see Appendix, p. 199), suggests that the workhouse provided one room for living and eating and four rooms for sleeping. Living in the house seems to have been a temporary rather than a permanent measure, but when paupers moved in they brought their goods and chattels with them. Widow Arnold's inventory, taken on her entry into the house, read:

> The eimatri [inventory] of wido arnold
> One bras pot and tin cetel
> One bedsted and cirtings
> One flock and straw three blankets
> Tow old sacks and pilo
> One gound tow pectcots [petticoats] one pare of stays
> One clok and hat one table chair
> One cofer and box pothoke and belos
> One shet tow shifts three trenchers
> One candelstek one cinmil
> Tow cups tow hanketers [hankerchiefs]

The appendix also shows that inventories carried lists of occupants. In 1796 there were 16 paupers: 8 adults, including 2 old widows, 3 old men and 3 mothers, the latter's 6 children and 2 sisters, Margaret and Mary Primmet, aged 8 and 11. They received a total of 15s a week between them and presumably had to pay for everything out of this allowance. A small garden may have been used to grow some of their own food.

Between 1766 and 1796 a person with the title of workhouse master seems to have been given a contract for maintaining the inmates. Before this all people receiving weekly relief were referred to as pensioners, with no distinction made between indoor and outdoor relief. Masters were given a lump sum quarterly to look after the daily needs of the poor in the house. These masters did not live in the workhouse and also had another occupation. They appear to have been from the labouring classes and took on this work as an extra source of income. John Cowland, the first workhouse master, was given £84 a year. He continued as master for nine years, although on the militia list he was called a farmer and labourer during this period. The amount he was given to carry out his task rose to £105 five years later. In contrast, most masters did the job for about three years. Their occupations are also given in militia lists as farmer or labourer, or in one case victualler.[20] Richard Smith was master from 1781 to 1787. He was a farm servant until his marriage to Sarah Primmet in 1766 and then he was initially described as a labourer. Seven years later, when he had four children, he was described as 'poor'. His circumstances must have changed because by 1778 he was a farmer and then workhouse master. He was not a rich man at his death, however: his wife received one guinea from the overseers to help bury him. After 1796 the role of master seems to come to an end and the paupers were given a weekly sum to maintain themselves. This sort of detailed prosopography of workhouse masters and staff is largely missing from the existing historiographical literature.

There is only one year – 1758 – when food for the workhouse was recorded. This was before the role of workhouse master was introduced. The occupants seem to have enjoyed a fairly good diet, especially if they were growing their own vegetables. Throughout 1758 Edmund Simpkins the butcher supplied between two and six stone of meat every week – beef at 3d a pound and pork at 7d a pound. The total bill for meat for the year was £13 7s. Overseers were paying for up to nine stone of beef at a time. It is not clear how it was stored or who the meat was intended for. Cheese was 3d a pound, with 15lbs being ordered at a time from Mr Turner. A total of £3 6s 8d was spent on cheese during the year. Flour was a guinea a sack, or 5s a bushel; presumably this was for breadmaking, as '6 faggots and straw to heat the oven' were also delivered. At the beginning of the year a quern was purchased for the workhouse and there is one account of five loads of wheat being delivered at £1 a load. The paupers seem to have been brewing their own beer, as malt, barley, hops and yeast were also bought.

As is usual for the Old Poor Law, there are no records of whether inmates worked in the workhouse, but for three years from 1774 Francis Arnold was paid £1 10s so that his barn could be used by the workhouse poor. It is possible that it was used as a workroom for plaiting or spinning, as a spinning wheel is found in the two surviving inventories. In 1796 Mrs Kingsley taught the 'Smith girl to plait' and five years later Ann Smith taught the Wright children, who were in the workhouse. From 1802 straw was delivered to the workhouse and it is possible that some inmates were engaged in plaiting. Such deliveries continued until March 1829, although no people are recorded as living in the house after 1820. It is possible that the activity simply provided a small supplementary income for any outpensioners.

The number of occupants in the house fluctuated as residents came and went. There are seasonal variations, with the availability of work during the summer reducing numbers needing relief, and a slight increase in residents and outpensioners during the winter. Between 1796 and 1809 the total amount paid to outpensioners was twice that given to those in the house. In April 1802, when the two classes are individually listed, there were 16 outpensioners (of whom half were widows) and 7 indoor paupers. Between 1809 and 1818 the amounts paid to the two groups were about the same, at £110 each, but by April 1820 all payments to indoor paupers had ceased. At that time there were 27 named outpensioners, 7 of whom were widows, 17 men, 2 younger women and 1 a single mother. Payment to outpensioners continued until the end of the records in the accounts, but the abrupt end to Pirton's engagement with the workhouse, in stark contrast to the increasing use of the institution in other communities, perhaps tells us something about the nature of the poor law in its dying years.

Conclusion

National returns of Poor Law expenditure in 1802/03 show that expenditure had doubled over the previous 20 years and that one in nine of the population was receiving some sort of relief, mainly outdoors.[21] Pirton follows this trend closely. By 1804 average wages for farm labourers in Hertfordshire were around 8s per week in summer and 6s in winter,[22] but their purchasing power had decreased. Agricultural labourers, the dominant occupational group in the area, continued to be the worst paid, worst fed and worst housed of all working communities.[23]

From the early nineteenth century it must have been obvious to Pirton ratepayers that the Old Poor Law was failing to provide work for the poor. It was much easier for the overseers to hand out relief rather than arrange for the finding and supervision of parish work for gangs of men. The 1832 Poor Rate Returns noted that, of all the money spent on relieving the poor in England and Wales, only one-twentieth was spent on paying for work, even taking into account work on the roads and in the workhouse.[24] Pirton was no exception. By the 1780s officials had adopted the roundsman system throughout the slack winter months. The able-bodied unemployed circulated round the employers of the parish to do whatever work they could find, with employers paying a proportion of the wage agreed while the remaining portion was paid by the overseers on a scale from 1s to 3s a week. Able-bodied men who at one time would have asked for relief only when they were sick now became regular recipients of relief. By 1821 the overseers' account book shows that throughout the year – except at harvest time – the wages of between 7 and 18 men were being supplemented by between 2d to 4d a day. In 1831 the total cost of one week of relief in the winter was £10 14s 10d. The outpensioners cost £3 7s 6d and the rest £7 7s 4d. Supplementing the wages of the able-bodied cost £4 18s 4d. This amount of relief compares with the much lower level in a similar week in 1795 of £1 19s 6d and in 1731 of £1 4s.[25]

It has been claimed by Dunkley and Boyer that it was the under-employed male, and men overburdened with large families in particular, who came to dominate the relief lists after 1790.[26] Possibly as a result of growing poverty the overseers of Pirton introduced an allowance for families with more than three children in 1800. This was paid to families whether they were in employment or not. It was agreed 'To allow to every person having one child 6d per week and for every child above one, 9d per head to nine years of age. All trades men exempt but Francis Crouch and Henry Walker jun.' The allowances were a temporary solution and the arrangement ran for a year. It was restarted in December 1816, after which it lasted until March 1818, and was paid to 15 families. This second allowance was for '6d per head for those families that have got three children or more under twelve years of age'. One family in the village had seven children, but three or four children were more normal. It was thought at the time that the arrangement led to early marriages, large families and higher claims for relief.[27] The child allowance added around £1 4s to the overseer's weekly bill.

Against this backdrop it is perhaps unsurprising that welfare historians have come to talk about a crisis of the Old Poor Law between the 1790s and 1830s, in which an ever more vocal and insistent cohort of the dependent poor lost their legitimacy in the eyes of an ever more burdened ratepaying group. In Pirton paupers could certainly challenge authority, as did John Wright and his wife, who, it is recorded in the accounts of John Kingsley:

> came to me [17 June 1809] for relief on account of being very
> ill and I relief im of 5 shillings and on the 19th [he] set off to
> the Hay Cuntry and [he] sent is whife up to me for 7 shillings

more saying that if I did no relief her he would go before Mr
Whitbread [a local JP].

These threats to bring in the justices are familiar from the work of Peter
King.[28] And yet there is also a competing reading of the evidence, one in
which the parochial authorities went to great lengths to treat the sick and
aged poor with dignity, to ensure decent burials and to pay for food and
medical treatment which may have been somewhat in advance of that
which the independent labouring classes could themselves have obtained.
Long-term commitment to a parochial workhouse also seems to have
meant a commitment to care rather than discipline, and consideration
of the detailed contours of outdoor relief clearly testifies to a group of
officials who carefully calibrated their resources to the micro-needs of
their parishioners. This was not enough to prevent the development of
inter-generational poverty and, in the case of the mothers of illegitimate
children, was not always done with the best of sentiments. Yet, at the very
time that others have seen a crisis of sentiment, this rapidly growing open
village, potentially representative of so many in eastern and midland
England, seems to have simply tried to do its best.

Appendix

An inventory of the household goods and the linnen & wearing apparel belonging to the paupers in Pirton workhouse taken & appraised April ye 13th 1796 by order of Mr Handscombe overseer

Room over the Dwelling House

A corded bedstead & straw bed
Flock bed bolster one pillow
A blanket a coverlid & 2 sheets
A bedstead and straw mat
A straw bed a flock bed & 2 bolsters
A blanket a coverlid
One new sheet one old sheet
A cofer & some old tools
Sundry pieces of old bedsteads
A corded bedstead as before
Two flock beds one bolster
A blanket a coverlid
One old one new sheet
A corded bedstead &mat
Straw bed & flock bolster
Two blankets
Two sheets
John Wrights box with rags in it
One old cofer a lace pillow
Six sheets off ye beds
Judy Goldsmiths box in a trunk a bacco
box little drawers & a fork a chaff knife
old sack

Dwelling House

Two pot hooks 2 pairs of bellows
Three pair of old tongs
A long table & 4 small tables
One large cofer two lesser cofers
Seven old chairs two childrens chairs
Two small stools one reel
Ten wooden dishes six spoons
Eleven trenchers a bowl & two ladles
Nine iron candlesticks
Seven earthen platers a few cups &
saucers & basins
Three black pitchers
A washing tray a spade
A few knives & forks & 4 pieces of
tinware
A large brass pottage pot & cover
A bell mettal bell two tin kettles

Wearing Apparel

12 shirts & shifts great & small
Four childrens frocks 2 pin cloths 2
aprons
Two gowns two petticoats

Three cloaks four bonnets 4 hats
Six handkerchiefs
Twelve caps various sizes
Three childrens petticoats
Eleven pair of stockings great & small

Room next the dwelling house below

Corded bedstead a straw bed
An old feather bed two flock bolsters
Two blankets &two coverlids
Two old bedsteads not put up
A bag with old feathers
An old table three pieces of spinning wheels
A wooden rake a lye latch one old chair

Further house

A corded bedstead
A feather bed & bolster
A blanket a coverlid
Two sheets
A small feather bed
A cofer a stool & 2 small tubs
Two small tables
Six chairs a linnen wheel
A cupboard 2 pair of bellows
A pot hook & tongs
A pick axe
Three wooden dishes & some earthen cups & two tin kettles

A frying pan a skillet a pottage pot

Jonas Goodwins House

A bedstead a small feather bed & bolster
A blanket a rug a table a chair
A small cofer a pothook tongs & bellows
Two old sheets
A spade a mattock

List of Paupers

Jonas Goodwin
William Nicholas
Catherine Nicholas
A cloak a hat
A shirt & shift
3 aprons 3 caps 3 handcherchiefs
A bed gown & 2 pair of stockings
Old coat & shirt belonging to Jonas Goodwin
Judy Goldsmith
Two children
Mary Hudson & one child
Mary Wright her three children
John Wright
Mary & Margaret Primmet
Alice Campkin with her bedstead bedding & 2 sheets
2 new shirts a pair of new shoes and a good petticoat

The whole valued by S Eames at £16 18s 0d

Notes

1. For examples of micro-studies see S. Hindle, *On the parish? The micro-politics of poor relief in rural England c.1550–1750* (Oxford, 2004) and S. Williams, *Poverty, gender and life-cycle under the English Poor Law 1760–1834* (Woodbridge, 2011).

2. The Excel spreadsheets used during the preparation of this chapter can be accessed by contacting the webmaster at enquiries@pirtonhistory.org.uk. Further information about the research being undertaken by the Pirton Local History Group can be found on the website www.pirtonhistory.org.uk. This website also has a database that allows users to search for information about the people of Pirton.

3. Hertfordshire Archives and Local Studies, Hertford (hereafter HALS) DP/80/11/1–4 Overseers' Account Books.

4. L. Munby, *Hertfordshire population statistics 1563–1801* (Hitchin, 1964).

5. HALS 1841 Census Folio 1–2 District 14 Piece HO107445.

6. E. Wallace, *Children of the labouring poor: the working lives of children in nineteenth-century Hertfordshire* (Hatfield, 2010), p. 55.

7. Hansard, Debate on labourers' wages, 25 March 1824 Series 2 Vol 10 cc1413–1415.

8. HALS 61351 Letter from John Woolston overseer for Pirton 1824 replying to government commission into labourer's wages.

9. C. Emsley, *Crime and society in England 1750–1900* (London, 1987), pp. 27–9.

10. The overseers' account books records payments such as that of April 1750 'pd £2 8s for going processioning'. This refers to the refreshments bought for the perambulating of the bounds at Rogation tide.

11. See A.J. Gritt, 'The census and the servant: a reassessment of the decline and distribution of farm service in early nineteenth-century England', *Economic History Review*, 53 (2000), pp. 84–106.

12. On doctoring contracts see S. Williams, 'Practitioners' income and provision for the poor: parish doctors in the late eighteenth and early nineteenth centuries, *Social History of Medicine*, 18 (2005), pp. 159–86.

13. On nursing see S. Williams, 'Caring for the sick poor: poor law nurses in Bedfordshire, c. 1770–1834', in P. Lane *et al.* (eds), *Women, work and wages, c.1650–1900* (Woodbridge, 2004), pp. 123–43.

14. On smallpox inoculation see S. King, *Poverty and welfare in England 1700–1850: a regional perspective* (Manchester, 2000), pp. 126–39.

15. For bastardy-prone sub-societies of this sort see S. King, 'The bastardy prone sub-society again: bastards and their fathers and mothers in Lancashire, Wiltshire and Somerset, 1800–1840', in A. Levene *et al.* (eds), *Illegitimacy in Britain, 1700–1920* (Basingstoke, 2005), pp. 66–85.

16. HALS 1841 census Folio 1–2 District 14 Piece HO107445.

17. 80 two-gallon buckets made one load.

18. HALS DP/80/18/1 Inventory 1796. For other work on the structure and visual representation of workhouses see K. Morrison, *The workhouse: a study of poor law buildings in England* (Swindon, 1999).

19. *An abstract of returns of the overseers of the poor 1777*, www.workhouses.org.uk.

20. HALS DP/80/17/1 Militia lists.

21. M. Rose, *The English Poor Law, 1780–1930* (Newton Abbot, 1971), p. 39.

22. A. Young, *General view of the agriculture of Hertfordshire 1804* (Newton Abbot, 1971), p. 217.

23. J.L. and B. Hammond, *The village labourer 1760–1832* (London, 1911), p. 226.

24. *Copy of the Report Made in 1834 by the Commissioners for Inquiring into the Administration and Practical Operation of the Poor Laws Presented by both Houses of Parliament by Command of His Majesty.*

25. On these labour systems see G. Boyer, *An economic history of the English poor law, 1750–1850* (Cambridge, 1990).

26. S. Williams 'Malthus, marriage and poor law allowances revisited: a Bedfordshire case study, 1770–1834', *Agricultural History Review*, 52 (2004), p. 66.

27. *Copy of the Report Made in 1834 by the Commissioners.*

28. See P. King, 'The summary courts and social relations in eighteenth-century England', *Past and Present*, 183 (2004), pp. 124–72.

A note on the history of the London Foundling Hospital

Jennifer Sherwood

THE LONDON FOUNDLING Hospital was one of the world's first incorporated charities. Established for the 'Maintenance and Education of Exposed and Deserted Young Children', it was set up in 1739 by Royal Charter, granted by George II, after 17 years of tireless campaigning by Captain Thomas Coram, a retired sea captain, who, distressed by the sight of abandoned children on London's streets, sought to remedy the situation.[1] The Hospital was first established in Hatton Garden, but soon a new site of 56 acres in Lamb's Conduit Fields, owned by the earl of Salisbury, was chosen. A building large enough to house 400 children was envisaged and a design by Theodore Jacobsen, who gave his services free of charge, was selected. The building generally reflected the purpose for which it was built and the needs of its children. The overall effect was one of simplicity and utility and the only areas with any decoration were administration and public rooms, the Court Room, Committee Room and the Picture Gallery. Only the Court Room, which was used for Board meetings and official functions, had really profuse decoration, with an elaborate ceiling designed by William Wilton.

From the very beginning art and music played an important part in the life of the Hospital. At the instigation of William Hogarth the walls of the Court Room and other public rooms were adorned with works by English painters and sculptors. In April 1747 there was a public opening of the works of art. The annual exhibitions at the Hospital, which followed, led later to the foundation of the Royal Academy. Hogarth, a founding governor, donated his painting of Coram to the Hospital, designed the Seal of Corporation (which depicted the finding of Moses in the bulrushes by Pharoah's daughter), the coat-of-arms (showing a lamb with a sprig of thyme in its mouth, which was to become the symbol of the Hospital[2]) and also the uniforms for the children.

Although the Chapel was not used for regular services until April 1753 it had been used for benefit concerts since 1749, when, for the first concert, Handel 'generously and charitably offered a performance of vocal and instrumental musick', the proceeds of which were to be used to complete the Chapel. In 1750 Handel became a governor and gave the Foundling Hospital an organ for use in the chapel. On his death he bequeathed the Hospital a 'fair copy of the score and all parts of his oratorio call'd the Messiah'. It became fashionable to attend services at the Foundling Hospital to enjoy music, look at paintings and survey orphans.[3]

The original policy of the governors, set out in an Act of Parliament of 1740, was to take in 'as many children as they shall think fit'. The overwhelming numbers of children applying to the Hospital led to the introduction of a balloting system by coloured balls. This policy was in its turn suspended when Parliament granted the Hospital £10,000 on condition that the Foundling Hospital accepted all children offered to it. This situation led to the establishment of regional hospitals to cope with the high number of children. After 1760 balloting combined with individual assessment was reintroduced.

By 1795 the dual purpose of the Foundling Hospital had become explicit: 'The Foundling Hospital has two objects, to preserve and educate infants otherwise exposed to perish, and to restore the mothers to a course of Industry and Virtue ... to the benefit of the child and the parent.' In 1801 the governors passed a resolution stating that the 'principal object of the Hospital is the maintenance and support of illegitimate children'. Orphaned children of soldiers or sailors were the only exception to this rule.

In the early days of the Foundling Hospital the education was very much craft orientated. The girls went into domestic service and the boys were apprenticed. In the later years some girls became teachers and many boys joined regimental or naval bands, carrying on the musical tradition of the Hospital. From the earliest days children were fostered in the country as infants until the age of 5, when they entered the Hospital. Hertfordshire, with its close proximity to London, received its share of foundling children (see Chapter 9, p. 211). Although the chief source of evidence of the names of supervisors and wet nurses in the countryside is to be found in the Foundling Hospital archives, housed in the Metropolitan Archives,[4] additional confirmatory information can be obtained by perusing local burial registers[5] and other local evidence. In local studies it becomes obvious that the supervisors of the wet nurses came largely out of the aristocracy,[6] upper middle classes or clerical classes. Rectors and rectors' wives figure large among their numbers, as David Allin and Yvonne Tomlinson show in their chapters for this volume.

A letter sent by Mrs Jeffries,[7] wife of the Rector of Berkhamsted St Peter, to the Secretary of the Foundling Hospital tells us something of the life of the foundlings in the countryside:

> Sir, – I intend sending Mary Johnson up to the Hospital next
> Thursday by the Waggon. I have today had information of her
> having got the Itch. I therefore give you notice of her coming that
> care may be taken of her. The girl takes on sadly at leaving her
> Nurse,[8] that I hope she will be us'd with tenderness, tho' she has
> that disagreeable distemper. I have inclosed patterns of the Lace[9]
> the Children make, there is no other employment for them at this
> place, the Nurses teach them to Read and say their Catechism, but
> most of them are backward in Reading, and it cannot be expected
> that common Nurses are capable of teaching them well.

By the early part of the nineteenth century the Foundling Hospital had reached a settled order of internal economy and administration, only departing from the model to keep up with 'progress'.[10] Alterations were made with the aim of providing better accommodation, improving the health and conditions of the children and paying more attention to their future careers. A new infirmary was established, an improved diet was introduced and there was increased interest in the welfare of the apprentices. The age of apprenticeship was raised and a library was established for older children. The idea of summer camps was introduced in 1892, although it was not until 1931 that the camp near Folkestone was purchased. The isolation of the children from the outside world did not, however, lessen and the stigma of illegitimacy remained as strong as ever.[11] Nevertheless, the benefit to the children of a month in the country away from London during the summer camp was obvious. This, coupled with the improved railway system in and out of London, led the Foundling Hospital to consider moving away from the metropolis (see Chapter 11).

Notes

1. R.K. McClure, *Coram's children: the London Foundling Hospital in the eighteenth century* (London and New Haven, CT, 1981); R.H. Nichols and F.A. Wray, *The history of the Foundling Hospital* (London, 1935), p. 13; R. Harris, *Enlightened self-interest* (London, 1997).

2. Symbolising courage and purification.

3. McClure, *Coram's children*, pp. 71–2.

4. For example, London Metropolitan Archive (hereafter LMA) A/FH/A/09/005/001/1.

5. See A. Kaloczi, 'The St Albans Foundling Hospital babies, 1756–1760', *Herts Past and Present*, 3rd series 4 (2004), pp. 3–7.

6. Letter, 3 May 1787, from Countess of Marchmont to Matron of Foundling Hospital requesting 'that Mrs Jones send cloaths by Windmills Waggon as usual' for five foundlings ranging in age from three to five years. See Dacorum Heritage Trust Museum Store (hereafter DACHT) 1490.

7. John Jeffries, rector of St Peter's Berkhamsted, 1756–98.

8. Evidence of fondness for foster parents can be found throughout the time of the Foundling Hospital: A. Levene, *Childcare, health and mortality at the London Foundling Hospital, 1741–1800: 'left to the mercy of the world'* (Manchester, 2007), p. 204; G. Aspey, *All at sea: memories of a Coram boy* (Emsworth, 2010).

9. Lace-making was the main cottage industry in eighteenth-century Berkhamsted.

10. Nichols and Wray, *History*.

11. McClure, *Coram's children*.

CHAPTER NINE

Foundling Hospital children at nurse in Hertfordshire in the eighteenth century

David Allin

THE FOUNDLING HOSPITAL (Figure 9.1) received a Royal Charter from George II on 17 October 1739, thanks largely to the dogged determination of Thomas Coram, a shipwright and semi-retired merchant who had campaigned for such an institution for over 17 years (Figure 9.2). He had been shocked at finding babies abandoned on the streets of London, some of whom were dead, others dying. Foundlings were taken in as babies (at first they had to be no older than two months, later the age limit was raised) to the hospital's headquarters in London. In order to encourage mothers to hand over children instead of abandoning them in the streets no questions were asked and the children were given new names. These infants were then sent to nurses (foster mothers) in the country, who were supervised by unpaid inspectors. In the first few years the children were usually kept at nurse until they were about 3 years old, but after a while it was decided it would be better for them to stay in the country until they were 4 or 5. The foundlings were then returned as 'grown children', either to the London hospital or to one of the six branch hospitals (Ackworth, Shrewsbury, Aylesbury, Westerham, Barnet and Chester) established between 1757 and 1763. These were not hospitals in our sense, but institutions similar to orphanages in which the children were brought up. In fact, the Shrewsbury Hospital was always called the Orphan Hospital. The children were then apprenticed, normally at the age

Figure 9.1 A view of the Foundling Hospital, London. Engraving by B. Cole for *A Survey of the Cities of London and Westminster and the Borough of Southwark* by John Stow (1754). From 1745 all the foundlings had to be taken to this building in Bloomsbury before they could be accepted.

of 10, 11, 12 or 13, the boys until they were 24 (lowered to 21 in 1767) and the girls until they were 21 or married.

In recent years the Foundling Hospital has attracted considerable academic attention. Alysa Levene, for instance, has undertaken detailed work on the life-chances of foundlings, while Samantha Williams has analysed the rhetoric in petitions made by mothers for the admission of their children.[1] The tokens that sometimes accompanied abandoned children, and which have been retained in the archives, have similarly been subject to detailed scrutiny and an exhibition.[2] My book deals with the early years of the Foundling Hospital and builds on the work of Ruth McClure, though, unlike Mrs McClure's book, it deals with the branch hospitals as well as the London hospital.[3] Yet a considerable amount remains to be done. While much is known about the hospital itself, its admissions policy and even the numbers of children involved, the ways in which country nurses were found, the experiences of children in the provinces and the nature of the inspection regime are much less well documented, except in the case of Berkshire, thanks to Dr Gillian Clark's excellent edition of the correspondence of the Foundling Hospital inspectors in that county.[4]

The current chapter deals with these matters, drawing on the particular experiences of Hertfordshire. It uses the Foundling Hospital's extensive records in the London Metropolitan Archives, especially the Disposal

Figure 9.2 Portrait of Captain Thomas Coram, 1751. The original painting by Balthasar Nebot is dated 1741, the year in which the first babies were accepted to the Foundling Hospital. © Foundling Museum.

Books,[5] which record the names of the children sent to the country in chronological order as well as the places and the names of their nurses and inspectors; the Inspection Books,[6] which list the children sent to the various inspections with the names of their nurses and inspectors, the deaths at nurse and the dates when a child that survived was returned to London or to one of the branch hospitals; the letters sent by inspectors to the Foundling Hospital;[7] and the letters from the Secretary Thomas Collingwood to inspectors.[8] Other sources used include the General Registers,[9] the Accounts Audited (1741–87),[10] the State of the Children Quarterly and then Annually[11] and the minutes of the General Committee[12] and the Sub-Committee.[13]

Hertfordshire as a destination

In the initial years after its foundation (1741–56) the hospital accepted 1,384 children.[14] Its activities were, however, hampered by reliance on funding from legacies, donations and subscriptions. Thus, although the substantial sum of £115,489 had been raised by the end of 1755,[15] the charity never had enough money to take in all the children brought to the London headquarters. For every child accepted, three or four had to be rejected. The governors therefore appealed to Parliament for help and statutory funding was agreed provided the hospital took in *all* the children brought to it under the age to be specified by the governors.[16] This was the period of 'General Reception', which lasted from June 1756 to March 1760.

Parliament had probably expected a three- or four-fold increase in the number taken in each year. In fact, 14,934 'parliamentary children' (as they were sometimes called) were accepted during the three years and ten months during which this policy of indiscriminate admission was followed – more than forty times the number taken in per month in the previous period.[17] One surely unexpected result was that large numbers now came from outside London. In fact, they probably comprised almost half of the 'parliamentary' children accepted.[18] In turn, the governors soon realised that it would be impossible to house all the 'parliamentary children' that survived their time at nurse in the hospital in London, leading to the establishment of six branch hospitals.

The more urgent task, however, was finding enough country nurses and enough inspectors to supervise them. Over *nine times* as many children were sent to nurse in this period than before the General Reception (12,464: 1,326; see Table 9.1).[19]

Table 9.1   Number of children at nurse in the country at selected dates.

Date	No. children
31 Dec 1756	1,463
24 June 1757	2,386
29 Sept 1759	5,549
31 Dec 1762	4,375
31 Dec 1765	2,458
31 Dec 1767	1,640
31 Dec 1769	241

Note: The great majority were 'parliamentary children'. A very small number had been taken in before the General Reception and rather more after the General Reception.
Source: A/FH/A/09/012/001 and 002 The State of the Children Quarterly and then Annually.

Table 9.2   Comparative county figures.

County	Number of inspections	Number of foundlings
Surrey	39	3089
Middlesex	68	1861
Essex	33	1846
Hertfordshire	27	1210
Berkshire	29	1202
Kent	22	1020

Source: State of the Children Quarterly and then Annually, except for Hertfordshire for which the Books of Inspection have been used. Allin, The early years, Chapter 9.

Table 9.3   The number of 'parliamentary children' sent to Hertfordshire.

Period of reception by the Foundling Hospital	Number sent	Inspectors they were sent to	% of all children sent to country nurses
2 June 1756–31 Dec 1756	42	5	2.7
1 Jan 1757–31 Aug 1757	158	13	7.2
1 Sept 1757–3 April 1758	167	14	6.9
1 May 1758–31 Dec 1758	323	17	14.1
1 Jan 1759–31 Aug 1759	322	18	15.2
1 Sept 1759–25 Mar 1760	198	19	10.8
Total number sent to Hertfordshire 1210			9.7

Notes: Percentages corrected to one place of decimal.
Source: Books of Inspection.

For the first time[20] Hertfordshire played a vital role in looking after the foundlings at nurse. The county was one of only six (see Table 9.2) that took more than 1,000 'parliamentary children' (Table 9.3). The same six counties took almost three-quarters of all the children sent to nurse. More and more children were sent to Hertfordshire. In all it took just under 10 per cent of the 'parliamentary children' and it did so on an increasing trajectory. Between 24 June 1757 and 31 December 1760 there were always more than 100 children at nurse in Hertfordshire and on four dates (see Table 9.4) there were more than 400.

Hertfordshire inspections

There were 27 inspections taking children directly from London during the General Reception.[21] As the number of children sent to Hertfordshire increased, more inspections were set up (see Table 9.5), although some closed before the period of indiscriminate admission ended.

Table 9.4   Number of children at nurse in Hertfordshire at selected dates.

Date	Number	% of all children at nurse
31 Dec 1756	39	2.7
24 June 1757	138	5.8
29 Sept 1759	600	10.8
29 Sept 1760	609	11.0
31 Sept 1761	514	10.4
31 Dec 1762	442	10.1
31 Dec 1763	299	7.8
31 Dec 1764	262	8.2
31 Dec 1766	196	8.0
31 Dec 1767	88	6.5
31 Dec 1768	62	6.4
31 Dec 1769	13	5.4

Source: The State of the Children Quarterly and then Annually.

Table 9.5   The number of inspections in Hertfordshire.

1 July 1756	1
31 Dec 1756	5
31 Dec 1757	13
29 Mar 1759	23

Source: Books of Inspection.

The inspectors in Hertfordshire, like those in other counties, had to recruit the nurses and make sure they were looking after the children properly. They had to pay them (usually once a month) from funds provided by the Foundling Hospital and submit the accounts at least once a year; these were carefully scrutinised. When more clothes were needed they had to write to the Hospital for them. They had to deal with the children's illnesses. For minor ailments they probably just gave advice to the nurses. In more serious cases a local apothecary or surgeon might be called in, although, as we shall see, some of the inspectors were themselves apothecaries or surgeons. Inspectors had to inform the governors in cases of serious diseases, especially measles and smallpox. When a child died the Hospital had to be informed and the inspector had to arrange for the funeral. Children reaching the age to be returned to London left on transport arranged for them by the inspectors. In the case of children sent to the branch hospitals at Ackworth and Shrewsbury, these hospitals sent their 'caravans' (see Chapter 10, Appendix, p. 262–4) to collect them.

Although there were just 27 inspections during the General Reception period, turnover of personnel meant that 36 inspectors were individually responsible for running them. In one case, that of Richard Lloyd's Aston inspection, some of the children were hived off to Thomas Neats. It is not clear whether Lloyd secured the governors' approval for this. John Atkinson (Hatfield) got a Mr Dunne to supervise the children in his inspection, apparently without consulting the governors. In addition to these 36 inspectors a number had deputies who had to take their place if they were ill or away. A Mrs Harris, for example, stood in for Mrs Barker (Abbots Langley),[22] and a Mrs Dean looked after Mrs Johnson's charges[23] at Berkhamsted. Thirteen of the inspectors were women. The Foundling Hospital was the first major charity to give women an official role of considerable importance in what today we would call voluntary social work. This is all the more remarkable in that women were not eligible to become governors.

We can get an idea of the social position of some of the inspectors from Dury and Andrews' map of Hertfordshire of 1766, since it notes 'Noblemen's and Gentlemen's Seats'.[24] Thirteen of the inspectors (see Table 9.6) were either owners of houses shown on the map or were related to the owners. Mrs Cowper's husband William Cowper was MP for Hertford from 1768 until his death on 27 August 1769. Mrs Martha Brassey, who took over the Hertingfordbury inspection from Mrs

Figure 9.3 Portrait of Taylor White, 1758. Pastel by Francis Cotes. White (1701–72) was governor from 1739 until 1772 and held the key post of treasurer (1745–72) during the General Reception and its aftermath, when 1200 children were sent to Hertfordshire. © Foundling Museum.

Cowper, was the widow of Nathaniel Brassey, who had served as MP for Hertford from 1734 to 1761.[25] The home of Miss Mary Arnott (Hertford inspection) is not listed, but she presumably came from the same social class. She was related to Matthew Robert Arnott, Esq. and was acquainted with Mrs Cowper.[26] The home of Mrs Anne Barker (Abbots Langley) is also not shown, but she was probably well off as she spent several months

Table 9.6 Social status of inspectors.

J. A. Bucknall, Esq.	Oxhey Place
George Prescott, Esq.	Cheshunt*
Richard Lloyd, Esq.	Aston
The Hon. Mrs John Robinson Lytton, taking over from John Robinson Lytton, Esq.	Knebworth Place
Mrs Maria Cowper	The Park, Hertingfordbury
Miss Amelia Halsey, taking over from Frederick Halsey, Esq.	Great Gaddesden
Miss C. Jansen, taking over from William Jansen	Cheshunt Nunnery (or Priory)
Mrs Meliora Shaw	Cheshunt House
Mrs Frances Harcourt	Berkhamsted
Mrs Dorothy Gardiner	Thunderidgebury

* It has been assumed this is the George Prescott who ran the Hoddesdon inspection. Hoddesdon is quite near Cheshunt.

at Bath in the winter of 1758/9.[27] Elizabeth Jeffreys, who took over from Mrs Harcourt, was the wife of John Jeffreys, the rector of Berkhamsted.[28] Mrs Prudence West (Barnet) is the subject of Yvonne Tomlinson's chapter in this volume (see p. 234).[29]

Four inspectors were clergymen. One of them, the Revd Thomas Whitehurst (Hitchin inspection), had a fortune of £10,000. He had taken a curacy but this was only for 'the sake of Employment in his Profession'; we do not know whether he was accepted as one of the gentry.[30] Jabez Hirons (St Albans) was a Congregational minister. The Revd Benjamin Preedy (also St Albans) was rector of St Albans Abbey and headmaster of St Albans School. The Revd William Hatfield was the inspector at Lilley.[31] Six of the laymen – Joseph Law (Redbourn), Daniel Van De Wall (Welwyn), P.B. Roberts (Barnet),[32] John Heaviside (Hatfield), William Bayley (Tring) and Henry Churchill, taking over from Thomas Whitehurst (Hitchin) – were apothecaries and/or surgeons.

Table 9.7 provides a summary of Hertfordshire's part in looking after the General Reception children sent to nurse. All the inspections are listed, along with the inspectors, the number of nurses employed in each inspection at one time or another, the number of 'parliamentary children' that passed through each inspection and the number that died at nurse. As some nurses were employed in more than one inspection the number of nurses cannot be calculated by adding up the number of nurses employed in the various inspections.

Table 9.7   A summary of 'parliamentary children' sent to Hertfordshire.

Inspection	Inspector/s	No. of nurses	No. of 'parliamentary children'	% died
Abbots Langley	Mrs Anne Barker	1	10	20.0
Aston	Richard Lloyd, some to Thomas Neats	75	130	58.5
Barnet	Mrs Prudence West	81	138	42.0
Barnet	P.B. Roberts	46	63	63.5
Berkhamsted	William Johnson, then Mrs Letitia Johnson	10	25	64.7
Berkhamsted	Mrs Frances Harcourt, then Mrs Jeffreys	7	17	60.0
Cheshunt	Mrs Meliora Shaw	19	32	33.3
Cheshunt Nunnery	William Jansen & Miss C Jansen	1	2	Nil
Codicote	James Cooper	49	68	45.5
Great Gaddesden	Frederick Halsey, then Miss Amelia Halsey	12	17	52.9
Hatfield	John Heaviside	36	36	50.0
Hatfield	John Atkinson, then Mr Dunne	41	49	71.4
Hemel Hempstead	Mrs Elizabeth Crompton	6	8	37.5
Hertford	Miss Mary Arnott	10	12	50.0
Hertingfordbury	Mrs Maria Cowper, then Mrs Martha Brassey	6	6	33.3
Hitchin	Revd Thomas Whitehurst, then Henry Churchill	32	37	44.4
Hoddesdon	Geo. Prescott, Esq.	4	6	16.7
Knebworth	John Robinson Lytton Esq., then the Hon Mrs J. R. Lytton	94	137	44.9
Lilley	Revd William Hatfield	43	63	52.4
Northaw	Mrs Leman	10	10	80.0
Oxhey	John Arkell Bucknall, Esq.	15	39	71.8
Redbourne	Joseph Law	92	146	47.9
St Albans	Jabez Hirons	46	74	54.0
St Albans	Revd. Benjamin Preedy	25	33	48.5
Thunderidgebury	Mrs Dorothy Gardiner		3	33.3
Tring	William Bayley	6	7	28.6
Welwyn	Daniel Van De Wall	37	40	40.0
			1210	50.2

Source: Books of Inspection.

Table 9.8   Inspectors taking additional children.

Inspection	Foundlings	Parish children*
Barnet (Mrs West)	10	–
Hertingfordbury (Mrs Cowper)	2	8
Lilley (Rev. Mr Hatfield)	1	–
Redbourn (Mr Law)	3	10

*Source: Books of Inspectors.

When an inspection closed those children who were not thought ready to be sent to the London hospital or one of the branch hospitals as 'grown children', because they were either too young or in a poor state of health, were transferred to one or more of the other inspections.[33] In order to avoid double counting, these children have not been added to the number under the new inspection or inspections. Deaths of children have been listed under the original inspection, although some died after being transferred to another. In most cases the same nurses were employed in looking after them. In the case of the Revd Benjamin Preedy's St Albans inspection all the children have been classed as first-destination children, as they seem to have been sent directly to St Albans, even though some had for a time been listed under Mrs Georgiana Spencer's Althorp inspection in Northamptonshire. To do otherwise would mean they were not counted at all.[34] Where two inspections are recorded at the same place they were quite separate from each other. The only inspection listed here where children were sent before the General Reception was that of Mrs Shaw at Cheshunt (three children – not counted here).[35] The only inspection in Hertfordshire established in the eighteenth century after the General Reception was Lady Marchmont's at Hemel Hempstead. She took 89 children from 7 June 1775 to 6 June 1796.[36] Four inspectors (see Table 9.8) who had taken 'parliamentary children' also took children accepted by the Hospital after the General Reception. Of these, 15 were foundlings classed as 'children of the Hospital' and 18 were children sent by London parishes under the terms of Hanway's Act of 1767.

Experiences

Table 9.7 shows that about half the 'parliamentary children' in Hertfordshire died at nurse. This would not have shocked contemporaries. Everybody knew how dangerous the first few years of life were, even for children whose parents were wealthy, and many of the babies handed over to the

Foundling Hospital were in a wretched state of health, as Alysa Levene has
suggested elsewhere.

The inspectors did not always record the cause of death or what they
believed to be the cause of death, sometimes stating merely that the child
had died. In some other cases they stated the child had been ill but not
what the illness was. On 4 November 1759, for example, Mrs Letitia
Johnson (Berkhamsted), in reporting the death of Catherine Gardiner to
Mr Blackbeard, the Foundling Hospital clerk, said only that she had been
ill 'for this year and a half & everything she has had which was thought
to do her good'.[37] In some cases inspectors, when reporting the deaths of
children, stated that they had received the best possible treatment. For
other children the symptoms were described. Thus, on 4 February 1759
Mrs Johnson wrote to Mr Blackbeard

> to inform you of the death of Sarah Chandler, she dy'd the first of
> this Month & Maud Bettison I expect will every day as she is very
> ill,[38] it seems to be one disorder which carrys' em all off .... They all
> break out in perfect sores which fall upon their Lungs or Bowels.[39]

A number of deaths were attributed to fevers, but we do not know their
nature, though worm fever is mentioned in one case. Fits were said to be
the cause of some deaths, while Mr Heaviside (Hatfield) reported several
deaths from gripes and purging. On 5 February 1758, for instance, he
wrote that

> I am sorry to inform you that Wm Baldwin (at first Nurs'd by
> Sarah Albon, & lately by Sarah Greenham) died on the 19th of
> last month & Barth: Stone, nurs'd by Susan Sawyer died on the
> 2nd of this instant, both of gripes & purging; which are indeed
> [the] distemper that has carried off all those that have died under
> [my] care, whether tis owing to the poor living of the Nurses now
> [at] this time of Scarcity, or what other cause I am not able to
> determine; but all that I have been able to do has been ineffectual
> to save these, tho' many others have been ill of the same disorder,
> who have done well.

Two of Mrs West's children also died of watery gripes.[40]

Whooping cough was also common. On 24 September 1759, for

example, Mrs Harcourt (Berkhamsted) reported that two of the children looked after by Mary Trensham had died (Sarah Poultrey and Beatrice Watts), although she had taken the greatest care of them.[41] A few months later she reported the death of Susan Barker from the same disease.[42] There were also deaths from measles. On 2 June 1761 Mrs West reported that 'On my being absent from Home for a few Days I found two children dead at my return [Phoebe Thornton and Ann Role] that had for some time been in a declining state after the measles.'[43]

The disease that caused the most anxiety was smallpox. Ebenezer Ash (Mr Law's inspection) died on 26 October 1761, Edith Ford (Mrs Shaw's inspection) on 25 December 1763 and Elias Carter (the Revd Mr Hatfield's inspection) on 14 July 1764.[44] But some children who caught the disease 'in the natural way' survived, including Judith Rich and William Perkins (Mr Roberts' Barnet inspection).[45] On 14 January 1767, in a letter to Mrs Leicester, the Matron, Mrs Maria Cowper (Hertingfordbury) reported that 'Martha Bright has had the small pox and likewise George Watson, both now in good health.'[46] In turn, the governors were anxious that those children who had not caught the disease 'in the natural way' should be inoculated. Inoculation must have saved the lives of many of the foundlings, though it did not always 'take'. Some children were inoculated while still living in the country. On 15 April 1768, for example, Mrs Cowper sent the following account to Collingwood:

> I have not till this day been able to come to any certainty
> concerning the Inoculation of the Children under my care. It was
> Judg'd necessary, to lodge e'm all together at some House, from the
> Town of Hertford, for fear of communicating the disease to the
> People there. I have at last got a proper place. The woman will let it
> for 5s p. week, but she is not capable to look after the children but
> one of my Foundling Nurses, is entirely so, accordingly I propose
> she will go with them – 8 days or 10 at the farthest, will be the time
> we sh l [shall] have occation to remove them for …[47]

On 24 June she reported that 'John Wm Gray is at present under Inoculation (with five more)'.[48]

The fears of local people sometimes made it difficult to arrange for the children to be inoculated, as the following report of the Revd Mr Hatfield (Lilley) of 16 September 1766 shows:

> I reced a letter this morning from Mr Kirby of Luton to desire a
> list of the children under my Inspection for inoculation. I tho't
> it proper to let you know beforehand, that the several Parishes
> where they are nurs'd are unwilling to receive them again for fear
> of Infection. Mrs Edwards of Arsley was here the Morn to whom
> I show'd the letter, & she will not permit the 2 Children I have in
> that Parish to be return'd either afterwards for the same reason,
> they must be convey'd directly to London from Mr Kirby's. For I
> can't consent to have 'em return'd to their Nurses. The People in
> the neighbourhood are almost as much afraid of the small Pox as
> of the Plague, and it has been so great an Expence to the parishes
> that they will not suffer any Foundlings to remain there.[49]

The governors tried to make sure that the children who had not been
inoculated at nurse were inoculated when they returned to London as
'grown children'.

The effectiveness of inspectors

As one would expect, the lowest death rates were usually in the smallest
inspections. It was easier for an inspector with only a few nurses to keep
a close watch on the way the children were being looked after. Nine of
the inspections where one-third or fewer children died took ten or fewer
children, though the inspection with the highest death rate of all was
Mrs Leman's (Northaw), where eight out of the ten children died. The
governors, though, would not have been able to recruit enough inspectors
if each had looked after only a few children. Even if they *had* been able
to, the administrative problems in dealing with more than 100 inspectors
would have been insuperable.

In the other inspections there was no correlation between the number
of children cared for and death rates. The death rate for Mrs Shaw's
Cheshunt inspection was only 31.2 per cent; for J.A. Bucknall's Oxhey
inspection (not much bigger than Mrs Shaw's) it was 71.4 per cent. An
inspection where most of the children arrived in the last few months of
the General Reception might well have a higher death rate than one where
the majority arrived in the early months, since the percentage who died at
nurse in Hertfordshire rose throughout the period (see Table 9.9). In the
early days, when the numbers sent to Hertfordshire were manageable, it
may have been easier to find good nurses and to supervise them properly.

Table 9.9   Percentage of 'parliamentary children' that died at nurse in Hertfordshire period of reception.

Period	Number	% died
1 Jun 1756–31 Dec 1756	42	28.6
1 Jan 1757–31 Aug 1757	159	44.0
1 Sep 1757–3 Apr 1758	166	45.2
1 May 1758–31 Dec 1758	323	50.2
1 Jan 1759–31 Aug 1759	316	52.2
1 Sep 1759–25 Mar 1760	204	59.0
	1210	50.2

Source: Books of Inspectors.

It is also possible that the children sent to Hertfordshire toward the end of the General Reception were in poorer health than those sent earlier.

The variation in death rates for children sent to different inspections in the same period, however, is so marked that the period when children were sent to Hertfordshire cannot be a complete explanation of why some inspectors were more successful than others. Some of the children sent to some inspectors were in a worse state of health than those sent to others. In the larger inspections, however, it seems likely that the proportion of healthy and unhealthy children sent in the same period probably did not differ very much. It may be that some inspectors were unable to find good nurses in their areas. The fact that death rates of inspections in the same town varied sharply, however, suggests that much depended on how conscientious an inspector was.

In Berkhamsted there was little difference between the death rate in Mrs Johnson's inspection (60 per cent) and Mrs Harcourt's (64.7 per cent), but in other places the difference was much greater. Thus, in Hatfield only 50 per cent of John Heaviside's children died at nurse, but the death rate for John Atkinson's inspection was 71.4 per cent. John Heaviside proved to be one of the most conscientious inspectors. On 30 April 1757, soon after he had been appointed, he wrote to the governors arguing that the relative merits of wet and dry nurses should be given a fair trial.[50] He did his best to look after the children. In February 1758, for example, when two children had died of 'gripes and purging,' he asked whether Dr Cadogan, one of the Foundling Hospital's physicians, knew of any effective treatment.[51] In January 1760 he said he would be able to see those nurses who lived in Hatfield every day 'that they want no assistance either from diet or medicine'.[52] All the Hertfordshire inspectors that were apothecaries or surgeons gave medical advice to their nurses without payment, but Heaviside went further and made no charge for the medicines he provided.[53] The governors were so impressed with this gesture that he was elected a governor on 31 December 1760, a most unusual honour for an apothecary.[54]

John Atkinson became an inspector in the spring of 1759, when, as we have seen, death rates were rising in Hertfordshire. The main reason for the high death rate in his inspection, however, seems to have been largely his own fault. He took little interest in his inspection. Without consulting the Foundling Hospital he passed the work of supervising the nurses to his brother-in-law, a Mr Dunne. In February 1760 Heaviside wrote to the Secretary that Dunne, who was a local shopkeeper, had refused to allow any nurse to keep a child unless she took her whole wages in goods from his shop and that many children had suffered by the practice.[55] Atkinson's inspection was brought to an end on 16 October 1761.[56]

There were also markedly different death rates at Mrs Prudence West's Barnet inspection, where 42 per cent died, and Mr Roberts' inspection, also in Barnet, where the death rate was 63.5 per cent. Mrs West's record was remarkable, especially since she was in charge of the second largest inspection in the county. No other inspector taking more than 50 children had a better record. In a letter dated 19 May 1760 she said she spent 'the greatest part of my time in looking after the children'.[57] On 17 January 1761 the governors decided that five children in the Foundling Hospital, all aged about 5, who appeared to be in a 'declining State of health,' should be sent to her 'as she has distinguished herself for her great attention to children in such circumstances'. If she could not take all five, one or two should be sent to Mr Heaviside.[58] Not only was Mrs West an excellent inspector, she also persuaded the governors to set up a small branch hospital (the Barnet or Hadley hospital) which she managed and which is the subject of Yvonne Tomlinson's chapter (see p. 234).

Roberts seems to have been a reluctant recruit. In a letter to Jonas Hanway Mrs West said he was the only person she could prevail on to become an inspector in Barnet. She reported that his medicines cost less than was usual and that he had recommended medicines of a simple kind that she could make up herself at no cost to the charity.[59] We do not know why so many of Mr Roberts' children died. Perhaps, as a busy apothecary, he did not have enough time, though other inspectors who were apothecaries and/or surgeons – Joseph Law, Daniel Van De Wall, John Heaviside and William Bailey – all had a better record in keeping their children alive. A number of Roberts' children were transferred to Mrs West's inspection at Michaelmas (29 September) 1763.

Mrs West's record was impressive, but two of the other three large inspections had death rates below the average for the whole county. For Mrs Lytton's Knebworth inspection it was 44.5 per cent. Lytton, though, served as an inspector for only just over two years. On 16 September 1759 she said that she would give up at Michaelmas. A week later she explained that she would be so little at Knebworth for several months together 'that tis impossible for me to take *that* care of the children which I always *have done*'.[60] Since no one could be found to take over Mrs Lytton's inspection many of the children were transferred to Van De Wall's inspection and a number were sent to Mr Chase at Luton in Bedfordshire.

In the largest inspection of all, Joseph Law's at Redbourn, 70 of the 146 'parliamentary children' died (44.5 per cent). Law acted as an inspector for 11 years (28 April 1758 to 23 April 1769), and 80 of his letters to the Foundling Hospital in that period have survived (as well as 5 written after his inspection came to an end). Many of them show his concern for the children. At one time or another he supervised 92 nurses. This would have been a heavy workload for a man of leisure, but Law was an apothecary who had to earn his own living. As we have seen, Mr Law also took ten children sent by London parishes in 1767 following Hanway's Act of that year.

The record of the other inspector supervising a large number of children, Richard Lloyd at Aston, was not so good: 76 of the 130 children died (58.5 per cent). The few letters that survive were all sent from Devonshire Street in London, so he may have spent more time in the capital than at his country house in Aston. In October 1759 he said that if he had realised how much trouble the duties of an inspector would be he would never have volunteered.[61] It may have been a desire to lighten the workload that led him to appoint Thomas Neats to look after the children at Watton. Neats, like Dunne, forced the nurses to take their pay in goods from him. He disappeared owing the Foundling Hospital £31 7s 3d.[62] Some of Neats' children were transferred to the care of Mrs Gardiner of Thundridgebury and the rest to Van De Wall in May of that year.[63]

Only 40 per cent of the children sent directly to Van De Wall's Welwyn inspection died. His letters show that he was anxious to do his best for the children and for conscientious nurses. In 1767, however, the governors became concerned because he had not sent in his accounts.[64] It was not until May 1769, after numerous reminders from the Secretary, Thomas Collingwood, that they were sent. He owed the Hospital £23 11s 3d. On 13 November 1770 he admitted that he could not repay the money – 'as you are Guardians of orphans for Godsake do not prosecute me for if you do my wife and six children must inevitably come to the parish'.[65] In May 1782 the debt was written off, as were Neats' debt and a debt by Miss Halsey of Great Gaddesden of £10 1s 0d.[66]

The nurses

The inspectors collectively employed about 700 nurses to look after the 'parliamentary children'.[67] They had to be married: most were probably the wives of husbandmen and farm labourers. The overwhelming majority of foundlings were only a few days or a few weeks old and nearly all, therefore, went to wet nurses, although those that survived would, of course, be weaned eventually. The Foundling Hospital tried to ensure that a wet nurse had only one child at a time that had not been weaned or could not 'go alone' (which probably means a child who was incapable of doing anything for itself). But with these exceptions there was no objection to a nurse looking after more than one child at a time.

There seems usually to have been little difficulty in recruiting enough nurses. In a letter of May 1759 Mrs Maria Cowper (Hertingfordbury) said she could supply the Hospital with wet and dry nurses,

> but the consequence of that, wou'd be, that I must inspect the children, and tis impossible for me to undertake the care of more than three I already have if you w'd have Nurses without an Inspectress it often falls in my and Miss Arnott's too to hear of them.[68]

In another letter she said that women 'come frequently to Miss Arnott and myself from 9 or 8 miles off, if such may be order'd by the Foundling Hospital and trusted themselves, you may have them at any time'.[69] The governors, however, would not consider employing nurses without inspectors to supervise them.

One reason why there was usually no shortage of nurses was that during the General Reception period they were fairly well paid. They earned 2s 6d per week, at a time when farm labourers in Hertfordshire earned about 6s a week.[70] In time, however, the governors succeeded in reducing the pay of some of the nurses. On 18 June 1764 William Hatfield, the inspector at Lilley, reported that 'some Nurses are ready to keep their children at 2s. a week'.[71] A year later, however, his nurses refused to accept a further reduction to 18d.[72] The nurses did not have to buy clothes for the foundlings: they were provided by the Hospital. The governors canvassed the inspectors to see whether the nurses would agree to providing the clothes themselves if they were given an extra 3d a week, but this scheme was not adopted except by Richard Lloyd at Aston, who tried it for a while (before the General Committee had come to a decision) on the grounds that it would cut costs for the Hospital and save the inspectors trouble.[73]

On 14 July 1756 the governors had decided that nurses whose charges were still alive after a year in their care should be given a premium of 10s.[74] Extra payments were also sometimes given to nurses for looking after seriously ill or disabled children. In October 1759, for example, Mrs Cowper gave Mary Trussil an extra 2s 6d for looking after Thomasine Edmonton – 'she having such an extraordinary fatigue, night and day, in carrying it backwards and forwards'.[75] In another case the Secretary informed Miss Arnott that the committee were glad that two children had recovered from the smallpox, 'and do agree to your giving the Nurse a gratuity of 10s for her trouble'.[76]

A nurse looking after just one child for four or five years would have increased the family income considerably, although in many cases children died after only a few weeks or months at nurse. The gain to the family also depended on the cost of living. In normal times, when the cost of necessities was not exceptionally high, 2s 6d a week would have easily covered the cost of looking after a foundling. The Foundling Hospital did not, however, increase the nurses' pay when the cost of living rose. In times of high prices 2s 6d may not even have covered the cost of feeding the older children, as William Jansen argued in 1765. On 9 February 1767 Joseph Law reported that Judith Hynnard was prepared to take a child at 2s a week, 'though, I cannot see how she Can Support it for that as the Necessarys of life are all so much dearer than usual'.[77] Not all areas of Hertfordshire benefited from the extra income provided by looking after foundlings, as there was not a single inspection to the north and east of a line running from Hitchin to Thundridgebury via Aston, while in places such as Tring and Oxhey only a few nurses were needed (see Figure 9.4). Places where many children

Hitchin

Aston

Lilley

Knebworth

Thundridgebury

Codicote

Welwyn

Hertford

Hertingfordbury

Redbourn

Great Gaddesden

Hatfield [2]

Hoddesdon

Tring

St Albans [2]

Cheshunt

Berkhamsted [2]

Cheshunt Nunnery

Hemel Hempstead [2]*

Abbots Langley

Northaw

Oxhey

Barnet

*Including one inspection set up for post-General Reception children

Figure 9.4 Map of foundling hospital inspections in Hertfordshire. © David Allin.

were looked after, such as Redbourn, Barnet and Knebworth, must have benefited most.

We do not know enough about most of the nurses to make confident generalisations about their conscientiousness. Valerie Fildes has examined a sample of 99 wet nurses from 16 parishes in Hertfordshire who nursed 232 foundlings between 1756 and 1757. The number of foundlings taken ranged from one to six (no nurse would have looked after six at one time and very few would have been looking after more than three at one time). Fildes suggested that 'in the majority of cases [the typical nurse] was a good experienced mother whose own children survived infancy and a successful foster mother'.[78] Yet, as we have seen, *half* the 'parliamentary children' died at nurse. Only about 280 of the nurses (two-fifths of the total) did not lose a single child and 50 of those taking two, 7 of those taking three and 5 of those taking four did not succeed in keeping *any* of them alive.[79] In many cases, as we have suggested, the death of a child may not have been the fault of the nurse. Sometimes an inspector urged the Hospital to give her another child. On 8 February 1759, for example, William Johnson (Berkhamsted) recommended Rose Gower even though Sarah Chandler had died – 'poor Woman she has had bad luck but I am sure it is not for her want of Care'.[80] On 15 November Frances Harcourt, in charge of the other Berkhamsted inspection, reported that 'Lorance Hall who was nursed by Mary Castle died last week he was bursten when she had it [almost certainly he had suffered a rupture] ... Mary Castle is a good nurse & shall send her for another child next Monday ...'.[81] On 4 December 1759 she reported that a second child in her care, John Gore, had just died and 'I believe he has been taken great care of, and that she is a very good nurse if you chuse it ... will send her up for another child. John Gore has been ill ever since he came.'[82]

Where three or four children who were sent to a nurse all died, however, the nurse may have failed to look after them properly. Mary Mould, a nurse living in Stapleford under Mr Lloyd's inspection, took in three boys between 15 February and 15 May 1759. By 9 June all three were dead. Similarly, the two boys and one girl entrusted to Mary Lewis of Ridge (Mr Roberts' Barnet inspection) all died. All four boys looked after by Elisabeth Gray of Burley (Bucknall's Oxhey inspection) died. Only one of the five children sent to Ann Wright at Stevenage (Mrs Lytton's inspection) survived. One cannot help thinking that the inspectors were at fault in sending children to these nurses[83] unless they were confident that the nurses had been unlucky rather than incompetent.

Certainly, Mrs West argued that deaths were often due to poor nursing. She believed that a number of children seemingly in good health that died suddenly had been 'overlaid' (i.e. suffocated as a result of sleeping in the same bed as the nurse). She was also critical of some wet nurses. In May 1760 she declared that

> tho' I am a great enemy to the taking of a child from the Breast,
> but many of these People give the Children so little, its impossible
> it can be of any advantage, & what other nourishment they have
> has more resemblance to a Poltice than Brest milk some time I
> find Bread crum'd with water, out of a Tea Pot, that they have been
> drinking themselves out of ...

She added that

> there is hardly a Week passes without my moving some of them,
> what becomes of those that are never look[ed] after they must be
> many of them very miserable for the poor in general are so bad
> that any thing that is left wholly to their mercy must stand very
> little chance of being well used.[84]

In October 1762 she said that 'The children who were allowed to play in
the open air were much healthier than those who were kept shut up in the
nurses' cottages.' Indeed, she had restored a number of children to health
by moving them from unsatisfactory to good nurses.[85]

In a letter dated 29 October 1761 the Revd Thomas Whitehurst (Lilley)
stated that he had removed 'the following Foundlings from their nurses
owing entirely to the Negligence, Immorality and dirtiness of the Persons
to whom they were entrusted'. One child was removed from Ann Steward
and three from Lydia Cooper.[86] In June 1759 Joseph Law of Redbourn had
removed Mary Probyn from Sarah Harrison at Hemel Hempstead to Mary
Peacock of Redbourn,

> having been Credibly Inform'd of her going a whole Day & Night,
> without anyone to care for the Child … it Appear'd to be the most
> wretchedly Emaciated Creature my Eyes ever beheld […] 'being
> Undress'd it had all the Appearance of a Child Almost Starv'd to
> death with Several ulcers on the Privities, Little Mortification on
> her Hips (owing to Negligence) and one of its Thighs Broken.[87]

Cases of unsatisfactory nursing may have been fairly common, but
cases of shocking neglect seem to have been rare. Probably most nurses
looked after the foundlings in much the same way as their own children.
Certainly, we know that some inspectors had a high regard for some of their
nurses. On 6 January 1760, for example, John Heaviside, in arranging for
nurses to go to London to collect four children, said, 'One of them (Mary
Piper) I shall desire you to give two to, she being particularly carefull and
understanding in all the disorders of children.'[88] On 24 September 1764
Amelia Halsey of Great Gaddesden stated that she would be very willing
for Hannah Crowley to have another child 'as she is a very good Nurse
and takes very good care of the Children'. On 21 May 1765 William Jansen

(Cheshunt Nunnery), when returning Henry Marshall and Charles Abrey to the Hospital, added,

> I can't send them away without giving due Praise to the poor good
> Woman [Nurse Brewett], who, tho' every article of Life is dearer than
> at London, has not Starv'd 'Em as may be seen, & tho' They're now
> 7 years old, & can Eat near enough as Men, has only the Scantiest
> Allowance for their Maintenances as she had at the beginning.[89]

Two years later, on 19 July 1767, Mrs Cowper said that 'the three Nurses I had before appointed, are well known to me, as very proper nurses, two of Them, have Nurs'd Children of my own and therefore to be depended on'.[90]

Some nurses became so fond of the children that it was a wrench to part with them. On 16 June 1761 Mrs Lytton reported that she had petitions from many nurses '(who had children from my Inspection) to have the Children continued with them ... I find a degree of Affection in many of the Nurses of the Children that is seldom to be equall'd in the Parents of the Poor.'[91] Similarly, on 2 October 1764, Mrs Cowper reported that one of her nurses, Elizabeth Forbes, became so distraught on learning that the child she was looking after, Richard Breakspeare, was to be returned to London that she ran off with him. He was eventually found and sent to the Hospital.[92] Others were luckier. On 6 November 1768 Benjamin Preedy, one of the St Albans inspectors, wrote that 'The bearers [Mary] Livermore and [Ruth] Morris are so concerned at the Children to be taken from them [Edward Southbrook and Sarah Bowles] that they wait on you to know if they may keep them for nothing.'[93]

There is no way of knowing how many nurses were exceptionally good, how many were adequate and how many were unsatisfactory. We can, however, compare Hertfordshire's record in keeping foundlings alive with that of other counties. Table 9.10 is confined to the nine counties taking the largest number of foundlings. Only inspections taking 20 or more 'parliamentary children' have been counted.

Clearly Hertfordshire's record was far better than that of the first four on the list and not substantially worse than Kent and Staffordshire, which had the lowest percentage of deaths for the larger inspections. Of the 12,464 'parliamentary children' sent to the country 7,696 died at nurse (61.4 per cent), while only 50.2 per cent of the 'parliamentary children' sent to Hertfordshire died at nurse. The governors had made the right

Table 9.10   Hertfordshire's record compared with that of other counties.

County	Number of foundlings	Number died	% died
Surrey	2985	1792	60.0
Essex	1751	1011	57.7
Middlesex	1623	1097	67.6
Berkshire	1121	645	57.5
Hertfordshire	1108	571	51.5
Kent	968	478	49.4
Yorkshire	695	364	52.4
Hampshire	506	259	51.2
Staffordshire	376	186	49.5
	11132	6403	57.5

Source: Disposal Books.

decision in sending so many children to that county.[94]

After the General Reception ended there was a sharp decline in the number of children sent to Hertfordshire. It was only in the early twentieth century, with the opening of the Berkhamsted Hospital, that Hertfordshire again played an important role in the history of the Foundling Hospital (see Chapter 11, p. 272).

Notes

1.   Levene, *Childcare, health and mortality at the London Foundling Hospital, 1741–1800: 'left to the mercy of the world'* (Manchester, 2007); S. Williams, '"A good character for virtue, sobriety and honesty": unmarried mothers' petitions to the London Foundling Hospital and the rhetoric of need in the early nineteenth century', in A. Levene *et al.* (eds), *Illegitimacy in Britain, 1700–1850* (Basingstoke, 2005), pp. 86–110.

2.   J. Styles, *Threads of feeling: the London Foundling Hospital's textile tokens, 1740–1770* (London, 2010).

3.   R.K. McClure, *Coram's children: the London Foundling Hospital in the eighteenth century* (London and New Haven, CT, 1981); D.S. Allin, *The early years of the Foundling Hospital, 1739/41–1773* (London, 2011), pp. 119–54, available at www.foundlingmuseum.org.uk/collections.

4.   Gillian Clark (ed.), *Correspondence of the Foundling Hospital Inspectors in Berkshire 1757–1768* (Reading 1994).

5.   London Metropolitan Archives (hereafter LMA) A/FH/A/10/003/004–007. See the Foundling Hospital Index, vol. 2, pp. 318–19.

6.   LMA A/FH/A/10/004/001–002, microfilm X041/001A-002A. Index, vol. 2, p. 319.

7. From 1759 inspectors' letters were kept, although it is likely that some have not survived. There are four or five letters for 1758 (mixed in with the 1759 letters). Very few letters survive prior to 1758 and only one of these was from a Hertfordshire inspector. Index, vol. 1, pp. 64–85.

8. LMA A/FH/A/06/002/001–003 Copy Book of letters, vols 3–5 covering the period 4 September 1760 to 1 October 1785. The first two letter books have disappeared. Index, vol. 1, p. 201.

9. LMA A/FH/A/09/002/001–004, microfilm X041/003–004, index, vol. 2 p. 277–549.

10. LMA A/FH/A/04/001/002, Index, vol. 1, p. 50.

11. LMA A/FH/A/09/012/001–002, Index, vol. 2, p. 285.

12. LMA A/FH/K/02/005–014, microfilm X041/015–012, Index, vol. 3, p. 745.

13. LMA A/FH/A/03/005/002–011, Index, vol. 1, pp. 22–3.

14. LMA General Register.

15. LMA A/FH/A/04/001/002.

16. The petition is printed in R.H. Nichols and F.A. Wray, *The history of the Foundling Hospital* (London, 1935), p. 48.

17. LMA General Register.

18. Allin, *The early years*, pp. 113–16.

19. LMA A/FH/A/10/003/004–007.

20. By the eve of the General Reception (1 June 1756) only eight children had been sent to Hertfordshire.

21. LMA A/FH/A/10/004/001–002.

22. LMA A/FH/A/06/001/012/002/38 Letter of Mrs Barker, 24 March 1759.

23. LMA A/FH/06/001/018/009/33 Letter of Mrs Johnson, 10 August 1765.

24. 'A Topographical Map of Hartford-shire' by Dury and Andrews (1766), reproduced by Hertfordshire Record Society, 2004.

25. See *The History of Parliament, 1754–1796 Members*, vol. II.

26. LMA A/FH/A/06/001/012/003/99 Letter of Mrs Cowper to the Foundling Hospital, received 29 May 1759.

27. LMA A/FH/A/06/001/012/002/38 Letter of Mrs Barker to the Foundling Hospital, 24 March 1759.

28. Mrs Jennifer Sherwood provided this information.

29. The National Archives Will Prob 11/1381 Will signed and sealed 30 November 1792 and proved 11 September 1802.

30. LMA A/FH/A/06/001/012/008/120 Letter of the Revd William Hatfield recommending Whitehurst for the position as inspector, 9 May 1759.

31. For Hirons and Preedy and their connection with the Hon. Georgiana Spencer see A. Kaloczi, 'The St Albans Foundling Hospital babies, 1756–1760', *Herts Past and Present*, 3rd series 4 (2004), pp. 3–7.

32. Yvonne Tomlinson has pointed out to me that a Philip Bodlam Roberts appears in Mrs West's and her sister Elizabeth's wills. It is quite likely that this was the full name of P.B. Roberts.

33. In a few cases children were transferred to Samuel Chase's Luton inspection in Bedfordshire.

34. See Kaloczi, 'The St Albans Foundling Hospital'.

35. Five pre-General reception children had been returned before the period began.

36. LMA A/FH/A/10/003/004–007 Disposal Books.

37. LMA A/FH/A/06/001/010/009/18.

38. Her death was reported three days later. LMA A/F/A/06/001/012/009/22.

39. LMA A/FH/A/06/001/012/009/23.

40. LMA A/FH/A/06/001/012/008/10 (Heaviside) and A/FH/A/06/013/021/58 (Mrs West, 20 February 1760).

41. LMA A/FH/A/06/001/012/008/36.

42. LMA A/FH/A/06/001/013/008/66.

43. LMA A/FH/A/06/001/014/019/24.

44. LMA A/FH/A/10/004/001–002.

45. LMA A/FH/A/06/001/016/016/8 Letter of 13 February 1763. William Perkins died at the Barnet Hospital on 22 May 1764, but not of smallpox.

46. LMA A/FH/A/06/001/020/003/29.

47. LMA A/FH/A/06/001/021/003/2. This plan was approved by the General Committee on 23 April.

48. LMA A/FH/A/06/021/003/65.

49. LMA A/FH/A/06/001/019/008/33.

50. LMA A/FH/A/06/001/010/7.

51. LMA A/FH/A/06/001/012/008/10.

52. LMA A/FH/A/06/001/013/008/86.

53. LMA A/FH/A/06/001/013/008/81 Letter of 29 Sept 1760.

54. See Nichols and Wray, *History*, p. 374.

55. LMA A/FH/A/06/001/013/008/85.

56. LMA A/FH/A/06/002/001 Copy Book of Letters, vol. 3, 16 October 1761.

57. LMA A/FH/A/06/001/013/021/59.

58. LMA A/FH/A/03/005/004.

59. Ibid., 21 February 1761.

60. LMA A/FH/A/06/001/012/011/60.

61. LMA A/FH/A/06/001/012/011/57.

62. LMA A/FH/A/06/001/013/129 Letters of Lloyd – 28 January 1760; A/FH/A/06/001/014/011/30 21 February 1761; A/FH/A/06/001/014/011/29 5 April 1761. Sub-Cttee 21 February 1761, 7 March 1761 and 14 March 1761 – A/FH/A/05/004 and letters to Lloyd of 11 June 1761 and 26 August 1761 – Copy Book of letters, vol. 3.

63. LMA A/FH/A/10/004/002 Book of Inspection, vol 2.

64. LMA Sub-Cttee A/FH/A/03/005/006.

65. LMA A/FH/A/06/002/002 Copy Book of letters, vol. 4 Nov: 28, 1767 & 13 May 1769; A/FH/A/06/001/025/020/1 Van De Wall to the governors – 13 Nov 1770.

66. LMA A/FH/K/01/002 microfilm X041/010 Gen. Cttee. 8 May 1782.

67. LMA A/FH/A/10/004/001–002. A determined attempt has been made to avoid counting nurses more than once, but there may be cases where the re-occurrence of the same name at the same place has not been spotted. Where the same name occurs in more than one inspection, but the place given is different, it is hard to

know whether the same person is referred to. In these cases it has been assumed that they were different persons. The actual number of nurses may therefore have been somewhat lower than suggested here.

68. LMA A/FH/A/06/001/012/003/95.
69. LMA A/FH/A/06/001/012/003/99 Undated letter received by F. H. 29 May 1759.
70. LMA The Gen. Committee on 12 April 1758 stated that nurses near London were paid 2s 6d a week. In Yorkshire and Staffordshire the pay was only 2s a week. See E.C. Connel, 'Hertfordshire agriculture', MSc dissertation (London, 1968), for Hertfordshire wages. Quoted by V. Fildes, *Wet nursing: a history from antiquity to the present day* (Oxford, 1988), p. 174.
71. LMA A/FH/A/06/001/017/008/36.
72. LMA A/FH/A/06/001/018/008/95 Letter of June 8 1765.
73. LMA A/FH/A/06/001/013/012/9 Letter 22 Jan 1760.
74. LMA A/FH/A/03/002/004 Gen. Cttee, 14 July 1756.
75. LMA A/FH/A/06/001/012/003/97.
76. LMA A/FH/A/06/002/001 Copy Book of letters, vol. 3, 6 March 1762.
77. LMA A/FH/A/06/001/020/012/19.
78. Fildes, *Wet nursing*, pp. 174–89.
79. LMA A/FH/A/10/004/001–002.
80. LMA A/FH/A/06/001/012/009/22.
81. LMA A/FH/A/06/001/012/008/51.
82. LMA A/FH/A/06/001/012/008/54.
83. LMA A/FH/A/10/004/001–002.
84. LMA A/FH/A/06/001/013/021/59 Letter of May 1760.
85. LMA A/FH/A/06/001/015/019/73.
86. LMA A/FH/A/06/001/014/019/32.
87. LMA A/FH/A/06/001/012/001/72.
88. LMA A/FH/A/06/001/013/008/86.
89. LMA A/FH/A/06/001/018/019/2.
90. LMA A/FH/A/06/001/020/003/27.
91. LMA A/FH/A/06/001/014/001/25.
92. LMA A/FH/A/06/001/017/003/35, A/FH/A/06/001/017/003/43 and A/FH/A/06/001/017/003/44 Letters of 20 Oct, 9 Oct and 25 Oct 1764.
93. LMA A/FH/A/06/001/021/005/3.
94. Allin, *The early years*, p. 144.

CHAPTER TEN

Prudence West and the Foundling Hospital in Barnet, 1757–71

Yvonne Tomlinson

A S DAVID ALLIN has suggested in the preceding chapter, one of the surprising features of the recent upsurge of writing on the Foundling Hospital has been the relative failure to engage with the personalities, motivations and work of the provincial inspectors who placed and monitored children sent out from London. Mostly male, inspectors were largely professionals such as clergymen, surgeons and apothecaries, but little is known of them apart from their professions, and that female inspectors were of independent means – a 'considerable number of them were women, particularly upper class women – the wives of governors and their social circle'.[1] In a report dated 1 October 1740, however, the General Court of Governors stated that the Foundling Hospital's 'General Plan', among other things, should involve 'the Fair Sex, who altho' excluded by Custom from the management of Publick Business, are by their natural tenderness and compassion peculiarly enabled to advise in the care and management of Children'.[2] Prudence West was one such recruit, employed as a volunteer[3] by the Foundling Hospital as inspector of 'nurseries' in Barnet, Monken Hadley and parts of south Hertfordshire from at least 1757 to 1771.[4] The nurseries were, in fact, groups of women in or near small towns and villages, who cared for the children in their own homes. Recruitment of wet and dry nurses almost certainly formed part of inspectors' responsibilities. In addition to organising and managing the workforce and paying wages and other allowances, they also monitored the children's development, health and wellbeing. For the period 1762–8 Prudence West was also the voluntary manager of the Barnet branch hospital. The daughter of Prudence and

James West, a skinner,[5] she lived in Chipping Barnet and was described in her will as a widow.[6] She had two unmarried sisters, Elizabeth and Sarah West, and she must therefore have married a man with the same surname as her own. None of them named children as beneficiaries other than those of relatives. The family were nonconformists and had a burial vault in Bunhill Fields cemetery in London.[7] Information about Mrs West's marriage and that of her parents is elusive. She and her sister Elizabeth and previously her parents owned property in Barnet, Elizabeth, Prudence and Sarah in Staffordshire and Elizabeth and Sarah in Worcestershire, so they could have originated from any of those counties and it may be due to their nonconformist religion that further information has been difficult to find. Vice-Admiral Temple West was her uncle and she was the cousin of his son, Colonel Temple West,[8] who inherited a substantial property known as Blue House and a house called Cockfosters in East Barnet from his father.[9]

The correspondence between Mrs West and the governors of the Foundling Hospital, London is a rich repository, opening a door into the day-to-day lives of not only herself but also the children in her charge and the nurses and other individuals who carried similar responsibilities to her own. Encompassing all aspects of care of children in both the nurseries and the Barnet branch hospital,[10] these letters provide the main source for this chapter. Highly descriptive, they evidence Mrs West's deeply caring attitude, from which a picture of a hard-working independent woman with firm views and a strong sense of commitment is easily drawn. In terms of the organisation of everyday matters in Barnet and in the hospital in London they are enlightening on many aspects: the lives and work of children, country nurses and hospital staff; education and industry; clothing and shoes; provisions and furnishings; finance and logistics; locality and travel; health and sickness; and, inevitably, death. Most importantly, clearly discernible experiences of the children, including the fate of some, can be gleaned and are recounted here.

Mostly written by Thomas Collingwood, the Foundling Hospital Secretary, the return letters from the committees of governors are informative as to the administrative functions of the organisation and, as would be expected, are directive, formal and polite.

Admission to the Foundling Hospital, London

Admission to the London hospital was usually by reception of a child from its mother. This was sometimes by recommendation, and Mrs West made

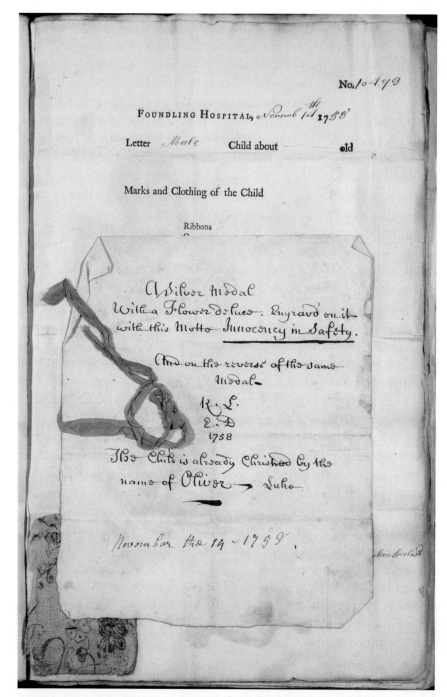

Figure 10.1 Billet made out in respect of Luke Perkins with textile and note tokens. These accompanied the child when he was admitted to the Foundling Hospital. © Coram.

such a recommendation on at least one occasion.[11] Admission numbers were allocated – these were the identifying link between the children and their names and circumstances, if known. The number, along with any personal information, was carefully recorded on a billet sheet (see Figure 10.1) and the billets stored chronologically. At least during the eighteenth and early nineteenth centuries a lead seal – something not easily removed – was stamped with the number for the child to wear around its neck at all times; one such disc is still in existence at the Foundling Museum.[12] If the children were known to have been baptised they were renamed; otherwise they were baptised by the hospital soon after admission and their baptismal names were recorded in the General Register.

During the eighteenth century and up until 1810 a variety of tokens were left with some children.[13] These served as identifiers in the event of the children being restored to their family. Extensive studies by Janette Bright, Gillian Clark and John Styles provide much information on the range of tokens left with the children, which formed unique means of identification for each child. One type was a note, the detail and content of which varied greatly, sometimes giving reasons for abandonment. Information recorded on the notes was, for example, baptismal name and date, or possibly parents or date of birth. In some instances such information was provided by the person who formally delivered the child to the hospital. One example of a note token provides the birth details of the child renamed as Honour Watson, no. 6584, who was in the care of Mrs West, which reads: 'Jane Quin born the 27th March 1757 in the parish of St Sepulchre Decebr. 7'.[14]

Sometimes other types of token were left as well as or instead of a note, such as engraved mother-of-pearl, textiles – often pieces of clothing – or halved objects such as one sleeve or medals and coins. The 'overwhelming majority' of such tokens were textiles.[15] Leaving such objects was encouraged by the Foundling Hospital and the small objects, described by Bright and Clark as 'tangible tokens',[16] such as coins and medals, were particularly important in the case of illiterate mothers.[17] Most of the tokens were left between 1741 and 1760[18] and some were described on the billets. The items were stored in a labelled packet created by folding the billet, which recorded the date of admission and number on the outside. The tangible tokens were removed in the 1850s or 1860s to be displayed at the London hospital, and means of correlating these objects with children were thus lost.[19] Many years of painstaking work by Bright and Clark, consulting the billets and every other possible documentary source for descriptions, has enabled the matching of some of the tokens held by the Foundling Museum with the billet. Unfortunately, it is clear that some tokens are now missing from the collection and matches will never be achieved. After the tokens were removed for display the billets were bound together in books.

It is as a result of the hospital's rigorous recording processes that today there is a vast collection of information about many of the children. Written and textile tokens are still attached to some billets but those tangible tokens that were removed are only rarely described. It is important to note that suggested baptismal names recorded on note tokens were never used and that some children were left with no identifiers.

The tokens left with Luke Perkins were a coin, two pieces of textile and a note. He was admitted to the London hospital on 15 November 1758 and transferred to South Mimms (part of Mrs West's Barnet inspection) on 23 November, where his dry nurse was Sarah Corral. There is a 'piece of yellow ribbon' attached to a note giving details of his baptism as Oliver Luke and a swatch of floral textile attached to the billet.

Styles explains that, at this time, ribbons were love tokens, as were items such as coins, and these were sometimes worn together by the recipient. The objects left with Luke Perkins reflect a popular choice by the parents of the foundlings – indeed, ribbons represent almost one-third of the textiles left with them – which act as a message of love for their deserted child.[20] The note accompanied a silver medal with the words 'INNOCENCY IN SAFETY', with the initials RL and ED inscribed on the reverse; 'The token is a coin from the reign of Charles II and the inscriptions are just as described on his billet' (Figure 10.2). In 1763 there was a successful petition made by his father for his return, to whom he was apprenticed in husbandry.[21] His father's name was Richard Luke of Eynesbury, and therefore it is almost certain that the RL inscribed on the coin token were his father's initials and ED those of his mother.[22]

The forward correspondence is silent on Luke, but is not in the case of a little girl who heads a list in the committee's letter of 31 October 1767.[23] Ann Thaxted, admission no. 1791, had been admitted to the London hospital on 28 June 1756 and was now 'of a sufficient Age to be App[rentice]d out'. The coin provided as a token and left with this child in 1756 (see Figure 10.3) was originally a shilling of the reign of James I; it had been 'rubbed almost smooth on one side before being engraved' with the name Elizabeth Harris.[24] Ann was placed with Ann Ludford, a dry nurse of South Mimms on 18 May 1758, then transferred to the Barnet hospital on 9 March 1763;

Figure 10.2 A coin token which accompanied Luke Perkins when he was admitted to the Foundling Hospital. © Foundling Museum.

Figure 10.3 A coin token which accompanied Ann Thaxted when she was admitted to the Foundling Hospital. © Foundling Museum.

she was finally transferred back to London in the autumn of 1767 but died of measles the following year, aged 12.[25]

During the first five years of the children's lives after admission to the Foundling Hospital care was given by country nurses, after which they were sent to the London or branch hospitals.[26] This invaluable group of women, it seems, did a very good job in caring for the children, who became part of their family, playing with and looking after animals and carrying out small farmyard tasks with their foster sisters and brothers.[27] Levene explains that, in doing this work, a family income may have been supplemented by as much as 25 per cent; it also had the benefit of representing year-round income, unlike agricultural work.[28] Fortunately, nurses were supervised and greatly supported by the inspectors, as the job of raising children, many of whom arrived in a very sorry state, carried a great deal of responsibility. Clark explains that some children arrived with syphilis, but showing no symptoms, and that there was evidence of ringworm, head-lice or fleas and scabies. The hospital's medical officer declared that 'one fifth of those admitted were so emaciated as to make it doubtful that they could be reared'. Unsatisfactory diets also meant that the children were vulnerable.[29] Levene believes that, although much maligned, most of the nurses were conscientious and caring, and overseen by equally conscientious inspectors, which ensured a 'rigorously supervised and sympathetic relationship' between the Foundling Hospital and its nurses.[30] Efforts were made to ensure they were not overburdened, usually breast-feeding only one infant at a time; however, the sizes and ages of the nurses' own families could have meant that they were caring for a large number of children.[31] Inherent risks included contracting a variety of infectious diseases, such as smallpox and measles. Prevention of infection with syphilis was taken very seriously; however, in the event of infection the nurses were treated by the organisation, sometimes in the London hospital's infirmary.[32] A gratuity paid for one nurse's 'extraordinary trouble'[33] indicates the latitude extended to Mrs West, who was best able to assess the degree and extent of care required in nursing such vulnerable children. There are nonetheless areas of concern expressed in Mrs West's letters. She comments on how some nurses fed the children, suggesting that 'many of the nurses I believe live wholly on Tea for if I goe morning, noon, or night I find every meal to be of that'.[34] Occasionally more serious issues arise, as, for instance, where she suspects that dead children had been 'overlaid' by their nurses (see Chapter 9, p. 227) or where more general neglect is indicated. An example of another issue is one raised by a foundling child, Vertue Lambeth. Mrs West explains that 'the account the Child gives of her being sent abeging is without the least foundations strange indeed it is a Child should make up such a story'. The placement was apparently well supervised, if partly informally, as, according to Mrs West, the nurse was 'overlook'd by many Neighbors & a place we Daily pass'. This report seems to have come as some surprise to Mrs West, who believed that 'every person in the Parish, would witness to Her being, the most tender, & affectionate, to the Children, as well, as a very sober, good, woman, in every Carractor'.[35] Her defensive attitude is not surprising, as a slight on one of her nurses would reflect badly on her. Apparently there was no loss of confidence in the nurse as, following an illness, the committee wrote on 5 April 1766[36] that Vertue Lambeth 'wants the Country Air for the recovery of her Strength, be pleased to send up the Nurse to Town that formerly had the Care of her'. Unfortunately, by 12 September[37] Vertue was 'at the Point of Death with Glandeloes Consumption' and died the following day.[38]

By contrast, some of the letters demonstrate the emotional bond that developed between nurses and their charges. One extract is emphatic in its moving plea, which had come from the nurse herself. The prospect of separation is described in Mrs West's letter read to the committee on 23 March 1768.[39] A Mrs Crook, who cared for Prudence Way, wanted to keep her 'for any price rather than part with her'. From a very young age the child, among others, had been cared for by this nurse, and Mrs West believed that Mrs Crook deserved to keep Prudence in thanks. She also thought that the child could be placed as an apprentice when she was old enough to leave the hospital. Only occasionally, however, were the children allowed to stay and Pugh describes the sense of loss which must have been felt by both nurses and children when they were returned to London.[40] While the children themselves have no voice, it is perhaps not unreasonable to believe that the feelings of the foundlings placed with their nurses in the 1760s were similar to those of the children raised by the Foundling Hospital in the twentieth century, a topic discussed in Jennifer Sherwood's chapter for this volume (see pp. 278–87).

The Foundling Hospital, Barnet

There was particular pressure on the Foundling Hospital during the General Reception period (analysed by David Allin, see p. 000), when unrestricted admissions supported by a government grant[41] created an urgent need for more nursing capacity, which would eventually put pressure on the London hospital. Two years previously Mrs West had notified the committee of 'a good House in this Neighborhood that wou'd be very fitt for the purpose, that by standing in a lonely place is never lett'.[42] Clearly bearing this in mind since then, Mrs West's response to the pressures resulting from the General Reception was to set up the Barnet hospital, to which end she made

detailed proposals to the committee on 6 September 1762.[43] From the seeds
of an idea first sown two years previously, her plans for the Barnet branch
hospital developed rapidly. On finding a suitable building in 'a delightfall
sittuation at the farther end of Hadley' she described a suggestion made to
her that, as 'the number of children is much greater then all the Hospitals
can contain … I will if the gentleman of the Committee gives me direction
to do it take a House that is about a mile from me.' Mrs West explained
that it was 'a pleasant walk' and she would be able 'to visit it constantly'. She
thought it 'extreemly fitt for the purpose' and described its remote position,
'a small distance from any House', in an open aspect and with 'a fine view
of the Chase'.[44] There was a 'good Orchard garden & a conveenence for
play ground for the Children a dry cosway to the Church & a large pue in
it'[45] – ideal, then, for the children's religious education. The rent was £12 a
year, with 'a rite of keeping cows in the Chase'[46] – perfect for the children's
nourishment. (The subject of cows was also raised later, when Mrs West was
rethinking that fresh milk could be beneficial to her charges and when she
asked whether houses could 'be obtained near commons for the Keeping
[of] Cows'.)[47] Conceding that she would need to take boys as well as girls,
her estimate was that the house would accommodate 40,[48] although the
children numbered at least 42 on one occasion.[49] By 23 September Mrs
West knew that 'the allowance of Parliment for each Child … [was] £7::10::
per Annum'. Granting her permission, the committee's letter stated that,
if her estimated costs of caring for the children 'does not exceed that sum
… it should be carried into execution'.[50] While theoretically the hospital
was governed by the committee, in practice it was managed by Mrs West;
this was both remarkable and exceptional, as women were not eligible to
become governors and it was the only hospital to be run by a woman.[51]

Inevitably, once the concept had been agreed, there was protracted
correspondence about the plans for occupation and operation. During the
last four months of 1762 each party wrote ten letters – Mrs West's were
often particularly lengthy – and some issues were unresolved for some
time. The following thematic discussions simply give a flavour of the topics
encompassed, but they are highly informative of Mrs West's requirements
and of the governors' deliberations and decisions.

'[W]hat will be the Value of the Furniture wanting?'[52] On 16 September
1762[53] the committee wrote asking Mrs West to advise them of various
arrangements and costs. They required her assurance that the 'Scheme'
would be 'practicable without too great an Expence' and they were keen

to confirm the likely expenditure so that 'the owner of the House may have an immediate answer'. Her response covered various aspects and she estimated that the cost of furniture would 'be but triffling, except the Beds'.[54] Requisites were many and various and some items arose repeatedly, including tables and chairs, a copper, a bath stove and grates, to be fitted by a 'bricklore'.[55] When issues were not quickly resolved her frustrations were forcefully expressed in many letters, and may have been justified; however, the immense pressures on the London staff must be taken into account when delays and misunderstanding arose, in these and all other circumstances. She also demonstrated compliance in respect of clothing, stating that the children would be dressed in the same way as they were in the London hospital.[56] In cases of ill health, the children would be moved into isolation under the care of a nurse, with a payment of 4d per week. Any 'extraordinary expence that may attend sickness', Mrs West believed, would be alleviated by exercise and diet. She expected few illnesses except smallpox and imagined that, in respect of those previously uninfected, 'it will be thought best for them to be sent up to be Enocalated at the Hospital some at a time'. She declared most of the children to have had whooping cough[57] and, triumphantly, she announced: 'I ... [have] not Buried one this twel[v]e months out of 74'.[58]

'[T]he children can come as soon as they please.'[59] Ever eager, on 5 November 1762[60] Mrs West expressed the desire to press on with her new venture, as the house was ready for occupation. 'A month agoe I had an order to take the House, upon which I ordered the Landlord to begin the repairs: it's now reddy if they send the beds for the Children.' On occasions the relationship between Mrs West and the committee was tense and the repairs seem to have been a bone of contention. Her final comment expressed her feelings succinctly: 'You & I have taken a great deal of pains about this foolish affair. Wish we may have any thanks for it.'[61]

'[Y]ou must send Books for the Children and two for to keep the accounts in.'[62] Anxious that the children arrive soon, on 16 November 1762[63] Mrs West pressed the committee, as it was for the want of a variety of objects that occupation could not proceed: 'I received the Shoes safe pray forward the things that are to make the cloth[e]s for the children ... hope the Committee will order the Beds to morrow if half were sent, the Children might be taken in part of them.' Having received some items, arrangements included one of the nurses living in the house 'to keep it aird'. Among other items, chairs, tables, fenders and shovels were to be provided by the matron and her assistant. Mrs West was instructed by the committee in their letter of 9 December 1762[64] to arrange for them to be valued and that the hospital would obtain their own valuation in order to pay for them; it is made clear that the items would then become the London hospital's property. This matter became an issue at the end of their occupancy.

Eventually most of these matters were resolved and, on 19 December 1762,[65] the committee was advised that the first of the children had moved into the Barnet hospital. A nurse was with them, probably from Mrs West's inspectorate. Mrs West confirmed: 'have lent them Beds & sheets till yours come cannot take in more tell they come'. The nurse must have been very busy on that day, probably working on her own, as Mrs West expected the matron and her assistant the following day. Understandably anxious, she continued: 'beg you'l forward the things as the Beds are greatly wanted'. It can only be wondered where she obtained so many beds and sheets.[66] It was not only beds which were needed, as evidently clothing for children still with Barnet nurses was inadequate and she still had not received other essential items previously requested, including boys' clothing, shoes and stockings, flour and a copper. We also learn from this letter that 'the water comes into the Kitchen that they may wash [there]'. The presence of water raises the question as to what kind of building had water inside in the mid-eighteenth century. It is likely that there was a well inside the building, 'quite a significant feature' of houses in the locality 'of that period that can still be seen today.' A 'piped supply of water came late to Barnet, in the late 19th century'.[67]

The children were to be transferred into the hospital from local nurses. Mrs West advised that 'some are almost naked for want of cloths & am unwilling to give them to spoil before they come in the House'.[68] Further supplies were requested for 4-year-olds on 26 December[69] when, with some frustration, she again reminded the committee of the urgency of the need for essential items, including 'knives & forks for the children'. Most prominent among the essential furnishing and equipment, beds feature in nine of Mrs West's ten letters written in the period leading up to occupation. They were very late in being delivered, despite Mrs West's almost constant reminders. Her suggestion made previously for transportation, on 22 October 1762,[70] paints an interesting picture of the furniture travelling north: 'When the Beds are got reddy they & any thing elce may come in a returned Hay cart.' At last, on 30 December,[71] very good news was received, as all items were 'ready to be sent to the Hospital at Barnet'.

The committee commented that, as there were 'frequent opportunitys of returned Carts it would be a saving to the Hospital' if Mrs West would arrange for a driver to call for 'a Load' and to advise when the driver might arrive.

Having received the children, a further concern was the matter of their education and improvement. First mentioned on 6 September 1762,[72] the committee learned that 'two Gentlewomen of my intimate aquaintance that are Sisters I propose puting into the Bigest end with twenty Children at first'. At 'the lesser end of the House I have an other Person to put in, that I propose to give ten at first, think it will be better to sepparate Familys' (there is no further specific mention of another person working there in the same capacity). Mrs West explained that they were 'very Fitt for it as they always managed their own Children extremely well & are very neet & handy women'. She confirmed that they would teach the children 'every thing they Learn in the Hospital at a resonable price over & above the two & Sixpence given for their Board'. The gentlewomen were of very intimate acquaintance indeed – her cousins, in fact.[73] On 17 September 1762[74] Mrs West expressed the view that the teaching allowance should be not less than '4 pence a Head' but thought that the London hospital might 'alow more when the Children are biger'. They would be taught 'Plain work marking Darning kniting & spinning & Reading'.[75]

However, there was soon to be disagreement on this subject. The process of agreeing terms of employment for the Mrs Cullarnes was to be troublesome. When Mrs West attended a sub-committee meeting held on Saturday 30 October 1762 she took from it an understanding that salaries of £20 per annum were agreed for 'Mary' (actually Martha) Cullarne, the proposed Matron, with £15 for Sarah as assistant matron.[76] Immediately following the meeting Mrs West had reported this to her cousins; however, she learned from the committee's letter, written by Thomas Collingwood on 4 November 1762,[77] that the General Committee thought otherwise. The wages proposed were thought by the committee to be 'too great', but they were 'willing to give a Salary after the rate of £15. a year to Mary Cullarne, & £10 to Sarah, her Sister, solong as they continue in the service of this Hospital … and that a Maid Servant be appointed at the Wages of £4 a year'.

Demonstrably both furious and embarrassed, on 5 November 1762[78] Mrs West wrote a lengthy, vituperative letter to Jonas Hanway, with some underlining for emphasis:

I am Surpris'd the Gentlemen shou'd desire to Beat down these
poor women, as the first Price is so much lower than what I see
they give at Alsbury' [Aylesbury]. I don't know how to make the
proposal now offer'd to them … [the committee] must consider
these women are not only to teach 40 Children (a greater fatigue
than the hardest labour) but they are besides <u>to assist in doing</u>
<u>every other office for them</u>, which will be a constant employment
every minute of the Day.

She further exclaimed: 'Their Charactor & acquaintance in Life with
People of the best Fashion wou'd render it an easy thing for them, to obtain
a place to wait of a Lady, which would be more profit & not any thing
like the trouble.'[79] They were, she added, obliged to board out their two
boys when taking up their posts. Two weeks passed and, on 18 November
1762,[80] Mrs West learned that the committee upheld their decision not to
pay the Cullarnes the rates she had proposed; however, 'it was agreed to
give a gratuity to the said Mistress and her assistant at the expiration of a
year if the said persons should be thought deserving'.

    Mrs West was asked to pay them £5 each on 29 December 1763, so the
gratuity was duly received;[81] however, the disagreement did not end there.
Both the committee and Mrs West believed that the children should be
industrious, but they disagreed as to whether the matron and her assistant
should 'profit' from the children's needlework, although it is not mentioned
in the letter how such profit would come about. On 11 October 1762[82] she
wrote very firmly and extensively. Her arguments follow several different
tangents, furthering her views on profits and allowances for the children's
clothing; linking the two, she felt that, if no profit was to be made, and if
'the Children are not allow'd to work, knit & spin, for their own [wear]',
the allowance of 15s per annum was insufficient. Her case was not very
well made, however, and her arguments labyrinthine. By 1759 the London
hospital's employees and the older girls were making most of the children's
clothes,[83] but it is possible that the Barnet hospital children were not old
enough at this stage as, of the initial intake, the oldest was aged six. Despite
her efforts, as with the Mrs Cullarnes' salaries, she did not win the battle.
The committee's letter of 9 October advised that the General Court did
not approve of her proposal and that 'the School Mistresses should not be
allow'd the profit of the Children's Labour'.[84] Work nonetheless continued
to be an important part of the hospital regime in Barnet, as elsewhere.

Mrs West needed to plan for the children's agreed needlework programme by ordering cloth well in advance of supplies running out. Her requests were frequent and mostly comparatively uninformative, but her letter of 19 December 1762,[85] written when advising that the first of the children had moved in, wasted no time in planning the children's work and gives a good idea of their tasks: 'the Children I think may assist in making [towels and tablecloths] they have hem'd some of the [check] for aprons, beg you'l send some cloth to make them Shifts if its not two thick'. Much industry is later evidenced in her letter of 24 October 1766,[86] when she advised Dr Watson that 'three Hundred & nineteen, shirts & shifts, they have made for London hospital, besides doing all their own work'. It seems that the Barnet hospital was a hive of industry and that children may have made a sizeable contribution to the institution's productivity.

Life in the Barnet hospital

Fewer letters were exchanged following the opening of the Barnet hospital.[87] Those that were sent, however, offer substantive information to help us understand how it functioned, the work of Mrs West, the nurses, the matrons and the committee and, most importantly, the lives of the Barnet children.

Naturally, requirements for children's clothing and shoes were frequent subjects of Mrs West's letters and mostly the requests seem to have been for the very young children at nurse.[88] As was the case for the period before the hospital opened, the children's clothes while at nurse were still in a sorry state and on 10 March 1763[89] Mrs West asked Mr Collingwood

> Pray desire Mrs Leicester[90] to send me Cloths for ten Children of
> 4 years old that are out of the House the shifts, caps and pining
> Cloths if they are cut out and sent unmade will serve for work for
> the Girls in the House beg she will send me some Flanelling to
> make Petticoats have made up all the Old Coats that woud doe but
> many of the Children come into the House with such old things
> they will not make any thing.

The precise manner in which the children were dressed when at nurse is not clear from Mrs West's letters, but it is almost certain that they were supplied with identical clothing to that worn by the children resident in the London hospital.[91] Such clothing is described by McClure as clean and warm, but with 'no frills'.[92] Mrs West took a pride in their appearance, but she was determined to allow the children much time to play outside, which must have benefited them greatly: 'many of my Children … are very active, & run much in the Road'.[93] This caused their shoes to wear out very quickly, and these needed frequent replacement, as did their clothes, with inherent monetary costs. Furthering her cause, she believed that there should be no 'unresonable confinment' to save expenditure on such items.

Babies were sent out to the country almost as soon as they were received at the London hospital, many in a very poor state of health. This practice was decried by both the London hospital apothecary and matron of the nurseries, and Mrs West advocated their care within the London hospital for a longer period: 'if they are obliged to go the next day into the Country, or perhaps the same day, it must be a great deal too much for their little frames to bear'.[94] The children were often weak when received in London, where they were exposed to disease. They might already have travelled to London only to be sent on further journeys to their nurses, although the committee decided in January 1758 that 'no children be sent at too great a distance in the Country to Nurse, who may not be thought capable of bearing the fatigue'.[95] Levene comments that during the General Reception period the children may have arrived in the country in reduced states of wellbeing. She believes that long journeys may have contributed, although speed of placement with a country nurse reduced risk.[96] Attitudes towards the provision of a healthy environment for the children were shared by the committee with those responsible for the care of parish children and Jonas Hanway's 1767 Act, *Better Regulation of the Parish Poor Children*, laid down this requirement.[97] Therefore, children aged over 4 years who were sick, or delicate children usually resident in the London hospital, were also sent to the country 'for the air'. Similarly, Mrs West believed that children benefited greatly from spending time in the country and often extolled the virtues of such arrangements, on one occasion apparently suggesting that more properties be purchased which were similar to the Barnet hospital:

> their has not been a sick child in the House the great Health they
> enjoy convinces me that vast numbers of Lives woul'd be saved
> ware they all divided into small Body's insted of being crouded
> togeather into large ones and cou'd Houses be obtained near
> commons for keeping Cows.[98]

This was certainly a sound idea, as the children suffered from a 'dangerous concentration of infection' in the hospitals.[99] If the committee was not already aware of Mrs West's thoughts on the subject they must have been in no doubt on receipt of her comments in a letter dated 21 August 1766.[100] After visiting children who had been inoculated in London she felt that the London hospital's 'school Rooms' were kept 'so Close I thought them more like Ovens, then places for Children to breath in'. At 'Home' (in Barnet), she explained, 'they have every Window open'. In terms of physical activity, on 11 October 1762[101] she emphasised the nurses' contribution, adding that 'the number of Children I have recover'd from the weakest state' by transferring them to nurses 'that have time to give them great exercise convinces me that their is hardly any so bad but may be recoverd by it'. On 18 April 1762 she had written that one child received from London who became breathless easily 'soon got the better of it by runing about here'.[102] Such a lifestyle would not be mirrored when they returned to the London hospital, where exercise was limited enough for boys, but much more so for girls.[103]

In the same letter of 18 April 1762[104] Mrs West also commented that 'Children of Weak Habits' improved with plenty of warm milk and 'as much exercise as they can [bear]'. This is one of many occasions when the committee was reminded of the benefits of much activity and nourishing food. As children who returned to London from the country often became ill, doctors wondered if their previous diet had been better. The advice was that country nurses should feed the children 'any kind of mellow Fruit, either raw, stewed or baked; Root of all sorts, and all the Produce of the Kitchen Garden'.[105] The London hospital's diet sheet did not specify how much and what kind of food they would have eaten while at nurse, but a document written by Mrs West describes her views that good nourishing food developed the children's strength: 'as to Diet I propose the Children shou'd have … supper Meat one Day Puding an other or any thing the seson affords'.[106] There is no indication of how much fresh garden produce was served to the children in London, but it is comforting to think that the Barnet children might have eaten at least seasonal fruit such as apples, pears and plums – perhaps they picked fruit from the trees of Barnet Hospital's own 'orchard garden',[107] which would have helped to keep them healthy.

Dr William Cadogan condemned food given to babies such as 'Butter and Sugar' and 'roast Pig'. For the first three months he encouraged breast-feeding only, at a maximum of four times daily, and recommended that weaning should not take place under the age of one year.[108] Some foundling babies were unable to suck, as was often found on admission.[109] On 26 February 1760[110] Mrs West wrote of such a child, Sophe (Sophia) Hanway, who had been very ill and had had 'fitts', but, fortunately in this case, she reassured the committee: 'I have very narrowly watch it, & it can now suck very well & I hope its out of dainger'. Sophia died on 1 June 1761.[111]

Some children were returned to London if they were very sick. Many had one of the very unpleasant conditions that were rife at the time, of which Mrs West wrote frequently. On 24 April 1761[112] she reported that none of the children requested were fit to return, one because of smallpox, another with measles and the rest with 'the Itch' (scabies) – a disease a nurse feared she had herself contracted – because of which they were 'shifted out of there infected cloth[e]s'. On 12 May 1763 Mrs West was 'oblig'd to put one out' for the same reason: 'she is Honour West that came from your House for the Air'.[113] The committee learned on 19 October 1763 that 13 were not well enough to be dispatched to London,[114] when in her letter Mrs West described their illnesses and resulting difficulties. Apart from measles and scabies, two children had also 'just recover'd of the small Pox' and these ailments had 'brought sound disalation to the Familys' where they were nursed. She also explained that 'the last that came has a very bad Head'. So concerned was she about the sickness they brought to Barnet that she had doubts about the future reception of children from London. Of the 13, she advised that 'as soon as they are Tolerable will send them Home'.

Clearly Mrs West was practised in recognising serious illness, some of which was life-threatening. Mrs West was concerned that Bridget Hill, having been sent to London due to ill health, would deteriorate while amongst other sick children;[115] however, the committee advised her by return of post[116] that Bridget would have been worse had this not been arranged. Mrs West consulted Mr Roberts,[117] her fellow Barnet inspector, when necessary and carried out treatments suggested by him, but she also applied an assortment of preparations recommended by the London Hospital. Not often wanting to seek advice, known remedies, she thought, would suffice in most cases.[118] Use of rhubarb specifically as directed by the committee is evident in her letter of 1 December 1767[119]: 'Your children are all well but the youngest looks poorly as if it had Worms Mrs Ripley has given it Rubarb but has not found it void any.'[120]

There were very worrying numbers of deaths, especially during the General Reception period, despite Herculean efforts made by the organisation to prevent disease. From the 1740s, at a time before common practice, the Foundling Hospital managed a massive inoculation programme against smallpox – a significant and innovative measure from which workhouses took a lead – and were isolated immediately. This is described by Levene as 'a case of an early medical trial using the children of the poor'[121] (see also Chapter 9, p. 219). Usually children were sent to London to be inoculated but Mrs West actively sought out preventative and isolation measures and, following her request,[122] on 4 June 1767 Mr Sutton was approved by the London hospital to inoculate some children locally, as he 'had charitably inoculated several of the Children of this Hospital … at 5s 3d' per child.[123] Local inoculation seemed a sensible alternative to the London hospital, where other diseases might be caught. Isolation was achieved by keeping inoculated children in separate 'chambers' within the Barnet hospital, a process that was highly successful. Levene explains that 'The role of inoculation in the decline of smallpox as a killer disease has been debated, but the hospital lost only a tiny proportion of its inoculation patients, compared with a relatively high toll among the non-immune foundlings.'[124] By 28 July 1767 the committee was advised that six children had been inoculated successfully and that they were all 'got well'.[125] Where children were sent to London Mrs West worried about their fate, enquiring on 5 October 1766,[126] for example, 'how my poor children goe on that went up to be inoculated & when they will be returnd'. In an undated letter received on 20 October[127] she wrote: 'I wonder that I do not hear something of the children that went up to be inoculated sure they must be fitt to return.'[128]

For those children who did not return to health the correspondence provides some vivid descriptions of illness: 'William Whatley[129] no.16634 died this morning of a Glandulos Consumption he has been a long time a most dismall object with soars and loss of flesh.'[130] Henry Salt's story is particularly moving. He was in Barnet only a short time, having previously been cared for in Aylesbury, but it is informative to consider his pitiful condition as a very sad example of what some children endured. In a letter of 22 April 1762[131] the committee informed Mrs West that Henry, whom she had returned to the London hospital, had a 'foul Bone in the foot thought to proceed from the Evil which is not infectious'. This is probably a reference to scrofula, or the King's Evil, in fact an infectious tuberculous condition of the lymph glands. It was believed that 'the Country air may be of great service to him'. Henry almost certainly had congenital syphilis, which caused a serious eye condition[132] – he was also described as 'paralytic from a distortion of the spine'.[133] Unfortunately, he died on 29 April 1764. Other children died locally and Mrs West almost certainly arranged their funerals. Thomas Coram, named for the founder of the Foundling Hospital, was buried in Barnet on 26 April 1764[134] and some were buried in other parishes. Special efforts were made to help Luke Bolton, among others, but he was buried on 28 November 1766. Mrs West had sent food for him but reported he 'is dead Buried at Barnet Friday he was so weak when he came & had such a loss of apitite that hardly any Chicken Broth or Sagoe I sent him could he gett down'.[135] The stories of these children demonstrate not only their dreadful condition but also Mrs West's deep concern for their wellbeing and attempts at treatment.[136] The committee sent children to her inspection as she had 'distinguished herself for her great attention to Children in such Circumstance'.[137]

Transportation, travel, finance and futures

The letters also provide us with an opportunity to consider issues which have rarely been discussed in the depth they deserve, one of which is transport (see also Appendix, p. 262). Arrangements sometimes did not go according to plan, as Mrs West related to John Tucker, Treasurer's Clerk at the London hospital,[138] when attempting to meet a request: 'You should give more notice when these Children are to come up its been a great hurry to me as they were 4 mile from me 3 miles from each other was obliged to fetch them in a Post Chais last night and 4 of them lay at our House'.[139] From this it is assumed that she took them into her own home overnight.

Following requests from the committee, or on instruction from inspectors, local nurses accompanied children – largely newly admitted babies – on their journey from London to Barnet. As is evident from the committee's letters dated 2 July 1763[140] to both Mrs West and Mr Roberts, nine children from her own inspection and five from Mr Roberts's were to be prepared for the 'Caravan'[141] arriving in Barnet on the following Monday. The complications which arose from these travel arrangements are recounted by Mrs West on 8 July 1763.[142] Also addressed to Mr Tucker, her description conjures up a pitiful image:

> I wrote it down particularly and I sent the woman in the Cart to
> Potters-bar with directions to send George Diston to Yorkshire
> yett when they came their they could not gett any Body to Read

Writing and tould the Woman she was to send her Biggest Girl
which was Deborah Blackbeard no. 6065 that came for the air
I inform you of it as you may send an account how the mistake
happen'd … its such a Grieff to the Poor Woman to part with
Children they have had long with them I cannot help being much
consern'd for the Poor Children that happen'd to be taken from
good nurses the Grief some Children suffer.

If 'an account' was provided, it was not recorded in the *Copy Book of Letters*. The effects were not only in terms of practical difficulties but also on the physical wellbeing and emotions of the children who were to be removed and their nurses, as Mrs West indicates. Almost certainly the child was to be sent to the Ackworth branch hospital,[143] a journey of approximately 160 miles. The journey was no doubt quite uncomfortable and there is evidence that such journeys took their toll; however, the journeys were broken, arrangements being made in advance for accommodation of the children and nurses.

Transport issues were not confined to the carriage of the children; if Mrs West was to do her job efficiently she needed to travel around her inspection area. She commented that the Barnet hospital was about a mile from where she lived and, although most of the children were placed with local nurses, her inspectorate role required travel to neighbouring areas as far away as Hatfield, a distance of approximately 11 miles. She mentioned among her early suggestions about the hospital that she could visit it 'constantly', which, along with the spread of her nursery, would have made for a good deal of travelling. It is possible that she journeyed into London and elsewhere by commercial coach and horses, but she may have had a post-chaise for local travel.

Travel was not the only onerous aspect of the job. Mrs West was responsible for finances in respect of both her inspection role and in running the Barnet hospital. Naturally, accurate record-keeping was essential but, by no means a gifted accountant, Mrs West baulked at the idea of accounting for a 'Hospital'. She felt herself 'quite unfitt for the undertaking' and could see no point in itemising all purchases.[144] There were also many changes in arrangements which she found tiresome and very frustrating. These included security and payment methods, examples of which are mentioned in the committee's letter of 5 December 1767,[145] when 'Four Bank Post Bills' of £25 were sent: 'for the more Security I thought Proper to Cut them asunder' – the two sets of halves would then have been sent separately. Mrs West raised objections to other security measures as they were difficult to manage and suggested using this same method of cutting the bills in half on several other occasions. The committee's proposed alternative was to nominate a person who could act as her collection agent, but this she was not prepared to do: 'Inspectors, that are of traids, may give Bills to those they deal with, but I have no Transactions with any Body, in Town, cannot possable doe it.'[146]

Some expenditure could be planned, such as payment of nurses and rent for the Barnet hospital, but in addition, for example, Mrs West paid local tradesmen such as a blacksmith and a bricklayer[147] for repairs. Fees were payable to apothecaries[148] and churchmen and to undertakers for the children's funerals. One such undertaker, Mr Beatty of Barnet, was owed £40.[149] Often it was a few weeks before reimbursements were made by the committee to Mrs West and her letters are peppered with requests and reminders. The most frequently mentioned figure was £100 (worth approximately £7,500 in today's terms), but on one occasion she advises, 'I am near 2 Hundred pound out of pocket.'[150] To be able to afford to spend £100 repeatedly is an indication of Mrs West's means, given the governors' recruitment as inspectors of 'ladies and gentlemen of easy fortunes'.[151] Between 4 October 1762 and 29 February 1768, the period of the Barnet hospital's existence, reimbursements totalled £2,240. Overall, from 19 May 1760 to 3 May 1770, the amount of reimbursements was £3,280.[152] Whatever her circumstances, it is evident that outlays were reimbursed later than Mrs West wished, as she often reminded the committee: 'pray send me soon one Hundred Pound for the use of the Children under my Care.'[153]

The letters also allow us to pick up a theme begun in David Allin's chapter: apprenticeship. The age at which the children were apprenticed seems to vary over the years, but when they were ready to be apprenticed some children were sent back to London for preparation, although others were placed directly from Barnet.[154] Mrs West believed that their good health made the children attractive apprentices and advocated local placements, which were more healthy than those in town. She pointed out that 'most of them gon would have been apprenticed at Hadley had they remaind'.[155] Some applications, mostly for girls in respect of 'household business', were made to Mrs West by local people and she consulted with the committee on these occasions. Although not necessarily typical, the following cases are interesting as they outline the experience of a few foundlings placed locally and also reveal changes in the organisation's policies. Such changes were possibly due to large numbers of General Reception children by then requiring placement.

Honour Watson's placement was comparatively easy. It was proposed by Mrs West on 16 June 1767[156] that Honour might be placed with a 'Man and Woman that keep a shop in this town, He sells coals and his Wife chan[d]lery goods, & earthen Ware'. The letter was about three girls and the committee was prepared to accept her advice. An annotation reads: 'Ask West what she would recommend as to paying a sum not exceeding £7 with each Child.' She recommended £7 over two years for Honour and the same sum for Hope Millington over three years, which was agreed.[157] Mrs West was able to report to Taylor White on 28 July[158] that Honour was 'bound to Thos Augur'.[159]

Hope Millington is a rather different case. On 24 October 1766 Mrs West proposed that Hope should be apprenticed to her own nurse. Awaiting news of Hope's recovery from her smallpox inoculation, she wrote: 'pray be so good, to get her returnd, for the Woman will be almost distracted, & wou'd take Her as soon as she is a little taught'.[160] It was seven months before there is evidence of the matter being raised again: 'I think she would be well dispos'd of as the woman and her Husband are middle aged people.' Mrs West went on to explain that they were 'very industreous', that they had 'no Child of their own' and were 'very fond both of them of this child'.[161] Six weeks later she explained that Mr Macey was 'a labouring man, they are not 40 years old'.[162] Unusually for apprenticeship masters and mistresses, they were childless – children were mostly placed with experienced mothers.

On 1 August 1767[163] the committee refused the proposal of Mr Macey of South Mimms as he was a day labourer and therefore not of the usually required status. This was surprising as, in 1760, for the first time, apprenticeships were arranged with the husbands of nurses with whom the children had been nursed.[164] Standards were maintained as to the calibre of masters and some children had to leave the families, so this is an example when the change of policy was probably advantageous to the child – according to Levene, 'approximately 5.5 per cent of all foundling apprenticeships were to the nurse's husband or someone else of the same name in the same place.'[165] However, on 1 December 1767[166] Mrs West announced: 'I paid … two [pounds] to Macy with Hope Millington.' From this it can be assumed that the committee had a change of heart – the apprenticeship had commenced on 18 November 1767.

The story of Judith Scarborough's apprenticeship is similarly illuminating. It begins on 16 June 1767,[167] when we learn that 'she is chose by a Lady of Fortune'. Judith's duties included sewing and knitting, for a fee of £7 for the whole period, the length of which was not stated.[168] Six months later lack of funding was a problem, as the committee learned on 13 December 1767: 'Judith Scarborough … would have been taken this week, but [for your] informing me no money will be given till the Parliments Pleasure is known' – this meant that Judith had to 'stay a little longer'. Unfortunately, plans had changed: 'as Mrs Woodhouse the lady that fixd on her last Summer, is gone to an Estate they have in Glostershire & has not sent me what she intends I think my self not obligd to keep Her'.[169] This implies that Mrs West believed that Judith should be returned to London. Presumably their letters had crossed in the post, as Mrs West was obviously not aware of these plans being abandoned. On 12 December 1767[170] the committee had already decided that 'the Child Judith Scarborough No 5198 may be imediately returned to this Hospital.' Clearly, attempts to progress the placement took a very long time. Judith's feelings are unrecorded, but this experience must, at the least, have been unsettling. Eventually different arrangements were made and, three months later, on 5 March 1768,[171] her apprenticeship was arranged to an apothecary, Mr William Wilson of Barnet, with an apprenticeship fee of £3.[172]

Elizabeth Hillyard's story is a little different, in that she was placed in London. The process was initiated by Mrs West when she advised the committee on 28 September 1766[173] that the child was wanted as an apprentice by a Mr West, 'Dyer', and his sister, who were probably her relatives. She confirmed that they were 'People of exceeding good Carractor I think their cannot be any objection to his having the Child … I tould Him their was not any [money] given.' Mr West, of St John Street, London, was invited to attend a committee meeting the following Wednesday to sign the indenture papers.[174] Other close family connections are also observable. The foundling Ann Hampstead was later employed in the West household as a servant and was named as a beneficiary in Prudence West's will and in that of Prudence's sister, Sarah West. Prudence bequeathed some furniture and a £5 annuity and Sarah bequeathed her clothes. There were also even more direct connections. Mrs West's letter of 23 March 1768[175] announced to the committee: 'Prudence West will take

Figure 10.4 Detail from the indenture binding the foundling Prudence West to Mrs Prudence West, manager of the foundling hospital in Barnet and Barnet inspector. Admission no. 16108 © Coram.

my self ... my mother lett her be in Her House that she might gett health & strenth by good norishment'[176] – the child was a foundling named after Mrs West. The indenture papers (see Figure 10.4), signed on 23 March, show that Prudence, aged 8, was apprenticed on 18 March 1768 to 'Mrs Prudence West of Barnet ... Widow'.[177] Mrs West's decision to keep her namesake seems to have been a successful arrangement, as Prudence the foundling was a beneficiary in the wills of Mrs West and her sisters. Mrs West bequeathed a £5 annuity and a 'toilet table'. In 1769 Elizabeth West bequeathed £100, to be paid at the age of 21, and Sarah West bequeathed a £5 lifetime annuity in 1782. Prudence the foundling continued to live in Barnet and married James Rolf, a whitesmith of the parish of South Mimms, in Chipping Barnet on 7 October 1779.

Of course, not all apprenticeships were successful, but these detailed cases provide a useful corrective to a literature that has usually concentrated on the problems with rather than the benefits of the apprenticeship system.

Closure

By 12 January 1768[178] the death knell was tolling for the Barnet hospital. The pressures caused by the General Reception were diminishing as those children taken in were placed in apprenticeships and the need for the branch hospitals was coming to an end. The committee had decided that this branch should close:

> you will be pleased to return Twenty Children from the Hospital
> at Hadley, to this Hospital as soon as Convenient … and by order
> of the Committee to desire that the Matron & Servants in the
> Hospital at Hadley may have Notice that they will be discharged at
> Lady Day next.[179]

Mrs West was not happy about the children returning to London. Letters requiring their prompt return were sent for two months from the middle of January, including this letter of 30 January 1768: 'with relation to sending part of the Children from the Hosp'l at Hadley imediately … the orders … for that Purpose must be complied with'.[180] A kind but firm hand was needed to ensure compliance:[181]

> the Orders … for removing the Children from the Hospital at
> Hadley [must] be carried into execution … and the Committee
> hope for your kindness in making proper disposition for quitting
> that Hospital at the time above-mentioned, and that you will send
> to this Hospital a few of the Child:n from thence imeadiately, and
> continue sending a few, as conveniensy may best suit you till they
> are all removed.

On 5 March[182] the committee's instruction was sent for the conveyance of children to London. However, this was delayed for two weeks and on 17 March 1768[183] Mrs West was given the following directive: 'all the Children be ret:d imediately from Barnet'. In fact, some did not return until the following week, and a few sick children mentioned in Mrs West's letter, read to the committee on 23 March 1768,[184] were sent to stay with their nurses. Molly Roberts was:

> in a poor State of Health & wou'd be death to Her to leave the Air
> Shall send her & Sally Budley to her Nurse … the last coach full

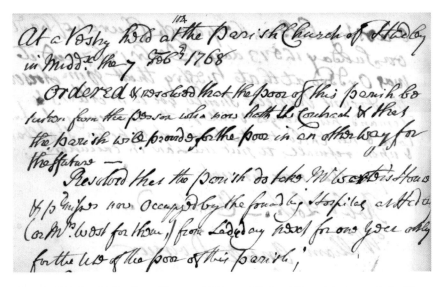

Figure 10.5 Monken Hadley Vestry Minutes of 7 February 1768, p. 104, resolving to use the building then occupied by the foundling children 'for use of the poor' when empty. © Barnet Archives and Local Studies.

> now you have all from Hadley except Ann Wager shall send her
> with the others she is next to a dwarf by being ricketed in infancy
> runing in the Air is the best thing to make her groe.

It is reassuring to know that, if Ann Wager was so disabled as to be unable to fare on her own as an adult, the Foundling Hospital would have cared for her for the rest of her life.[185]

This still left the issue of the building itself. The committee wrote letters to the overseers of the parish of Monken Hadley with proposals. On 15 March 1768[186] the overseers were advised that, if they wished to purchase the goods then in the Barnet hospital, a person would be sent to take an inventory. 'I thought this information necessary that you may get an Appraiser on your part, otherwise they will all be brought to Town.' On closure the Monken Hadley parish officials offered £60, which was accepted;[187] in fact, at least some of the furniture remained, as will be seen. Two days later the overseers were advised that 'the Key of the Hadley Hospital [should] be delivered to the Landlord' and that, on 18 March, Mr Tucker would carry out an 'Apprasement of the Goods'.[188] Mrs West explained in her letter, read to the committee on 23 March

1768,[189] that she was unable to return the key as the landlord lived 60 miles away.

The parish officials had already discussed the premises at their meeting on 7 February 1768 (Figure 10.5).[190] It was minuted that 'the Parish will provide for the Poor in an other way for the ffuture' and that 'the Parish do take Mr Warter's House and premises now occupied by the foundling Hospital at Hadley … from Ladyday next for one year only for the use of the poor of this parish'.[191] Repairs were agreed and, one week later, the vestry minutes record that all provision for the poor would be reviewed, that the cost of repairs was £10 and that the premises would be let to the parish at £10 per annum, £2 less than the rent paid by the Foundling Hospital.

It has already been mentioned that the matron and her assistant purchased furniture remaining when the Barnet hospital closed, at least some of which had been bought from them by the Foundling Hospital when the Barnet branch first opened. Mrs West explained in her letter of 1 February 1768 that this was required as the 'Mrs Cullarnes intend to try to rais a School for Little Children'.[192] Following appraisal in March there was disagreement between Mrs West and the committee about the valuation of the goods purchased by the Cullarnes and in her letter dated 17 November 1768[193] she left the committee with a precise indication of her feelings: 'I should never have desired any abatement, on Mrs Cullarnes goods, being sertain, it woud be injustice to them if I did not.' In other words, she felt obliged to propose an abatement as the goods had been over-valued: 'Mr Tucker had so little time to take His Inventory, that [he] made mistakes' and he had not seen how many items 'was wore out'. Were he 'to look over them again', she continued, 'I know he must acknowlidge that 13 Pound is the full value.' She was without doubt a major source of irritation by this time, as on the outside of this letter was written, almost certainly by Thomas Collingwood: 'Give 40/- to Mrs West get rid of her.' This decision was politely relayed to her one week later: 'the Gent:m agree to give Mrs Cullen, 40S: in the Acct of the Goods which You'll be pleased to pay her.'[194]

Conclusion

Significantly, Mrs West had supervised more children than any other Hertfordshire inspector with the exception of Mr Law of Redbourn (see Chapter 9, p. 288ff). She clearly believed that the children were best brought up in the country and close to families and a neighbourhood which had become their own. She probably fought hard for the hospital to remain open and certainly objected to the children's return to London. This period must have been very difficult for her, having dedicated more than five years to the running of the hospital alongside the care of the children, which was carried out with a generous portion of individuality.

There were issues between herself and the London hospital committee, but Mrs West speaks clearly to us from the past, defending her position and that of her charges. The committee certainly found her difficult at times: forthright, dogmatic and argumentative is how they might have described her, but with these traits came empathy, diligence, hard work and determination. Despite their circumstances, many of the Barnet children thrived, both in the hospital and at nurse. For a while she still had the 'nursery' children and nurses to oversee, and her expertise continued to be paramount to the survival of those children who followed Hope, Luke, Thomas and the two Prudences, among so many others, some of whose lives we are privileged to have witnessed. As evidence of letters drafted to Mrs West from the committee has not been found after 1771 it is assumed that her work finished in that year. The treasure trove of Mrs West's letters provides many things: a glimpse into the past, not only of the children but also of their nurses and their surroundings, and allowing us insight into her belief that the children needed and deserved much attention to both mind and body, in concordance with the opinion of her peers. Besides this, the letters illustrate the complications and frustrations of her task and her dedication in carrying it out – and all as a volunteer. Set against our relatively poor understanding of the role, character and achievements of foundling inspectors, the story of Mrs West is truly one with wider import.

Appendix

Transportation of the children

Difficulties and concerns similar to those experienced by Mrs West when arranging transportation of the children are covered by two authors in particular and give a broader picture of the problems faced by those involved in such arrangements, organisers and travellers alike. See Clark, *Correspondence … Berkshire*, and Nichols and Wray, *The history of the Foundling Hospital*.

On 4 October 1761 Mr Hughes explained that 45 children aged 3 and 4 were to be conveyed to the Shrewsbury Foundling hospital in a caravan 'without the laps of their nurses'. He was very worried about this and stated that there should be a 'proper no. of women to take care of them in the carravan'. He also expressed his view about the 'hardship to the nurses to have the children taken from them before they are 5 years old' (Clark, *Correspondence … Berkshire*, pp. 137–9, A/FH/A/06/001/014/008/72).

John Grant, clerk to the governors, describes some Chertsey nurses' 'most lively sorrow in parting with' the children. He also mentions the nurses' refusal to co-operate without payment. Many of the children were too sick or still suckling and were not sent as instructed as he deemed the journey too long. In a letter written on 18 July 1759 he also describes the difficulties of transporting 29 children in two caravan journeys from Surrey to Yorkshire (Nichols and Wray, *The history of the Foundling Hospital*, p. 104).

Some idea of the caravan may be deduced from Mr McClellan's letter to the Foundling Hospital, London, dated October 1761 (McClellan was apothecary at the London hospital 1759–97[195]), describing how he made the caravan as comfortable as possible for its journey to Shrewsbury. He reported that nurses from the Shrewsbury branch hospital would travel with 12 children; 14 had been collected for the journey but he felt that the nurses could not manage this number. He ensured that plenty of straw was 'laid at the bottom' of the caravan, that it was 'well defended from the Badness of the Weather by a good Covering' and provided biscuits (Nichols and Wray, *The history of the Foundling Hospital*, p. 108).

In his letter to the London hospital dated 2 June 1761, John Tucker, the Treasurer's Clerk, provides a very moving vignette of a group of children and their nurses who were accommodated overnight in 'the Inn at Baldock' on their journey to Ackworth. Here he describes the concern shown by soldiers assisting with the difficult process of placing the children in the caravan. Their nurse gave the children bread and butter and ale to drink from a spoon before putting them to bed with bedding and linen 'which were very sweet and clean'. He reported that the soldiers 'were very fond of the Children & took great care in handing them into the Caravan, & pitied the poor Women for having so much trouble in taking care of so many Children'. It is later mentioned that a 'sober good Motherly Woman' in Watton was employed to travel with the children 'in the Caravan and to take care and see that the Children were well treated'; the woman was to return with those who would form 'the last Cargo of Children' (Nichols and Wray, *The history of the Foundling Hospital*, p. 106).

The vehicle mentioned here may have been the Ackworth branch hospital vehicle often mentioned in the correspondence, once described by Mrs West as 'the Yorkshire cart'. The term 'cart', which she used on three occasions[196], usually refers to a two-wheeled vehicle, although it can also mean a carriage, car or chariot.

Caravans were vehicles with covers and the Foundling Hospital's caravans were probably similar to covered stage wagons, which carried freight as well as passengers. This type of vehicle was a precursor of the stage coach, which was enclosed, whereas the stage wagon was not. This would explain the need to provide 'a good Covering' for the children's journey. The phrase 'long coach', used in the committee's letter dated 5 March 1768, almost certainly refers to the same vehicle. This term is cited as being synonymous with 'caravan'.

Marc Allum, BBC television's *Antiques Road Show* expert, gave his view in an email to the author on 4 January 2012, which has been summarised as follows: he surmised that, whatever the vehicle type, they would have been practical, basic and inexpensive and were possibly covered military-style wagons, possibly even supplied by the military. He also suggested that they might have been hired; however, John Caldicott, Honorary Secretary of the Old Coram Association, advises that the Ackworth branch hospital had its own 'caravan', made especially for transporting the children, so it is possible that transfers between Yorkshire and other inspection areas and branch hospitals at least may have been by this method.

There are some considerations arising from the above. References throughout the correspondence are to 'the caravan' rather than 'a caravan', implying that it was probably a vehicle owned by the organisation, be it in London or Ackworth, so Marc Allum's suggestion that it might have been 'hired in' or been a military vehicle seems unlikely.

The description of an attempt to make the vehicle as comfortable as possible for the journey, with weather protection, certainly indicates that it was not enclosed, but for it to travel frequently to and from Yorkshire, probably across many unmade roads, indicates that it may have been robust. The fact that children were to travel without the comfort of their nurses' laps may indicate that there was not enough room for all who travelled together to be seated comfortably and raises questions about the number of seats, if any at all.[197]

Notes

1. See G. Clark (ed.), *Correspondence of the Foundling Hospital inspectors in Berkshire 1757–68* (Reading, 1994), p. xxvi, and G. Pugh, *London's forgotten children: Thomas Coram and the Foundling Hospital* (Stroud, 2007), p. 42.

2. R.H. Nichols and F.A Wray, *The history of the Foundling Hospital* (London, 1935), pp. 29–30.

3. Payments were introduced at the beginning of the nineteenth century. See R.K. McClure, *Coram's children: the London Foundling Hospital in the eighteenth century* (London and New Haven, CT, 1981), p. 250.

4. It is probable that the first child transferred from London to Mrs West's inspection was Margaret Blisse, on 19 March 1757. See London Metropolitan Archives (hereafter LMA) A/FH/A/10/004/001 *Inspection Book No. 1 1749–1758*, p. 37, microfilm X041/001. The last letter written by Mrs West to the committee was dated 5 May 1770 (A/FH/A/06/001/023/021/18) and the last record of a letter written to her by the committee was 2 April 1771. See LMA *Copy Book of Letters No. IV.* A/FH/A/06/002/002. No letters from Mrs West to the Foundling hospital were found in the boxes held at the LMA for 1759, 1771 or 1772. Retention of inspectors' letters seems to occur only from *c.*1759.

5. The National Archives (hereafter TNA) Prob 11/944 and Prob 11/770.

6. TNA Prob 11/1381.

7. TNA Prob 11/1097 and Prob 11/1129.

8. See the will of Elizabeth West, Prudence West's sister, wherein Temple West the younger was named as a beneficiary. TNA Prob 11/1097.

9. See British History online, Victoria County History of Middlesex, http://www.british-history.ac.uk/source.aspx?pubid=87&page=2. The Blue House appears on a map

prepared for the Duchy of Lancaster in 1776 and both properties are shown on a facsimile tracing from the original in the Bodleian Library of Enfield Chase dating from 1658. The facsimile is signed by Edward Ford, July 1874, held in Enfield Local Studies Library & Archive, Thomas Hardy House (First Floor), 39, London Road, Enfield, EN2 6DS.

10. A list of the names of children who were in the care of the Foundling Hospital, in both Mrs West's and Mrs Roberts's inspection, is held in Barnet Museum, 31 Wood Street, Barnet, Hertfordshire, EN5 4BE. This list will be under review and may not be complete.

11. LMA A/FH/A/06/002/001 31 March 1764 *Copy Book of Letters From 4 Sep. 1760 to 19 Nov 1767 No. III.*

12. Later this may have changed to numbers being sewn onto their clothing. I am grateful to J. Bright for this information, provided in an email to the author, 19 June 2012.

13. I am grateful to J. Bright for this information, provided in an email to the author, 24 June 2012.

14. LMA Billet book A/FH/A/09/001/077. St Sepulchre Church is in Holborn.

15. See J. Styles, *Threads of feeling: the London Fondling Hospital's textile tokens, 1740–1770* (London, 2010), p. 17.

16. See J. Bright and G. Clark, *An introduction to the tokens at the Foundling Museum* (London, 2011), p. 9.

17. See Styles, *Threads of feeling*, p. 15.

18. See Bright and Clark, *An introduction*, p. 3.

19. Ibid., p. 8.

20. See Styles, *Threads of feeling*, pp. 43–4.

21. His apprenticeship commenced after returning to the London hospital on 19 October 1763. I am grateful to D. Allin for information on this and the nurse, provided in letters to the author dated 16 and 22 February 2012, and to information provided by J. Bright and G. Clark in February 2012.

22. An excommunication order was made by the Rev. Timothy Neve, archdeacon of Huntingdon. An extract from the record of this decision dated 5 June 1754 is as follows: 'Of Eynsbury Richard Luke for not appearing to answer Articles for being the reported Father of Bastard Child born of the Body of Eliz[abe]th. Dixey'. There is also a 'Letter denunciatory of excommunication: Eynesbury parish. Elizabeth Dixy' dated 21 September 1753. This must have been in respect of a previous birth as Luke Perkins was received in 1758, almost definitely as a baby. See Cambridgeshire Archives Online Catalogue: http://calm.cambridgeshire.gov.uk/ArchiveCatalogue/ Refs: Richard Luke (AH13/268/227), Elizabeth Dix[e]y (AH12/267/217).

23. LMA A/FH/A/06/002/001 *Copy Book of Letters No. III.*

24. The evidence is somewhat confusing, as the accompanying vicar's note describes his baptism of a child called Mary Harris in Harmondsworth, Middlesex, born on 6 June and baptised on 7 June of that year. According to the parish register the baby was born to Elizabeth Harris and her husband John, a felon recently transported. In the view of Bright and Clark the vicar transposed the names of mother and daughter; they also believe that 'the match between the dates on the note and the coin are good'. See Bright and Clark, *An introduction*, p. 22.

25. Ann's death confirmed by J. Bright in an email to the author dated 12 February 2012.

26. For her calculated mean average age of 5.2 years of children returned to London or sent to branch hospitals from country nurses see A. Levene, *Childcare, health and mortality at the London Foundling Hospital, 1741–1800: 'left to the mercy of the world'* (Manchester, 2007), p. 109.

27. McClure, *Coram's children*, pp. 94–5, and Clark, *Correspondence*, p. xxxvii.

28. Levene, *Childcare, health and mortality*, p. 135 in respect of income.

29. Clark, *Correspondence*, p. xxviii.

30. Levene, *Childcare, health and mortality*, p. 114.

31. Ibid., p. 113.

32. McClure, *Coram's children*, p. 93.

33. See the committee's letter dated 22 April 1762 LMA A/FH/A/06/002/001 *No. III.*

34. LMA A/FH/A/06/001/013/021/59 19 May 1760.

35. This letter is not dated; it was read to the committee on 15 January 1766. LMA A/FH/A/06/001/019/020/49. Vertue was in the care of Martha Tuffe of Monken Hadley.

36. LMA A/FH/A/06/002/001 *No. III.*

37. LMA A/FH/A/06/001/019/020/59.

38. Ibid. Death recorded in LMA A/FH/A/10/004/001, p. 392.

39. This letter is not dated. LMA A/FH/A/06/001/021/018/40.

40. See Pugh, *London's forgotten children*, p. 60.

41. Growing numbers resulted in the need for government grants of £546,000. See Pugh, *London's forgotten children*, p. 48.

42. 19 May 1760. LMA A/FH/A/06/001/013/021/59.

43. LMA A/FH/A/06/001/015/019/69.

44. This is Enfield Chase.

45. Almost certainly St Mary the Virgin church.

46. The right to graze cows on Enfield Chase 'carried over after the dischasement on 1st January 1779, when such rights became the grazing rights of Monken Hadley Commoners, known as stints today'. I am grateful to William Pumfrey, Monken Hadley resident, for this information, provided in writing to the author 6 August 2012.

47. LMA A/FH/A/06/001/016/020/34, 15 August 1763.

48. LMA A/FH/A/06/001/015/019/69, 6 September 1762.

49. See Mrs West's letter dated 1 February 1768. LMA A/FH/A/06/001/021/018/44.

50. LMA A/FH/A/06/002/001 *No. III.*

51. I am grateful to D. Allin for this information, provided in writing to the author 17 July 2012.

52. LMA A/FH/A/06/002/001 *No. III*, 16 September 1762.

53. LMA A/FH/A/06/002/001 *No. III.*

54. LMA A/FH/A/06/001/015/019/71, 17 September 1762.

55. Ibid.

56. Ibid.

57. Ibid.

58. Here Mrs West probably refers to 74 children. Ibid.

59. LMA A/FH/A/06/001/015/019/76.

60. Ibid.
61. Ibid.
62. LMA A/FH/A/06/001/015/019/81.
63. Ibid.
64. LMA A/FH/A/06/002/001 *No. III.*
65. LMA A/FH/A/06/001/015/019/74.
66. The children would not each have had their own bed as it was not the hospital's practice. However, A. Levene explains that, later, 'In June 1780 all children with "diseased heads" were ordered to sleep in separate beds in order to prevent infection.' See Levene, *Childcare, health and mortality*, p. 157.
67. I am grateful to William Pumfrey for this information, provided on 6 August 2012.
68. LMA A/FH/A/06/001/015/019/74, 19 December 1762.
69. LMA A/FH/A/06/001/015/019/75, 26 December 1762.
70. LMA A/FH/A/06/001/015/019/79.
71. LMA A/FH/A/06/002/001 *No. III.*
72. LMA A/FH/A/06/001/015/019/69.
73. The names Martha, Elizabeth and Sarah Cullern appear as beneficiaries in the wills of Prudence (TNA Prob 11/1381) and her sisters Elizabeth (TNA Prob 11/1097) and Sarah West (TNA Prob 11/1129), wherein they are variously described as relatives and cousins. No mention of their relationship with Mrs West is made in the correspondence.
74. LMA A/FH/A/06/001/015/019/71.
75. The level of education given by the Foundling Hospital was far superior to that of poor children at the time, but limitations were enforced in keeping with contemporary views, which ensured that such children were not educated to a level where they might forget their place in society. Allin lists skills acquired by girls in London which led to apprenticeships, which included embroidery. See Allin, D., *The early years of the Foundling Hospital, 1739/41–1773*, pp. 180–1.
76. LMA A/FH/A/06/001/015/019/76, 5 November 1762.
77. LMA A/FH/A/06/002/001 *No. III.*
78. LMA A/FH/A/06/001/015/019/76.
79. Ibid.
80. LMA A/FH/A/06/002/001 *No. III.*
81. LMA A/FH/A/06/002/001 *No. III.*
82. LMA A/FH/A/06/001/015/019/73.
83. McClure, *Coram's children*, p. 194.
84. See LMA A/FH/A/06/002/001 *No. III*, 9 October 1762.
85. LMA A/FH/A/06/001/015/019/74.
86. LMA A/FH/A/06/001/019/020/38.
87. Apart from 1763, which is probably to be expected, during the first year of its operation; in 1766, where there was much illness and discussion about apprenticeships; and in 1767, also owing to apprenticeship arrangements.
88. See Mrs West's letter of 13 September 1762 for an example of her detailed request. LMA A/FH/A/06/001/015/019/70, 13 September 1762.
89. LMA A/FH/A/06/001/016/020/30.

90.   'Matron of the Infirmarys'. Nichols and Wray, *History*, p. 270.

91.   Clark, *Correspondence*, p. xlii. Country nurses collected the children from the London hospital and they were taken to nurses' homes in Berkshire with clothes for one year. They were required to return any outgrown clothes to London.

92.   McClure, *Coram's children*, p. 190.

93.   LMA A/FH/A/06/001/015/019/73, 11 October 1762.

94.   McClure, *Coram's children*, p. 102.

95.   Levene, *Childcare, health and mortality*, p. 99.

96.   Ibid., p. 80.

97.   A. Levene, *The childhood of the poor: welfare in eighteenth-century London* (Basingstoke, 2012), p. 46.

98.   LMA A/FH/A/06/001/016/020/34, 15 August 1763.

99.   Levene, *Childcare, health and mortality*, p. 202.

100. LMA A/FH/A/06/001/019/020/72.

101. LMA A/FH/A/06/001/015/019/73.

102. LMA A/FH/A/06/001/015/017/68.

103. See Pugh, *London's forgotten children*, pp. 60 and 66, for discussion about exercise in the London hospital.

104. LMA A/FH/A/06/001/015/017/68.

105. See Pugh, *London's forgotten children*, p. 61.

106. This letter is not dated and may precede Mrs West's letter of 5 November. LMA A/FH/A/06/001/015/019/80.

107. LMA A/FH/A/06/001/015/019/69, 6 September 1762.

108. Pugh, *London's forgotten children*, p. 58.

109. See Clark, *Correspondence*, p. xxviii.

110. LMA A/FH/A/06/001/013/021/58.

111. LMA A/FH/A/06/001/014/019/24.

112. LMA A/FH/A/06/001/014/019/25.

113. This probably means that she placed the child with a nurse instead of in the Barnet hospital. LMA A/FH/A/06/001/016/020/31.

114. This letter has no reference number.

115. LMA A/FH/A/06/001/019/020/7, 13 June 1766.

116. LMA A/FH/A/06/002/001 *No. III*, 14 June 1766.

117. This is John Roberts, apothecary. See Chapter 9, p. 222, regarding Mrs West recommending Mr Roberts as an inspector. He seems to have been assisted by a P.B. Roberts, as several letters to the Foundling Hospital reveal.

118. LMA A/FH/A/06/001/015/019/71, 17 September 1762. See A. Vickery, *The gentleman's daughter: women's lives in Georgian England* (London and New Haven, CT, 1998), p. 156, where it is explained that housekeeping included rudimentary medicine.

119. LMA A/FH/A/06/001/020/020/74.

120. LMA A/FH/A/06/001/020/020/74. Mrs Ripley's name does not show in the inspection lists; she may have been employed in the Barnet hospital. One of the 'medicines' was rhubarb for 'Worms'. It was also recommended 'In Looseness' and 'at Intervals', 'To Open the Body'. See Nichols and Wray, *History*, p. 134.

121. See Levene, *Childhood of the Poor*, p. 8, where she mentions experiments in inoculation against smallpox and 'electric therapy' at the Foundling Hospital. Elsewhere, Levene explains the hospital was 'often in the vanguard of new medical ideas and practice', see Levene, *Childcare, health and mortality*, p. 157.

122. LMA A/FH/A/06/001/020/020/12, 28 May 1767.

123. LMA A/FH/A/06/002/001 *No. III.*

124. Levene, *Childcare, health and mortality*, p. 164.

125. LMA A/FH/A/06/001/020/020/31, 28 July 1767.

126. LMA A/FH/A/06/001/019/020/35.

127. LMA A/FH/A/06/001/019/020/36.

128. At least 25 of the Barnet hospital children were inoculated. I am grateful to D. Allin for this information.

129. Probably named after George Whatley, Treasurer of the London Foundling Hospital.

130. LMA A/FH/A/06/001/016/020/34, 15 August 1763.

131. LMA A/FH/A/06/002/001 *No. III.*

132. I am grateful to G. Clark for this information, provided in an email to the author dated 21 January 2012.

133. See Clark, *Correspondence*, p. 96.

134. See Mrs West's letter dated 30 April 1764. LMA A/FH/A/06/001/017/019/4.

135. See Mrs West's letter dated 30 November 1766. LMA A/FH/A/06/001/019/020/41.

136. D. Allin's chapter shows the percentage of children who died in Hertfordshire inspections. See p. 221.

137. See sub-committee minutes 17 January 1761 (LMA A/FH/A/03/005/004, p. 160).

138. See Nichols and Wray, *History*, p. 109.

139. This letter was not dated. It was received at the London hospital on 28 July 1764. LMA A/FH/A/06/001/017/019/41. See also Mrs West's letter of 18 April, 1762, where she mentions travelling with a child with suspected smallpox in a post-chaise. LMA A/FH/A/06/001/015/017/68.

140. LMA A/FH/A/06/002/001 *No. III.*

141. LMA A/FH/A/06/001/019/020/17.

142. LMA A/FH/A/06/001/016/020/29.

143. I am grateful to D. Allin for this information, provided 17 July 2012.

144. LMA A/FH/A/06/001/015/019/79, 22 October 1762, and LMA A/FH/A/06/001/016/020/31, 12 May 1763.

145. LMA A/FH/A/06/002/002 *No. IV.*

146. LMA A/FH/A/06/001/019/020/41, 30 November 1766.

147. See Mrs West's letter dated 14 April 1768. LMA A/FH/A/06/001/021/018/45.

148. The apothecary had been paid by Mrs West and his bill was sent in evidence to the London hospital. See Mrs West's letter dated 7 January, 1768. LMA A/FH/A/06/001/021/018/52.

149. See Mrs West's letter dated 23 Nov 1768. LMA A/FH/A/06/001/021/018/41.

150. LMA A/FH/A/06/001/019/020/41, 30 November 1766.

151. See McClure, *Coram's children*, p. 88.

152. Information gleaned from both Mrs West's and the committee's letters. Interpretation

was complex and every effort has been made not to double-count figures; however, as there are some gaps in the correspondence it is likely that the total figure was higher.

153. LMA A/FH/A/06/001/020/020/31, 28 July 1767.
154. Apprenticeship records found so far which are associated with Barnet children are shown in a list held at Barnet Museum.
155. LMA A/FH/A/06/001/019/020/38, 24 October, 1766.
156. LMA A/FH/A/06/001/020/020/38.
157. LMA A/FH/A/06/001/020/020/30, 14 July 1767.
158. LMA A/FH/A/06/001/020/020/31.
159. Thomas Augur was a parish official. See Barnet Archives and Local Studies Centre (hereafter BALSC), Monken Hadley Vestry Minutes, 16 November 1759.
160. LMA A/FH/A/06/001/019/020/38.
161. LMA A/FH/A/06/001/020/020/12, 28 May 1767.
162. This letter is not dated. It was received by the committee 14 July 1767. LMA A/FH/A/06/001/020/020/30.
163. LMA A/FH/A/06/002/001 *No. III.*
164. See Clark, *Correspondence*, pp. lvi and lviii.
165. See Levene, *Childcare, health and mortality*, p. 142, n. 32.
166. LMA A/FH/A/06/001/020/020/74.
167. LMA A/FH/A/06/001/020/020/38.
168. See table of apprentices' names and fees, 1 July 1767. LMA A/FH/A/06/001/020/020/71.
169. LMA A/FH/A/06/001/020/020/11.
170. LMA A/FH/A/06/002/002 *No. IV.*
171. Ibid. I am grateful to D. Allin for this information, provided in a letter to the author dated 22 February 2012.
172. LMA A/FH/A/06/002/002 *No. IV.*
173. LMA A/FH/A/06/001/019/020/60. It is possible that this Mr West was related to Mrs West. A person named Edward West, of the same address, appears in her will. In the will his occupation is noted as that of dyer. (However, the apprenticeship records show that Elizabeth's master was a lapidary. I am grateful to D. Allin for this information, provided in writing to the author 26 June 2012.)
174. LMA A/FH/A/06/002/001 *No. III,* 12 January 1767.
175. LMA A/FH/A/06/001/021/018/40.
176. Mrs West's mother was also Prudence. Prudence West the foundling was named after Mrs West in the same way that many children were named after governors or their friends. See J. Brownlow, *The history and objects of the Foundling Hospital: with a memoir of the founder* (London, 1865) www.ebooksread.com/(Brownlow), p. 44.
177. LMA A/FH/A/12/004/047/1 – part of bundle.
178. LMA A/FH/A/06/002/002 *No. IV.*
179. 25 March.
180. LMA A/FH/A/06/002/002 *No. IV.*
181. Ibid, 4 February 1768.
182. Ibid.
183. Ibid.

184. This letter is not dated. LMA A/FH/A/06/001/021/018/40.

185. See McClure, *Coram's children*, p. 218.

186. LMA A/FH/A/06/002/002 *No. IV*.

187. See Nichols and Wray, *History*, p. 180.

188. LMA A/FH/A/06/002/002 *No. IV*, 17 March 1768.

189. This letter is not dated. LMA A/FH/A/06/001/021/018/40.

190. BALSC Monken Hadley Vestry Minutes, 7 February 1768. The workhouse shows a map prepared for the Duchy of Lancaster in 1776 and therefore is the location of the Foundling Hospital building. A copy is held at Barnet Museum.

191. Ibid. Hugh Petrie of Barnet Archives believes that the name of the person mentioned in association with the building on the minutes dated 14 February 1762 is Warter.

192. LMA A/FH/A/06/001/021/018/44.

193. LMA A/FH/A/06/001/021/018/39.

194. LMA A/FH/A/06/002/002 *No. IV*, 24 November 1768.

195. I am grateful to D. Allin for this information, provided in a letter to the author dated 16 February 2012.

196. LMA A/FH/A/06/001/016/020/29, 8 July 1763; A/FH/A/06/001/016/020/32 23 July 1763; A/FH/A/06/001/019/020/17 ('Yorkshire cart' – not dated, in 1766 bundle).

197. Research on the caravans continues and any additional information on the subject will be available through Barnet Museum.

CHAPTER ELEVEN

The last years of the Foundling Hospital – Berkhamsted, 1935–55

Jennifer Sherwood

WHILE MUCH OF the history of the Foundling Hospital in the eighteenth and nineteenth centuries is relatively familiar, the same cannot be said of the later development of the institution, and it is this period that is the focus of the current chapter. In researching the last years of the Foundling Hospital in Berkhamsted it has been possible to draw not only on official documents, minutes and correspondence but also on the personal memories, written and spoken, of former foundlings, many still alive today.

The early twentieth century and a changing climate

Just as in other areas of Hertfordshire, foundlings had been fostered with nurses in Berkhamsted for the first years of their lives (see p. 216). Changes in the governance of the Foundling Hospital together with changing patterns in the country at large at the beginning of the twentieth century were to bring Berkhamsted to the centre of the stage.

During the course of the nineteenth century London had expanded tremendously. The Foundling Hospital, sited on what were once fields, was now in the centre of the metropolis. Early in the twentieth century increasing pollution in the area of the Foundling Hospital and new ideas about the importance of cleaner air and country living led the Hospital to look for a new site. By 1912 the governors were prepared to sell the 56-acre site to London University, but this plan was later dropped; however, after the First World War developers were keen to obtain the site and an offer from James White to buy the site was finally accepted in 1925. Jacobsen's

Hospital was demolished apart from the southernmost colonnades, the southern range and the pedestal for Thomas Coram's statue. The carving of the Hospital Arms, designed by Hogarth and sited in the pediment of the western colonnade's pavilion, was destroyed.[1] Only a few elements of the main buildings were saved and later incorporated in the new London headquarters in Brunswick Square.[2] A number of other items were stored in readiness to be incorporated in the new Foundling Hospital. These included the main staircase from the Girls' Wing, the remains of Thomas Coram (deposited at Kensal Green Cemetery), the organ (placed with Messrs Hill & Sons of Camden), the turret clock (stored with Messrs Thwaite & Read) and many others.[3] The children themselves were temporarily housed in St Anne's School, Redhill,[4] while a new permanent site was sought.

In searching for an appropriate site for the new Hospital the governors were concerned to provide for the health and wellbeing of both the children and the staff, and set certain criteria:

> They sought a site in the country, with an area of not less than 150
> acres, not more than forty miles from London, not on clay soil
> but on gravel if possible and also with mains drainage, company's
> water, gas and electric light, a site with altitude not less than 200
> feet above sea-level, near a village and main-line railway station
> and preferably within easy access of London.[5]

Six sites were considered, including Stowe and Ashridge,[6] before the Ashlyns Hall estate was chosen. In May 1928 the report of the sub-committee considering sites stated the following:

> This is a site of two hundred acres, situated on the south side
> of the North Western Railway, about a mile from the station,
> and from the town of Berkhamsted. It is in many respects a
> suitable site, has gas and water and stands at an altitude of five
> hundred feet. An objection to the property is the fact that there
> are two footpaths across the estate which might interfere with the
> development but possibly these might be diverted by arrangement
> with the local authority. The main drainage system is within
> close proximity to the site. The land is well-timbered and level,
> giving excellent sites for buildings and playgrounds and adjoins
> the playing fields of the Berkhamsted Schools. The proximity of

this important school may be of great advantage both from the educational and social point of view. The town of Berkhamsted is quite large enough to provide many amusements for the Staff, and the station is easily accessible. The price is £25/30,000 for two hundred acres. The house, which is comparatively small, is not likely to be adaptable, and might have to be pulled down, but it is of minor importance.[7]

The sub-committee of the Foundling Hospital governors went to considerable lengths to meet the challenges of bringing 400 children and staff to a new neighbourhood. The quality of the water supply was assessed through an analysis by the British Drug Houses Ltd 1928. Permanent hardness was six but 'bacteriologically the water appears a good one.' Boring was carried out by geological survey contractors Le Grand, Sutcliff and Gill Ltd, who reported that there was a remote risk of subsidence because of chalk pockets in the clay.[8]

The health needs of the children and staff were very carefully considered and a study of the *53rd Annual report on the sanitary condition of the Middlesex and Hertfordshire combined sanitary district* for the year 1926 by H. Hyslop Thomson, County Medical Officer of Health, led to the conclusion that 'the health of the district is on the whole satisfactory'. This was reiterated in a letter from General Foot of Whitehill, Berkhamsted, to Sir Roger Gregory of the Foundling Hospital stating that his doctor had confirmed the 'healthy nature of the area'.[9] In fact, local landowners showed considerable interest in the possibility of the Foundling Hospital coming to Berkhamsted and were in the main very supportive. On 21 June 1928 General Foot again wrote to Sir Roger offering support and providing local knowledge. Geoffrey Blackwell[10] of Haresfoot, whose land abutted on Ashlyns, wrote on 11 October 1928, reassuring the Foundling Hospital about drainage for the playing fields. The minor problems (which arose because part of the land was outside the town boundary), difficulties arising from the Town and Country Planning Act of 1926 and Berkhamsted's Town Plan, were all resolved by careful negotiations to modify anything that might restrict the governors from erecting all necessary buildings in connection with the new Hospital. As far as the Town Plan was concerned, Edward Penny, deputy clerk to Berkhamsted Urban District Council, explained in a letter dated 14 December 1928 that the plan was only to prevent 'indiscriminate building of cheap housing' and would not apply to the building of the

Hospital: 'My information is that everyone on the Urban Council is most keen that the Foundling Hospital should establish itself in Berkhamsted.'[11]

The matter of the two footpaths was perhaps the greatest obstacle to be overcome. On 12 May 1928 the Foundling Hospital's solicitors wrote to Mr Haynes of the chemical firm Cooper, McDougall and Robertson, the largest employer in the town, requesting help and advice over the matter of the footpaths. As a result the Secretary of the Foundling Hospital wrote on 17 July 1928 that 'it was agreed I should apply to the Berkhamsted Council for the closing of the footpaths and the dropping of the Town Planning Scheme offering the Council four acres of land in return for the closing of the footpaths'.[12] This was finally accepted in spite of objections raised by the Commons and Footpaths Preservation Society, and the playing field known as Velvet Lawn, adjacent to the present Thomas Coram Middle School, was given to the town.

There remained one further problem to be resolved. The report on the site had stated: 'there is a reservoir in the centre of the property supplying water to Bottom Farm and adjoining cottages.' The Great Berkhampstead Water Works Company offered to close the reservoir and supply the farm and cottages from the main. To meet the water requirements of the very large increase in population occasioned by the arrival of the Foundling Hospital the Kingshill Water Tower was opened on 1 November 1935.[13] The Foundling Hospital finally completed purchase of the Ashlyns Hall estate, comprising Ashlyns Hall, the Model Farm and most of the Park, on 18 November 1929.

Erecting the new buildings

In spite of an enthusiastic letter from Geoffrey Blackwell of Haresfoot to Sir Roger Gregory on 23 October 1928 saying 'I am very much interested in modern architecture and it seems to me that you have an opportunity of putting up buildings that should be a glory for generations to come, and an example of the best that our age can do', John Mortimer Sheppard, a little-known architect, was chosen to design the buildings. The same thoroughness evident in the choice of a site was obvious in the design and erection of the buildings. While every attempt was made to re-invoke the spirit of the original Foundling Hospital, the Committee was keen to incorporate ideas displayed in recent buildings of a similar nature. They visited Merchant Taylors' School, Moor Park, the Girls' Masonic School, Rickmansworth, Lady Margaret Hall, Oxford and the YWCA, Tottenham

Figure 11.1 The official opening ceremony for the new Foundling Hospital buildings on the Ashlyns Hall estate, Berkhamsted, 1935. Prince Arthur of Connaught and other dignitaries meet some of the young girls. DACHT BK5660 Berkhamsted Local History and Museum Society.

Court Road. Lady Margaret Hall was chosen as the most suitable model.

The buildings were begun in autumn 1932 and erected by Messrs Walter Lawrence & Son. They were constructed of locally manufactured multi-coloured narrow bricks dressed with Bath stone. Accommodation comprised dormitories, classrooms and recreation rooms for boys and girls, a chapel, a large assembly hall, dining halls, a gymnasium and swimming bath, administrative offices and a boardroom. The classrooms were light and airy, and were specially designed to give the children the benefit of the morning sun. There were also a large band-practice room, technical workshops, kitchens and a boiler house. The buildings provided for between 200 and 250 boys and an equal number of girls, with accommodation for the necessary teaching and administrative staff. Adequate playing fields were laid out to either side of the site.[14] The foundation stone was laid on 30 June 1933 by HRH Prince Arthur of Connaught KG and the children were transferred to the new buildings in July 1935 (see Figure 11.1).

Whilst the Foundling Hospital Committee was aware of modern developments in architecture, at the same time it was keen that many features of the old Hospital should be incorporated in the new, thus embodying the spirit and the ethos of the original Foundling Hospital. Detailed correspondence between Hardwick H. Nichols, secretary of the Foundling Hospital, and the architect Mortimer Sheppard bear this out. A photograph of the former coat of arms of the Hospital, designed by Hogarth, was sent with the comment that the new ones should be based on this.[15] As far as possible everything that had been salvaged from the demolition and either stored or put to use at the Redhill School was to be incorporated in the new buildings. The staircase which had been outside the Secretary's room in the Girls' Wing was to be re-erected in the new Hospital.

In considering the plan for the Band Room it was stipulated that 'the columns should be the same as in the old building': there was one in store at Redhill which could serve as a reference. The busts of the musicians from the old Band Room were to be installed in the new one.[16] The original light pedestals from London that had been used to light the road for carriages were placed alongside the main drive of the new Foundling Hospital. At the stipulation of the Land Registry the Foundling Hospital was required to place 20 boundary posts around the estate. These were modelled on the earlier boundary posts (which featured the Foundling Hospital lamb with a sprig of thyme in its mouth – see p. 204) from the London site, one of which had been salvaged. These boundary posts, especially those on Brickhill Green, Sandpit Green and Long Green, caused particular concern with the local council, which stated that the freehold in these areas of common land belonged to the Duchy of Cornwall.[17]

It was hoped that a large picture by Raphael, 'The Murder of the Innocents', at the time on loan to the Victoria and Albert Museum, could be placed in the new Foundling Hospital. 'It would be good to get it back to hang in Berkhamsted.'[18] The statue of Thomas Coram was to be placed on the grass court in front of the administrative block and would require a new pedestal.[19] The importance of the history of the Foundling Hospital and above all that of its founder to the governors was particularly evident. It was decided that the tomb of Thomas Coram and his mortal remains, together with the other memorials to former governors, would have to be placed in a specially erected crypt under the new chapel. As a letter to Sheppard from Secretary Nichols stated, 'The Committee have authorised you to construct a crypt under the chapel in accordance with the plans you submitted at a cost not exceeding £1,200 for the purpose of fixing memorial tablets from the old Hospital chapel.'[20]

The most important treasures and artefacts brought from the original Foundling Hospital were to be housed in the chapel or the crypt. All the stained-glass windows within their original leading were intended to be reinstated in the new chapel. Owing to lack of space, however, only the oldest windows were placed in the new chapel; those left over, mainly with armorial bearings, were placed in the windows of the concert hall.[21] The 'old Governors' pews' were to be reused, and the remaining seating was to be adapted and reused at the front of the chapel balcony. The old communion rails were to be fixed across the new chancel. It was proposed to hang a picture of Christ presenting a little child by Benjamin West (1738–1820), previously over the altar in the London Foundling Hospital, above the altar. All these arrangements were duly carried out, the statue of Coram was erected and his coffin placed in the crypt, together with the other memorial tablets and the bust of Handel. In creating the new Hospital a great deal of respect for its founder and forefathers is evident, while at the same time due regard was paid to the best use of materials and the avoidance of unnecessary expenditure.

Life in the Berkhamsted Foundling Hospital

For the children transferring from Redhill to the new buildings at Berkhamsted the change must have been quite significant. Not only were they in new buildings, which were larger than those at St Anne's, but the grounds were extensive and, to the children, remote from civilisation. With the large iron gates kept locked at all times, the children felt cut off from the outside world.[22] The grounds of St Anne's were large but the building was close to the station and the railway line ran adjacent to the grounds. There was not the same feeling of being in the countryside (see Figure 11.2) and of remoteness from the local community.

As had been the case from the early days of the Foundling Hospital the children spent the first five years of their life with foster parents, where they enjoyed the semblance of a normal family life within the local community, either with foster brothers and sisters or the children of their foster parents. Although it was not always the case, many foundlings look back to those early days with fond memories of their foster parents, the only parents they knew.[23] Some of the children spent a short time in the local primary school before transferring to the Foundling Hospital.

The entry for these small children was a traumatic one, with the parting in many instances equally difficult for the foster mothers. The new children

Figure 11.2 Aerial view of the Berkhamsted Foundling Hospital buildings and grounds, taken in the 1940s. DACHT BK10627 © Berkhamsted Local History and Museum Society.

were brought to Berkhamsted by coach in May each year, accompanied in most instances by their foster mothers. On leaving the coach the children were formed into a crocodile and, clutching the single toy they were permitted to bring with them, led into the school. The doors were shut firmly behind them. The child was not going to use that main door again until the day he or she left. No goodbyes or farewells were permitted. The foster mother had gone. The child was alone. Many remember that as the unhappiest first memory of their time in Berkhamsted.

The children were bathed before being given a very close haircut and fitted out with the infants' school uniform, 'all the while under the supervision of the stern and unbending staff'.[24] 'We were all bathed on the day of our arrival like lambs being herded through a sheep dip. The smell of carbolic soap lingered for days and seemed to permeate everything.'[25] Things had been done that way for two centuries and were not to change until after the end of the Second World War, when educational and social reforms were to alter dramatically the way the Foundling Hospital operated. In the 1930s and 1940s the children were still living under the harsh conditions that had been maintained since the foundation of the Hospital in the eighteenth century. The children became accustomed to a 'life devoid of any love or affection'.[26]

Certain allowances were made for the infants, however. The boys were housed on the girls' side of the school for their first year. They were not yet subjected to the harsh discipline and bullying from older children that they would suffer when they moved to the boys' side. The bigger girls were encouraged to befriend the infants and play games with them in the playground. A senior girl slept in each infant dormitory and in the morning would on occasion invite one of the infants into her bed for a cuddle before the day started. The charge nurses, although very strict, were known by their Christian names. The class teachers (see Figure 11.3) were more aloof and stricter than the nurses.

The infants were encouraged to play together and taken for walks in the countryside. As well as lessons, they were taught by the nurses to lace their boots and mend holes in their socks. As infants the children were well fed, bathed twice a week, well clothed and kept warm in winter. They were kept busy, so were never bored. In August they went to summer camp

Figure 11.3 An infant class in progress in the 1940s. Note the coloured picture tiles on the walls. DACHT BK10621 Berkhamsted Local History and Museum Society.

by the sea and at Christmas time they were taken to Bertram Mills' circus in London.[27] Birthdays were marked only by the arrival of cards and gifts from foster parents. No mention of a birthday was ever made by any of the staff. On Christmas Day a special lunch was served and afterwards, in the concert hall, each child was given a present provided by the governors. The presents were taken from around an enormous Christmas tree. Films were shown once a week and, if suitable for them, the infants were allowed to attend.[28]

When an infant misbehaved his or her name was recorded with a pencil on the corner of their nurse's starched apron and at bedtime the nurse called out the names of the children she had collected in the course of the day and punishment was administered accordingly with the back of a hairbrush on the bare behind. An extra tick was added if a child misbehaved more than once and the punishment was increased.

> This was a daily ritual enacted before we knelt at the foot of our
> beds and with eyes closed sang the evening vesper:
>> Glory to Thee my God this night
>> For all the blessings of the light
>> Keep me O keep me King of Kings
>> Beneath Thine own almighty wings.[29]

Until the outbreak of war foster parents were able to visit once every three months but many were unable to do so because of difficult journeys. Others ceased to visit because they found the change in their children too distressing. The children had become cool and detached. Children, when deprived of love and affection, learn to do without it and often in later life find it hard to show such emotions. The boys, particularly, learned to restrain tears and then later found it impossible to show emotions or to cry. Any presents or confectionery brought by the foster parents for the children on these visits were taken away and given out over a period of time by the headmaster. Many of the presents went missing.

After that first year in the Infants' Department boys and girls were permanently and rigidly segregated. The only glimpse obtained of the opposite sex was in the school chapel (see Figure 11.4), attended twice every Sunday. Boys and girls who had been brought up together as foster brothers and sisters were allowed no time together for the rest of their school life. Many foundlings mention the pain of this separation.

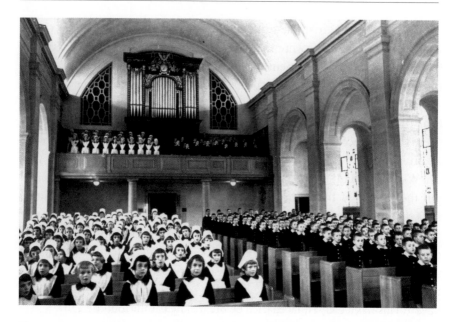

Figure 11.4 Boys and girls, strictly segregated, in the school chapel in the 1940s. DACHT BK10614 Berkhamsted Local History and Museum Society.

On arrival in the Junior Department boys and girls were exposed to the full rigours of institutional discipline from the staff and bullying from senior boys and girls. A number of former foundlings, both boys and girls, relate instances of bullying, which was sometimes physical and sometimes meant going hungry because of having to hand over food to older boys. A clip round the ear or a slap in the face would be administered for the slightest misdemeanour. Corporal punishment by stick or hand was so entrenched that children would involuntarily flinch at the approach of any member of staff. They were equally afraid of being bullied by older boys. This habitual nervous twitching in the presence of authority was to persist in many of the boys even after conditions had improved after the War. [30]

There was frequent emotional abuse and children were often humiliated. Gordon Aspey wrote years later that he feared humiliating punishments more than the cane, being made to stand on a chair for an entire lunchtime, perhaps, for talking during a meal. Girls were sometimes punished for talking in the dormitory after lights out by being made to stand in front of an open window with their nightdresses over their heads until they were shivering with cold. Staff were aware of bullying inflicted on the younger children by both older boys and girls, but made no effort to intervene. For the children it was difficult at times to distinguish punishment from bullying. It was all part of the life that they endured. Again, it was only after the War, when changes were introduced, that such behaviour stopped.

The children were well fed, in principle, with plain wholesome food, but with the active physical life they led were always hungry. This was particularly so when rationing was introduced during wartime. Both girls and boys talk of taking raw vegetables from the garden vegetable store and supplementing their diet with wild fruits found in the school grounds. One girl mentions climbing a large oak tree, the branches of which overhung the fence. In the field on the other side was an apple tree. One snack only was allowed at eleven o'clock on weekdays. Biscuits were brought to the classroom, one or two for each pupil. Sometimes the teacher would eat them all himself, saying that the children hadn't worked hard enough or their behaviour hadn't been up to standard. The younger boys would often have to save their biscuits to give to an older boy. The same applied to meals, when a younger boy was 'ordered' to save his portion and hide it in his uniform to give to the monitors.[31] He then went hungry to bed.

It should be remembered that this harsh regime, with corporal punishment and bullying, was no different from that of a number of other similar boarding institutions of that time, such as preparatory schools, public schools and charitable institutions. Corporal punishment was still used in schools for a number of years after the period we are studying. The obvious and crucial difference between the children of the Foundling Hospital and those at public or prep schools was that the children in the Foundling Hospital did not go home in the holidays. During the War they did not even go to summer camp, so had no escape from the school environment. There was also the historic attitude to the children and their illegitimate birth. 'We were often reminded that we should be grateful to the Foundling Hospital and our position in life was to serve.'[32] When at School 'we were constantly reminded of our disadvantaged position in life and of how we should be grateful for the help given and in return show some respect and humility.'[33]

Even in this harsh regime one or two individuals stand out as showing some kindness. This was particularly so among ancillary staff, who had no responsibility for the children.[34] In most cases punishment did not break the children's spirit. One girl is reported to have said to a teacher or nurse who was caning her, 'One day I shall be bigger than you. Then you'd better watch out!'[35] Pupils even managed to turn punishment into fun, as is reported by several former girl pupils. Detentions were carried out on Saturday afternoons, normally the only free time during the week. They were given when a pupil had acquired a certain number of black marks, which could occur for quite trivial offences. Tasks given included washing the walls and polishing the floors in the lengthy corridors, for which strips of blanket were given. These provided an excellent opportunity for racing speedily down the corridors while polishing the floors at the same time. A lookout was posted at either end to warn of the arrival of a member of staff.

Like all children, they 'played up' those in command. The girls played 'musical beds' when they changed beds in the dark to confuse the nurse on duty. One particularly bold pupil played Oliver Twist and in the middle of the meal said, 'Please Miss, may I have some more? I'm hungry!' which evoked the expected outburst of anger. In spite of the strict regime and the knowledge that harsh punishment would be exacted for misdemeanours, one of the boys tells of a midnight feast being held, but it was probably a rare occurrence. Additionally, some of the boys indulged in illicit smoking behind the Band Room. This could only be done on sunny days when the sun's rays were strong enough to ignite the tip of the cigarette. This was done with the aid of a magnifying glass or the lens of spectacles. Cigarettes were made from short lengths of bootlace wrapped in toilet paper.[36]

Real friendships among the girls have lasted in many instances for very many years. Boys tended to run around in gangs but were not encouraged to make close friends. After breakfast each day the children went into the playground or, in bad weather, into the playroom. There were no toys as such. The children improvised by making a ball from paper and string and would play football. In the 1940s an illustrated article appeared in *Picture Post* that showed the children playing with toys. These vanished when the photographers departed.[37]

The boys and girls from the Junior School onwards still wore the uniform which had been worn by foundlings for over two centuries with very little change. Although this appears anachronistic by today's standards, it was not unique. Eton College and Christ's Hospital School also maintained their traditional uniforms. For the foundling boys this consisted of dark brown long trousers and jacket. The jacket had from the neck down brass buttons embossed with the school emblem of a lamb. Only the top button was fastened and the front flared down to the waist, revealing a scarlet waistcoat also adorned with brass buttons with the school emblem but fastened up to the neck. The final adornment was a stiffly starched white collar worn on the outside of the jacket and a large black bow tie. Heavy army-style boots were worn.[38] This uncomfortable uniform did not, however, impede the rough and tumble of the playground. In fact, it could be advantageous when shinning up drainpipes to retrieve a precious, badly worn tennis ball from the flat roof or to peep down at the girls in the indoor swimming pool.

The girls, likewise, still wore the uniform of the eighteenth century and this, together with the uniform hairstyle of a short bob with a fringe, left little opportunity for individuality. White caps with white aprons over their brown skirts and tops and, for outside wear, red capes gave the impression of little maids, later to be in service.

The school had the advantage of a very fine gymnasium and swimming pool, which was unusual at that time, and a competitive spirit was encouraged. School teams competed successfully against neighbouring schools. A regimented, even draconian, approach was used in the teaching of sport and woe betide the child who did not exert himself or herself or had no aptitude for sport. It was the same when it came to learning to swim: the PE master

> would push the learners to the deep end of the pool with a large broom. Then he would shout, 'Let go of the broom and swim! … If you do not let go, then I will!' The surface of the water would boil with panic-stricken learners desperately lunging towards the side of the pool and safety.

Occasionally a strong swimmer was sent into the pool to rescue a gradually submerging boy, who was then comforted with words to the effect, 'You will learn to swim even if we both drown in the process.'[39]

Music played a central role in the life of the school, as it had done from the earliest days of the Hospital. The focus was on singing and the school military band. No theory of music was taught. There were no individual instrumental lessons, nor were the piano or string instruments taught. The Hospital choir was magnificent and had a fine reputation. Every weekday afternoon except Mondays the school band could be heard practising in the Band Room, sited on the edge of the boys' playground. Only boys over 12 were allowed to join and no choice of instrument was given: the bigger boys were allocated the larger instruments or whichever instrument was needed to maintain the balance of the band.[40] The magnificent 'Handel'[41] organ played for services in the chapel enhanced the beauty of the music and a number of ex-pupils have mentioned the solace and escape from everyday life that the music brought them twice each Sunday.[42]

The education at the Foundling Hospital remained elementary until changes were introduced after the War, being restricted to the 'three Rs' – reading, writing and arithmetic – and with a strong emphasis on religion. In these basics the children were well educated. Numeracy, grammar and religion were given a high profile. Algebra, trigonometry and geometry were not covered and science, history and geography were very limited. In the later years a few girls had the opportunity to attend local grammar schools, having passed the 11-plus scholarship exam. I have found no evidence that boys had a similar opportunity. Those remaining at the Hospital school even when the curriculum was broadened had no possibility of being entered for external exams.[43]

Before the Second World War the whole school spent the month of August under canvas by the sea a few miles from Folkestone. The journey there was carried out like a military exercise. The boys and girls were marched in regimental formation behind the school band to Berkhamsted station and put on a train to Folkestone. On arrival at Folkestone the band again led the marching column through the town to the campsite, where everything was already prepared. At the end of the month the same procedure was followed in reverse. On Sundays while in camp the whole school marched again behind the band to and from Folkestone parish church. The summer camp was a welcome break from the daily school routine, but stopped abruptly with the onset of war. During the war the government introduced a scheme, 'Holidays at Home', in which local authorities were encouraged to provide entertainment during the holiday period. The school band contributed to this by playing in a fairground in the town centre.[44]

From the early days of the Foundling Hospital boys had been placed in apprenticeships on leaving school and girls went largely into domestic service. This was still the case when the Berkhamsted Hospital was established. In September 1936 18 boys in their fourteenth or fifteenth year were placed out as apprentices, of whom 9 had passed the exam to become apprentices in the Army Ordnance Corps; 5 entered various regimental bands; 2 were apprenticed in engineering works in Reading; and 2 became agricultural apprentices. In 1941 10 boys were placed at Vickers Armstrong in Weybridge and an engineering company in Redhill. Another 14 were placed in regimental bands. These were typical of the placements for male foundlings in the 1930s and 1940s. Although most of the boys placed in the army went into regimental bands, a considerable number were placed at the Army Technical School in Chepstow, with the Royal Ordnance Corps and in the Army Apprentices School.[45]

Girls were mainly placed as apprentice domestic servants in respectable homes, where they were visited regularly until coming of age, but after the Second World War girls were sometimes placed in clerical positions with commercial firms and fewer became domestic servants. In the later years some of the girls who had gone to grammar school were able to proceed to teachers' training colleges. Of the girls going into domestic service some were sent to the Foundling Hospital's Domestic Economy School, Roselawn, at Chislehurst, where they received intensive training in 'modern housewifery'. They were then placed in respectable households to continue their apprenticeships. By early 1938 Roselawn became too expensive to run and soon after, the Foundling Hospital founded another domestic economy school in Craven Hill Gardens, Bayswater, London.

Every year apprentices from the Foundling Hospital were required to obtain 'certificates of good conduct' from their commanding officers, employers and mistresses and received rewards commensurate with their length of service. On completion of indentures, each foundling attended a thanksgiving service at the school's chapel and received five guineas if their conduct had been satisfactory throughout.[46] The placement of foundlings in apprenticeships continued until the 1950s and the closure of the Hospital. The inculcation of the work ethic was all-important and excluded most other considerations. The need for children to have a stable family life and a happy upbringing did not merit recognition.[47]

Wartime in the Foundling Hospital

The period 1935–9 was one of relative calm for the Foundling Hospital in Berkhamsted. Difficulties on several fronts began to occur with the outbreak of the Second World War and the need for large-scale evacuation of children from London. As early as February 1939 the Foundling Hospital received a request from the government to prepare accommodation in their Berkhamsted buildings.[48] Fifty girls from Chiswick Central School were evacuated to Berkhamsted and used one of the dormitories as classroom accommodation during the day. Consequently the foundlings had to be moved into other areas, leading to overcrowding. This also led to some confusion of command, as the schoolchildren were working with both school and institutional authorities under one roof. For the foundlings the atmosphere became even more depersonalised and regimented.

As in many schools during the War, there were staffing difficulties. Many of the younger teachers were called up for war service and older or less experienced teachers came in their stead. The problem was particularly difficult in the Boys' School, but also affected the Girls' School to a lesser extent. For the children and adults alike, rationing meant that food allocations were more stringently applied. Summer camps ceased and visits from foster parents, where they had existed, were no more.

The Foundling Hospital survived the war years unscathed, except for one incident when a German bomb fell on the southern extremity of the school grounds, fortunately causing little damage and no injury. Berkhamsted itself, only 30 miles from London, suffered the occasional bombing raid. On these occasions the boys were taken to the woodwork room, a semi-basement room, and the girls to another basement area. Here a section was set up with palliasses, pillows and blankets for the children to sleep on until the all-clear siren sounded.[49] Part way through the War the Americans arrived in Bovingdon Airfield, about three miles away. At night their searchlights could be seen and it was possible to hear aircraft taking off and returning from their missions. The airmen were very kind to the foundlings, giving them presents and holding the occasional tea party.[50]

The War and its aftermath shook the structure of the Foundling Hospital. Financial difficulties and the required introduction of new legislation, affecting both the education of children and the management of orphans, were to lead to changes in the governance of the Foundling Hospital and eventually to its demise.

Social Service Legislation

In 1933 the Children & Young Person's Act had come into force. This extended the state's responsibility for children in care to the age of 17 and brought them more directly under the control of the Home Office.[51] It now had statutory power over the children of the Foundling Hospital, a factor that was gradually to become significant as time went on and to alter the balance between charitable and state child-welfare organisations.[52] Evidence of more direct state intervention did not become apparent until early in 1945 when the Hospital secretary, H.H. Nichols, received a report from the Home Office drawn up as a result of an inspection.[53] This criticised the way in which the school was being run, objecting especially to the early institutionalisation of the children and the lack of contact with foster parents. The report was also critical of the educational standards. The governors maintained that the criticisms 'were exaggerated and unfair' and that now was not 'the time for drastic alterations', especially ones that would cost money. The charity's finances were stretched to their limits in the period of post-war austerity. A special sub-committee of governors was established in February 1945 to consider the criticisms made. Legal advice was sought and appeared to be reassuring: the charity was a child-saving institution so some aspects of the 1944 Education Act might be avoided, especially the need to give all children the same educational opportunities. The legal adviser claimed that while the Schools were conducted along the 'lines of an institution there was no cause for anxiety apart from the difficulties which have arisen through the War and the reduced staff'.[54]

This somewhat entrenched attitude of the governors towards change had been apparent for some years. The headmaster of 40 years, Mr Holgate, had retired in December 1943. The new headmaster had proposed a radical revision of the curriculum to provide a secondary education for the older boys. This was delayed pending a careful review of the financial situation. There was also some resistance from the governors to the idea of a universal secondary education for foundlings because of their low social status. The new head had also proposed replacing the traditional uniforms with more normal dress, but this was refused; frustrated by the resistance to change, he resigned. The subsequent appointee, as head of the Boys' School only, also resigned after a year. In January 1945 the name of the school was changed, as a result of a referendum held among former pupils, to the Thomas Coram Schools, with the charity retaining the name Foundling Hospital. The problems, however, continued.

The sub-committee of governors made a number of recommendations as a result of the Home Office Report. They thought that it was desirable to appoint a person with experience in residential schools as headmaster. The governors also recommended that the children should remain with their foster parents until the age of six, and that they should spend the holidays with them on a regular basis.[55] This policy was implemented at Easter 1945.[56] It was intended that this would bring the Hospital more into line with boarding schools.

Figure 11.5 Boys and girls, dressed in the redesigned school uniform, together in the library, 1949.
DACHT BK6882 Berkhamsted Local History and Museum Society.

Mr E.E. White, who had previously been headmaster at the London County Council School at St Margaret's, Great Gaddesden, was appointed head of what was now known as the Thomas Coram Schools. He took up his appointment in September 1945 and it was under his headship that many changes were implemented. The school uniform was changed in favour of traditional clothes of the period (see Figure 11.5). The boys wore grey trousers and jackets, white shirts and grey socks, the girls dresses and modern gym-slips and blouses.

> No longer would Saturday be bath night with boys bathing two
> at a time in the same bath, nor would the teachers eat separately
> from the children. The wards where the children slept were
> brightened, adding furniture and allowing the children to separate
> the beds into units of five or six and to decorate the walls in bright
> colours … With our own pocket money we were allowed to visit
> the Berkhamsted shops.[57]

Gordon Aspey[58] also wrote of these changes: 'The change – almost overnight – was dramatic, and school life suddenly became not only bearable but also enjoyable.' Time was needed to adapt to this sudden freedom. 'Being used to having every aspect of our lives controlled the effect on our behaviour was dramatic, and the staff found it very difficult to control us.'[59] Girl foundlings speak in similar vein about their experiences of the changes introduced and of the new opportunity to learn typing skills.

Children from that unknown institution on the hill, who had formerly only been seen walking in 'crocodiles', were now a part of Berkhamsted's community in a way they had not been before. Consequently, the Berkhamsted Citizens Association, founded in 1928, invited Mr White to speak to them in May 1947. In what was reported as 'a moving and intensely human' talk, Mr White said 'Every effort is being made to give each child a life as near to normal as was possible in the circumstances.' He referred to the changes that had taken place in the past two years. No longer were boys trained with the object of a great many being enlisted into army bands and no longer were girls prepared for domestic service. He wanted the children 'to have the finest training and to bring [the] schools in line with the best in present day education'. There was now a mixed primary school and some mixed classes in the senior school. A commercial section had been started for girls. The Band was no longer seen primarily as a way into the army, being reorganised as an orchestra for boys and girls purely as a cultural activity. Some boys still joined army bands, but a wider range of trades was now represented. Mr White ended his talk by thanking Berkhamsted residents for their kindly and tolerant welcome to the children:

> Two years was not a long time for the children to get the right
> attitude: they were not yet used to freedom, but it was good
> to know that the Coram School was no longer regarded as
> some isolated institution on the hill: it was becoming a part of
> Berkhamsted and he hoped the links would grow with the years.[60]

Educational Legislation

The Education Act of 1944 raised the school leaving age to 15 and introduced secondary education for all, dividing children among grammar schools, technical high schools and secondary modern schools according to the results of the 11-plus examination. The need to implement this Act had considerable implications for the Foundling Hospital, which was experiencing severe financial difficulties in the post-war years. Additional teaching staff were required in order to introduce a secondary curriculum and salaries had to be brought into line with the Burnham Scale. In 1947 the Foundling Hospital enquired from the Ministry of Education as to the availability of grants to meet the costs of education and administration of the schools, stating that 'until 1939 the governors had found no difficulty in meeting all the costs of the Schools from the corporate funds of the charity' and stressing that 'it is felt that the first objective of the charity must be to provide a home for the deprived child admitted to this Hospital.' From this point on protracted negotiations took place between the Foundling Hospital and Hertfordshire County Council regarding help with education costs. In a letter of February 1948 Secretary Nichols wrote outlining the current improvements at the Thomas Coram Schools:

> The schools are residential for boys and girls of six to fifteen
> years. The primary children are educated together and the seniors
> separately. The Secondary department has a technical bias for
> the boys with some commercial training for exceptional pupils.
> The girls' work has a dual bias, commercial and domestic science.
> There is a good musical tradition. The schools are recognised by
> the Ministry of Education as efficient for the purpose of Teachers'
> Superannuation.[61]

Coincidentally, Hertfordshire County Council required more accommodation for its local secondary modern pupils. A site had been earmarked before the war and architectural plans approved for a three-form-entry school.[62] Because of the expansion of Berkhamsted a five-form-entry secondary modern school might now be required. Additionally a two-form-entry technical school, preferably on the same site, was proposed. Accommodation for secondary pupils in the primary schools would have to be vacated as the expected increase in birth rate would require more primary places.

The request from the Foundling Hospital put a different perspective on the situation. A detailed memorandum dated 8 April 1948 and outlining various proposals was drawn up by John Newsom, County Education Officer. It was clear that no plan could be approved which envisaged the continued segregation of the foundling children in a school for them alone. Two suggestions were made. The first was that the LEA should avail itself of a relatively small number of vacancies in the primary and secondary departments of the school. This would mean that children from Berkhamsted would occupy a small proportion of places in an unreorganised school of special character. This was dismissed as 'obviously not a satisfactory proposal'. The second proposal suggested that the home should be confined to children of 11–15 years and the school to secondary education, providing a large secondary school in which the 'institutional' children would be in the minority. This second proposal was felt to have two major advantages: it would offer the 'institutional' children an education shared with ordinary children enjoying the normal advantages of family life; and it would offer the senior children of Berkhamsted excellent buildings and educational facilities. Reorganisation could be completed by September 1949. Any comparable provision would take far longer to implement.[63] The proposal was agreed in principle by the Foundling Hospital, although the governors were unhappy about the structure of the Board of Governors for the school. They also wished to keep a number of primary children in residence. These children would require schooling in the town. The Hospital also disliked the choice of the name 'Ashlyns', preferring to keep the name 'Thomas Coram'.[64]

In May 1949 the Hospital threatened to break off negotiations. In spite of these difficulties the school was opened in 1951 as a secondary modern school, although the lease had still not been signed. Hertfordshire County Council paid an annual rent of £5,500 plus a further £5,000 for services from that date. In the draft lease the county council agreed 'not to make any alterations or additions to the demised premises or the shared premises without consent in writing of the lessors and to keep these buildings in good and tenantable repair'. Local children were now educated alongside the residential children of the Foundling Hospital. The foundlings had not been told about these changes and in 'the early days found it very difficult to accept these "townies" into their home'.[65] Gradual integration through sports, music, art and drama broke down the barriers.

The Children Act 1948

The implementation of the Children Act of 1948 had a profound effect on the number of children coming into residence at the Hospital in Berkhamsted. Local authorities now had a duty to place a child in foster care, rather than in residential homes. This caused a steady dwindling of numbers, making the extensive buildings in Berkhamsted redundant. The governors sought legal advice as to whether they were bound by the terms of the lease to Hertfordshire County Council, as they were now considering selling the entire property. The situation was summed up by Mr Wilfred M. Hunt of Lincoln's Inn Fields thus:

> The policy of the Hospital has, I understand, changed since 1950 or so, and they now board out their children in foster homes and arrange for them to attend local schools, with the result that the number of their children available to go to such a school as the said Berkhamsted school is dwindling. By 1956 there will be none. Consequently the said school and the said assignment in reference thereto is now of no use to the Hospital for its own children, and it would prefer to sell the property.

Since the lease had never been signed 'there is no binding contract for a lease and either party is free to withdraw'.[66]

Conclusion

Negotiations between the Foundling Hospital and Hertfordshire County Council to sell the property were almost as protracted as those over the lease. At a meeting of the Foundling Hospital governors on 30 December 1953 it was reported that little progress had been made. A tentative offer of £175,000 had been turned down. It was decided that no more children should be sent to board at the Hospital and that all residential children and staff should be evacuated at the end of the summer term 1954.[67] On 12 May 1954 it was resolved 'that the school property at Berkhamsted of approximately fifty acres and including the staff houses in Coram Close be sold to Hertfordshire County Council for a sum of £225,000'.[68] The sale of the school was finally completed on 9 September 1955. Ashlyns School is now a Grade II listed building.

A great deal of discussion took place as to the future of the 'Handel' organ and the mortal remains of Thomas Coram, and of the memorials and fine artefacts which survived from the original Foundling Hospital. The remains of Thomas Coram and the organ were installed in the church of St Andrew's Holborn in London, but all other artefacts remain as a memorial to Thomas Coram and the institution which he established for the 'Maintenance and Education of Exposed and Deserted Young Children', which had had its last home in Berkhamsted. The Foundling Hospital as an institution had gone, its credibility and viability overtaken by the changing social and educational philosophy of the mid-twentieth century. The charitable work of the Thomas Coram Foundation continues today as *Coram*. Many of those who lived ten years of their lives in the Foundling Hospital in Berkhamsted have gone on to do well in adult life, in spite of unhappy earlier years. 'We had been taught that nobody is going to give you anything. If you want it, you'll have to get it yourself.'[69] 'The Hospital had not moved with the times. Our basic education was very good. We were well-educated to a certain standard, whereby we could go out and serve the community. What we lacked was love.'[70]

This detailed view of the experiences of foundlings and the development and decline of their institution in the twentieth century provides a counterbalance to the focus in the secondary literature on the eighteenth- and nineteenth-century incarnation of the Foundling Hospital.

Notes

1. R. Harris, *Enlightened self-interest* (London, 1997), p. 31.
2. The staircase from the Boys' Wing, and some architectural features of the Court Room, Committee Room and Picture Gallery.
3. Hertfordshire Archives and Local Studies, Hertford (hereafter HALS) DE/Cf/Q/2, Correspondence between Nichols, Secretary of Foundling Hospital and Sheppard, architect of new buildings.
4. This had been founded in 1702 as the Royal Asylum of St Anne's in Aldersgate for educating children of those who had once seen better times, moved to Streatham in the second half of the nineteenth century and to Redhill in 1884. St Anne's was closed in 1920 and offered for sale. It was purchased by the Foundling Hospital in 1926 for £25,500.
5. Quoted in R.H. Nichols and F.A. Wray, *The history of the Foundling Hospital* (London, 1935), p. 324.
6. Ashridge was rejected on the grounds that it was too remote to provide entertainment for the staff.
7. Ashlyns Hall still stands and is now a Grade II* listed building. Plans were drawn up to adapt the building as the sanatorium, but presumably this was either too expensive or too complicated. It became the headquarters for Nichols, the secretary of the Foundling Hospital.
8. From correspondence held at HALS DE/Cf/Q/2.
9. Ibid.
10. Of the Crosse & Blackwell family.
11. Among Ashlyns papers at HALS DE/Cf/Q/4.

12. Ibid.
13. Official opening ceremony of the Water Tower. Dacorum Heritage Trust. Collection of Berkhamsted Local History & Museum Society DACHT BK3898.123.
14. From the Foundling Hospital programme of arrangements for ceremony of laying the foundation stone, 30 June 1933, and architectural drawing of the Foundling Hospital, J.M. Sheppard & Partners. DACHT BK4012.1.
15. HALS DE/Cf/Q/9 Letter from Nichols to Sheppard, 29 January 1934.
16. HALS DE/Cf/Q/2 Letter from Foundling Hospital Secretary to Clerk of Works, 23 October 1934.
17. The manor and honour of Berkhamsted had been part of the Duchy of Cornwall since the time of the Black Prince. Although much of the area had been purchased by the Earls Brownlow, the freehold of the Greens mentioned above remained with the Duchy.
18. HALS DE/Cf/Q/2 Letter from Secretary to Sheppard, 1 April 1932.
19. HALS DE/Cf/Q/2 Letter from Sheppard, 12 November 1934. The former pedestal had been left at its former site in London.
20. HALS DE/Cf/Q/9 Letter to Sheppard, 11 January 1933.
21. HALS DE/Cf /Q/9 Letter from Secretary to Sheppard, 9 April 1934.
22. DACHT BK3895.118 Thomas Erskine, 'The childhood and early adult life of a foundling in the 1930s and 40s', Chapter V.
23. Ibid. and G. Aspey, *All at sea: memories of a Coram boy* (Emsworth, 2010).
24. DACHT BK3895.118, p. 24.
25. Aspey, *All at sea*, p. 56.
26. DACHT BK3895.118.
27. Both these outings ceased during the War.
28. Memories of former foundlings, written and recorded.
29. DACHT BK3895.118, p. 26.
30. Ibid.
31. Aspey, *All at sea*; DACHT BK3895.118 and interviews conducted for *Foundling Voices* lottery-funded project.
32. John Caldicott, 'My life as a foundling', *Your Berkhamsted* (May 2011), pp. 23–6.
33. DACHT BK3895.118, p. 14.
34. Memories of a former foundling, in conversation.
35. Interview for *Foundling Voices*.
36. DACHT BK3895.118.
37. This is reported by several ex-foundlings.
38. DACHT BK3895.118, p. 26, and others.
39. Aspey, *All at sea*, p. 61.
40. DACHT BK3895.118, p. 29 and interview for *Foundling Voices*.
41. The original organ was replaced quite early on in the history of the Foundling Hospital but continued to be referred to as the 'Handel' organ.
42. Interview for *Foundling Voices*.
43. DACHT BK3895.118, p. 32, and others.
44. Ibid., p. 30.

45. Minutes of Foundling Hospital Vol. 93, quoted in J. Ramsland, 'The decline and fall of the Thomas Coram Schools 1935–1954', *Journal of Educational Administration & History*, 27 (1995).

46. *Foundling Hospital Reports and Accounts for the year 1921* (London, 1922).

47. Ramsland, 'Decline and fall'.

48. Minutes Vol. 92, 21 February 1939, p. 109, quoted in Ramsland 'Decline and fall'.

49. Aspey, *All at sea*, p. 61, and other former foundlings in conversation.

50. Aspey, *All at sea*, p. 62.

51. Maurice Bruce, *The coming of the welfare state* (London, 1974), p. 289.

52. There was no obvious effect of this act until after the War.

53. Ramsland, 'Decline and fall'.

54. Ibid.

55. The Home Office had been very critical of the early age at which the children were institutionalised.

56. Ramsland, 'Decline and fall'.

57. Caldicott, 'My life'.

58. Aspey, *All at sea*, p. 63.

59. Caldicott, 'My life'.

60. Reported in *Berkhamsted Review*, June 1947.

61. HALS DE/Cf/Q/38.

62. Greenway First School and St Thomas More R.C. Primary School are now on this site.

63. HALS DE/Cf/Q/38 Confidential memo. There would be space for 340 children from Berkhamsted and 160 from Thomas Coram.

64. HCC chose the name Ashlyns in order to 'avoid any objections to association of the Berkhamsted school with the institution which has cared for children unfortunate in their parentage'. The name was retained for the residential premises.

65. Caldicott, 'My life'.

66. HALS DE/Cf/Q/46.

67. LMA A/FH/A/03.

68. LMA. A/FH/A/03 Minute Book, 12 May 1954.

69. *Foundling Voices*, interview with unnamed girl foundling.

70. Lydia Carmichael on Libby Purves' *Midweek*, Radio 4, April 2011.

CHAPTER TWELVE

Hertfordshire's relationship with certified industrial schools, 1857–1933

Gillian Gear

CERTIFIED INDUSTRIAL SCHOOLS were established by individuals, religious bodies and educational authorities following the passing of the 1857 Industrial Schools Act.[1] This act was intended to encourage the establishment of places that provided residential care and training for vulnerable and disruptive children to prevent their downward spiral into criminal careers. It was felt that through learning practical skills the children would be able to earn their living and through receiving a basic education and moral guidance they would be equipped for life as honest, upright citizens. In terms of the focus of this volume, those attending such schools comprise the most difficult group of people requiring 'care' in Hertfordshire. They constitute an interesting and important case study of the flexibility of care institutions and the ingrained sentiments of those paying for and providing care.

The name given to these schools was significant. The word 'certified' referred to the need for a 'certificate' to be granted, initially by the Education Department and then by the Home Office, to qualify for financial support. 'Industrial' referred to the industrial training that was given and 'school' to the basic education generally provided. The teaching staff in industrial schools did not have to hold teaching certificates. Some managers felt the standard of education merely needed to be basic, while others were more ambitious for their children.

Certified industrial schools were not the only schools to incorporate the word 'industrial' in their title. Schools of industry were generally earlier in date, parish-based and smaller. District Poor Law schools, established

Figure 12.1 Two ragamuffins. The Story of the Boys' Home, c.1890.

under the Poor Law system, often provided industrial training and some included 'industrial' in their title. These other schools can be confused with the certified industrial schools that are the subject of this chapter. All three elements described above need to be present for schools to fall within the scope of the certified-industrial-school system.

Attitudes towards the treatment of destitute and delinquent children underwent considerable change in the first half of the nineteenth century. Earlier it had been the practice to treat child and adult offenders in much the same way. Many children were being sent to prisons for frequent, short periods of time. It was becoming increasingly obvious that this was not solving the problem of young offenders but making mildly criminal children into serious offenders (Figure 12.1). Some people believed that punishment was an important element in the treatment of the children being brought before local magistrates, but others believed that society had failed these children and that, if caught early enough, they could be cured of any criminal tendencies and turned into useful citizens through residential care, education and industrial training. This resulted in the creation of two types of school, the reformatory school and the industrial school, which for most of their existence ran alongside each other under the supervision of the Home Office.

The 1854 Reformatory School Act[2] established homes providing training, care and education for older and more seriously criminal children but retaining an element of imprisonment. Courts would sentence the young offender to a short period of time in prison followed by a longer period in a reformatory school. The Industrial Schools Act of 1857 provided for the committal of younger, less criminal children brought before the courts to a period of time in industrial schools without the stigma of a term of imprisonment. Both reformatory and industrial schools provided residential care, education and training.

Children could also be admitted as voluntary cases to industrial schools, when money was often promised from those sponsoring the children. A system of inspection was established under the direction of the government inspector of reformatory and industrial schools and bodies such as the school boards also appointed their own inspectors to ensure that the children they sent were properly cared for. The pace at which industrial schools were set up was initially fairly slow, but the number of schools grew, peaking in the 1880s, before they slowly declined in popularity. In 1933 the remaining schools were merged into the new approved-school system as either senior or junior approved schools.[3]

Against this backdrop, the aim of the current chapter is to examine how the certified-industrial-school system was applied in Hertfordshire. It will identify and examine the schools run within the county and go on to find out how Hertfordshire's children were dealt with under the various industrial schools acts. In turn, detailed micro-studies such as this promise considerable advances in scholarship. Certified industrial schools are generally poorly understood; records are difficult to locate because the schools came under the Home Office rather than the Education Department and they were set up and run by a range of people and bodies. While there are some in-depth works published on individual schools the examination of the national picture is neglected. The author's PhD thesis attempted to fill this gap.[4]

The children

The range of children thought to be suitable for these schools changed over the period they ran – that is, from 1857 until 1933. The original aim of the 1857 Industrial Schools Act had been to 'Make better provision for the care and education of vagrant, destitute or disorderly children and for the extension of industrial schools, for children aged from seven to fourteen'.[5] In 1861 the lower age limit of seven years was dropped and the types of children that could be sent to industrial schools were defined as:

> Any child, apparently aged under fourteen, found begging or receiving alms
> Any child found wandering without a settled home or visible means of support or in the company of thieves
> Any unconvicted child, under the age of twelve, who had committed an offence punishable by prison, whom the justices thought should go to an industrial school
> or a child under fourteen whose parents stated they were unable to control him and who were prepared to pay the whole cost of his maintenance up to five shillings a week[6]

In 1866 the range of children was further extended to include convicts' children, those in bad company and disruptive children in workhouses, union, parish or district pauper schools or poorhouses.[7]

The 1870 Education Act allowed the newly formed school boards to make attendance at school compulsory in their district and they were enabled to establish their own industrial schools.[8] In 1871 the children of convicted mothers were added to the range of children who could be admitted. Under the 1876 Education Act[9] education became compulsory in all districts and as a result a further category of child was added, the truant child. Two new types of short-term industrial school, the day industrial school and the truant school, were opened to help deal with these children, although there were neither in Hertfordshire.

Nationally just 7 school boards set up 8 residential schools between them. In addition, 9 established 10 truant schools and 12 set up 1 day industrial school each. In districts where school boards had not already been established the 1876 Act provided for the setting up of school attendance committees. These committees had the same compulsory powers over attendance as the boards themselves. They ran until 1902.

In 1880 the range of children was further extended. Children living with prostitutes, those attending day industrial schools and those who were truanting or otherwise refusing to conform to school rules could be sent to residential industrial schools. Special industrial schools were established for mentally and physically handicapped children.[10] After 1908 all admissions came under the new Children Act.[11] That act added girls whose fathers had been convicted of the abuse of their daughters. Despite initial opposition, some children of soldiers killed during the First World War were also sent to industrial schools. Finally, children who had been found in the process of street trading contrary to locally introduced byelaws were added to the list.

Between 1857 and 1933 the pattern of the types of children being admitted changed. The number of destitute children decreased and that of young offenders increased. The proportion of children committed under the 1876 Education Act grew and in 1921 about one-fifth had been sent under that act. The London School Board (LSB) was a particularly active prosecutor, committing about a third of the children it sent to industrial schools under the 1876 Education Act. This was perhaps not as high a figure as might be expected, bearing in mind the nature of the board's role as an educational body.

The schools

Industrial schools were founded by four main groups: local magistrates; independent individuals supported by friends; educational authorities; and religious orders. To solve the problem facing local magistrates of dealing with destitute and delinquent children a few of them, such as those in Middlesex, set about providing and running their own industrial schools. About half of all industrial schools were established and run by independent philanthropic individuals who, with friends and local figures, formed management committees. After 1870 school boards set up industrial schools sub-committees with elected representatives and some founded their own schools. Some boards formed attendance committees that monitored attendance and took cases of truancy before the courts, as did boards of guardians. Roman Catholic orders established schools in cities such as Liverpool and Manchester, where there were large numbers of Irish Catholic children. The orders wanted to provide schools for their own 'flock' and tended not to have management committees with representatives from outside their own religious order. There was one Quaker-run school, Greenwood in Essex, for girls and one Jewish school for boys. Initially Jewish boys were sent to the Essex Industrial School but in 1900 the Jewish-run Hayes Industrial School was opened with places for 60 boys. Girls' schools tended to be smaller in size than boys' schools and were fewer in number. The Greenwood School was one of the larger girls' schools, catering for 70 girls, including some from Hertfordshire. Most girls' schools were smaller, like the Waifs and Strays school in Hemel Hempstead, which took just 20 girls.

By far the largest boys' school was the Feltham Industrial School, established by the Middlesex magistrates under their own act in 1854[12] and certified in 1867 for 700 boys. The larger schools tended to be those run by education authorities and were generally situated in or near to the large industrial cities rather than in more agriculturally based counties. The Bristol Industrial School for boys was certified in 1859 and in 1866, when it moved to Clifton Wood, it was certified for 180 boys and became known as the Clifton Industrial School. Shustoke Industrial School in Birmingham was certified in 1868 for 150 boys and recertified in 1914 for 166 boys. Schools founded by independent individuals were generally smaller, although the Boys' Home (initially founded in Euston Road, London in 1858 before moving to Hampstead in 1865) took between 120 and 140 boys.

The number of staff appointed by the managing committees depended on the size of the school. Usually a master and matron were the first to be appointed, followed by a schoolmaster and trade master. Other members of staff were appointed according to the needs of the individual schools.

There was no government requirement that teaching staff should be 'certificated' (qualified) and there was some criticism that the standard of education in industrial schools was not up to that of elementary schools.

Between 1857 and 1933 more than 220 schools were established. The majority of the schools were boys' schools, a smaller number were girls' schools and a very few were mixed-sex schools – generally these were the day industrial schools (see below) or those set up for the youngest children. The schools ran for varying lengths of time and were managed by management bodies that sometimes changed, as did the names and sites of some schools. This means it is not always possible to be certain of the exact numbers of individual schools or to trace the precise history of every school. The other types of certified industrial schools that had been established under the umbrella of the industrial-school system developed different characteristics. These were the day industrial schools, which, as the name suggests, provided education and training for children without providing accommodation, and truant schools, which took children for a short period of time and were, through a stricter regime, intended to discourage children from returning. There were also 'special' industrial schools established to cater for children with physical and mental handicaps, both referred to earlier.

Schools in Hertfordshire

Although all districts could make use of the industrial schools legislation, many areas chose not to establish their own but sent the children for whom they were responsible to schools set up by others and paid for their maintenance, training and education. Hertfordshire, like many other mainly agricultural counties, did not make a great deal of use of the Industrial School Act. Nevertheless there were five certified industrial schools in Hertfordshire and the county's children were sent to industrial schools both within and outside the county. The county schools were:

- The Boys' Farm Home, Church Farm, East Barnet, 1860–1933 (boys)
- Olive House, 27 George Street, Hemel Hempstead, 1884–1900 (girls)
- St Francis Industrial School (Special) Industrial School, Buntingford, 1919–1933 (boys and girls with mental health problems)
- Gisburne House Industrial School, Watford, 1912–33 (girls)
- St Elizabeth's School, Much Hadham, 1909–32 (boys and girls with epilepsy)

Figure 12.2 Boys working in the carpentry workshop at the Boys' Farm Home, Church Farm. *Boys' Farm Home Annual Report 1905.*

Just one of these schools, the Boys' Farm Home in East Barnet (see Figure 12.2), was established under the ethos of the early legislation. The other four opened after later legislation had extended the scope of the certified-industrial-school system. One, Gisburne House, was designed to take only London girls and the other three were run by organisations that specialised in taking children with specific problems.

The Boys' Farm Home was established in 1860 in East Barnet as a branch home of the Boys' Home, founded in 1858 in Euston Road, London. It was certified as a separate independent school by the Home Office in 1865. This school was also known as Church Farm. It continued to be run on the same site until 1938, by which time it had become a senior approved school. Today (see Figure 12.3) the buildings are used by Mill Hill County School as Oak Hill Campus.

This school was founded by a wealthy retired army officer, Lt Col W.J. Gillum, who had survived the loss of a leg during the Siege of Sebastopol and resolved thereafter to dedicate his life to establishing and running an industrial school to provide care and training for destitute and deprived boys. Gillum wrote in an appeal letter in January 1866 that the boys who

Figure 12.3 The former Boys' Farm Home buildings, East Barnet.

were admitted to his school were vagrant, destitute boys who had not been convicted of crime but were in great danger of being led astray if nothing was done for them. In 1866 in a letter to *The Times* he wrote that the home did not just take boys aged between 10 and 15 years of age, but had admitted some aged 7 and one aged 16.[13] The school stated that it tried to keep an even balance of children by having only 16 boys of any age. However, in 1876 there were 15 boys aged 10 to 12, 50 aged between 12 and 15 and 8 over the age of 15.[14]

Initially the school took on more voluntary cases than those committed under the government legislation that brought with it government financial support. Both the founder, Col. Gillum, and John Bowden, a long-serving master, liked the freedom to choose the boys they would accept, taking as many voluntary cases as they could. Gillum wrote, 'Most of our boys are admitted freely but we are greatly in need of funds. The home is specially for destitute boys. At present we do not take any under 10 years of age.'[15] Bowden told the government's 1897 Reformatory and Industrial Schools Committee that having voluntary boys improved the tone of the school. He cited as an example of the high standard of the children at his school the case of a boy who was the great grandson of an admiral.

Very few early admission records survive but it can be seen from a study of ten such records that just one boy was actually committed to the home under the Industrial Schools Act. At least one of the remainder was described as a 'semi-criminal', although he had not been prosecuted in return for his voluntary admission to Church Farm. Three other boys were described as 'the terror of the neighbourhood' and only one orphaned boy was described as 'respectable'.[16] Three of the boys were orphaned, three had lost their fathers, one his mother; the father of one was described as a lunatic and another of the fathers was blind; only one boy had what were described as 'decent parents' and he was too young to be prosecuted for the petty thieving that he had been doing.

The proportion of voluntary cases fell sharply in the mid-1890s, when there was a considerable drop in the value of donations and the managers had to take in a higher proportion of the committed and school-board cases which brought grants with them. The 1896 annual report showed that 55 of the 84 children had been committed and just 29 were voluntary cases.[17] A small proportion of voluntary admissions continued until 1933, at which time the Boys' Farm Home was the last industrial school admitting in this way.

Between 1870 and 1901 the London School Board was the main body sending children to the school. It did this by taking the case before a magistrate at one of London's police courts. In 1876 the Board sent 31 boys. At that time 6 other boys had been committed under the 1866 Industrial Schools Act and there were 42 voluntary cases.[18] Other children could be sent by boards of guardians, who would have made use of the court of Petty Sessions for truancy cases and the Quarter Sessions for more serious cases.

The details of the children attending the Boys' Farm Home have been extracted from the censuses from 1861 to 1901 and entered into a database. A total of 282 boys is listed in the four 10-yearly censuses. The total number of boys admitted during the 40-year period was probably more than double and possibly nearer triple that number, as boys generally stayed for between three and four years. The 1861 census showed just nine boys were living at the newly established home. Their ages ranged from 10 to 16, with three 10-year-olds, two aged 11, three 15-year-olds and one boy aged 16. By the time of the 1871 census the number of boys had increased to 57. Just over half, 30, had been born in London and Middlesex. The youngest boy was aged 11 years and there were three 16-year-olds. Otherwise their ages were fairly evenly spread. None of the boys had been sent by school boards since that avenue had yet to be opened up.

The accounts included in the annual reports for the same period show a breakdown of the school's income and the names of the bodies contributing to the maintenance of boys. These documents show the influence of the school's location, just into Hertfordshire and 11 miles from central London. The accounts lists donations, grants, subscriptions, special grants

Table 12.1   Origins of those in institutions.

Place	No. of boys	Place	No. of boys
London or Middlesex	140	Kent	15
Berkshire	3	Lincolnshire	2
Buckinghamshire	2	North Wales	1
Canada	1	Norfolk	1
Cornwall	1	Nottinghamshire	2
Devon	3	Oxfordshire	2
Dorset	1	Scotland	1
Essex	6	Staffordshire	1
Gloucestershire	2	Suffolk	5
Hampshire	3	Sussex	17
Hertfordshire	10	Warwickshire	1
Huntingdon	1	Wiltshire	3
India	1	Worcestershire	1
Isle of Wight	3	Yorkshire	1
Ireland	1	unknown	49

from the Secretary of State for boys sent under the Industrial Schools Act and for the teacher and contributions towards the cost of keeping boys sent by the London School Board and the Corporation of London, as well as the wages earned by the boys, which provided the home with additional income (there were several ways the boys earned money for the home; for example, some of the boys ran a milk round for the local community, sold milk, butter, eggs, livestock and vegetables and provided fencing for local landowners). Table 12.1 shows that of the 282 boys listed in census returns almost half, 140, had been born in either London or Middlesex. Of course, the census shows the boys' places of birth, not necessarily the districts from which they had been sent. It is quite possible that their families had moved to London from elsewhere by the time of their admission. However, the considerable range of birthplaces does suggest the existence of a wide capture network for troubled boys.

Despite the founder's desire to take a large proportion of voluntary cases, the school seemed increasingly to rely on the Home Office grants. By 1894, of the 50 boys who had been committed, 45 had been sent by the LSB. However there were actually 86 boys at the school at the time, presumably the difference was made up of voluntary admissions, and five had been committed through other boards or boards of guardians.[19]

Balfour's Education Act of 1901 abolished the school boards and the school attendance committees and put responsibility for elementary education under the counties, county boroughs and the larger boroughs and urban district councils as local education authorities. From 1901 to 1933 the annual reports' accounts showed the increasing range of bodies paying towards the cost of keeping children in the home. Once again, the greatest number of boys was supported by the government grants. They were closely followed by those boys sent by the London County Council (LCC), who continued the role of the former LSB. The Corporation of London also continued to pay for boys sent from the City.

In 1901 the annual accounts include payments by the Hertfordshire County Council, Middlesex County Council, Cambridge Corporation, Maidstone Education Committee and the Hitchin Guardians. Thereafter there was a remarkable increase in the number of other authorities who began to make use of the Boys' Home. The county councils included Hertfordshire, Middlesex, Derbyshire, Bedfordshire and Holland (Lincolnshire); the corporations, Bedford, London, Cambridge and Lincoln; the boroughs, West Ham, Cambridge and Luton; the education committees, Scarborough, Spalding and Maidstone; and the unions, Barnet, Edmonton, Hendon, Hitchin, Kettering, St Pancras, West Ham and Willesden.

Voluntary admissions frequently came at the request of individuals concerned about a boy's welfare. Applications for admission could be accompanied by a promise to make a donation. In 1915 a private sponsor, Alice M. Cowland, signed an agreement to pay £10 annually for six years in return for the admission to the home of Douglas Stuart Davidson. A local doctor, Dr Laseron of Tottenham, asked the committee to take in Henry Mortlock, an orphan, who was dependent upon his brother-in-law who was poor and dying of consumption. He was admitted and stayed at the home until 1873, when aged nearly 16.[20] Although not a particularly large school, Church Farm did help a large number of children because of the length of time that it operated. By the time it became an approved school under the 1933 Approved School Act, approximately 1,400 boys had attended the home.

Other schools can be dealt with in less depth. The Church of England Central Society for Promoting Homes for Waifs and Strays (Waifs and

Figure 12.4 Olive House, 27 George Street, Hemel Hempstead. *Our Waifs and Strays*, 1886, WS08. ©
The Children's Society.

Strays Society), later renamed the Children's Society, widened its work
of caring for children by setting up industrial schools for girls and boys.
According to their magazine, *Our Waifs and Strays*, in November 1885
they opened Olive House (see Figure 12.4) at 27 George Street, Hemel
Hempstead, for young girls under the age of 8 who had been 'rescued from
immoral surroundings'.[21] However, the school had actually been certified
as an industrial school on 7 October 1884 for 20 young girls. In May
1900 the school moved into new premises at Shipton-under-Wychwood,
Oxfordshire, and was recertified for 30 girls. The only census that covered
the period when the school was in Hemel Hempstead is that of 1901. It
showed 3 members of staff and 16 girls. Interestingly, no girl was actually
under the age of 8, as had been the Waifs and Strays Society's initial aim.
The 1901 census also appears to show that, despite the Waifs and Strays
Society being a national organisation, all the girls at the school had come
from London. One of the girls had been born in Deptford and another

three in Woolwich. The remainder were simply described as having been born in London.

Gisburne House Industrial School in Gammons Lane, Watford, ran from 1912 to 1933, too late for us to make use of the census to examine the range of children sent to it. However, as it was run by the LCC Children's Department, which in 1909 had taken over the role of the LSB, the girls would have all come from the London area. It was certified as an industrial school for 20 girls on 17 October 1912. In 1913 it was certified for 57 girls and in 1931 for 52 girls. In 1933 it became an approved school.

St Francis (Special) Industrial School ran at Hillside, Buntingford, where in 1919 it was certified for 40 children with mental health problems. It had replaced Thurlbury House, a Special Industrial School for mentally deficient Roman Catholic boys based at Woodford Bridge. It ceased certification in 1931 but in 1933 became an approved school and continued to run until 1956. The school may possibly have been run by the Sacred Heart Sisters; the building was sold in 1977 by them. At that time it was run as a home for people with learning disabilities, which was closed in 1992. No census material is available to identify the origins of children but in 1929, according to the *Annual Charities Register*, applications for admission could be sent to the Sister Superior; it was described as being for epileptic children and payment was according to circumstances. It seems likely that the children would have come from a wide area.[22]

St Elizabeth's School, Much Hadham, for Roman Catholic boys and girls, was established in 1903 in Perry Green, Much Hadham by the Congregation of the Daughters of the Cross of Liège as a Special School for epileptic children and was certified in 1909 for 30 girls and 30 boys. In 1929 it was certified under the Elementary Education (Defective and Epileptic Children) Act 1899,[23] but, confusingly, it was listed as a certified industrial school, presumably to enable government funding to be available. It seems to have left the industrial-school system in 1932 and continued to run as a registered charity. The 1911 census is the only one available for the period during which the school was open. In addition to 31 staff and 55 adult patients, the census lists 26 boys and 25 girls. The place where the children were born was not known for 34 children. Six children had been born in London and two in Liverpool. The others came from nine other places: Lanarkshire, Sligo, Birmingham, Worcester, Brighton, Southampton, Stafford, Glamorgan and Chelmsford. The range of the children's ages was very wide, but the greatest number were aged 13. The youngest children were aged 4 and 5. There were two aged 7, three aged 8, four aged 9, two aged 10, six aged 11, five aged 12, nine aged 13, seven aged 14, six aged 15 and four aged 16. The age of one child was unknown.

Committals of Hertfordshire children to certified industrial schools

The passing of the industrial school act does not appear to have had as significant an effect in Hertfordshire as it did in less rural counties. When in May 1879 advice was sought of the Essex Industrial School as to how Hertfordshire should make use of the new legislation, the reply was:

> in reply to your letter of the 30th I think the court of Quarter
> Sessions for your County would judging from statistics and
> experience of the London School Board find it to be the cheaper
> course to subscribe to the funds of some existing industrial school,
> able to receive inmates, rather than to establish Industrial Schools.[24]

This advice seems to have been taken on board and the county authorities did not establish schools of its own but did send Hertfordshire children to a considerable variety of industrial schools, making use of Col. Gillum's school in East Barnet as well as schools situated outside the county.

Thus, in 1879 the Boys' Farm Home was approached to agree a contract to take in Hertfordshire children. Colonel Gillum wrote that he was not prepared to enter into a contract 'to take any boys' as, at his school, each case was considered on its own merits.[25] Not to be put off, an 1876 Hertfordshire Quarter Sessions motion, moved by the Revd John Jessop and seconded by the Hon. Baron Dimsdale, recommended that a contract be made with the managers of the Halstead Industrial School to take girls from Hertfordshire for a sum not exceeding 2s 6d a week.[26] The school had been founded in 1866 by a Quaker, Lucy Greenwood, for destitute girls and it became a certified industrial school in 1869. She ran the school with the support of friends and fellow Quakers including Samuel Courtauld, Mrs Sydney Courtauld, Joseph Smith of Woolpits, William Brown of Halstead and Henry Rogers. The London School Board also used the school and their inspector George Ricks reported in 1894:

> [E]verything is satisfactory except the education in the
> schoolroom. And with regard to this school education I am afraid
> improvement is hopeless. The honorary secretary and general

manager tells me she does not think it good for the children to go beyond standard V, indeed she thinks standard IV would be far enough. She imagines that I want to push the children on to standard VI and she resents it. All I ask for is that the work so far as it goes, shall be intelligent and that the education shall be carried as far as possible under the circumstances.[27]

The following year Lucy Greenwood died. The two executors she had appointed persuaded the Quarterly Meeting of Essex and Suffolk to buy the property and appointed 12 trustees. A management committee was set up and the school ran until 1921. The executors were Wilson Marriage and Joseph Smith junior, the son of Lucy Greenwood's friend Joseph Smith of Pattiswick Hall. Joseph Smith became chairman of the house committee and Wilson Marriage acted as chairman of the managers.[28]

The Hertfordshire authorities also turned periodically to facilities further afield. The Essex Industrial School was established in 1872 in Baddow Road, Chelmsford and certified on 4 March 1873 under the 1866 Industrial Schools Act. In 1877 a grant of £5,000 from the Essex Quarter Sessions and one of £2,000 from the West Ham School Board enabled new premises to be built in Rainsford Road. It was recertified on 4 February 1879 for 150 boys and in 1924 for 130 boys. The boys came from a wide area, not just Chelmsford. Authorities sending boys included the Quarter Sessions of the Isle of Ely, Huntingdonshire, Norfolk and Lincolnshire; the Borough Councils of Bury St Edmunds, Cambridge, Hertford and Middlesex; the Folkestone Borough Bench; the Liberty of Havering; Mitford and Launditch Union; and the school boards of Ipswich, East Dereham and Chigwell. It became an Essex Home Approved School in 1933 and continued on its site until 1980.

Holme Court Truant School, Twickenham Road, Isleworth, was established jointly by the Chiswick and Heston School Boards. It was certified in 1891 for 65 children, recertified in December 1893 for 100 children and closed on 15 April 1921. It appears to have taken children from a much wider area than merely that of the founding school boards. In 1892 the London School Board made an agreement with the managers of Holme Court to accept its children and in 1894 the board sent 51.[29]

The North London Truant School opened in High Street, Walthamstow, London and was managed by the Tottenham, Hornsey and Edmonton School Boards. It was certified in 1884 for 85 children and was extended and recertified for 120 children in 1894. In 1933 it became the Northcotts Approved School and subsequently the Pishiobury Approved School, in Sawbridgeworth, Hertfordshire.[30] The 1891 census listed 37 children, of whom just one had been born in Hertfordshire and 19 in London or Middlesex.[31]

The Hitchin Board of Guardians seems to have favoured the use of the Mount Edgcumbe Industrial Ship School, Saltash, near Plymouth, for some of the troublesome boys brought before them. This ship school, which opened in 1877 as an industrial school for 250 boys, specialised in training boys for service in the navy. The anchored ship was used to accommodate the boys and staff, while a tender, the *Goshawk*, certified in August 1899, was used to teach naval skills. The boys came from a wide area, particularly London, and, it seems, also from Hitchin. The Edgcumbe stopped running as an industrial school in June 1920. The Hitchin Guardians also made use of other schools, such as the Boys' Farm Home in East Barnet.

Courts

Evidence of Hertfordshire children being sent to industrial schools through the courts shows up in both the Quarter Sessions and the Petty Sessions records. The former court seems to have dealt with the cases that involved larceny, under the 1866 Industrial Schools Act; the latter with cases of truancy, following the 1876 Education Act. That act had added truancy to the grounds for which children could be committed to industrial schools and provided for the setting up of short-term truant industrial schools.

The Hertfordshire Quarter Sessions were held in St Albans and Hertford. At these courts children under 15 charged with simple larceny could be tried by two justices of the peace.[32] The session records cover the period from August 1870 to March 1917, while those for the Liberty of St Albans begin in July 1870 and end in October 1916. Both Juvenile Courts appear to have made use of whipping and committal to reformatory schools to punish young offenders. The use of certified industrial schools was less common, but did occur. At the Hertford Court out of 1,058 cases just 5 resulted in the committal of a child to an industrial school. All these cases involved theft and one boy had been brought to court for two offences. The St Albans Court seems to have been more inclined to send children to industrial schools: 10 of its 965 cases resulted in the committal of a child to an industrial school. On two occasions the child had also been charged in another case. The St Albans Court appears to have used the Boys' Farm

Home in East Barnet and the accessibility of this school, just 11 miles away, may have influenced the Court's decision to send some children to an industrial school rather than a reformatory. Young offenders could also be sentenced to a short spell in prison followed by a period of time in a reformatory school or a certified industrial school. Below is a transcript (suitably anonymised) of an order made in 1916:

> Order of detention in a certified industrial school
> At the St Albans Juvenile Court
> In the county of Hertford
> Petty Sessional Division of St Albans
> F W T of […] Park Street St Albans who appears to the Court
> to be a child over the age of twelve years, but under the age of
> fourteen years having been born, so far as has been ascertained
> on the 8th day of October 1902 who resides in the district of the
> Education Authority for St Albans Division has been charged
> before the Court with the offence of Larceny which is punishable
> in the case of an adult by penal servitude or a less punishment but
> has not previously been convicted.
> … whereas the court is satisfied that the said child should be sent
> to a certified school, but having regard to the special circumstances
> of the case, should not be sent to a certified Reformatory School,
> and is also satisfied that the character and antecedents of the child
> are such that he will not exercise an evil influence over the other
> children in a certified Industrial School, and whereas the Managers
> of the certified Industrial School at the Boys' Farm Home, Church
> Farm, East Barnet are willing to receive the said child.
> And whereas the religious persuasion of the said child appears to
> the court to be Church of England
> It is hereby ordered that the said child shall be sent to the Boys'
> Farm Home aforesaid certified industrial school, to be there
> detained until he shall attain the age of sixteen years
> And it is further ordered that F W T residing at Park Street
> aforesaid, the father of the said child shall pay to the Chief
> Inspector of Reformatory and Industrial Schools, or his agents a
> weekly sum of 2s during the whole of the time for which the said
> child is liable to be detained in the School.
> Dated the 19th day of February 1916 signed Verulam[33]

The petty sessions involved different users. The 1870 Education Act provided for the establishment of school boards whose aim was to ensure the school attendance of the children in their districts. Where there were no existing school boards it was the board of guardians' relieving officers who acted as the districts' school attendance officers. In Hertfordshire there were nine poor-law districts – Barnet, Berkhamsted, Buntingford, Hemel Hempstead, Hertford, Hitchin, Royston, Ware and Watford – and it seems likely that in many of these places the guardians had to take responsibility for school attendance. To bring the new regulations regarding the compulsory school attendance of children to the notice of the people in their district the guardians put an advertisement in the *Herts Express* showing the provisions of the Education Act 1876. Attendance committees were duly established and attendance officers appointed. The new committees were instructed to make up a list of the names and ages of the children already attending their schools as well as a list of those children in their district who were not on the books of those schools. The local committees then had to try to get the parents of the latter children to name a school to which they would send their children and when parents refused to do so the local committees had to report this to the main school-attendance committee.[34] In turn, parents who did not ensure their children attended school were sent notices by the attendance officers, and if these did not succeed in ensuring a child attended school the parents were brought before the Petty Sessions. Sessions were held at Albury, Barnet, Bishop's Stortford, Buntingford, Cheshunt, Dacorum, Eastwick, Hatfield, Hertford, Hitchin, South Mimms, Odsey, St Albans, Shenley, Stevenage, Ware, Watford and Welwyn. For this chapter, the records of the Barnet Petty Sessions and the Barnet Attendance Committee have been subjected to particular examination.

From November 1866 to February 1892 the Barnet Petty Sessions met on Mondays at the Barnet Town Hall, which had been built in Union Street in 1862. The cases held at this court came from a larger area than just the town itself, very much along the lines of the area covered by the Barnet Poor Law Union. The court dealt with cases of minor offences by adults and children and, after 1876, these included charging parents or guardians with failing to ensure the attendance of children at school, sending children to industrial schools and charging employers for taking on children of school age. The person or body bringing the case was mainly one of the two attendance officers acting for the Barnet Board of Guardians, George

Thomas Tilbury or George Hitchings, or the Shenley School Board. The defendant was usually the father, but sometimes the mother, of the unnamed child or another person responsible for the child's care. The initial step was to ask the court to issue an attendance order. Failure to comply with the order would be followed by a fine. Should these actions fail to ensure the child's attendance, orders could follow for children to be sent to certified industrial schools or truant schools and the parent or guardian to be sent to gaol.

During the period from February 1881 to October 1893 the court records reveal at least 448 cases connected with the non-attendance of children or related to industrial or truant schools. Many of the parents being charged appeared before the court on more than one occasion. William Aldwin was brought to court 15 times. On 4 occasions an attendance order was issued and on 10 he was charged with non-compliance with an order. He was fined 8 times, the sums ranging between 1s and 3s, during the period from 1884 to 1888. Richard Cox was brought to court 28 times between 1882 and 1887. On 4 occasions an attendance order was issued and on 24 occasions he was charged with non-compliance with an order. He was fined 14 times. The sums involved were higher, at between 2s and 5s.

In 1881, of the 21 occasions when parents were brought to the court one-third were requests for attendance orders to be issued. Many cases were deferred while further information was sought but the other occasions were when truancy had continued and a case was brought against the parent or guardian for their failure to comply with an earlier order. Generally this involved the payment of a fine of something between 2s and 5s. This seems, on the whole, to have solved the situation; otherwise, the child reached the age when he no longer had to attend school.

There were times, however, when the use of the certified industrial school act was resorted to. In 1891 orders were made sending sons of Thomas Langdale and Sarah Pratchett to the North London Truant School, Walthamstow, until they each reached the age of 13. Thomas Lonsdale appears in the Petty Sessions records over several years. On 12 October 1891 the school-attendance committee brought him to court for non-compliance and an order was made that his child be sent to an industrial school. On 4 July 1892 Barnet attendance committee charged Lonsdale with refusing to return a child to an industrial school and the court decided that Lonsdale's child should be committed back to industrial school. Eliza Carter was charged with non-compliance with an order to

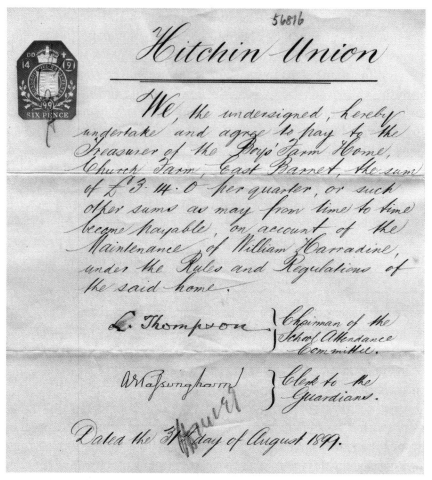

Figure 12.5 An example of a maintenance arrangement: Hitchin Board of Guardians' promise to pay maintenance to Boys' Farm Home for a William Harradine (1899).

send George Smith, who was in her charge, to school and it was agreed that he should be sent to a Truant School. Thomas Peak was charged with the non-attendance of his child and an order was given that he be sent to the Walthamstow Industrial School (North London Truant School) up to the age of 14. James March was ordered to pay towards the cost of the maintenance of his child. John Tinsley was brought to court and ordered to pay 1s a week and costs of 10s 6d for the support of a child in an industrial school. Figure 12.5 provides an example of a maintenance arrangement of this sort.

Unruly children could be sent by the courts to an industrial school. In 1903 Alfred May, aged 11, had been excluded from the South Mimms National School. The Board of Education 'could not consider that the grounds of exclusion of Alfred May were unreasonable' and proceedings were taken against Mrs May so that Alfred could be sent to an industrial school. Cases for the employment of children when they should have been in school were also brought by attendance officers to the Petty Sessions. In December 1888 George Hutchings brought a case against William Pratchett for employing a boy under the age of 10. Another case was brought in 1902 against Charles Field for employing William Walker, John Simmons and Henry Simmons. On that occasion the Barnet Bench refused to convict Mr Field for employing Walker. The attendance committee appealed to the Home Secretary, who said he had no authority over the Justices in respect of the case of William Walker. The following year William Walker was sent to a Truant School.

Conclusion

Although Hertfordshire had five industrial schools, just one – the Boys' Farm Home – ran for a significant amount of time and provided accommodation for a substantial number of boys. Nonetheless, the industrial-school legislation did play a part in the county's efforts to provide care and training for destitute and mildly delinquent children. It is difficult to establish exactly how many children attended Hertfordshire's industrial schools and even more difficult to discover how many Hertfordshire children were sent to schools outside the county. A rough estimate can be garnered by multiplying the average number of children by the number of years each school was open and dividing by four to allow for the fact that children stayed on average for four years. Church Farm School ran for 73 years and had an average of 80 children, suggesting a cumulative population of 1,460 boys. The Hemel Hempstead girls' school ran in George Street for just 16 years and was certified for 20 girls, and therefore the cumulative total of girls accommodated there is estimated at 80. Gisburne House ran in Watford from 1912 to 1933 and for most of that period the average number of girls was 57, suggesting that some 299 individuals may have passed through its doors. St Francis School, Buntingford, ran for 12 years and had 40 children (cumulative total estimated at 120), while the St Elizabeth school, Much Hadham, was certified as an industrial school for 32 years and took 51 children (perhaps 408 individuals). In short, perhaps

2–2,500 children passed through Hertfordshire's industrial schools. While such numbers are not huge they suggest that industrial schools had a role to play in the 'care' package available to the labouring classes and parochial or union authorities in the nineteenth and early twentieth centuries.

Notes

1. Parliamentary Papers (PP), 20 & 21 Vic, Cap XLVIII, An Act to make better Provision for the Care and Education of vagrant, destitute, and disorderly Children and for the Extension of Industrial Schools (Industrial Schools Act 1857).
2. PP, 17 & 18 Vic, Cap LXXXVI, *An Act for the Better Care of Young Offenders in Great Britain* (Reformatory Schools Act, 1854).
3. PP, 23 & 24 Geo 5, Cap XII, *Children and Young Persons Act* (Approved Schools Act, 1933).
4. Gillian Gear, 'Certified industrial schools in England, 1857–1933: "moral hospitals" or "oppressive institutions"?', PhD thesis (London, 1999).
5. PP, Industrial Schools Act 1857.
6. PP, 24 & 25 Vic Cap CXIII, An Act for amending and consolidating the Law relating to Industrial Schools (The Industrial Schools Amendment Act, 1861).
7. PP, 29 & 30 Vic, Cap CXVIII, An Act to consolidate and amend the Acts relating to Industrial Schools in Great Britain (Industrial Schools Amendment Act, 1866).
8. PP, 33 & 34 Vic Cap LXXV, An act to provide for public Elementary Education in England and Wales (Education Act 1870).
9. PP, 39 & 40 Vic Cap LXXIX, Elementary Education Act, 1876.
10. PP, 43 & 44 Vic Cap XV, Industrial Schools Amendment Act, 1880.
11. PP, 7 & 8 Edw. Cap LXVII, The Children Act, 1908.
12. PP, 17 & 18 Vic, Cap CLXIX, An Act for the provision regulation and maintenance of County Industrial Schools in Middlesex (The Feltham Act 1854).
13. Lt Col G.W. Gillum, *The Times* (14 April 1866).
14. Boys' Farm Home, *Annual Report* (1876) author's copy.
15. Hertfordshire Archives and Local Studies, Hertford (hereafter HALS) QS/Misc/B48.
16. Private hands, Boys' Farm Home, admission records.
17. Boys' Farm Home, *Annual Report* (1896), p. 7.
18. Boys' Farm Home, *Annual Report* (1876), pp. 7–8.
19. Boys' Farm Home, *Annual Report* (1894) and the London School Board (LSB) *Report of the Industrial Schools Committee* (1894) author's copy, table E (1), p. 38.
20. Private hands, Boys' Farm Home, correspondence file.
21. *Our Waifs and Strays* (Waifs and Strays Society [now Children's Society], 1886) p. 8.
22. The Charity Organisation Society, *Annual Charities Register and Digest* (London, 1929), p. 83.
23. PP, 62 & 63 Vic, Cap XXXII, An act to make better provision for the Elementary Education of Defective and Epileptic Children in England and Wales (1899).
24. HALS P.N. Dunville, letter to Hertfordshire Justices, May 1879.
25. HALS Lt Col. W.J. Gillum, letter regarding Boys Farm Home taking Hertfordshire children.

26. HALS QS/Misc/B/93/13.
27. LSB, *Report of the Industrial Schools Committee*, p. 63.
28. Essex Record Office, Greenwood Industrial School, Misc papers 1866–1921 T/P 139.
29. LSB, *Report of the Industrial Schools Committee*, p. xiii.
30. HALS Acc 2914 Approved school records (1884–1962).
31. The National Archives RG12/1358 folio 72.
32. Under 10 & 11 Vic, Cap LXXXII (Juvenile Offenders' Act, 1847) and 42 & 43 Vic, Cap XLIX (Summary Jurisdiction Act, 1879).
33. HALS QSC/43 Detention order, St Albans Division, Register of Juvenile convictions.
34. HALS BG/HIT/178-HIT/180.

Bibliography

Primary sources

Barnet Archives and Local Studies Centre
Monken Hadley Vestry Minutes, Vestry Books & Almanacs, microfilm, no reference
   number

Cambridgeshire Archives
R55/7 Tharp family of Chippenham

Dacorum Heritage Trust
DACHT 1490 Letter from Countess of Marchmont to Matron of Foundling Hospital

Dacorum Heritage Trust. Collection of Berkhamsted Local History & Museum Society
DACHT BK3895.118 Thomas Erskine, 'The childhood and early adult life of a foundling
   in the 1930s and 40s'
DACHT BK3898.123 Official opening ceremony of Water Tower
DACHT BK4012.1 Laying of foundation stone ceremony

Enfield Local Studies Library and Archive
Facsimile tracing from the original in the Bodleian Library of 'ENFIELD CHASE as now
   divided between the Commonwealth & Commons By Nick. Gunton and Edm Rolfe.
   1658'.

Essex Record Office (ERO)
D/ABW wills series, Archdeaconry Records, Commissary of Bishop of London Wills and
   online on the SEAX Database (henceforth ERO D/ABW)
D/ABW 43/54 Will of George Meade
D/ABW 43/125 Will of Robert Wilson
D/ABW 45/1 Will of Bennet Beltoft
D/ABW 45/67 Will of Henry Campe
D/ABW 48/112 Will of Henry Shuttleworth
D/ABW 48/130 Will of Anthony Wheeler
D/ABW 48/258 Will of Oliver Harvey
D/ABW 49/1 Will of George Channcy

D/ABW 49/256 Will of Anthony Cramphorne
D/ABW 49/330 Will of Thomas Haggard
D/ABW 52/67 Will of Henry Wootton
D/ABW 52/297 Will of Benedict Beawcock
D/ABW 55/62 Will of Prudence Bird
D/ABW 56/241 Will of John Miller
D/ABW 56/274 Will of William Bayford
D/ABW 56/275 Will of John Lyndsell
D/ABW 57/40 Will of Lucy Channcy
D/ABW 57/94 Will of William Sumpner
D/ABW 57/148 Will of John Parnell
D/ABW 57/164 Will of Leonard Knight
D/ABW 60/88 Will of Henry Neates
D/ABW 151/42 Will of Thomas Byrche
D/Z 15/1 Records of the Benevolent Medical Society for the United Counties of Essex and
     Hertford 1786–1804
Q/SBb 301 Quarter Sessions bundle 1780
Q/SBb 303 Quarter Sessions bundle 1781
Q/SBb 329 Quarter Sessions bundle 1787
Q/SBb 457 Quarter Sessions bundle 1819
T/P 139 Greenwood Industrial School, Misc papers 1866–1921

Hertford Museum
Andrews collection – printed note

Hertfordshire Archives and Local Studies
252.034/Le Bas Printed sermon
61351 Letter from John Woolston overseer for Pirton 1824 replying to government
     commission into labourer's wages
Acc 2914 Approved school records (1884–1962)
Acc 4104/17(Neg80/W/3a) in Local Studies Library image collection
Acc 4473/1a/37 by Stanley Kent; Local Studies Library image collection, by RCHME, *c.*1910
BG/HIT/178-HIT/180 Hitchin Board of Guardians, minutes of the schools attendance committee
DE/Bk/C/5 Baker papers
DE/Cf/Q/2 Correspondence between Secretary Nichols and Sheppard, architect
DE/Cf/Q/3 Further correspondence over site
DE/Cf/Q/4 Correspondence from Penny vice-chairman of BUDC
DE/Cf/Q/5–8 Supply of utilities to site
DE/Cf/Q/9 Correspondence over footpath and common land
DE/Cf/Q/38 Correspondence with HCC over possible grant and educational standards,
     reorganisation of schools
DE/Cf/Q/46 Negotiations with HCC over sale of Foundling Hospital
DE/Cr/21 *A catalogue of well-conditioned building materials fixtures and fittings up of
     Cheshunt Poor-House* by H Crawter & Sons Wednesday 18 October 1837

DE/Cr/109/1 *The liberty, manor and parish of Cheshunt* [tracing of 1785 plan] undated

DE/Cr/125/2 Field book to plan of *The liberty, manor and parish of Cheshunt* [original dated 1785] Undated [1852 or later]

DE/Ds/1/3 Orders relating to the Trustees at Cheshunt 1748 to 1778: Minute Book of the Charity School at Cheshunt Hertfordshire

DE/L/Q/5 The account of the Commissioners 1645

DE/L/Q/5 Will of Roger Daniels 1634

DE/L/3432–3445 Draft byelaws for School Attendance Committees and attendance returns, lists of pupils (1877–1878)

DE/Of/8/498 View of 'The College' – Receptacle for lunaties. View of 'Old House in Fishpool Street' – The Abbey Parish Workhouse *c.*1700–1800

DE/X3 Carrington Dairy

DP/3/12/1 Aldenham Overseers' Accounts

DP/4/8/1 Vestry minutes 1749–74, Great Amwell

DP/4/8/3 Vestry minutes 1772–1802, Great Amwell

DP/4/8/8 Bills and vouchers 1800, Great Amwell

DP/4/11/26 Rate Assessments 1802–1835, Great Amwell

DP/7/1/1/1 Ashwell Registers of Baptisms, Marriages and Burials

DP/7/12/1 Ashwell Overseers' Accounts 1667 to 1722

DP/7/12/2 Ashwell Overseers' Accounts 1722 to 1770

DP/7/18/1 Inventory of Ashwell Workhouse

DP/17/8/1 Vestry Meeting minutes, 1823–35, Bengeo

DP/17/12/1 Overseers' accounts 1632–1791, Bengeo

DP/18/5/1 Churchwardens Accounts, Bennington

DP/20/1/2 Register of baptisms, marriages and burials 1717–62, Little Berkhamsted

DP/20/8/1 Vestry minutes 1733–5, Little Berkhamsted

DP/20/8/2 Vestry minutes 1736–46, Little Berkhamstead

DP/20/8/3 Vestry minutes 1788–1858, Little Berkhamstead

DP/20/25/2 Maurice Hunt charity 1787–1891, Little Berkhamstead

DP/21/5/2 ff 34, 43 Bishop's Stortford Churchwardens' Accounts, Bishop's Stortford

DP/21/12/1 Overseers' accounts 1656–1772, Bishop's Stortford

DP/22/12/4 Overseers' accounts and vestry minutes 1826–1925, Bramfield

DP/23/8/1 ff 1, 5, 6, 9, 10, 13, 14 Braughing Vestry Minutes

DP/24A/8/1 Vestry minutes 1809–64, Hoddesdon

DP/24A/8/8 Vestry minutes 1642–1735, Hoddesdon

DP/24A/8/9 Vestry minutes 1735–69, Hoddesdon

DP/24A/8/10 Vestry minutes 1769–1809, Hoddesdon

DP/24A/8/11 Vestry order book 1763–91, Hoddesdon

DP/24A/18 Overseers' miscellaneous bills, requests and instructions, Hoddesdon

DP/24A/18/1 Overseers' miscellaneous bills, requests and instructions, bundle 1 1781–1798, Hoddesdon

DP/29/1/8 Cheshunt register of baptisms, marriages and burials 1747–1792

DP/29/4/1–2 Assessments for church rate, Waltham Cross Ward 1759, 1800

DP/29/4/3–8 Assessments for church rate, Cheshunt Street Ward 1791–1800

DP/29/4/9 Assessments for church rate, Woodside Ward 1813

DP/29/8/1 Cheshunt Vestry minutes 1731–1751

DP/29/8/48 Cheshunt Vestry minutes 1709–1731

DP/29/8/49 Cheshunt Vestry minutes 1752–1781

DP/29/8/50 Cheshunt Vestry minutes 1781–1786

DP/29/8/52 Cheshunt Vestry minutes 1816–1826

DP/29/11/156 Cheshunt overseers' assessments 1606 & 1630

DP/29/12/21 Cheshunt overseers' accounts 1734–1784

DP/29/13 & 14 Apprenticeship indentures for Cheshunt

DP/29/13 & 18 Cheshunt settlement examinations and certificates and removal orders

DP/29/14/1 Apprenticeship indentures for Cheshunt 1616–1806

DP/29/18/2 Cheshunt Workhouse Admittance Book 1753–1764

DP/29/18/27J removal order 6 October 1756, Cheshunt

DP/29/18/28 Cheshunt workhouse minutes 1753–1799

DP/29/18/29 Cheshunt workhouse minutes 1799–1817

DP/29/29/1 Cheshunt population returns 1821

DP/46B/5/1 Totteridge Overseers' Accounts

DP/48/8/2 Hertford All Saints Vestry minutes, Churchwardens' business

DP/48/8/8 Hertford All Saints Vestry minutes 1732–80

DP/48/8/9 Hertford All Saints Vestry minutes 1780–1816

DP/48/8/12 Hertford St John Vestry minutes 1752–70

DP/48/8/13 Hertford St John Overseers' accounts, Vestry minutes and orders relating to poor law matters 1768–78

DP/48/8/16 Vestry minutes 1740–62, Brickendon

DP/48/8/17 Vestry minutes 1762–76, Brickendon

DP/48/8/18 Vestry minutes and Overseers' accounts 1776–92, Brickendon

DP/48/8/20 Vestry minutes and Overseers' accounts 1820–9, Brickendon

DP/48/8/21 Vestry minutes and accounts 1829–44, Brickendon

DP/48/18/2 Hertford All Saints and Brickendon articles of agreement 1737

DP/48/18/3 Hertford St John and Brickendon agreement 1737

DP/49/8/1 Vestry minute book 1731–63, Hertford St. Andrew

DP/49/8/2 Vestry minute book 1763–81, Hertford St. Andrew

DP/50/8/1 Vestry book 1669–1813, Hertingfordbury

DP/50/8/2 Vestry minutes 1768–1814, Hertingfordbury

DP/50/8/3 Vestry minutes 1814–26, Hertingfordbury

DP/50/8/5 Vestry book 1723–48, Hertingfordbury

DP/50/8/6 Vestry minutes 1757–61, Hertingfordbury

DP/50/11/2 Table of annual amounts collected in poor, church and constables' rates 1723–1763, Hertingfordbury

DP/71/5/2 Little Munden Rate Book

DP/80/11/1–4 Overseers' Account Books, Pirton

DP/80/17/1 Certificates of service in militia and orders for payment of allowances 1793–1802, Pirton

DP/80/18/1 Inventory of contents of workhouse 1796, Pirton

DP/87/8/1 Vestry book, Royston, Cambs 1749–1773

DP/87/8/2 Minutes of joint annual vestry and Poor Law Committee meetings for united parishes (in Herts and Cambs) 1781–1798

DP/87/12/1 Royston Overseers' Accounts 1769–1809

DP/87/18/2 Letter and draft reply from Royston Vestry Clerk 1 and 4 May 1784

DP/87/18/2 and 18/3 Letters from Widow Mary Greenhow to Royston Vestry Clerk and letters written on her behalf by the Newmarket Overseer

DP/87/18/4 Miscellaneous papers 1778–1808

DP/87/18/8–35 Overseers' bills and vouchers 1782–1802

DP/87/18/10 Royston Overseers' Bills & Vouchers 1782–1807 Matthew Daniel's Bill May 1787–March 1788

DP/87/18/11 An Accnt of Doctors Bills from Easter 1782 to Easter 1789

DP/87/18/12 Royston Overseers' Bills & Vouchers 1782–1807 Thomas Nunn's Bill March 1788–April 1789

DP/87/18/15 Royston Overseers' Bills & Vouchers 1782–1807 Thomas Nunn's Bill April 1785–March 1786

DP/87/18/17 Royston Overseers' Bills & Vouchers 1782–1807 Daniel Crespin's Bill Nov 1795–March 1796

DP/87/18/18 Royston Overseers' Bills & Vouchers 1782–1807 Daniel Crespin's Bill March 1796–April 1797, 14 August 1796

DP/87/18/19 Names of the Poor in the Workhouse 7 February 1785

DP/87/18/19 Royston Overseers' Bills & Vouchers 1782–1807 Thomas Nunn's Bill April 1797–April 1798

DP/87/18/19 Royston Overseers' Bills & Vouchers 1782–1807 Daniel Crespin's Bill April 1801–April 1802, 7 July 1801

DP/87/18/20 Royston Overseers' Bills & Vouchers 1782–1807 Daniel Crespin's Bill April 1798–March 1799

DP/87/18/22 Royston Overseers' Bills & Vouchers 1782–1807 Daniel Crespin's Bill March 1799–April 1800, 18 April 1799

DP/87/18/26 Royston Overseers' Bills & Vouchers 1782–1807 Daniel Crespin's Bill April 1786 April 1787, 20 May 1786

DP/90/11/3 Rate assessments and accounts 1746–1761

DP/90/11/4 Rate assessments and accounts 1761–1795

DP/90/11/5 Rate assessments and accounts 1795–1801

DP/90/11/8 Rate assessments 1814–1818

DP/93/11/3 Poor rates and disbursements 1731–1741

DP/103/12/1 Overseers' accounts 1820–35, Stanstead St Margaret

DP/104/12/1 Accounts 1796–1808, Stapleford

DP/104/12/2 Accounts 1812–1920, Stapleford

DP/106/5/1 Parish book 1741–1814, Tewin

DP/110/8/1 Vestry minutes 1760–78, Thundridge

DP/116/5/1 Churchwardens' accounts 1763–1869, Ware

DP/116/8/1 Vestry minutes 1704–62, Ware

DP/116/8/2 Vestry minutes 1792–1827, Ware

DP/116/11/1 Poor Rate assessments 1790–1804, Ware

DP/116/12/1 Overseers' accounts 1724–9, Ware

DP/116/12/2 Overseers' accounts 1732–44, Ware

DSA4/6/2 Ashwell Tithe Map

Hertford Borough Records (HBR) Vol. 9 ff 102; 125 List of vagrants passed by the constables 1636; 127, 189; Vol. 20 ff. 136, 139v, 144r, 144v, 176, 178; Vol. 25 ff. 7–9; Vol. 26 Table of Apprenticeship enrolments ff. 46, 47, 50, 164, 167, 168, 184, 187; Vol. 46 ff. 896, 909–10; Vol. 48 ff. 29, 32, 34

PS/2/1/2/3 Barnet Petty Sessions

PS/2/1/6 Register of Summary Jurisdiction

QS Mil1 Ashwell militia lists, 1756 to 1786

QS/Misc/B/48 Reports re Essex Industrial School and Home for destitute boys (1873–79)

QS/Misc/B/93/13 Agreement Herts. County Quarter Sessions and Girls Industrial School, Halstead, Essex (1876)

QSB/2A/2B Quarter Sessions Books

QSC/8 Hertford Division, Convictions of Juveniles (29 Dec 1857–3 Feb 1894)

QSC/9 Hertford Division, Convictions of Juveniles (15 Nov 1893–31 Dec 1912)

QSC/34 St Albans Division, Convictions of Juveniles (16 Feb 1858–18 Feb 1884)

QSC/35 St Albans Division, Convictions of Juveniles (14 Jul 1884–28 Nov 1893)

QSC/36 St Albans Division, Convictions of Juveniles (13 Sep 1893–19 Aug 1913)

QSC/42 Hertford Division Register of Juvenile convictions (1857–1917)

QSC/43 St Albans Division, Register of Juvenile convictions (1857–1917)

QSR/112 letter dated 19 March 1889

UDC collections, Berkhamsted UDC 2, Hatfield UDC 7, Hitchin UDC 10, Hoddesdon UDC 11, Tring UDC 18

London Metropolitan Archives

A/FH/A/03 Minute Books of Foundling Hospital

A/FH/A/03/002/004 General Committee, 14 July 1756

A/FH/A/03/005/002–011 Nov 1754–Feb 1775 Sub-Committee Minutes

A/FH/A/04/001/002 1741–1787 Accounts Audited

A/FH/A/05/004 Estates and buildings sub-committee agenda and papers November 1953–July 1954

A/FH/A/06/001/010/001–A/FH/A/06/001/023/020 1759–1773 Letters sent by Inspectors to the Foundling Hospital

A/FH/A/06/002/001 1760–1767 Copy Book no. 3 of Letters sent by the Foundling Hospital

A/FH/A/06/002/002 1767–1770 Copy Book no. 4 of Letters sent by the Foundling Hospital

A/FH/A/06/002/003 1770–1780 Copy Book no. 5 of Letters sent by the Foundling Hospital

A/FH/A/09/001/077 Billet book December 1757

A/FH/A/09/002/001 Microfilm March 1741–February 1757 FH Nos 1–3595 X041/003 Vol 1 General Registers

A/FH/A/09/002/002 Microfilm X041/003 March 1757–July 1758 Nos 3596–9103 Vol 2 General Registers

A/FH/A/09/002/003 Microfilm X041/004 July 1758–May 1759 Nos 9104–12761 Vol 3 General Registers

A/FH/A/09/002/004 Microfilm X041/004 May 1759–Dec 1777 Nos 12762–17286 Vol 4 General Registers

A/FH/A/09/005/001/1 Memorandum Book of Foundling Hospital

A/FH/A/09/012/001 March 1741–Dec 1758 The State of the Children Quarterly and then Annually

A/FH/A/09/012/002 Jan 1759–May 1776 The State of the Children Quarterly and then Annually

A/FH/A/10/003/004 FH Nos 1385–4336 June 1756–May 1757 Nursery or Disposal Book

A/FH/A/10/003/005 FH Nos 4337–9266 May 1757–July 1758 Nursery or Disposal Book

A/FH/A/10/003/006 FH Nos 9267–14223 July 1758–October 1759 Nursery or Disposal Book

A/FH/A/10/003/007 FH Nos 14224–18991 October 1759–May 1812 Nursery or Disposal Book

A/FH/A/10/004/001 1749–1758 Microfilm X041/001 Inspection Book

A/FH/A/10/004/002 1756–1764 Microfilm X041/001 Inspection Book

A/FH/K/01/001 1739–1756 Microfilm X04/010 General Court Minutes

A/FH/K/01/002 1756–1767 Microfilm X041/010 General Court Minutes

A/FH/K/01/003 1767–1788 Microfilm X041/010 General Court Minutes

A/FH/K/02/005–008 Microfilm X041/015 Oct 1755–Dec 1763 General Committee Minutes

A/FH/K/02/009 Dec 1763–Jan 1766 Microfilm X041/016. A/FH/K/02/010 Feb 1766–Nov 1767 Microfilm X041/016. General Committee Minutes

A/FH/K/02/011–014 General Committee Minutes. (A/FH/K/02/011 1767 Nov–1769 Feb Microfilm X041/016; A/FH/K/02/012 1769 Mar–1770 Aug microfilm X041/017; A/FH/K/02/013 1770 Aug–1772 May Microfilm X041/017; A/FH/K/02/014 1772 Jun–1774 Aug microfilm X041/017)

CH/D/GIS/01–4, Records of Gisburne House Industrial (later Approved) School 1912–1954, minutes and papers, registers, reports

St John's College, Cambridge

D37 Terrier of Kirby Manor in Ashwell

The National Archives

J77/456/3889 Divorce Court File: 3889. Appellant: Allan MacLean. Respondent: Eva Augusta MacLean 1890

MH 51/735 The County Register: alphabetical record of proprietors of private madhouses, with a list of patients admitted 1798–1812

MH 94/11 Provincial licensed houses 1880–1900

PC 2/40 f 289 Registers of the Privy Council

Prob 11/770 Will of James West, Image Reference: 315

Prob 11/944 Will of Prudence West, wife of James, Image reference: 56

Prob 11/1097 Will of Elizabeth West, Image Reference: 432
Prob 11/1129 Will of Sarah West, Image Reference: 556
Prob 11/1381 Will of Prudence West
RG 12/1358 Registration Sub-District 5F Walthamstow 1891
SP16 Series: State papers for the reign of Charles I:SP16/182 f. 40; 183 f. 37; 185 f. 27;
    SP16/189 ff. 80, 98
SP28 Series: State Papers Commonwealth

University of Nottingham
PwF 230/1 Portland papers

Newspapers/Magazines/Directories
Bailey's British Directory ... for ... 1784, Vol. 4
Gentleman's Magazine
Hertfordshire Mercury
Herts Advertiser
Holden's Annual Directory (1811)
Kelly's Directories (1907–28)
The London and Provincial Medical Directory and General Medical Register (London, 1860)
Morning Post
Pigot's Directory of Hertfordshire (London, 1823–4)
The Reformer
The Times
Universal British Directory (Hertfordshire extracts) (London, 1791–8)
Universal British Directory of Trade and Commerce comprehending ... all the Cities, Towns and Principal Villages in England and Wales, Vol. 3

Parliamentary Papers
7 & 8 Edw. Cap LXVII (The Children Act, 1908)
9 Geo I, Cap VII, Act for Amending the Laws relating to the Settlement, Employment and Relief of the Poor (Workhouse Test Act 1723)
11 Geo I, Cap II (Enfield Chase or Galley Corner Trust, 1725)
23 & 24 Geo 5, Cap XII, Children and Young Persons Act (Approved Schools Act, 1933)
10 & 11 Vic, Cap LXXXII (Juvenile Offenders' Act, 1847)
42 & 43 Vic, Cap XLIX (Summary Jurisdiction Act, 1879)
17 & 18 Vic, Cap LXXXVI, An Act for the Better Care of Young Offenders in Great Britain (Reformatory Schools Act, 1854)
17 & 18 Vic, Cap CLXIX, An Act for the provision regulation and maintenance of County Industrial Schools in Middlesex (The Feltham Act 1854)
20 & 21 Vic, Cap XLVIII, An Act to make better Provision for the Care and Education of vagrant, destitute, and disorderly Children and for the Extension of Industrial Schools (Industrial Schools Act 1857)
24 & 25 Vic Cap CXIII, An Act for amending and consolidating the Law relating to Industrial Schools (The Industrial Schools Amendment Act, 1861)

29 & 30 Vic, Cap CXVIII, An Act to consolidate and amend the Acts relating to Industrial Schools in Great Britain (Industrial Schools Amendment Act, 1866)

33 & 34 Vic Cap LXXV, An act to provide for public Elementary Education in England and Wales (Education Act 1870)

39 & 40 Vic Cap LXXIX (Elementary Education Act, 1876)

43 & 44 Vic Cap XV (Industrial Schools Amendment Act, 1880)

62 & 63 Vic, Cap XXXII, An act to make better provision for the Elementary Education of Defective and Epileptic Children in England and Wales (1899)

Abstract of Answers and Returns under the Act for Procuring Returns Relative to Expense and Maintenance of the Poor in England, PP 1803–04 XIII, 378

Abstracts of the returns made by the overseers of the poor... (London, 1777)

Copy of the Report Made in 1834 by the Commissioners for Inquiring into the Administration and Practical Operation of the Poor Laws Presented by both Houses of Parliament by Command of His Majesty

Printed sources

Abraham, J.J., *Lettsom. His life times friends and descendants* (London, 1933).

Adams, J.M., 'The mixed economy for medical services in Herefordshire c. 1770–c. 1850', PhD thesis (Warwick University, 2003).

Agar, N., *Behind the plough* (Hatfield, 2005).

Allin, D.S., *The early years of the Foundling Hospital, 1739/41–1773* (London, 2011) www.foundlingmuseum.org.uk.

Alty, E.M., 'Cowper and St Albans', *Hertfordshire Countryside*, 30 (1975), p. 35.

Anon., *Journals of the House of Commons 1640–1666*, Vol. IV (London, 1803).

Anon., *Accounts of the Ashwell Overseers of the Poor Vol. 2 Part 1 1722–1752* (Ashwell, 1983).

Anon., *Accounts of the Ashwell Overseers of the Poor Vol. 2 Part 2 1752–1769* (Ashwell, 1983).

Archer, I.W., 'The charity of early modern Londoners', *Transactions of the Royal Historical Society*, 12 (2002), pp. 240–73.

Archer, P.C., *Historic Cheshunt* (Cheshunt, 1923).

Ashby, M., *The Hellard Almshouses and other Stevenage charities 1482–2005* (Hertford, 2005).

Ashdown, C.H., *St Albans historical and picturesque* (London, 1893).

Aspey, G., *All at sea: memories of a Coram boy* (Emsworth, 2010).

Baker, T.F.T. (ed.), *The Victoria County History of the county of Middlesex*, vol. 5 (London, 1976).

Barker-Read, M., 'The treatment of the aged poor in five selected west Kent parishes from settlement to Speenhamland, 1662–1797', PhD thesis (Open University, 1989).

Batchelor, H.R., *Hertfordshire and its ancient parishes… the parishes surrounding Hertford 1844* (W.R. Batchelor, 2003).

Beckett, J., *Writing local history* (Manchester, 2007).

Beier, A., *Masterless men: the vagrancy problem in England 1560–1640* (London, 1985).

Beier, A.L., *The problem of the poor in Tudor and early Stuart England* (London, 1983).

Birtchnell, P.C., *A short history of Berkhamsted* (Berkhamsted, 1972).

Boyer, G., *An economic history of the English poor law, 1750–1850* (Cambridge, 1990).

Bright, J. and Clark, G., *An introduction to the tokens at the Foundling Museum* (London,

2011).

Brown, A.F.J., *Prosperity and poverty* (Chelmsford, 1996).

Brown, W.N., 'The receipt of poor relief and family situation: Aldenham, Hertfordshire, 1630–90', in R.M. Smith (ed.), *Land, kinship and life-cycle* (Cambridge, 1984), pp. 405–22.

Brownlow, J., *The history and objects of the Foundling Hospital: with a memoir of the founder* (London, 1865) www.ebooksread.com/(Brownlow).

Bruce, M., *The coming of the welfare state* (London, 1974).

Brundage, A., *The English poor laws 1700–1930* (Basingstoke, 2001).

Buchan, W., *Domestic medicine: or a treatise on the prevention and cure of diseases by regimen and simple medicines…* 7th edn corrected (London, 1781; facsimile ECCO, 2011).

Burnby, J.G.L., *A Study of the English Apothecary from 1660 to 1760, Medical History*, Supplement No. 3 (London, 1983).

Burnett, J., *A social history of housing* (London, 1978).

Caldicott, J., 'My life as a foundling', *Your Berkhamsted* (May 2011), pp. 23–6.

Cawdell, M.J., *Royston St. John Hertfordshire burials from 1800–1852* (Royston, 2004).

Charity Organisation Society, *Annual charities register and digest* (London, 1929).

Charlesworth, L., *Welfare's forgotten past: A socio-legal history of the poor law* (Basingstoke, 2010).

Cherry, S., *Mental health care in modern England: the Norfolk Lunatic Asylum/St. Andrew's Hospital c.1810–1998* (Woodbridge, 2003).

Christie, O.F. (ed.), *Diary of the Revd. William Jones, 1777–1821: curate and vicar of Broxbourne and the hamlet of Hoddesdon 1781–1821* (London, 1929).

Clark, G. (ed.), *Correspondence of the Foundling Hospital inspectors in Berkshire 1757–68* (Reading, 1994).

Clark, G., 'Infant clothing in the eighteenth century: a new insight', *Costume: The Journal of the Costume Society*, 28 (1994), pp. 47–59.

Clarke, M., *Cold baths don't work. A history of mental health care in the Hitchin area* (Hitchin, 2011).

Clutterbuck, R., *The history and antiquities of the county of Hertford*, 3 vols (London, 1815–27).

Connel, E.C., 'Hertfordshire agriculture', MSc dissertation (London, 1968).

Cotton, N., *Observations on a particular kind of scarlet fever that lately prevailed in and about St Albans* (London, 1749).

Crassons, K., *The claims of poverty: literature, culture and ideology in late medieval England* (New York, 2010).

Curth, L.H. (ed.), *From physick to pharmacology: five hundred years of British drug retailing* (Aldershot, 2006).

Dasent, J.R. *et al.*, *Acts of the Privy Council of England 1600–1631*, 16 vols (London, 1906–64).

Digby, A., *Making a medical living: doctors and patients in the English market for medicine, 1720–1911* (Cambridge, 1994).

Dimsdale, T., *Remarks on a letter … by John Coakley Lettsom …* (London, 1779).

Dobson, M.J., *Contours of death and disease in early modern England* (Cambridge, 1997).

Dyston, R., 'The nature of urban poverty: an Oxford case study c. 1760–1835', PhD thesis (Oxford Brookes, 2007).

Earle, P., *An examination of the practice of blood-letting in mental disorders* (New York, 1854).

Edwards, J., *Cheshunt in Hertfordshire* (Cheshunt, 1974).

Ellis, W., *The country housewife's family companion…* (London, 1750; facsimile ECCO, 2011).

Emsley, C., *Crime and society in England 1750–1900* (London, 1987).

Falvey, H. and Hindle, S., *'This little commonwealth' Layston parish memorandum book 1607–c.1650 & 1704–c. 1747* (Hertford, 2003).

Fildes, V., *Wet nursing: a history from antiquity to the present day* (Oxford, 1988).

Firth, C.H. and Rait, R.S. (eds), *Acts and ordnances of the Interregnum 1634–1660*, 3 vols (London, 1911).

Fissell, M., *Patients, power and the poor in eighteenth-century Bristol* (Cambridge, 1991).

Forsythe, B., Melling, J. and Adair, R., 'The New Poor Law and the county pauper lunatic asylum: the Devon experience 1834–1884', *Social History of Medicine*, 9 (1996), pp. 335–55.

Foundling Hospital reports and accounts for the year 1921 (London, 1922).

Fuller, T., *The history of the University of Cambridge and of Waltham Abbey with the appeal of injured innocence* (London, 1840).

Gear, G., 'Industrial schools 1957–1933 with particular reference to Church Farm Industrial School, East Barnet', MA thesis (Middlesex University, 1985).

Gear, G., *Church Farm Industrial School*, Barnet & District Local History Society Bulletin 24 (Barnet, 1986).

Gear, G., 'Certified industrial schools in England, 1857–1933: "moral hospitals" or "oppressive institutions"?', PhD thesis (London, 1999).

Gestrich, A., Hurren, E. and King, S., 'Narratives of poverty and sickness in Europe 1780–1938: sources, methods and experiences', in A. Gestrich, E. Hurren and S.A. King (eds), *Poverty and sickness in modern Europe: narratives of the sick poor, 1780–1938* (London, 2012), pp. 1–34.

Goose, N., 'Workhouse populations in the mid-nineteenth century: the case of Hertfordshire', *Local Population Studies*, 62 (1999), pp. 52–69.

Goose, N., 'Poverty, old age and gender in nineteenth-century England: the case of Hertfordshire', *Continuity and Change*, 20 (2005), pp. 351–84.

Goose, N., 'Urban growth', in T. Slater and N. Goose (eds), *A county of small towns* (Hatfield, 2008), pp. 96–126.

Goose, N., 'The English almshouse and the mixed economy of welfare: medieval to modern', *Local Historian*, 40 (2010), pp. 3–14.

Great Britain Commissioners in Lunacy, *Report of the Metropolitan Commissioners in Lunacy* (London, 1844).

Great Britain Commissioners in Lunacy, *Further report of the Commissioners in Lunacy* (London, 1847).

Great Britain Commissioners in Lunacy, *Sixteenth Report of the Commissioners in Lunacy* (London, 1862).

Green, D., *Pauper capital: London and the poor law, 1790–1870* (Farnham, 2010).

Green, M.A.E. (ed.), *Calendar of State Papers Interregnum*, 13 vols (1875–86).

Gritt, A.J., 'The census and the servant: a reassessment of the decline and distribution of farm service in early nineteenth-century England', *Economic History Review*, 53 (2000), pp. 84–106.

Gruber von Arni, E., *Justice to the maimed soldier: nursing, medical care and welfare for sick and wounded soldiers and their families during the English civil wars and interregnum, 1642–1660* (Aldershot, 2001).

Hall, R., 'The vanishing unemployed, hidden disabled, and embezzling master: researching Coventry workhouse registers', *Local Historian*, 38 (2008), pp. 111–21.

Hammond, J.L. and B., *The village labourer 1760–1832* (London, 1911).

Hampson, E.M., *The treatment of poverty in Cambridgeshire 1597–1834* (Cambridge, 1934).

Harding, Rev F.A., 'Dr Nathaniel Cotton of St Albans', *Hertfordshire Countryside*, 23 (1969), pp. 46–8.

Harris, R., *Enlightened self-interest* (London, 1997).

Hayley, W., *The life and letters of William Cowper*, Vol. 1 (London, 1812), pp. 94–9.

Healey, J., 'Marginality and misfortune: poverty and social welfare in Lancashire c.1630–1760', D.Phil. thesis (Oxford, 2008).

Her Majesty's Stationery Office (HMSO) *Chronological table of statutes covering the period from 1235 to the end of 1973* (London, 1974).

Hill, J., *Hertfordshire militia lists: Cheshunt combining Street, Woodside and Waltham Cross wards* (Ware, 1999).

Hill, J., *Hertfordshire militia ballot lists: Royston 1758–66* (Ware, 2000).

Hinde, A. and Turnbull, F., 'The population of two Hampshire workhouses, 1851–1861', *Local Population Studies*, 61 (1998), pp. 38–53.

Hindle, S., 'Dependency, shame and belonging: badging the deserving poor, c.1550–1750', *Cultural & Social History*, 1/1 (2004), pp. 6–35.

Hindle, S., '"Good, godly and charitable uses": endowed charity and the relief of poverty in rural England, c.1550–1750', in A. Goldgar and R. Frost (eds), *Institutional culture in early modern society* (Leiden, 2004), pp. 164–88.

Hindle, S., *On the parish? The micro-politics of poor relief in rural England c.1550–1750* (Oxford, 2004).

Hindle, S., '"Waste children": pauper apprenticeships under the Elizabethan Poor Law c. 1598–1697', in Penelope Lane, Neil Raven and K.D.M. Snell (eds), *Women, work and wages in England 1600–1850* (Woodbridge, 2004), pp. 15–46.

Hitchcock, T., 'The English workhouse: a study in institutional poor relief in selected counties, 1696–1750', D.Phil. thesis (Oxford, 1985).

Hitchcock, T., 'Paupers and preachers: the SPCK and the parochial workhouse movement', in L. Davison, T. Hitchcock, T. Keirn and R. Shoemaker (eds), *Stilling the grumbling hive* (Stroud, 1992), pp. 145–66.

Hitchcock, T., 'Begging on the streets of eighteenth century London', *Journal of British Studies*, 44 (2005), pp. 47–98.

Honeyman, K., *Child workers in England, 1780–1820: parish apprentices and the making of the early industrial labour force* (Aldershot, 2007).

Hoskins, W.G., 'Harvest fluctuations and English economic history 1620–1759', *Agricultural History Review*, 16/1 (1968), pp. 13–31.

Houston, R., 'Vagrants and society in early modern England', *Cambridge Anthropology*, 6 (1980), pp. 18–32.

Humphries, J., *Childhood and child labour in the British Industrial Revolution* (Cambridge, 2010).

Hurren, E., *Protesting about pauperism: poverty, politics and poor relief in late-Victorian England, 1870–1900* (Woodbridge, 2007).

Hurren, E., *Dying for Victorian medicine: English anatomy and its trade in the dead poor c.1834–1929* (Abingdon, 2011).

Hurren, E. and King, S., 'Begging for a burial: death and the poor law in eighteenth and nineteenth century England', *Social History*, 30 (2005), pp. 321–41.

Innes, J., 'The mixed economy of welfare: assessment of the options from Hale to Malthus (1683–1803)', in M. Daunton (ed.), *Charity, self-interest and welfare in the English past* (London, 1996), pp. 139–80.

Innes, J., *Inferior politics: social problems and social policies in eighteenth-century Britain* (Oxford, 2009).

Johnson, S., *The rambler* (London, 1750–2).

Jones, C.E., 'A St Albans worthy: Dr. Nathaniel Cotton, 1705–1788', *St Albans and Hertfordshire Architectural and Archaeological Society Transactions* (1936), pp. 57–63.

Jones, K., *Lunacy, law and conscience 1744–1845. The social history of the care of the insane* (London, 1955).

Jones, K., *Mental health and social policy 1845–1959* (London, 1960).

Jordan, W.K., *Philanthropy in England, 1480–1660. A study of the changing pattern of English social aspirations* (New York, 1959).

Kaloczi, A., 'The St Albans Foundling Hospital babies, 1756–1760', *Herts Past and Present*, 3rd series 4 (2004), pp. 3–7.

Kelly, T.J., *Thorns on the Tudor rose: monks, rogues, vagabonds and sturdy beggars* (Jackson, WY, 1977).

Kent, J. and King, S.A., 'Changing patterns of poor relief in some English rural parishes circa 1650–1750', *Rural History*, 14 (2003), pp. 119–56.

Kilpatrick, R., '"Living in the Light": dispensaries, philanthropy and medical reform in late-eighteenth-century London', in A. Cunningham and R. French (eds), *The medical enlightenment of the eighteenth century* (Cambridge, 1990), pp. 254–80.

King, P., 'Pauper inventories and the material lives of the poor in the eighteenth and early nineteenth centuries', in T. Hitchcock, P. King and P. Sharpe (eds), *Chronicling poverty: the voices and strategies of the English poor, 1640–1840* (Basingstoke, 1997), pp. 155–91.

King, P., 'The summary courts and social relations in eighteenth-century England', *Past and Present*, 183 (2004), pp. 124–72.

King, S., *Poverty and welfare in England 1700–1850: a regional perspective* (Manchester, 2000).

King, S., 'The bastardy prone sub-society again: bastards and their fathers and mothers in Lancashire, Wiltshire and Somerset, 1800–1840', in A. Levene, T. Nutt and S. Williams (eds), *Illegitimacy in Britain, 1700–1920* (Basingstoke, 2005), pp. 66–85.

King, S., '"Stop this overwhelming torment of destiny": negotiating financial aid at times of sickness under the English Old Poor Law, 1800–1840", *Bulletin of the History of Medicine*, 79 (2005), pp. 228–60.

King, S., 'Negotiating the law of poor relief in England 1800–1840', *History*, 96 (2011), pp. 410–35.

King, S., 'Welfare regimes and welfare regions in Britain and Europe, c.1750–1860', *Journal of Modern European History*, 9 (2011), pp. 42–66.

King, S. and Stringer, A., '"I have once more taken the Leberty to say as you well know": the development of rhetoric in the letters of the English, Welsh and Scottish sick and poor 1780s–1830s', in A. Gestrich, E. Hurren and S.A. King (eds), *Poverty and sickness in modern Europe: narratives of the sick poor, 1780–1938* (London, 2012), pp. 63–94.

Lane, J., 'Eighteenth-century medical practice: a case study of Bradford Wilmer, surgeon of Coventry, 1737–1813', *Social History of Medicine*, 3 (1990), pp. 369–86.

Lane, J., *A social history of medicine: health, healing and disease in England, 1750–1950* (London, 2001).

Langton, J., *The geography of poor relief in rural Oxfordshire during the late eighteenth and nineteenth centuries* (Oxford, 2000).

Larkin, J. (ed.), *Stuart proclamations Vol. II royal proclamations of King Charles I 1625–1646* (Oxford, 1983).

Le Hardy, W., *Hertfordshire county records calendar to the sessions books, sessions minute books and other sessions records* (Hertford, 1931).

Lees, L. Hollen, *The solidarities of strangers: the English poor laws and the people, 1700–1948* (Cambridge, 1998), pp. 46–60.

Levene, A., *Childcare, health and mortality at the London Foundling Hospital, 1741–1800: 'left to the mercy of the world'* (Manchester, 2007).

Levene, A., 'Children, childhood and the workhouse: St Marylebone, 1769–1781', *London Journal*, 33 (2008), pp. 41–59.

Levene, A., 'Parish apprenticeships and the Old Poor Law in London', *Economic History Review*, 63/4 (2010) pp. 915–41.

Levene, A., *The childhood of the poor: welfare in eighteenth-century London* (Basingstoke, 2012).

Lloyd, S., *Charity and poverty in England, c.1680–1820: wild and visionary schemes* (Manchester, 2009).

Lobo, F.M., 'John Haygarth, smallpox and religious dissent in eighteenth-century England', in A. Cunningham and R. French (eds), *The medical enlightenment of the eighteenth century* (Cambridge, 1990), pp. 217–53.

Loudon, I., 'The nature of provincial medical practice in eighteenth-century England', *Medical History*, 29 (1985), pp. 1–32.

Loudon, I., *Medical care and the general practitioner 1750–1850* (Oxford, 1986).

McClure, R.K., *Coram's children: the London Foundling Hospital in the eighteenth century* (London and New Haven, CT, 1981).

McGranahan, L.M., 'Charity and the bequest motive: evidence from seventeenth-century wills', *Journal of Political Economy*, 108 (2000), pp. 1270–91.

Melling, J. and Forsythe, B., *The politics of madness: the state, insanity, and society in England, 1845–1914* (London, 2006).

Morrison, K., *The workhouse: a study of poor law buildings in England* (Swindon, 1999).

Munby, L., *Hertfordshire population statistics 1563–1801* (Hitchin, 1964).

Munk, W., *Roll of the Royal College of Physicians of London* (London, 1878).

Murphy, E., 'The metropolitan pauper farms 1722–1834', *London Journal*, 27 (2002), pp. 1–18.

Murphy, E., 'Workhouse care of the insane, 1845–1890', in P. Dale and J. Melling (eds), *Mental illness and learning disability since 1850* (London, 2006), pp. 24–45.

Newman, H.M., 'A home builder. A record of the Greenwood Industrial School, Halstead', *The Friends' Quarterly Examiner* (April 1922), p. 136.

Nichols, R.H. and Wray, F.A., *The history of the Foundling Hospital* (London, 1935).

Ottaway, S., *The decline of life: old age in eighteenth-century England* (Cambridge, 2004).

Owen, W., *Owen's new book of fairs, published by the king's authority: being a complete and authentic account of all the fairs in England and Wales* (London, 1788).

Oxley, G.W., *Poor relief in England and Wales 1601–1834* (Newton Abbot, 1974).

Page, F.M., *History of Hertford*, 2nd edn (Hertford, 1993).

Page, W. (ed.), *The Victoria County History of the county of Hertford*, 4 vols (London, 1902–14).

Palmer, C.J., *Perlustration of Great Yarmouth* (Great Yarmouth, 1872).

Parkinson, J., *Dangerous sports. A tale addressed to children* (London, 1800).

Parry-Jones, W., *The trade in lunacy: a study of private madhouses in England in the eighteenth and nineteenth centuries* (London, 1972).

Patriquin, L., *Agrarian capitalism and poor relief in England 1500–1860* (Basingstoke, 2007).

Perman, D., *600 years of charity: a brief history of the Ware Charity Trustees* (Ware, 1991).

Perman, D., *Scott of Amwell: Dr Johnson's Quaker critic* (Ware, 2001).

Perman, D., *A new history of Ware, its people and its buildings* (Ware, 2010).

Philipson, T., 'The sick poor and the quest for medical relief in Oxfordshire c. 1750–1835', PhD thesis (Oxford Brookes, 2009).

Philo, C., *A geographical history of institutional provision for the insane from medieval times to the 1960s in England and Wales: This space reserved for insanity* (Lewiston, NY, 2004).

Pound, J., *Poverty and vagrancy in Tudor England* (London, 1971).

Pugh, G., *London's forgotten children: Thomas Coram and the Foundling Hospital* (Stroud, 2007).

Quincy, J., *Pharmacopoeia officinalis & extemporanea: or, a complete English dispensatory, in two parts…*, 5th edn (London, 1724).

Quintrell, B.W., 'Making of Charles I's Book of Orders', *English Historical Review*, 95 (1980), pp. 553–72.

Ralls, S. and J., *Royston 1200–1800: a list of residents* (Royston, 2011).

Ramazzini, B., *Diseases of workers: the Latin text of 1713 revised with translation and notes by W.C. Wright* (Chicago, IL, 1940).

Ramsland, J., 'The decline and fall of the Thomas Coram Schools, 1935–1954', *Journal of Educational Administration and History*, 27/1 (1995), pp. 1–22.

Robin, J., 'The relief of poverty in mid-nineteenth century Colyton', *Rural History*, 1 (1990), pp. 193–218.

Rooke, P.E., *Cheshunt workhouse minutes transcribed and indexed* (Cheshunt, 1957).

Rose, M.E., *The English Poor Law, 1780–1930* (Newton Abbot, 1971).

Royston & District Family History Society, *Royston Burial Register 1678–1800* (Royston, 1998).

Scull, A., *The most solitary of afflictions: madness and society in Britain, 1700–1900* (New Haven, CT, 1993).

Sharpe, K., *The personal rule of Charles I* (New Haven, CT, and London, 1992).

Shave, S., 'The dependent poor? (Re) constructing individual lives "on the parish" in rural Dorset 1800–1832', *Rural History*, 20 (2009), pp. 67–98.

Short, D., *The history of the Ashwell Merchant Taylors' School* (unpublished MS, n.d.).

Short, D., *Snippets of Ashwell's history Volume 1* (Ashwell, 1997).

Short, D. (ed.), *Survey of the farm homesteads, private dwelling-houses, shops, cottages, etc. at Ashwell, Hertfordshire made August 1829* (Ashwell, 2007).

Short, D., 'Ashwell, an example of Anglo-Saxon town planning', in T. Slater and N. Goose (eds), *A county of small towns* (Hatfield, 2008), pp. 159–72.

Short, D., *Snippets of Ashwell's history Volume 2* (Ashwell, 2012).

Simmons, S.F., *The medical register for the year 1779* (London, 1779).

Simmons, S.F., *The medical register for the year 1780* (London, 1780).

Simmons, S.F., *The medical register for the year 1783* (London, 1783).

Slack, P., 'Books of Orders: the making of English social policy 1577–1631', *Transactions of the Royal Historical Society*, 30 (1980), pp. 1–22.

Slack, P., *Poverty and policy in Tudor and Stuart England* (Harlow, 1988).

Slack, P., *The English Poor Law, 1531–1782* (Cambridge, 1995).

Slater, T. and Goose, N. (eds), *A county of small towns* (Hatfield, 2008).

Smith, C., 'Family, community and the Victorian asylum: a case study of the Northampton General Lunatic Asylum and its pauper lunatics', *Family and Community History*, 9 (2006), pp. 23–46.

Smith, J.R., *The speckled monster* (Chelmsford, 1987).

Smith, J.T., 'Nine hundred years of St Albans: architecture and social history', *Hertfordshire Archaeology*, 11 (1993), pp. 1–22.

Smith, L., *Lunatic hospitals in Georgian England, 1750–1830* (London, 2007).

Smith, R.M., 'Ageing and well-being in early modern England: pension trends and gender preferences under the English Old Poor Law *c*.1650–1800', in P. Johnson and P. Thane (eds), *Old age from antiquity to post-modernity* (London, 1998), pp. 64–95.

Snell, K.D.M., *Parish and belonging: community, identity and welfare in England and Wales 1700–1950* (Cambridge, 2006).

Society for the Promotion of Christian Knowledge (SPCK), *An account of several workhouses for employing and maintaining the poor* (1732).

Sokoll, T., *Essex pauper letters 1731–1837* (Oxford, 2001).

Stringer, A., 'Depth and diversity in parochial healthcare: Northamptonshire 1750–1830', *Family & Community History*, 9/1 (2006), pp. 43–54.

Styles, J., *The dress of the people: everyday fashion in eighteenth-century England* (New Haven, CT, 2007).

Styles, J., *Threads of feeling: the London Fondling Hospital's textile tokens, 1740–1770* (London, 2010).

Suzuki, A., 'The household and the care of lunatics in eighteenth century London', in P. Horden and R. Smith (eds), *The locus of care: families, communities, institutions and the provision of welfare since antiquity* (London, 1998), pp. 153–75.

Thane, P., *Old age in English history: past experiences, present issues* (Oxford, 2000).

Thomas, A., 'Hertfordshire communities and central–local relations c. 1625–1665', PhD thesis (University of London, 1988).

Thomas, D.H., *Reformatory and industrial schools: an annotated list of the reformatory and industrial schools certified by the Home Office, 1854–1933* (Newcastle upon Tyne, 1986).

Thomas, E.G., 'The treatment of poverty in Berkshire, Essex and Oxfordshire, 1723–1834', PhD thesis (University of London, 1970).

Thomson, H. Hyslop, *53rd Annual Report on the sanitary condition of the Middlesex & Hertfordshire combined sanitary district, 1926*.

Thwaite, M.F., 'Doctor Nathaniel Cotton: physician and minor poet', *Hertfordshire Past & Present*, 6 (1966), pp. 29–33.

Tomkins, A., *The experience of urban poverty 1723–82* (Manchester, 2006).

Tuer, A.W., *History of the Horn-Book* (London, 1897).

Turnor, L., *History of the ancient town and borough of Hertford* (Hertford, 1830).

Vickery, A., *The gentleman's daughter: women's lives in Georgian England* (New Haven, CT, and London, 1998).

Wales, T., 'Poverty, poor relief and the life-cycle: some evidence from seventeenth-century Norfolk', in R.M. Smith (ed.), *Land, kinship and life-cycle* (Cambridge, 1984), pp. 351–404.

Walker, D., *A general view of the agriculture of the county of Hertford* (London, 1795).

Wallace, E., *Children of the labouring poor: the working lives of children in nineteenth-century Hertfordshire* (Hatfield, 2010).

Wallis, P.I. and R.V. (eds), *Eighteenth century medics: subscriptions, licenses, apprenticeships* (Newcastle upon Tyne, 1988).

Webb, S. and B., *English poor law history Part I: the Old Poor Law* (London, 1963).

Williams, S., 'Caring for the sick poor: poor law nurses in Bedfordshire, c. 1770–1834', in P. Lane, N. Raven and K.D.M. Snell (eds), *Women, work and wages, c.1650–1900* (Woodbridge, 2004), pp. 123–43.

Williams, S., 'Malthus, marriage and poor law allowances revisited: a Bedfordshire case study 1770–1834', *Agricultural History Review*, 52 (2004), pp. 56–82.

Williams, S., '"A good character for virtue, sobriety and honesty": unmarried mothers' petitions to the London Foundling Hospital and the rhetoric of need in the early nineteenth century', in A. Levene, T. Nutt and S. Williams (eds), *Illegitimacy in Britain, 1700–1850* (Basingstoke, 2005), pp. 86–110.

Williams, S., 'Practitioners' income and provision for the poor: parish doctors in the late eighteenth and early nineteenth centuries', *Social History of Medicine*, 18 (2005), pp. 159–86.

Williams, S., *Poverty, gender and life-cycle under the English Poor Law 1760–1834* (Woodbridge, 2011).

Wilson, A., 'The politics of medical improvement in early Hanoverian London', in A. Cunningham and R. French (eds), *The medical enlightenment of the eighteenth century* (Cambridge, 1990), pp. 4–39.

Winter, H., *The last of old St Albans* (1898).

Winters, W., *The history of the ancient parish of Waltham Abbey or Holy Cross* (Waltham Abbey, 1888).

Wise, S., *Inconvenient people. Lunacy, liberty and the mad-doctors in Victorian England* (London, 2012).

Young, A., *General view of the agriculture of Hertfordshire 1804* (Newton Abbot, 1971).

Index